VIZ GRAPHIC NOVEL
◆◆◆◆◆◆◆◆◆◆◆◆◆◆◆◆

NO NEED FOR FOR TENCHI!™

STORY AND ART BY
HITOSHI OKUDA

CONTENTS

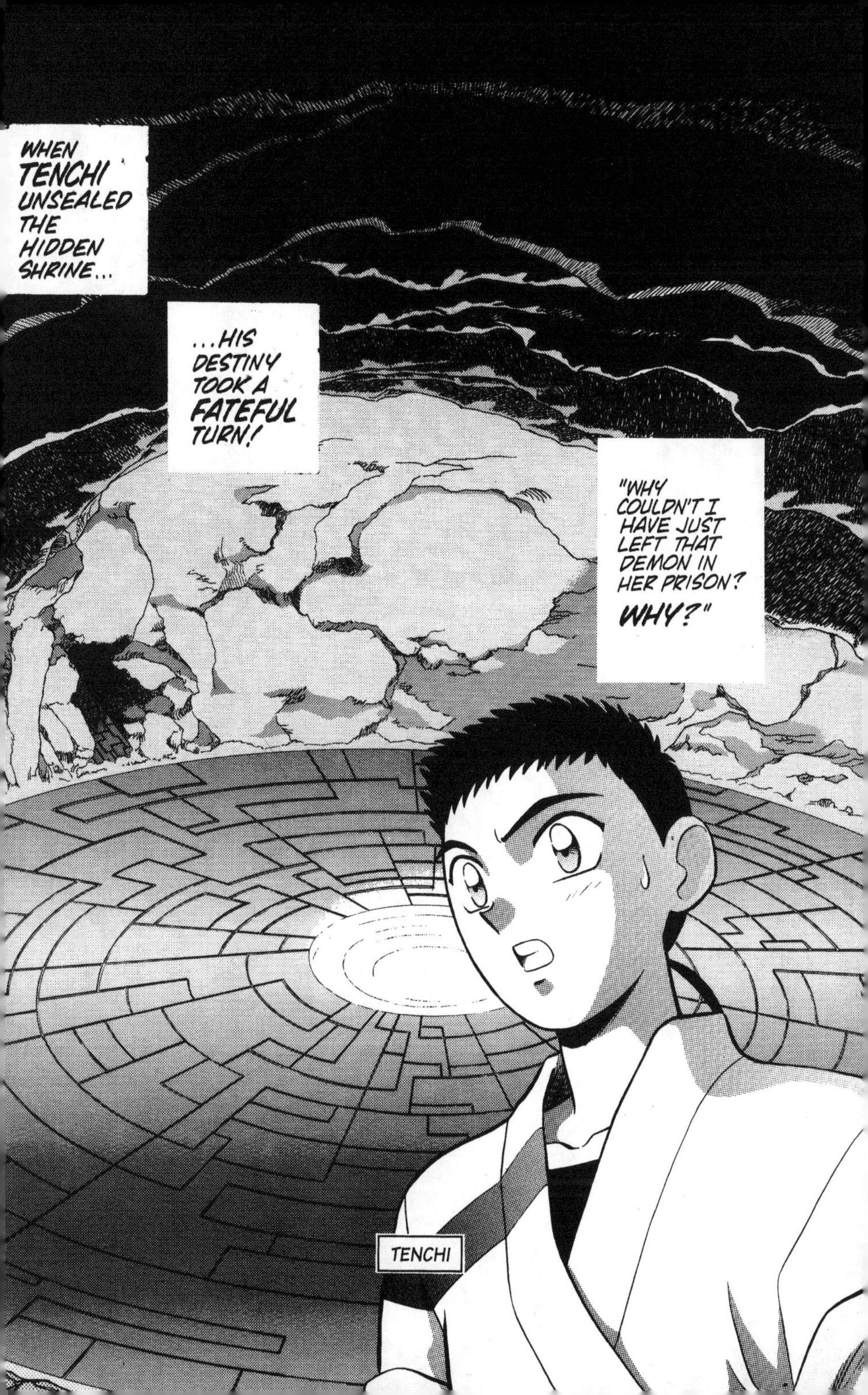
WHEN TENCHI UNSEALED THE HIDDEN SHRINE...
...HIS DESTINY TOOK A FATEFUL TURN!
"WHY COULDN'T I HAVE JUST LEFT THAT DEMON IN HER PRISON? WHY?"
TENCHI

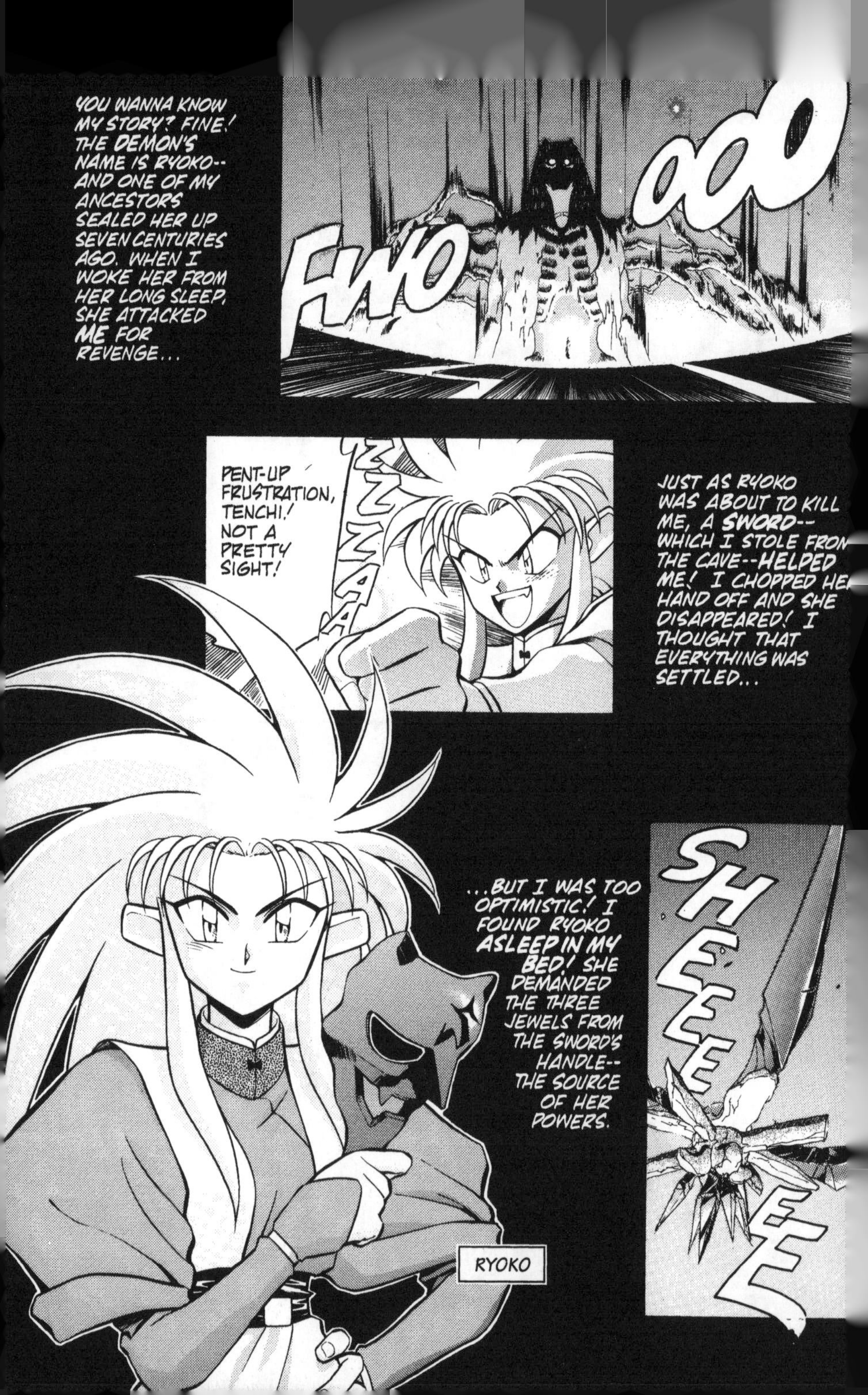
YOU WANNA KNOW MY STORY? FINE! THE DEMON'S NAME IS RYOKO--AND ONE OF MY ANCESTORS SEALED HER UP SEVEN CENTURIES AGO. WHEN I WOKE HER FROM HER LONG SLEEP, SHE ATTACKED ME FOR REVENGE...
FWOOOO
PENT-UP FRUSTRATION, TENCHI! NOT A PRETTY SIGHT!
ZZZAAA
JUST AS RYOKO WAS ABOUT TO KILL ME, A SWORD--WHICH I STOLE FROM THE CAVE--HELPED ME! I CHOPPED HER HAND OFF AND SHE DISAPPEARED! I THOUGHT THAT EVERYTHING WAS SETTLED...
...BUT I WAS TOO OPTIMISTIC! I FOUND RYOKO ASLEEP IN MY BED! SHE DEMANDED THE THREE JEWELS FROM THE SWORD'S HANDLE--THE SOURCE OF HER POWERS.
RYOKO
SHEEEEEEE

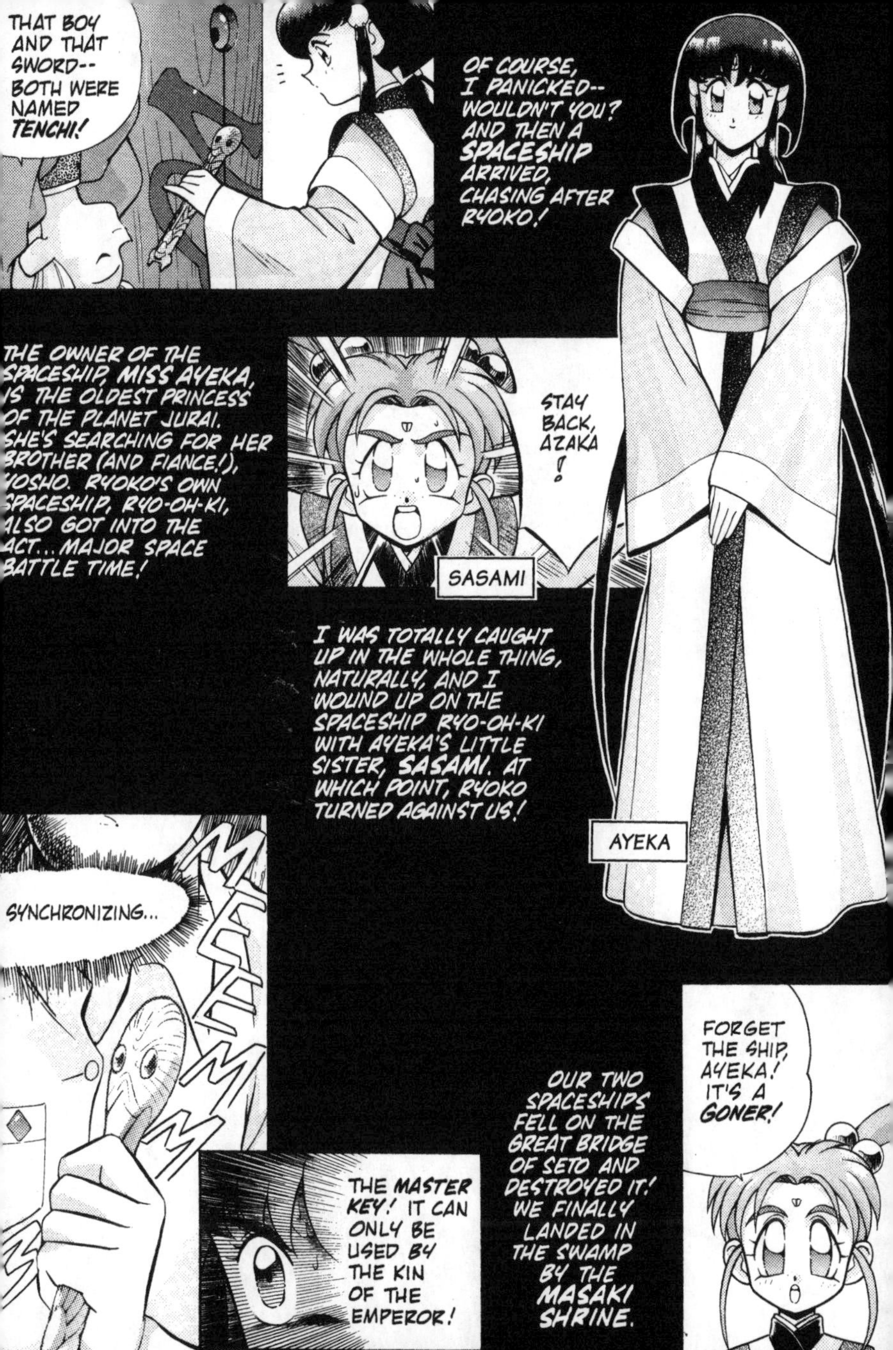
THAT BOY AND THAT SWORD-- BOTH WERE NAMED TENCHI!
OF COURSE, I PANICKED-- WOULDN'T YOU? AND THEN A SPACESHIP ARRIVED, CHASING AFTER RYOKO!
THE OWNER OF THE SPACESHIP, MISS AYEKA, IS THE OLDEST PRINCESS OF THE PLANET JURAI. SHE'S SEARCHING FOR HER BROTHER (AND FIANCE!), YOSHO. RYOKO'S OWN SPACESHIP, RYO-OH-KI, ALSO GOT INTO THE ACT... MAJOR SPACE BATTLE TIME!
STAY BACK, AZAKA!
SASAMI
I WAS TOTALLY CAUGHT UP IN THE WHOLE THING, NATURALLY, AND I WOUND UP ON THE SPACESHIP RYO-OH-KI WITH AYEKA'S LITTLE SISTER, SASAMI. AT WHICH POINT, RYOKO TURNED AGAINST US!
AYEKA
SYNCHRONIZING...
MEEEMM
THE MASTER KEY! IT CAN ONLY BE USED BY THE KIN OF THE EMPEROR!
OUR TWO SPACESHIPS FELL ON THE GREAT BRIDGE OF SETO AND DESTROYED IT! WE FINALLY LANDED IN THE SWAMP BY THE MASAKI SHRINE.
FORGET THE SHIP, AYEKA! IT'S A GONER!

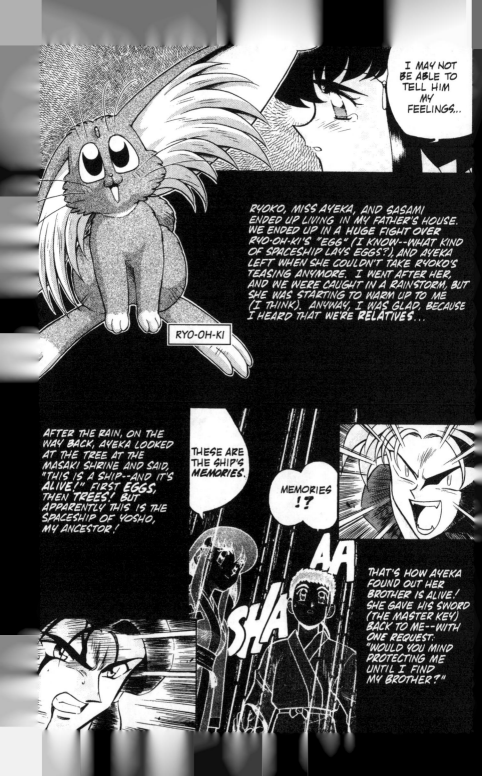

I MAY NOT BE ABLE TO TELL HIM MY FEELINGS...

RYOKO, MISS AYEKA, AND SASAMI ENDED UP LIVING IN MY FATHER'S HOUSE. WE ENDED UP IN A HUGE FIGHT OVER RYO-OH-KI'S "EGG" (I KNOW--WHAT KIND OF SPACESHIP LAYS EGGS?), AND AYEKA LEFT WHEN SHE COULDN'T TAKE RYOKO'S TEASING ANYMORE. I WENT AFTER HER, AND WE WERE CAUGHT IN A RAINSTORM, BUT SHE WAS STARTING TO WARM UP TO ME (I THINK). ANYWAY, I WAS GLAD, BECAUSE I HEARD THAT WE'RE **RELATIVES**...

RYO-OH-KI

AFTER THE RAIN, ON THE WAY BACK, AYEKA LOOKED AT THE TREE AT THE MASAKI SHRINE AND SAID, "THIS IS A SHIP--AND IT'S **ALIVE!**" FIRST **EGGS**, THEN **TREES!** BUT APPARENTLY THIS IS THE SPACESHIP OF YOSHO, MY ANCESTOR!

THESE ARE THE SHIP'S **MEMORIES**.

MEMORIES !?

AA

SHA

THAT'S HOW AYEKA FOUND OUT HER BROTHER IS ALIVE! SHE GAVE HIS SWORD (THE MASTER KEY) BACK TO ME--WITH ONE REQUEST: "WOULD YOU MIND PROTECTING ME UNTIL I FIND MY BROTHER?"

IT'S AN INSULT NOT TO TAKE A PEEK!

GRANDMA'S GONNA *KILL* YOU IF SHE FINDS OUT...

DON'T BE EMBARRASSED!

THE SEASONS CHANGED, AND AUTUMN ARRIVED. I'D GOTTEN KIND OF USED TO LIVING WITH AYEKA AND SASAMI AND RYOKO, AND WE DECIDED TO VISIT A RESORT IN OKAYAMA PREFECTURE. NATURALLY, RYOKO AND AYEKA DECIDED TO DUKE IT OUT AGAIN. RYOKO GATHERED UP SOME VICIOUS MONSTERS AND THEY GOT OUT OF CONTROL AND A BLACK HOLE APPEARED-- YOU GET THE PICTURE...

THAT'S WHEN I HELPED THE LADY WHO WAS ABOUT TO BE SUCKED UP BY THE BLACK HOLE...

THIS LADY, MIHOSHI, IS A MEMBER OF THE GALAXY POLICE. SHE CAME ALL THE WAY TO EARTH IN PURSUIT OF THE WANTED CRIMINAL KAGATO.

MIHOSHI

FINALLY, KAGATO APPEARED IN FRONT OF US! HE WAS WANDERING AROUND THE UNIVERSE ON A HUNT FOR THE GREATEST COSMIC POWER SOURCE. OF COURSE, THAT POWER COULD ONLY BE POSSESSED BY THE KIN OF THE JURAI EMPEROR. KAGATO WANTED THE SWORD AYEKA HAD FINALLY LET ME HAVE!

YOSHO

BUT THERE WAS EVEN MORE SHOCKING NEWS! TURNS OUT MY GRANDFATHER WAS ACTUALLY THE LEGENDARY YOSHO!

FINALLY, YOU APPEAR--

--FIRST PRINCE OF JURAI!

THANKS TO THE OLD MAN, WE MANAGED TO GET RID OF KAGATO, MOMENTARILY-- BUT RYOKO WAS TAKEN AS A HOSTAGE! I BORROWED THE SWORD FROM THE OLD MAN AND BOARDED THE SHIP RYO-OH-KI WITH AYEKA AND MIHOSHI...

...BUT KAGATO WAS JUST TOO POWERFUL! HIS SPACESHIP SOJA'S MAIN CANNON HIT MY SHIP, AND I PREPARED TO DIE...

KAGATO

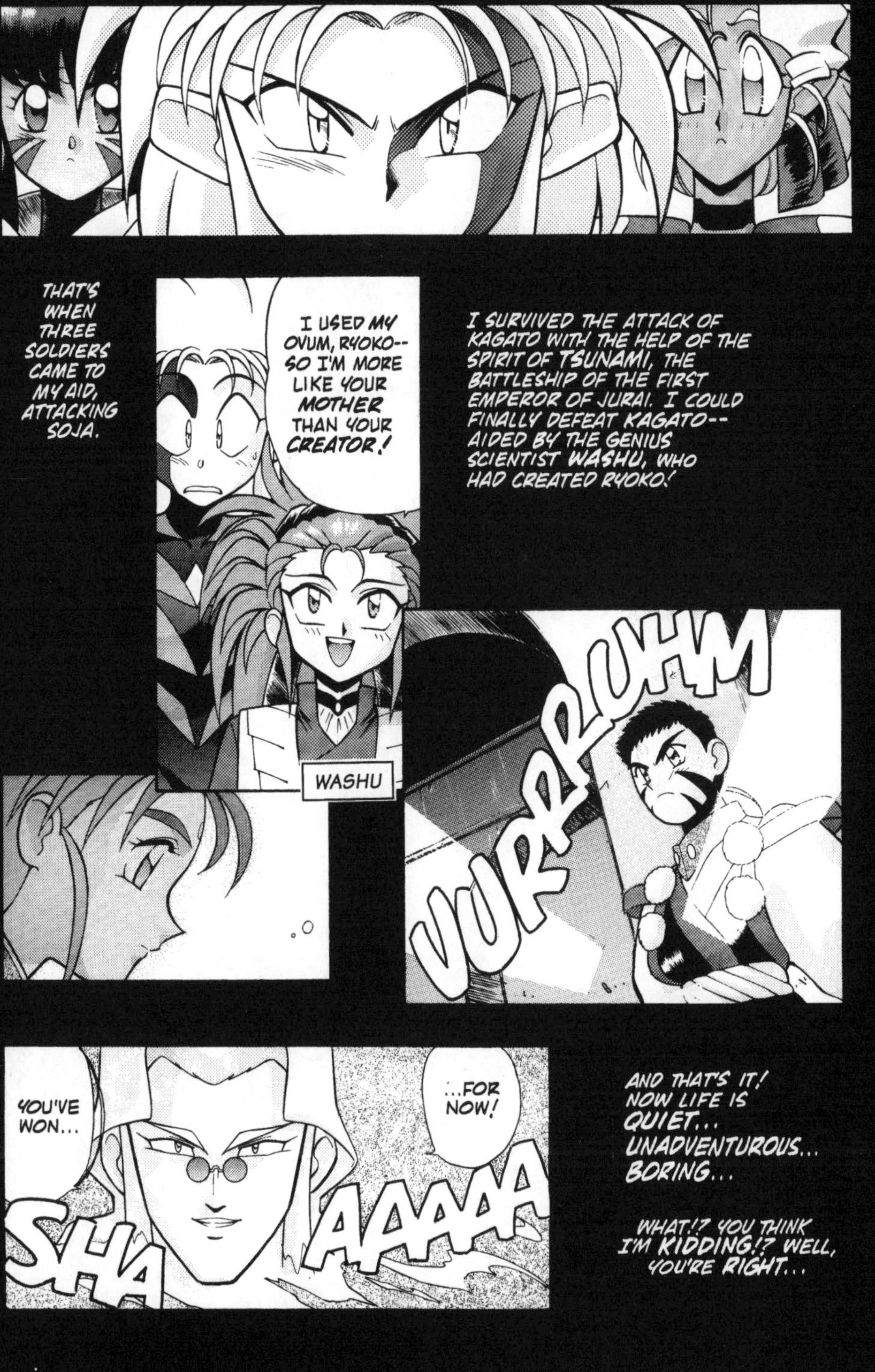

THAT'S WHEN THREE SOLDIERS CAME TO MY AID, ATTACKING SOJA.
I USED MY OVUM, RYOKO-- SO I'M MORE LIKE YOUR MOTHER THAN YOUR CREATOR!
WASHU
I SURVIVED THE ATTACK OF KAGATO WITH THE HELP OF THE SPIRIT OF TSUNAMI, THE BATTLESHIP OF THE FIRST EMPEROR OF JURAI. I COULD FINALLY DEFEAT KAGATO-- AIDED BY THE GENIUS SCIENTIST WASHU, WHO HAD CREATED RYOKO!
VURRUHM
YOU'VE WON...
...FOR NOW!
SHAAAAA
AND THAT'S IT! NOW LIFE IS QUIET... UNADVENTUROUS... BORING...
WHAT!? YOU THINK I'M KIDDING!? WELL, YOU'RE RIGHT...

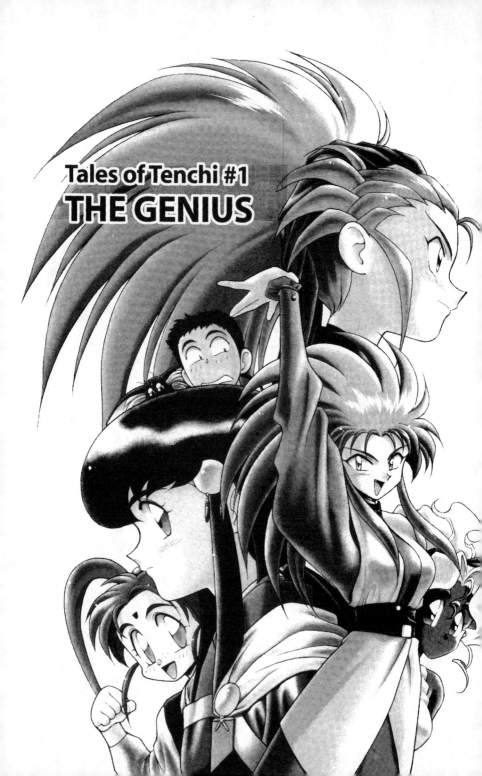

Tales of Tenchi #1
THE GENIUS

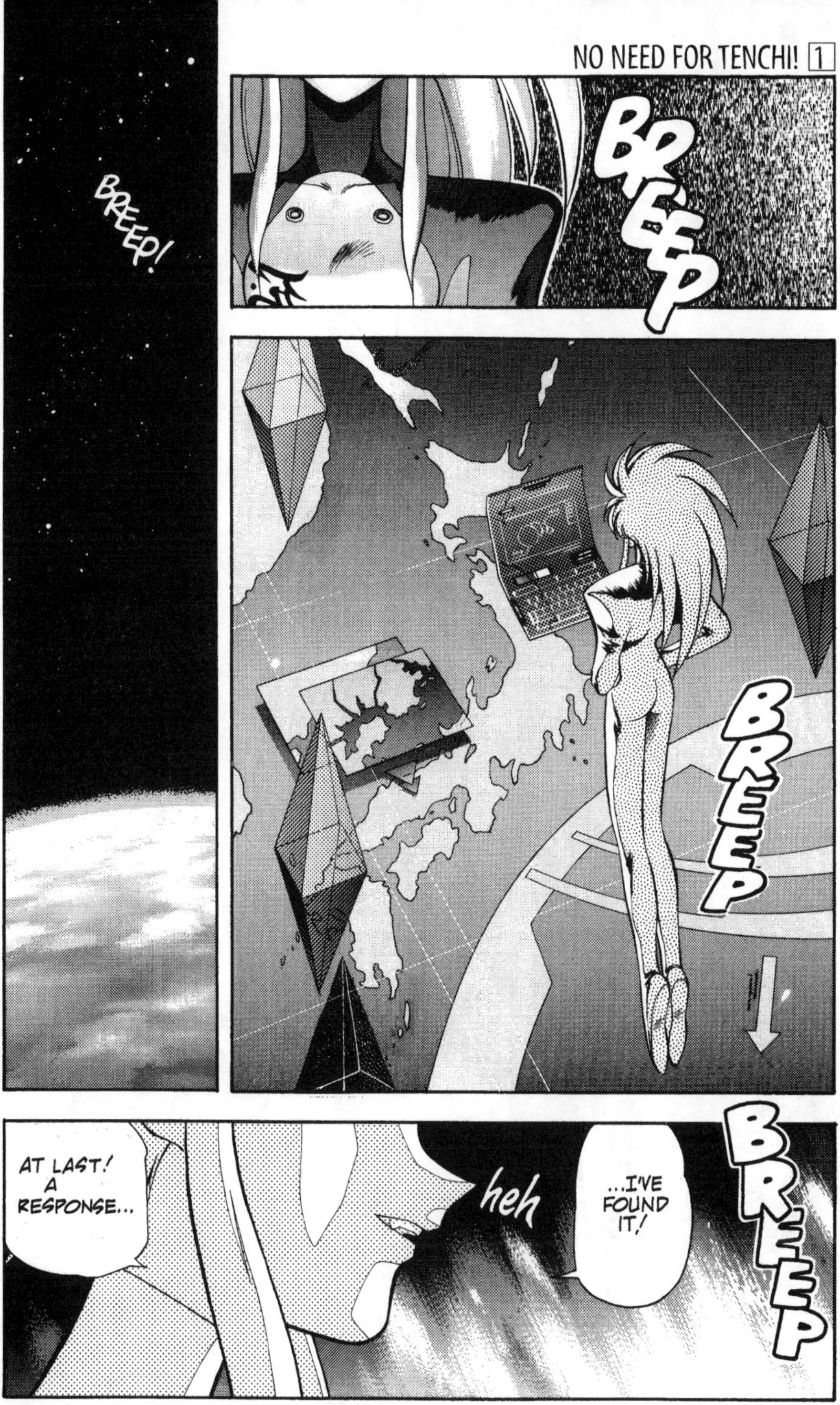
BREEP!
BREEP
BREEP
AT LAST! A RESPONSE...
heh
...I'VE FOUND IT!
BREEP

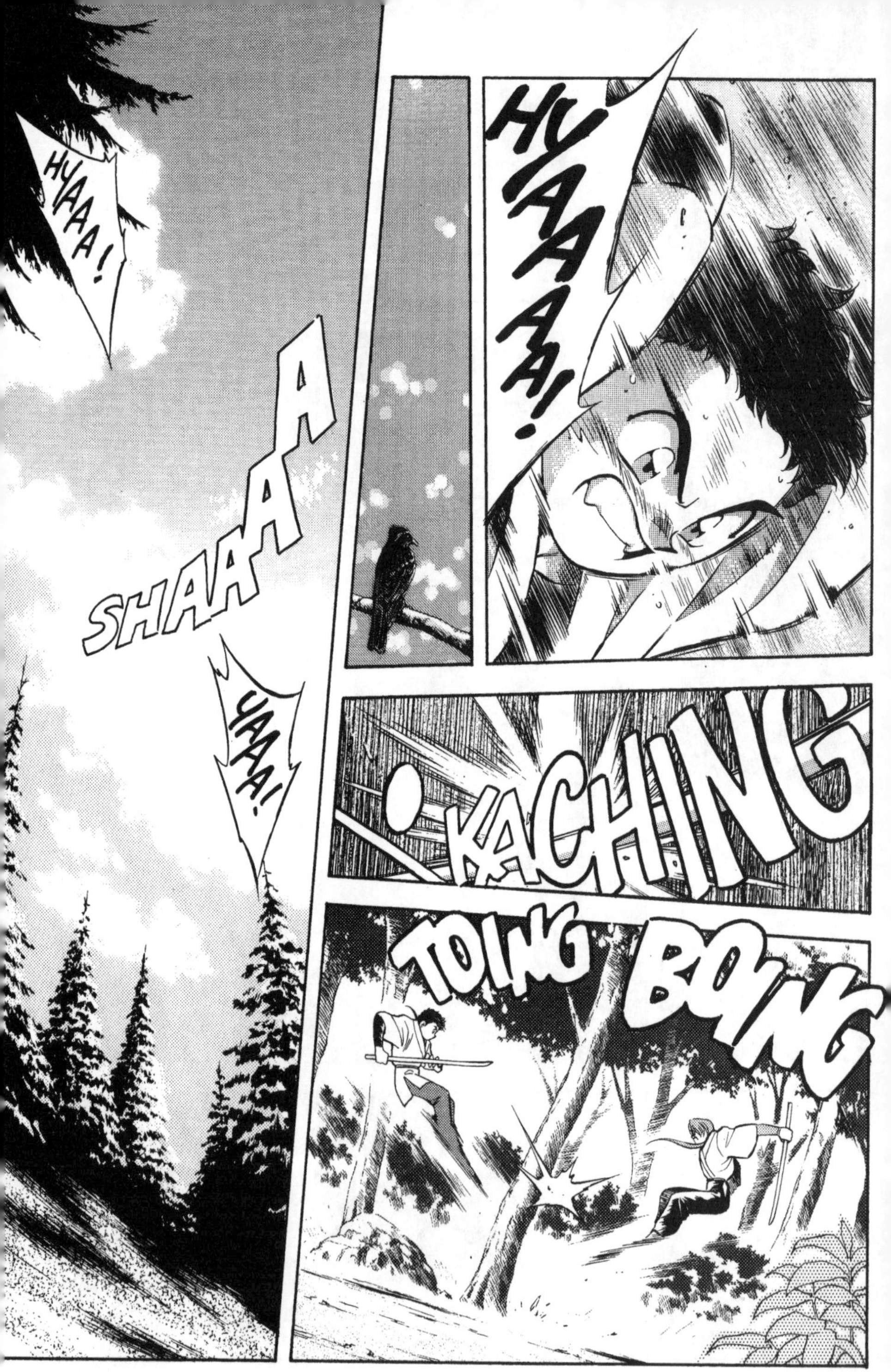
HYAAAA!
SHAAAA
YAAAA!
HYAAAAA!
KACHING
TOING
BOING

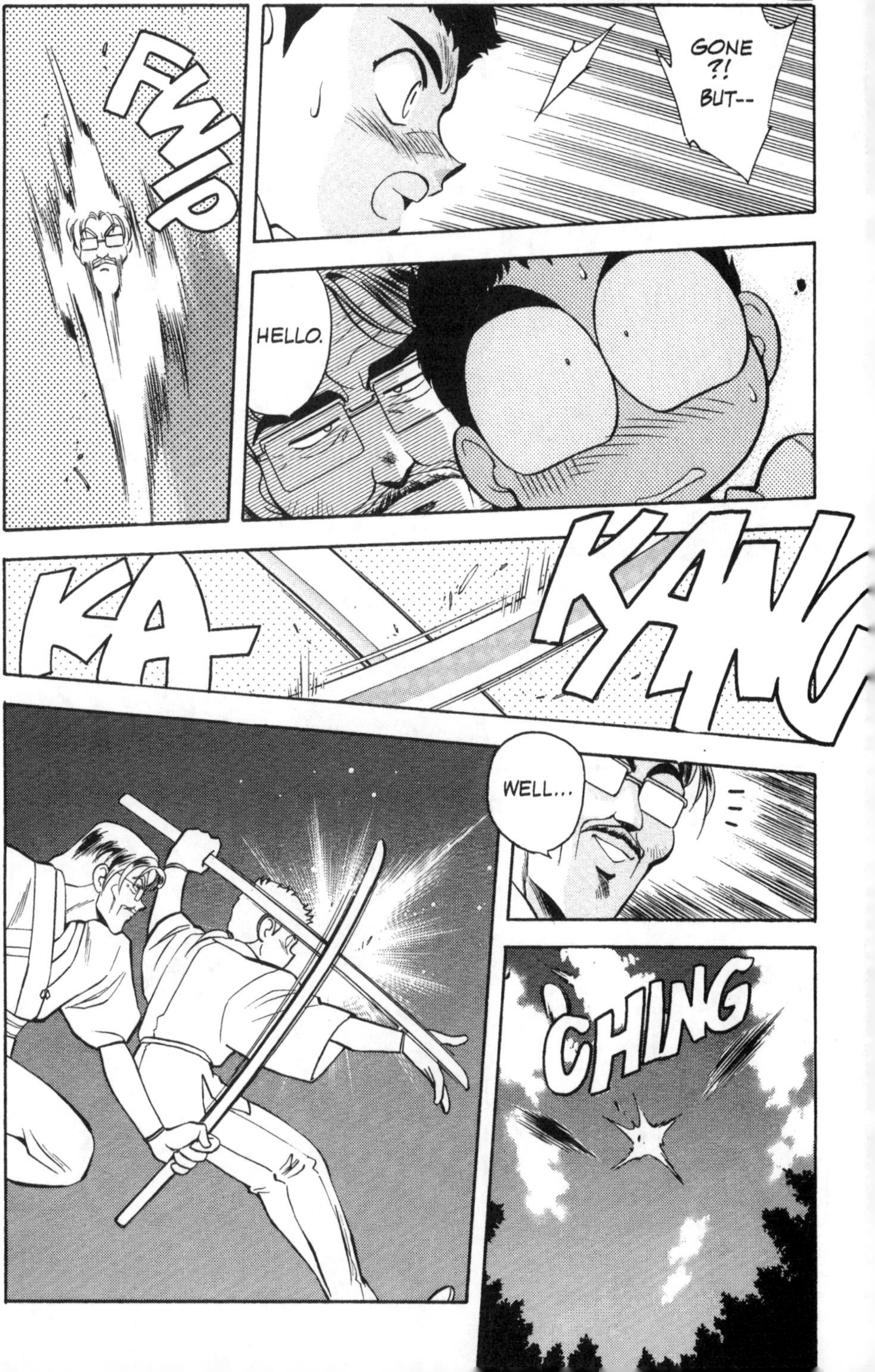
FWIP
GONE ?! BUT--
HELLO.
KA
KYANG
WELL...
CHING

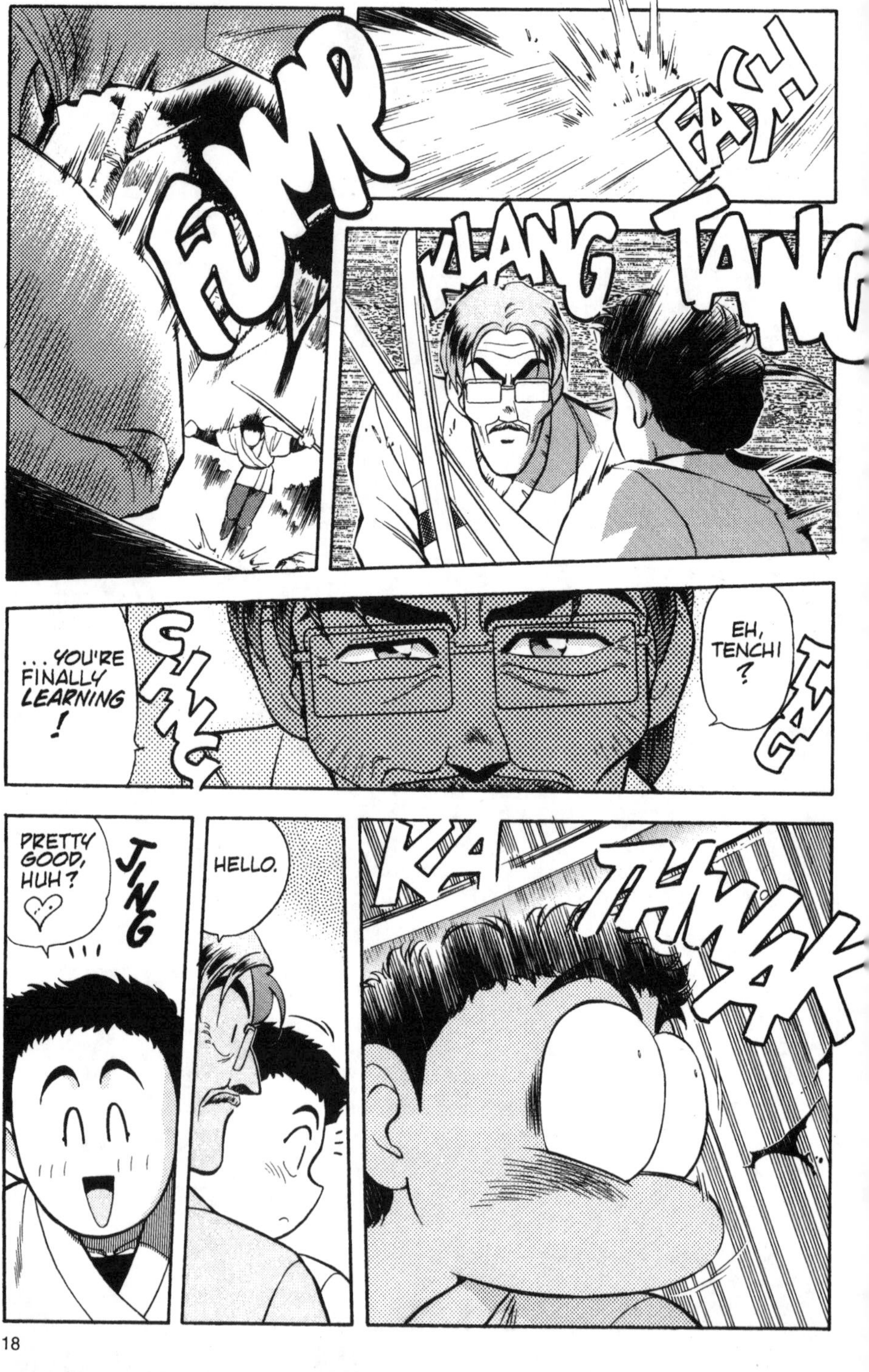
FUMP
FASH
KLANG
TANG
...YOU'RE FINALLY LEARNING!
CHING
EH, TENCHI?
PRETTY GOOD, HUH? ♡
JING
HELLO.
KA
THWAK

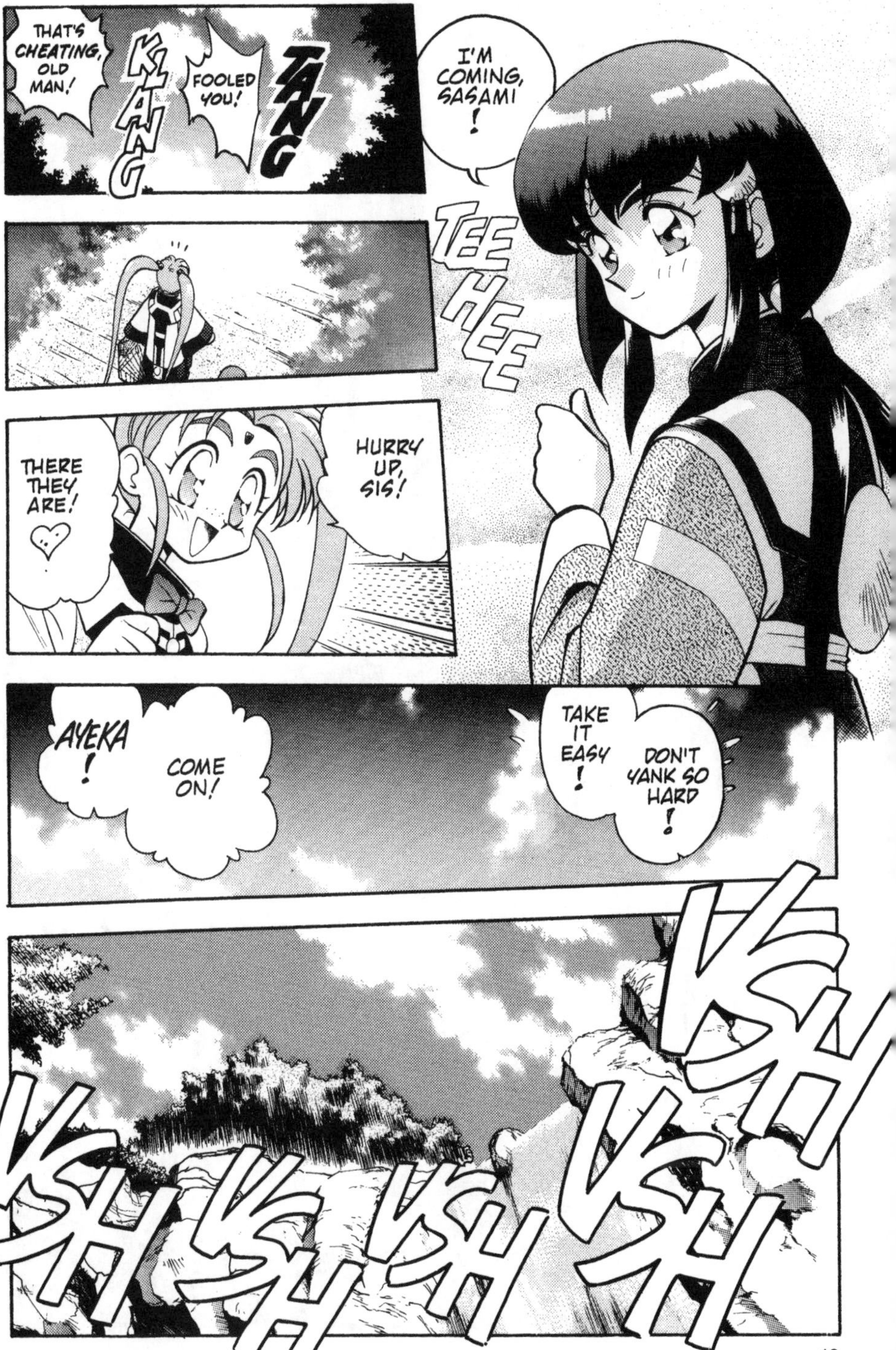

THAT'S CHEATING, OLD MAN!
KLANG
FOOLED YOU!
TANG
THERE THEY ARE! ♥
HURRY UP, SIS!
I'M COMING, SASAMI!
TEE HEE
AYEKA!
COME ON!
TAKE IT EASY!
DON'T YANK SO HARD!
VSH
VSH
VSH
VSH
VSH
VSH
VSH

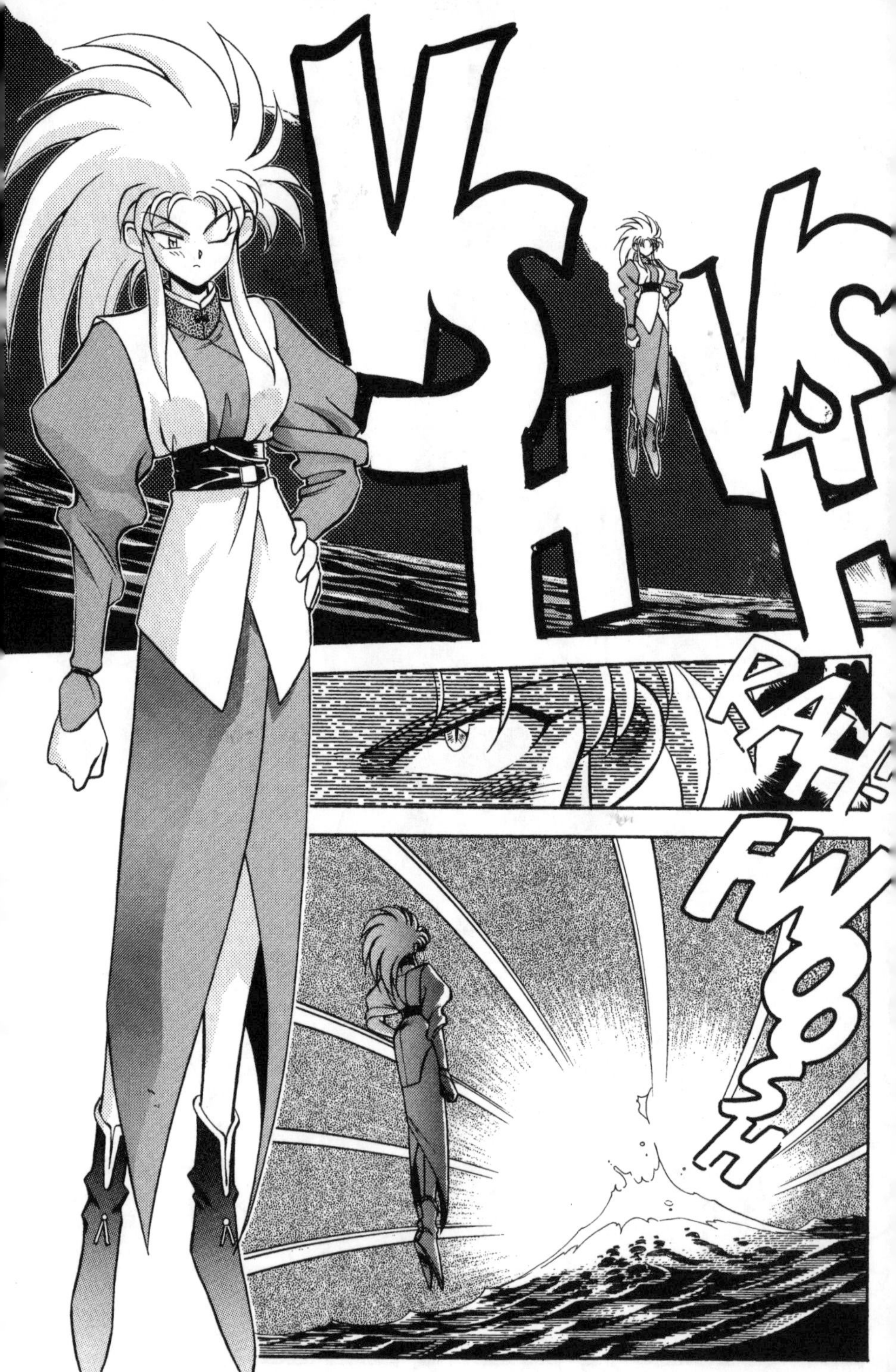
VSH
VSH!
RAH!
FWOOSH

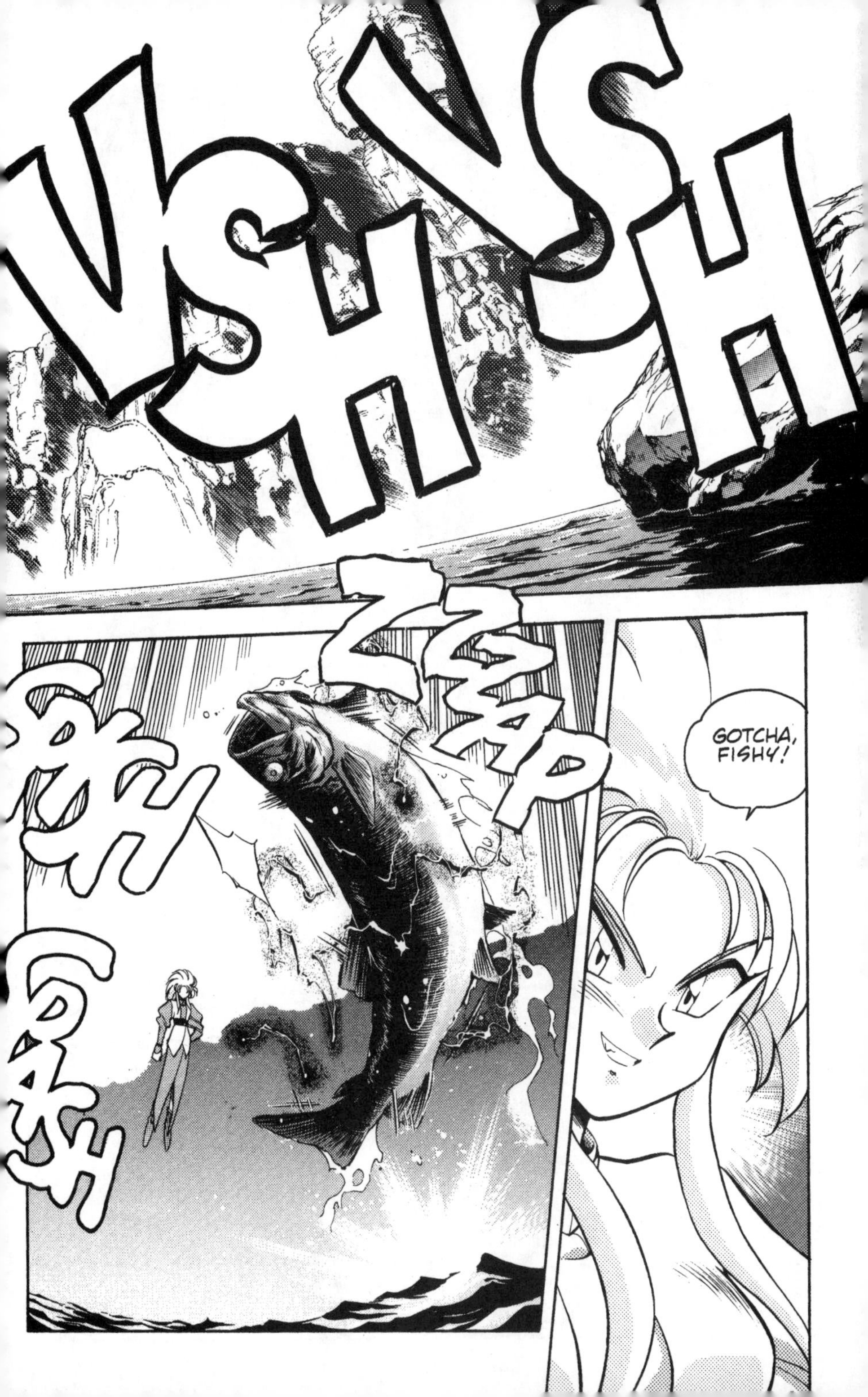
ZZAP
GOTCHA, FISHY!

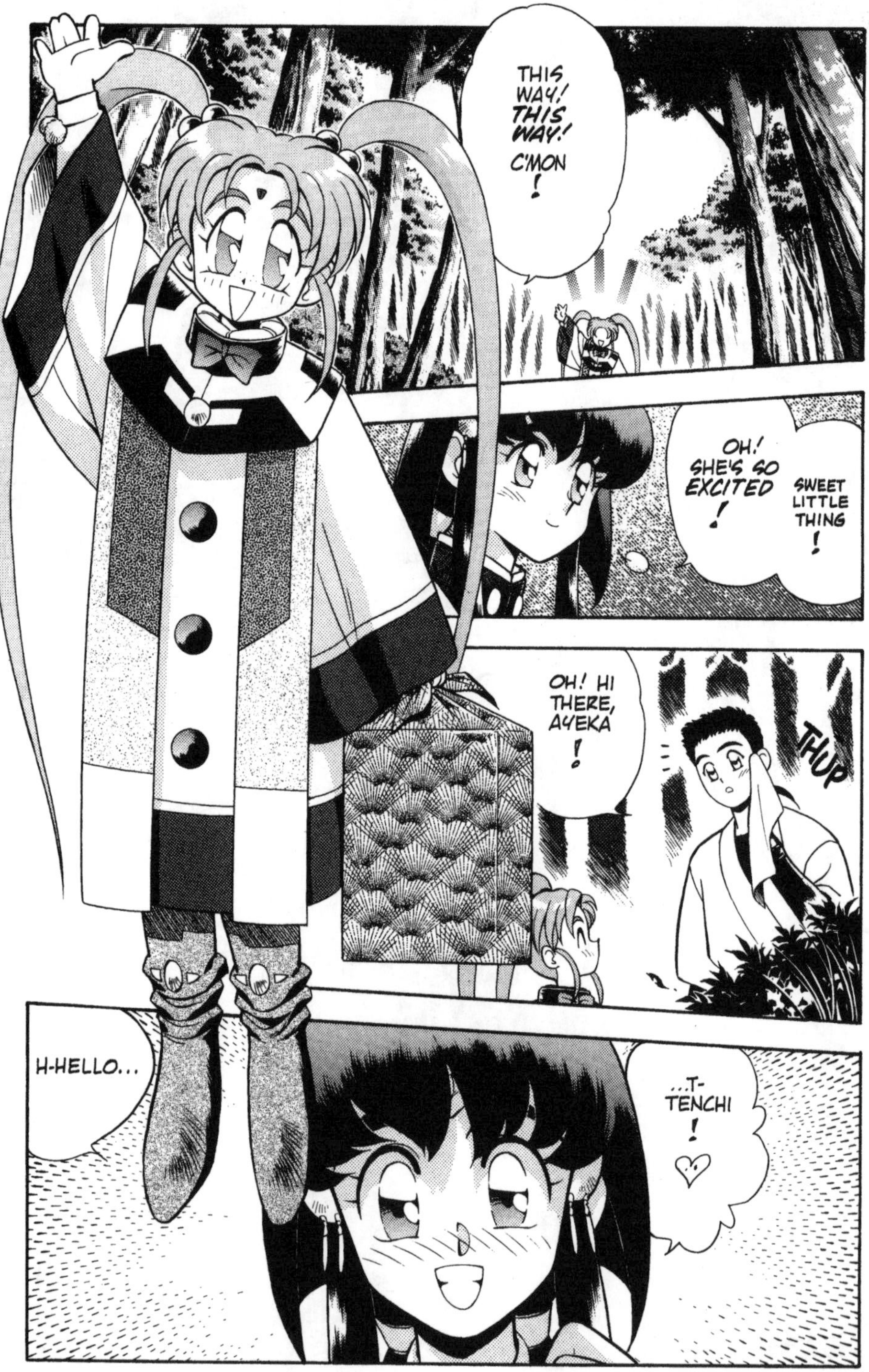
THIS WAY! THIS WAY! C'MON!
OH! SHE'S SO EXCITED!
SWEET LITTLE THING!
OH! HI THERE, AYEKA!
THUP
H-HELLO...
...T-TENCHI!

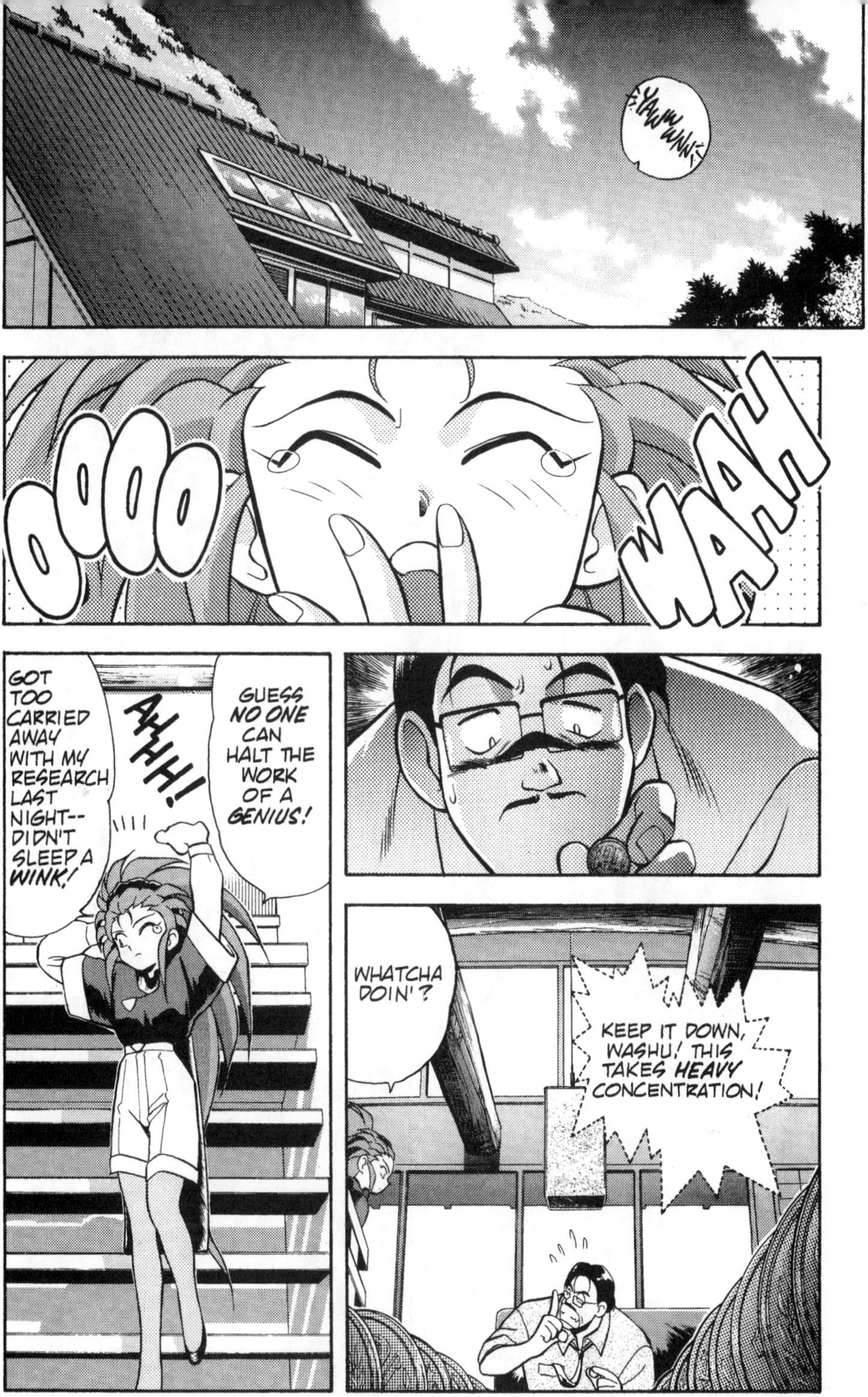
YAWWWN!
OOOO
WAAH
GOT TOO CARRIED AWAY WITH MY RESEARCH LAST NIGHT-- DIDN'T SLEEP A WINK!
AHHH!
GUESS NO ONE CAN HALT THE WORK OF A GENIUS!
WHATCHA DOIN'?
KEEP IT DOWN, WASHU! THIS TAKES HEAVY CONCENTRATION!

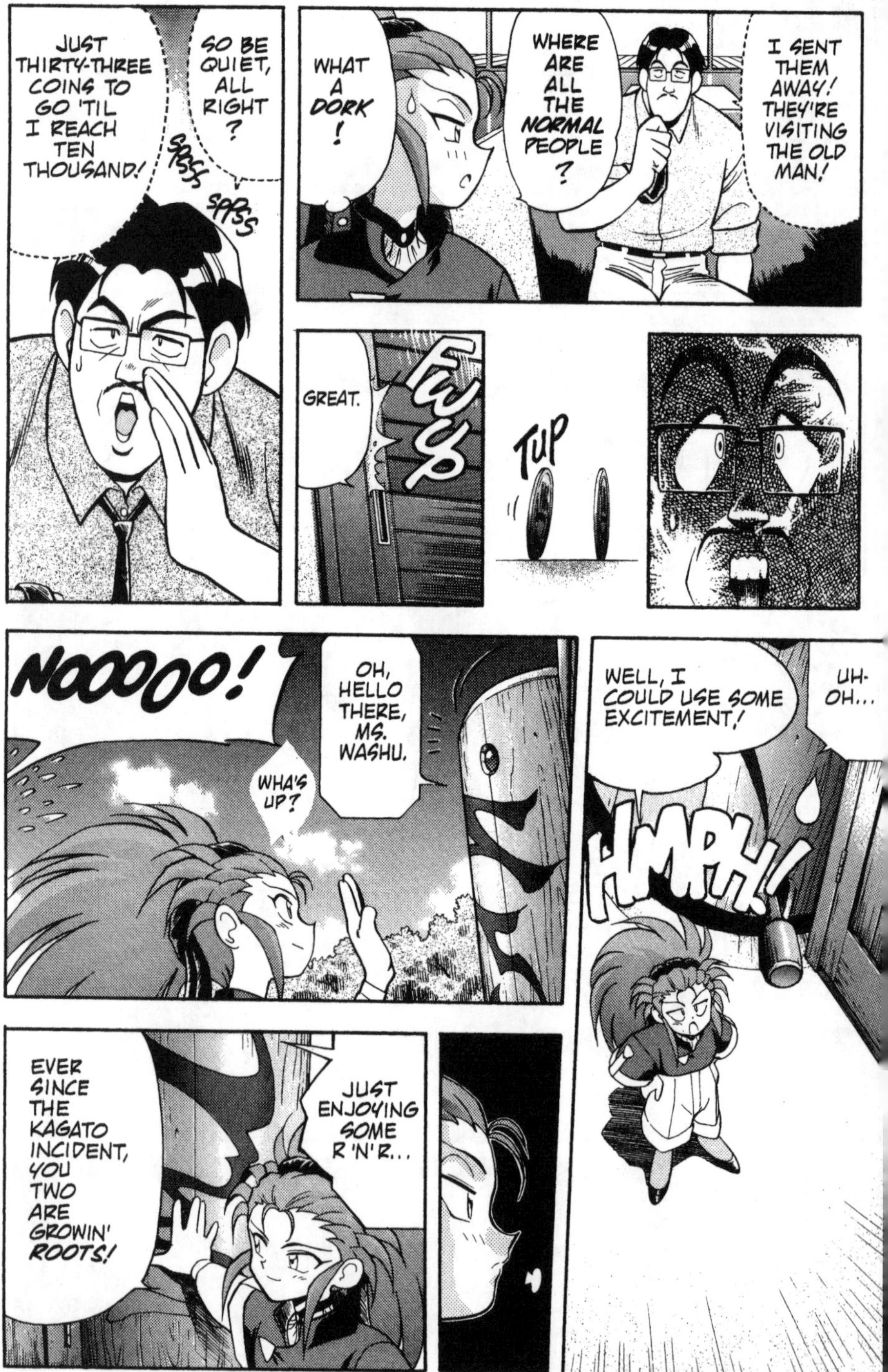
JUST THIRTY-THREE COINS TO GO 'TIL I REACH TEN THOUSAND!
SO BE QUIET, ALL RIGHT?
SPSSS
SPSSS
WHAT A DORK!
WHERE ARE ALL THE NORMAL PEOPLE?
I SENT THEM AWAY! THEY'RE VISITING THE OLD MAN!
GREAT.
FWUP
TUP
NOOOOO!
OH, HELLO THERE, MS. WASHU.
WHA'S UP?
EVER SINCE THE KAGATO INCIDENT, YOU TWO ARE GROWIN' ROOTS!
JUST ENJOYING SOME R'N'R...
WELL, I COULD USE SOME EXCITEMENT!
UH-OH...
HMPH!

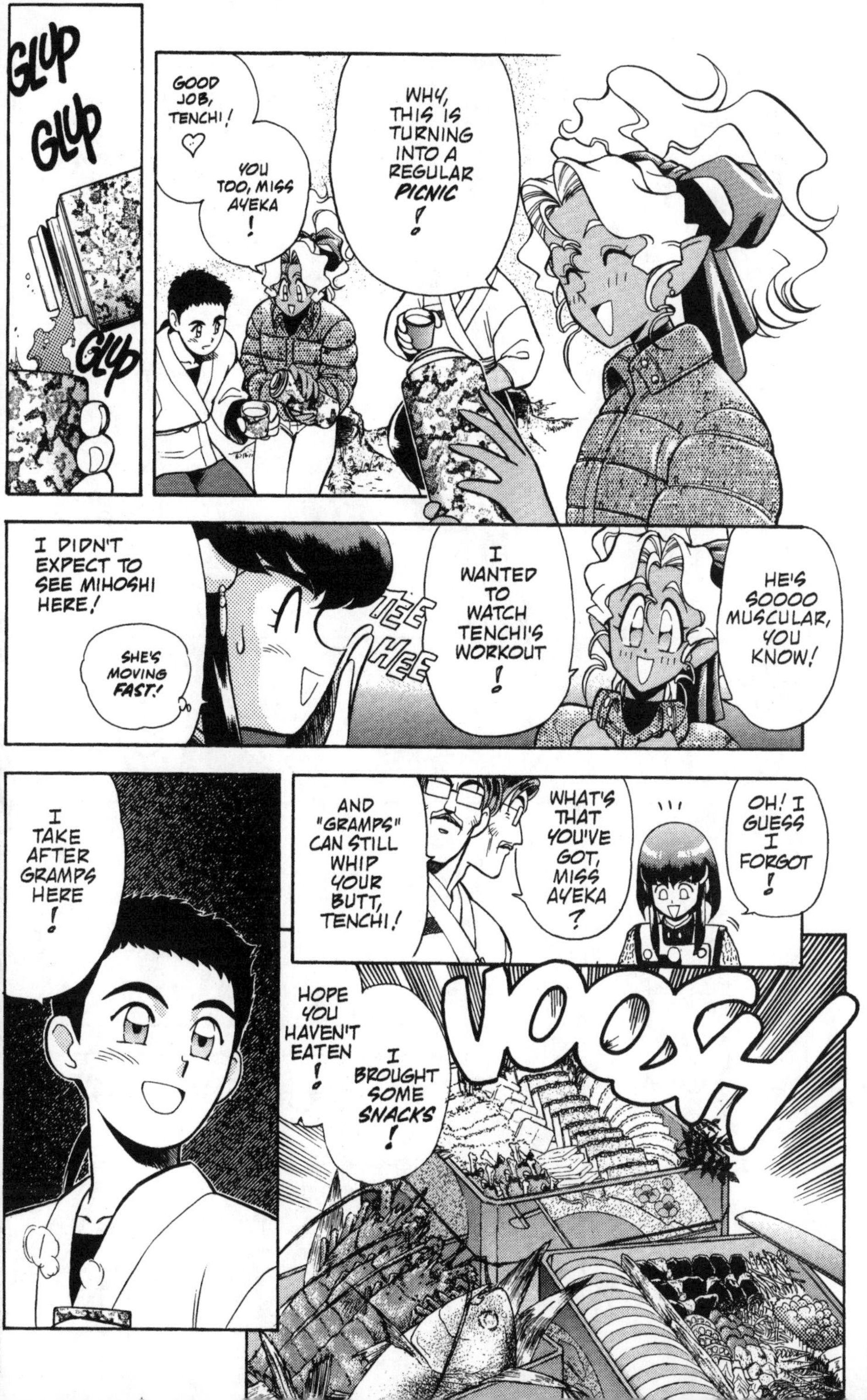
GLUP
GLUP
GLUP
GOOD JOB, TENCHI! ♡
YOU TOO, MISS AYEKA!
WHY, THIS IS TURNING INTO A REGULAR PICNIC!
I DIDN'T EXPECT TO SEE MIHOSHI HERE!
SHE'S MOVING FAST!
HEE HEE
I WANTED TO WATCH TENCHI'S WORKOUT!
HE'S SOOOO MUSCULAR, YOU KNOW!
I TAKE AFTER GRAMPS HERE!
AND "GRAMPS" CAN STILL WHIP YOUR BUTT, TENCHI!
WHAT'S THAT YOU'VE GOT, MISS AYEKA?
OH! I GUESS I FORGOT!
HOPE YOU HAVEN'T EATEN!
I BROUGHT SOME SNACKS!

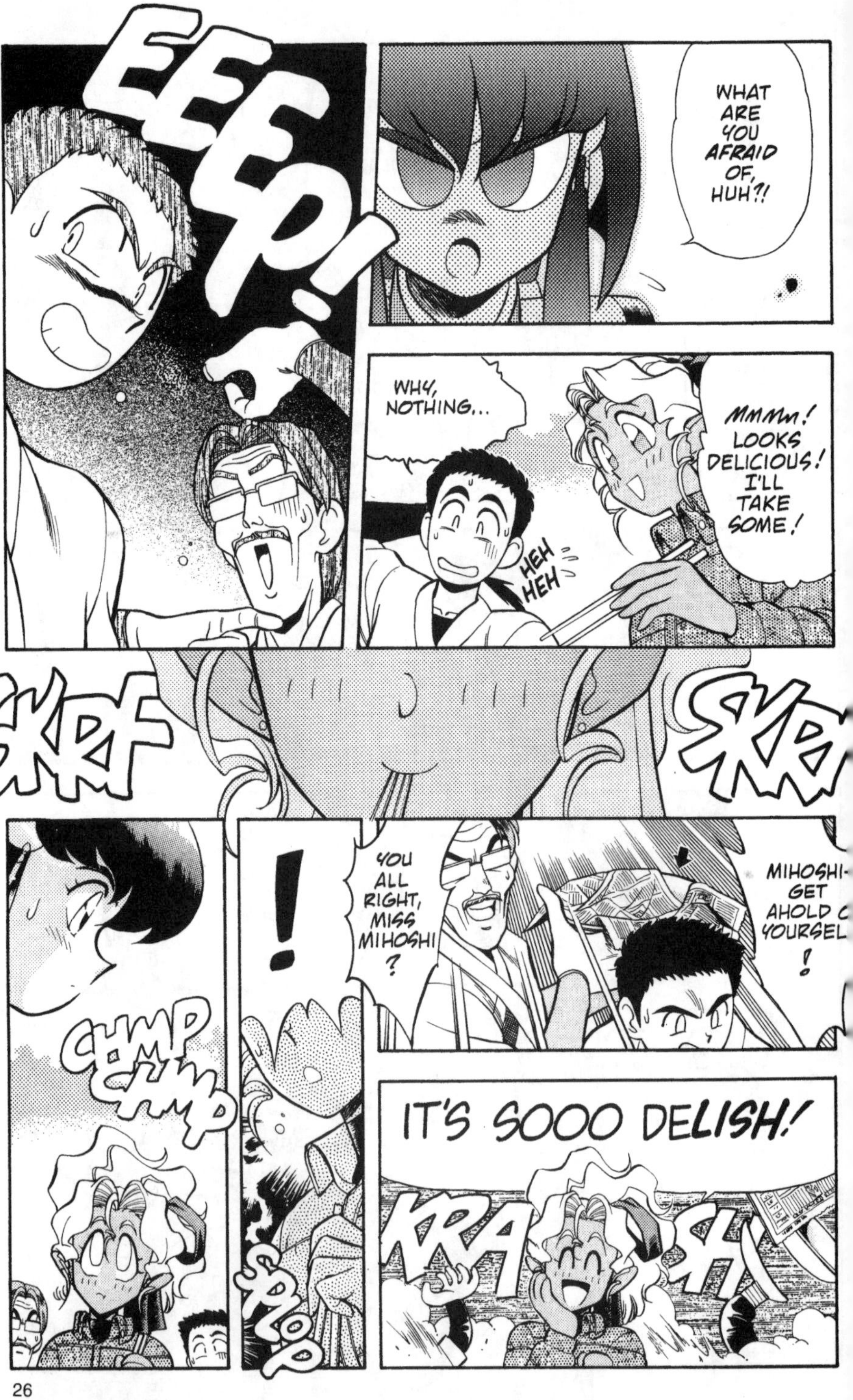
EEEP!
WHAT ARE YOU AFRAID OF, HUH?!
WHY, NOTHING...
MMMM! LOOKS DELICIOUS! I'LL TAKE SOME!
HEH HEH
SKRF
SKRF
CHMP CHMP
!
SPLOP
YOU ALL RIGHT, MISS MIHOSHI?
MIHOSHI-GET AHOLD O YOURSEL !
IT'S SOOO DELISH!
KRASH

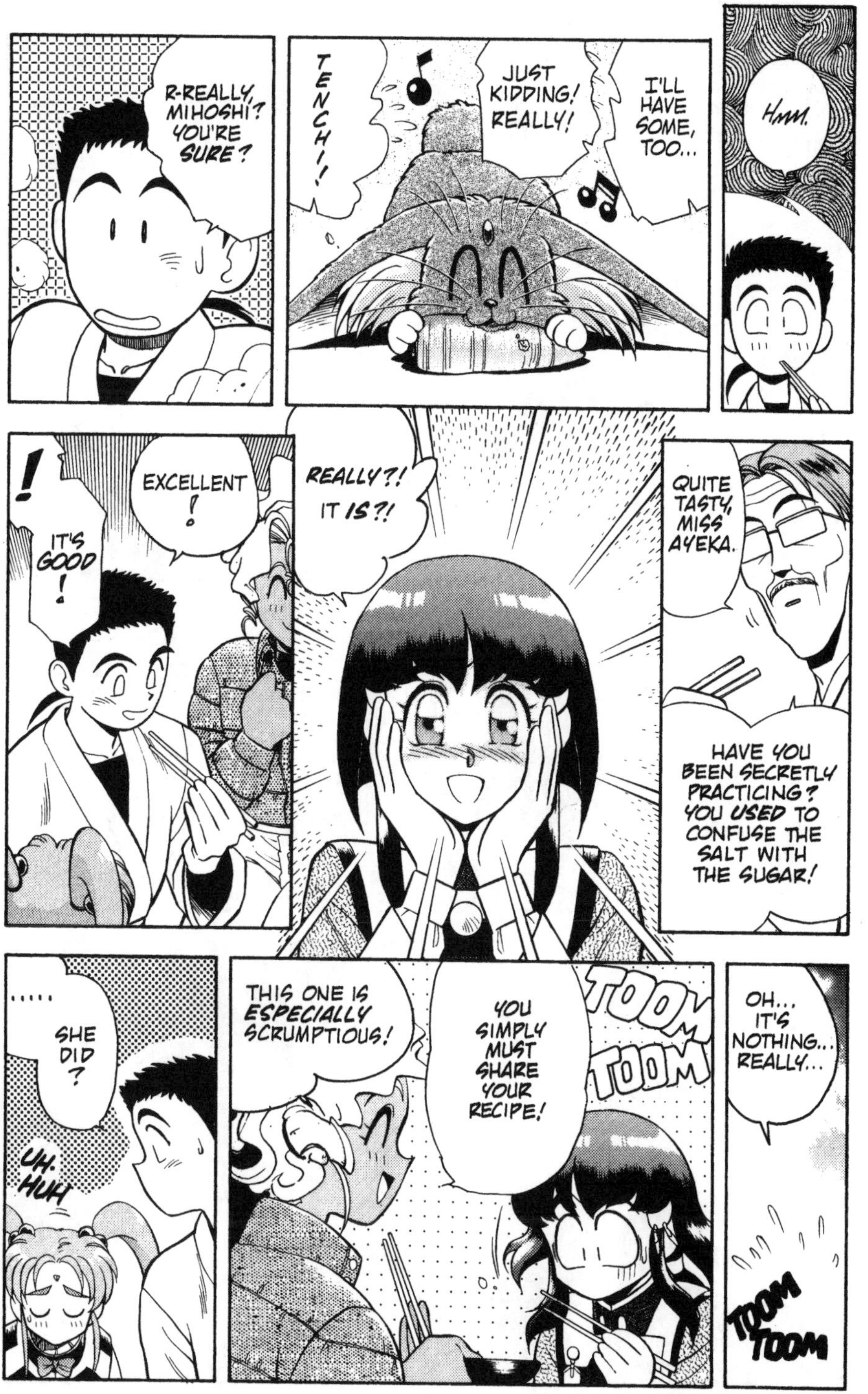
R-REALLY, MIHOSHI? YOU'RE SURE?
TENCHI!!
JUST KIDDING! REALLY!
I'LL HAVE SOME, TOO...
HMM.
!
IT'S GOOD!
EXCELLENT!
REALLY?! IT IS?!
QUITE TASTY, MISS AYEKA.
HAVE YOU BEEN SECRETLY PRACTICING? YOU USED TO CONFUSE THE SALT WITH THE SUGAR!
.....
SHE DID?
UH-HUH
THIS ONE IS ESPECIALLY SCRUMPTIOUS!
YOU SIMPLY MUST SHARE YOUR RECIPE!
TOOM TOOM
OH... IT'S NOTHING... REALLY...
TOOM TOOM

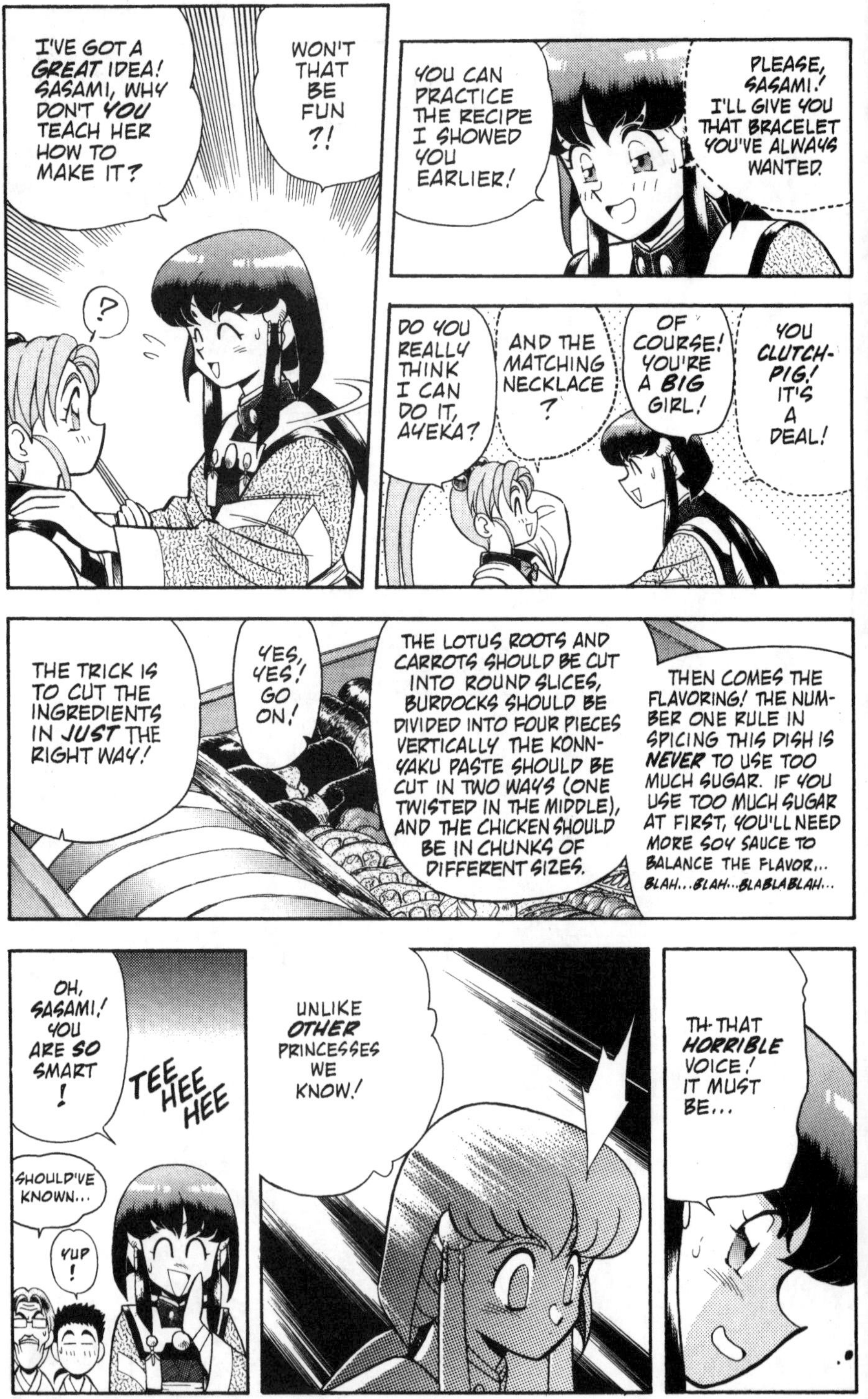
I'VE GOT A GREAT IDEA! SASAMI, WHY DON'T YOU TEACH HER HOW TO MAKE IT?
WON'T THAT BE FUN ?!
?
YOU CAN PRACTICE THE RECIPE I SHOWED YOU EARLIER!
PLEASE, SASAMI! I'LL GIVE YOU THAT BRACELET YOU'VE ALWAYS WANTED.
DO YOU REALLY THINK I CAN DO IT, AYEKA?
AND THE MATCHING NECKLACE ?
OF COURSE! YOU'RE A BIG GIRL!
YOU CLUTCH-PIG! IT'S A DEAL!
THE TRICK IS TO CUT THE INGREDIENTS IN JUST THE RIGHT WAY!
YES, YES! GO ON!
THE LOTUS ROOTS AND CARROTS SHOULD BE CUT INTO ROUND SLICES, BURDOCKS SHOULD BE DIVIDED INTO FOUR PIECES VERTICALLY THE KONN-YAKU PASTE SHOULD BE CUT IN TWO WAYS (ONE TWISTED IN THE MIDDLE), AND THE CHICKEN SHOULD BE IN CHUNKS OF DIFFERENT SIZES.
THEN COMES THE FLAVORING! THE NUM-BER ONE RULE IN SPICING THIS DISH IS NEVER TO USE TOO MUCH SUGAR. IF YOU USE TOO MUCH SUGAR AT FIRST, YOU'LL NEED MORE SOY SAUCE TO BALANCE THE FLAVOR... BLAH...BLAH...BLABLABLAH...
OH, SASAMI! YOU ARE SO SMART !
TEE HEE HEE
SHOULD'VE KNOWN...
YUP !
UNLIKE OTHER PRINCESSES WE KNOW!
TH-THAT HORRIBLE VOICE! IT MUST BE...

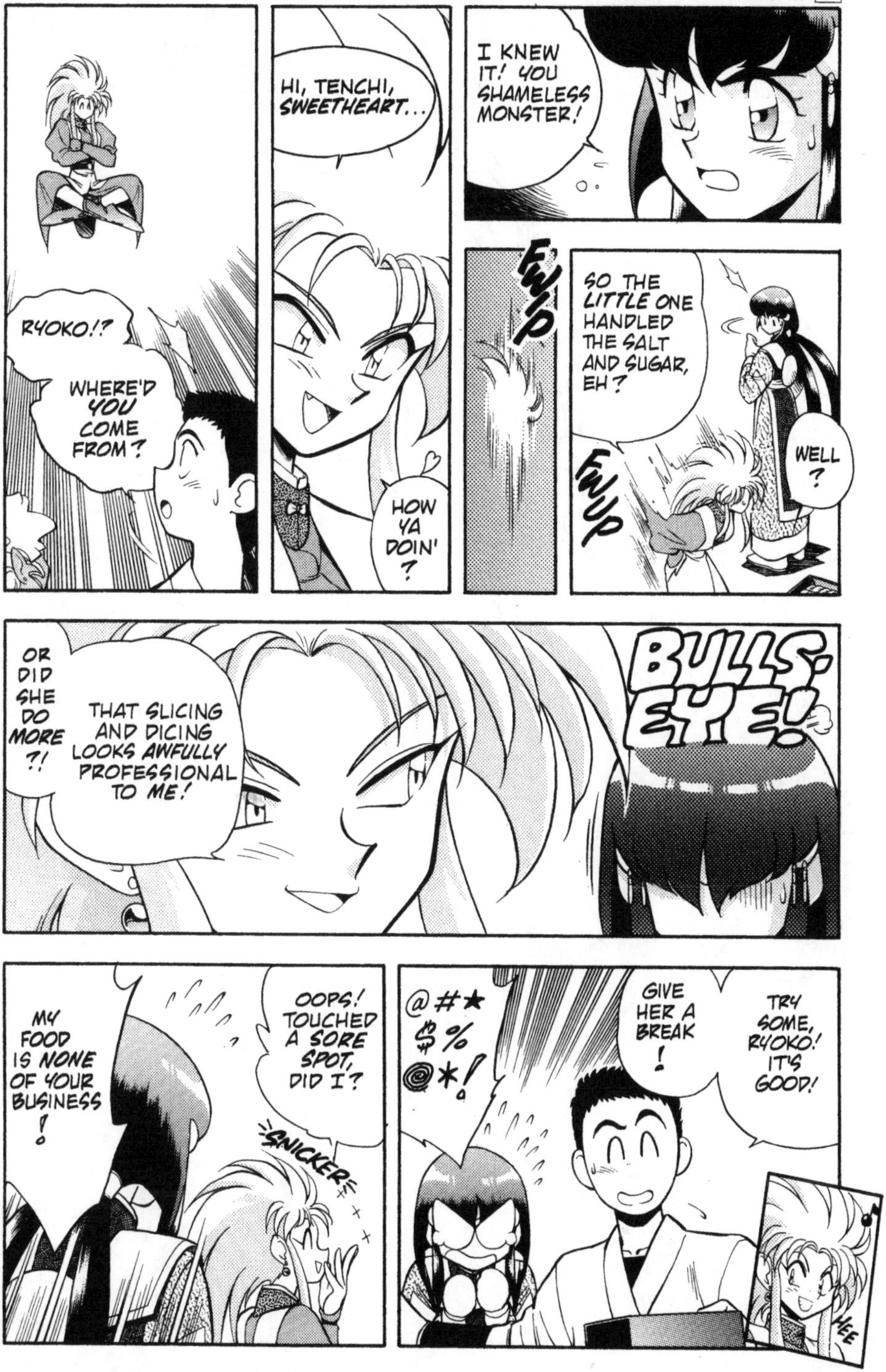
RYOKO!?
WHERE'D YOU COME FROM?
HI, TENCHI, SWEETHEART...
HOW YA DOIN'?
I KNEW IT! YOU SHAMELESS MONSTER!
FWIP
SO THE LITTLE ONE HANDLED THE SALT AND SUGAR, EH?
FWUP
WELL?
OR DID SHE DO MORE?!
THAT SLICING AND DICING LOOKS AWFULLY PROFESSIONAL TO ME!
BULLS-EYE!
MY FOOD IS NONE OF YOUR BUSINESS!
OOPS! TOUCHED A SORE SPOT, DID I?
SNICKER
@#★ $% @*!
GIVE HER A BREAK!
TRY SOME, RYOKO! IT'S GOOD!
HEE

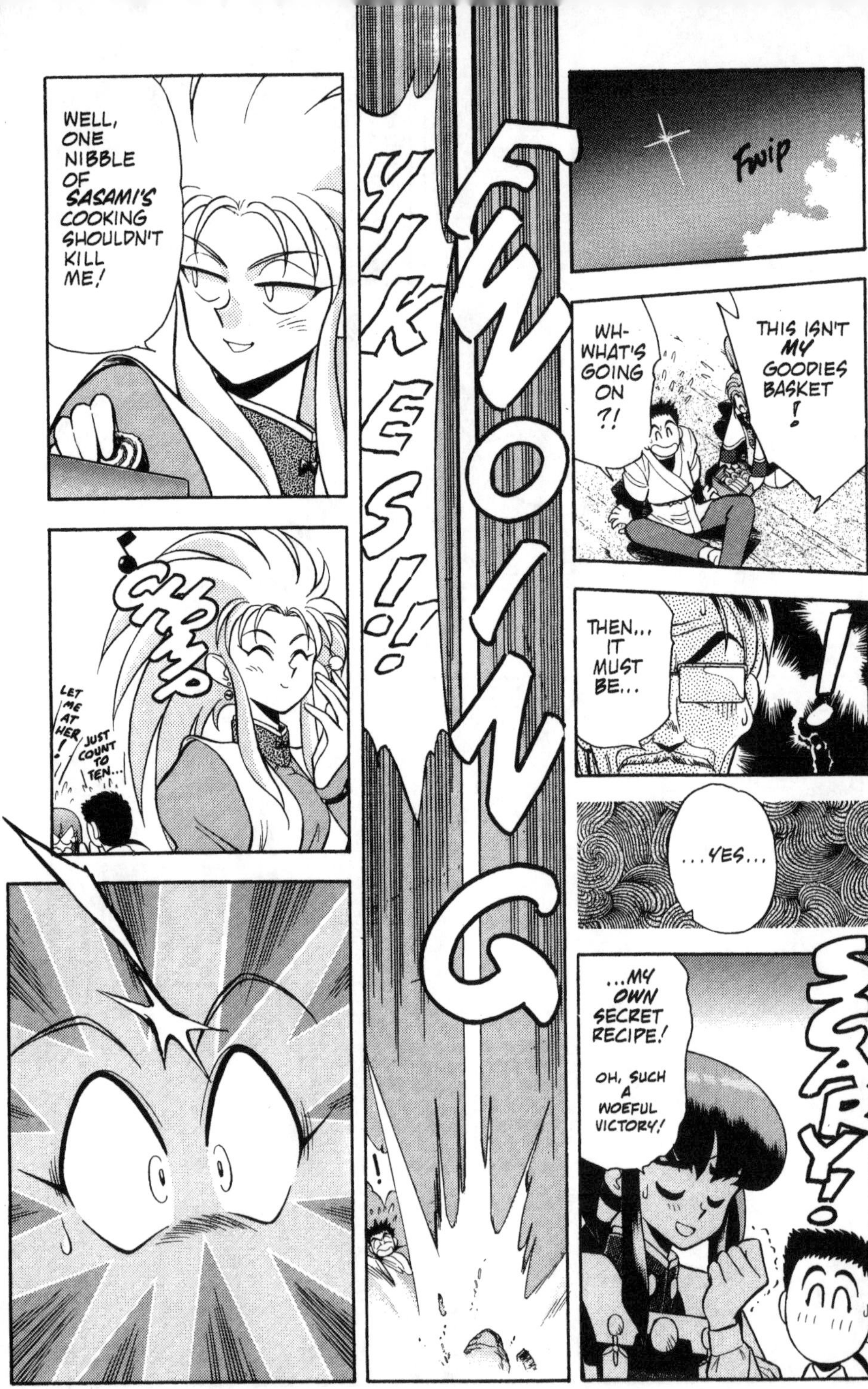
WELL, ONE NIBBLE OF SASAMI'S COOKING SHOULDN'T KILL ME!
CHOMP
LET ME AT HER!
JUST COUNT TO TEN...
YIKES!!!
FWOING
!
Fwip
WH-WHAT'S GOING ON ?!
THIS ISN'T MY GOODIES BASKET!
THEN... IT MUST BE...
!
...YES...
...MY OWN SECRET RECIPE!
OH, SUCH A WOEFUL VICTORY!
SORRY!

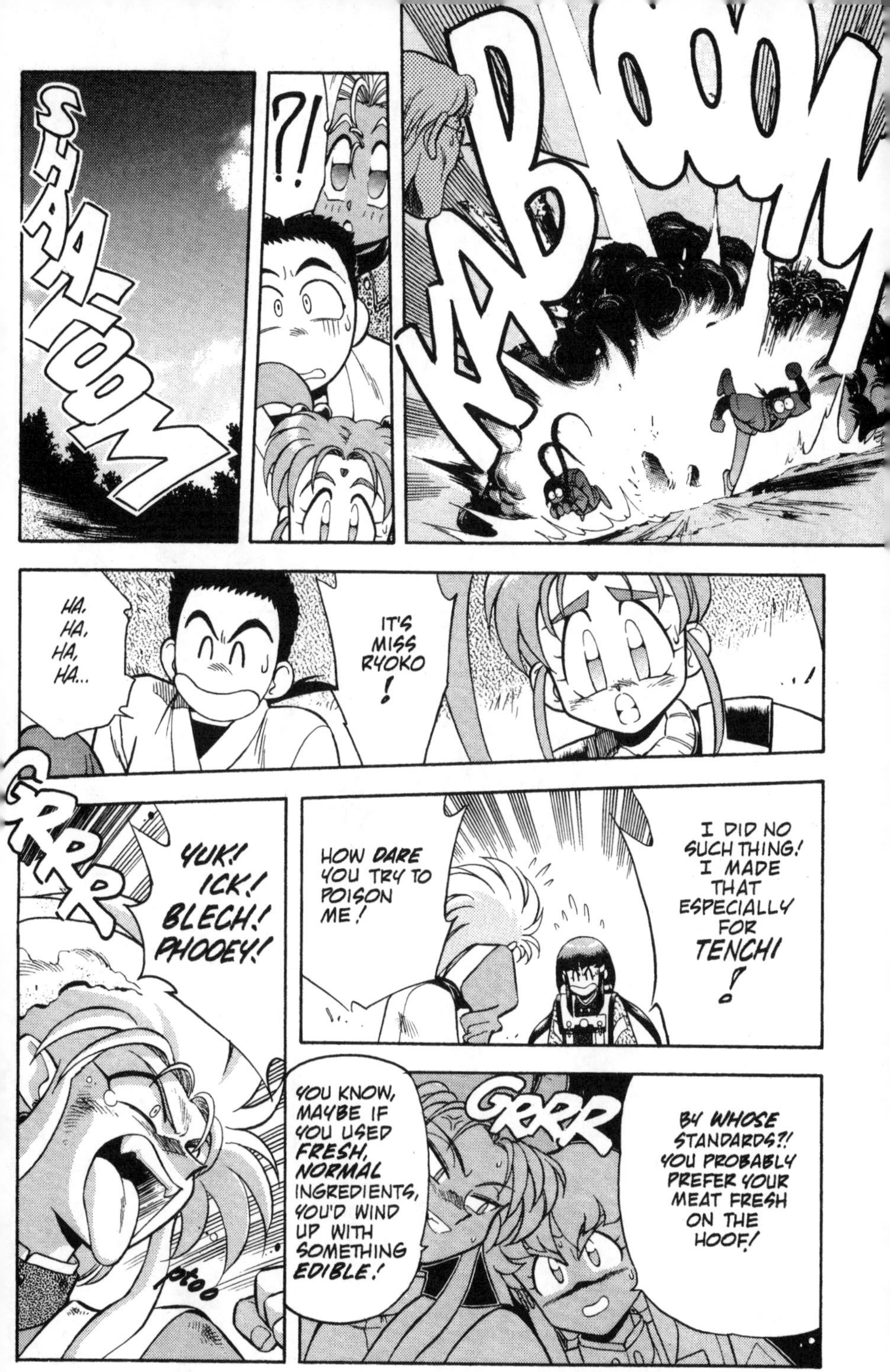
SHA-ATOOM
?!
KABLOOOM
HA, HA, HA, HA...
IT'S MISS RYOKO!
GRRR
YUK! ICK! BLECH! PHOOEY!
HOW DARE YOU TRY TO POISON ME!
I DID NO SUCH THING! I MADE THAT ESPECIALLY FOR TENCHI!
ptoo
YOU KNOW, MAYBE IF YOU USED FRESH, NORMAL INGREDIENTS, YOU'D WIND UP WITH SOMETHING EDIBLE!
GRRR
BY WHOSE STANDARDS?! YOU PROBABLY PREFER YOUR MEAT FRESH ON THE HOOF!

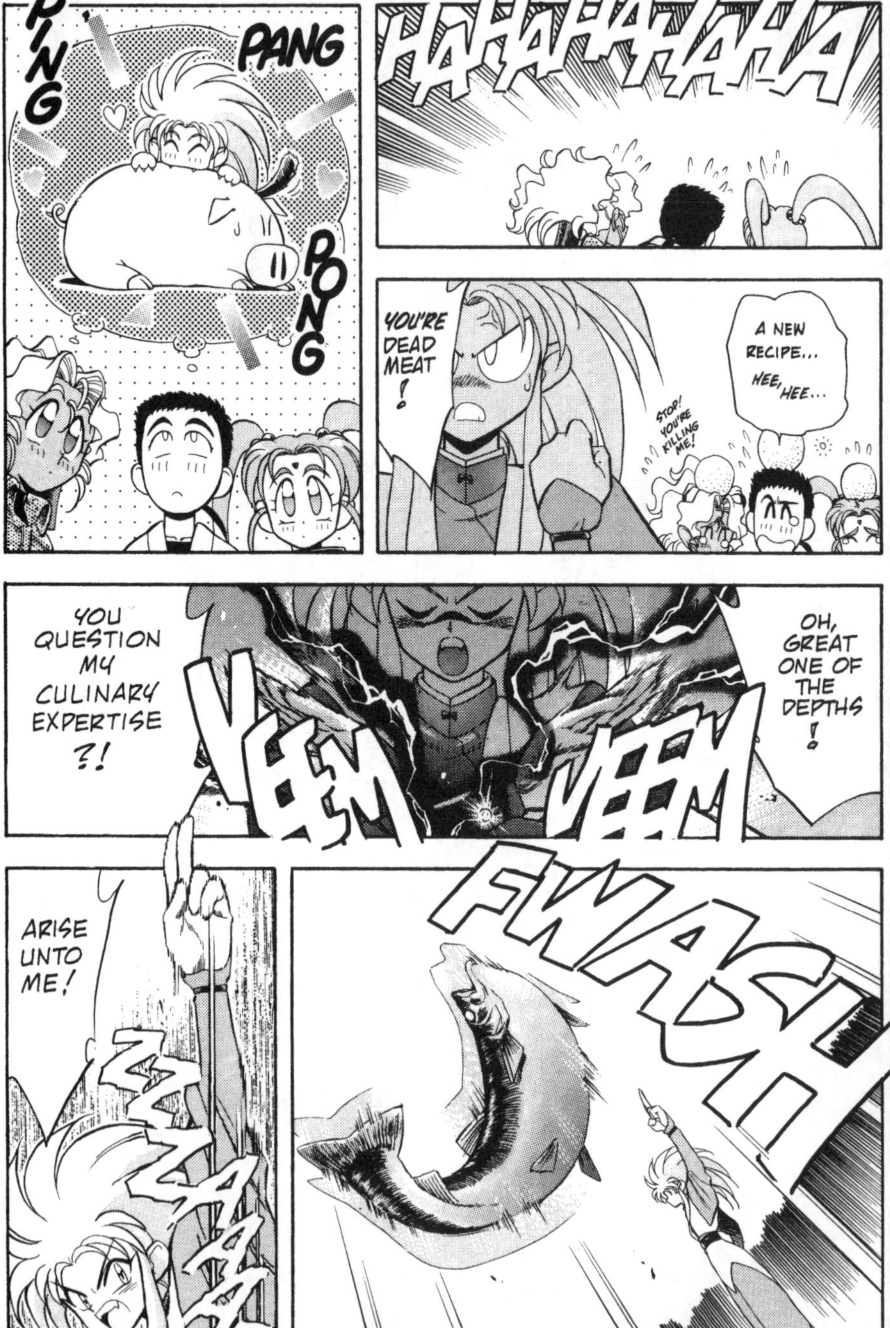
PING
PANG
PONG
HAHAHAHAHAHA
YOU'RE DEAD MEAT!
A NEW RECIPE... HEE, HEE...
STOP! YOU'RE KILLING ME!
YOU QUESTION MY CULINARY EXPERTISE ?!
VEEM
VEEEM
OH, GREAT ONE OF THE DEPTHS!
ARISE UNTO ME!
FWASH

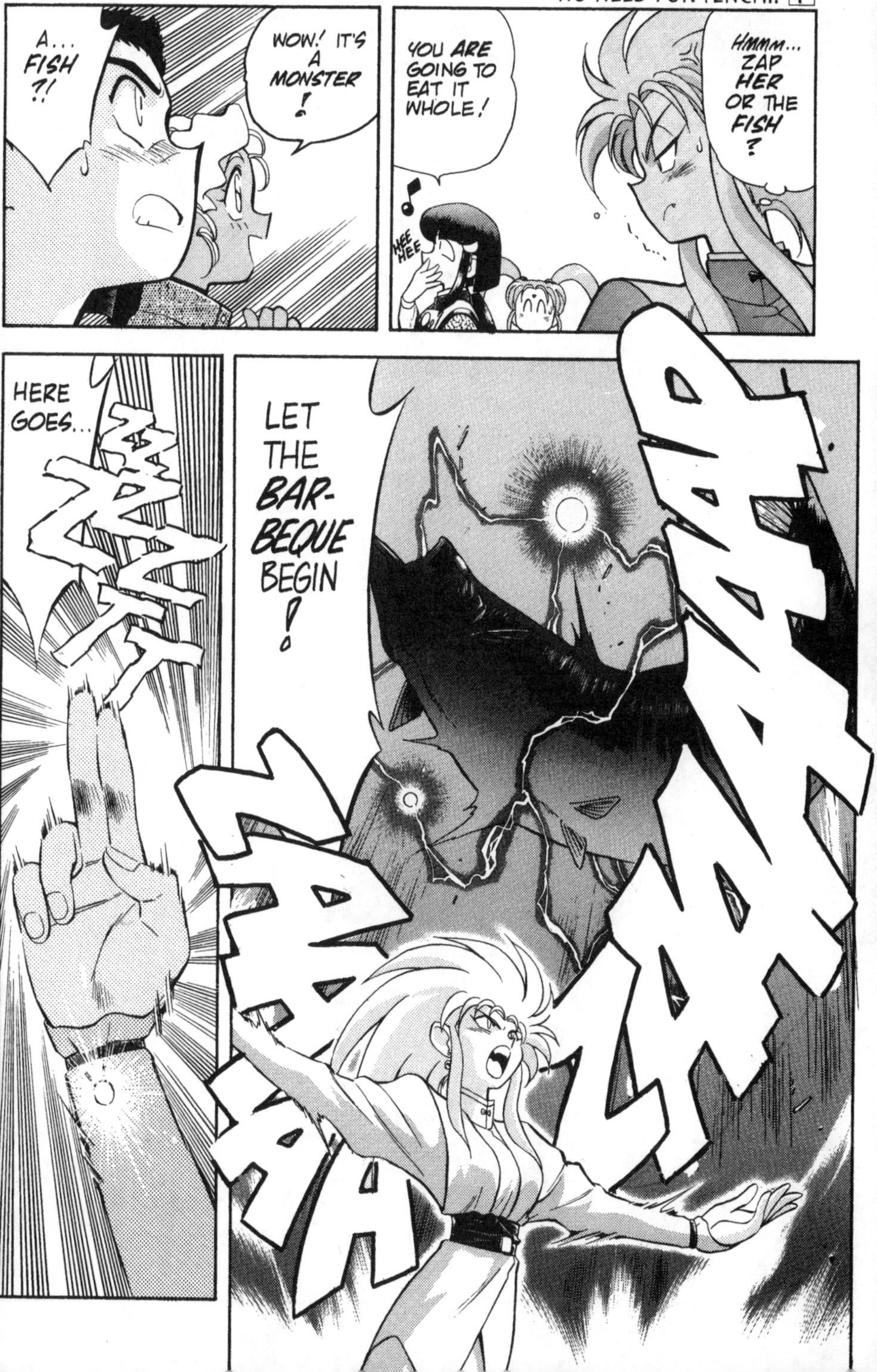
A... FISH ?!
WOW! IT'S A MONSTER!
YOU ARE GOING TO EAT IT WHOLE!
HEE HEE
HMMM... ZAP HER OR THE FISH?
HERE GOES...
LET THE BAR-BEQUE BEGIN!

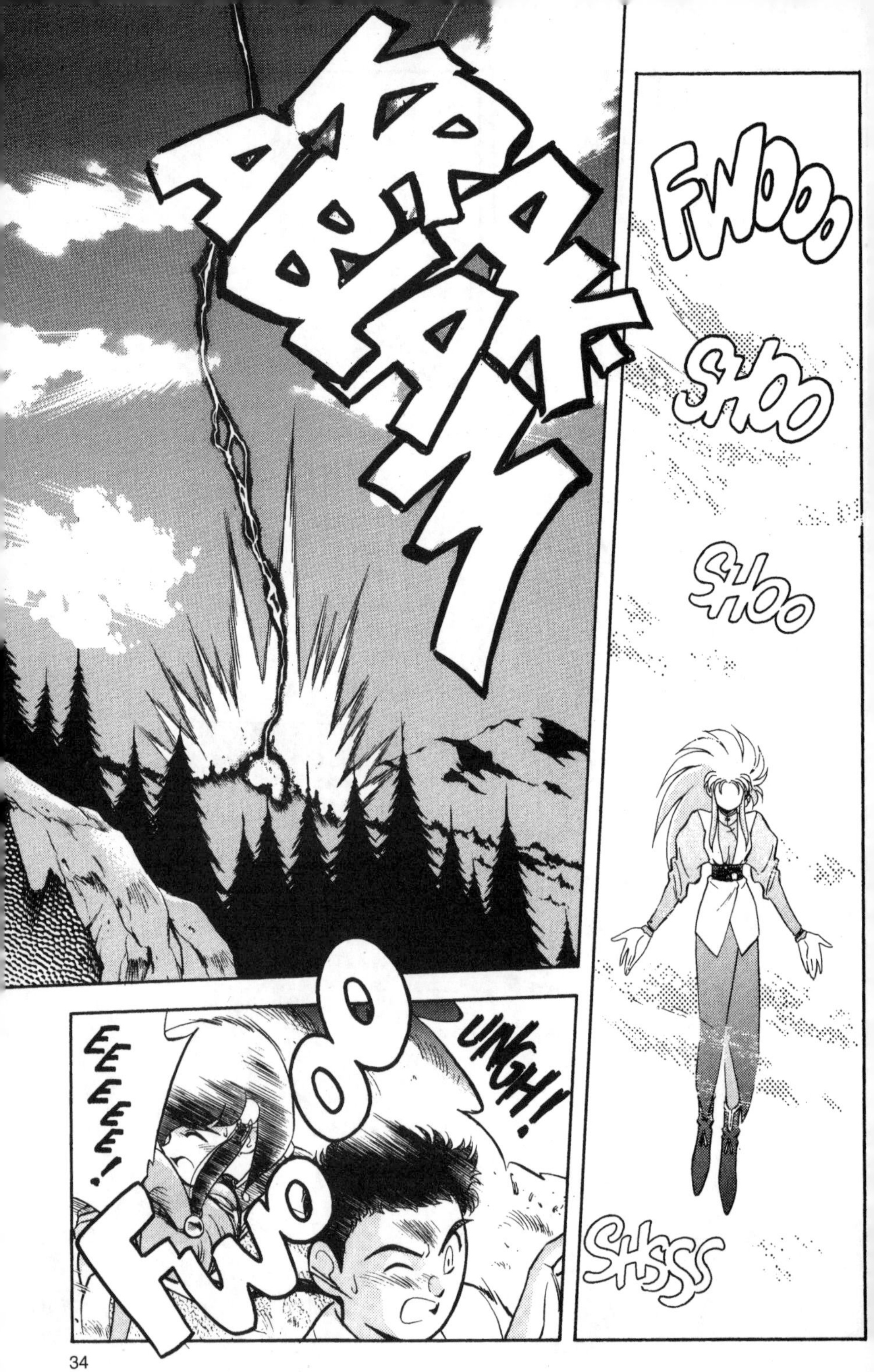
FWOOOO
SHOO
SHOO
SHSSS
EEEEEE!!
FWOOOO
UNGH!!

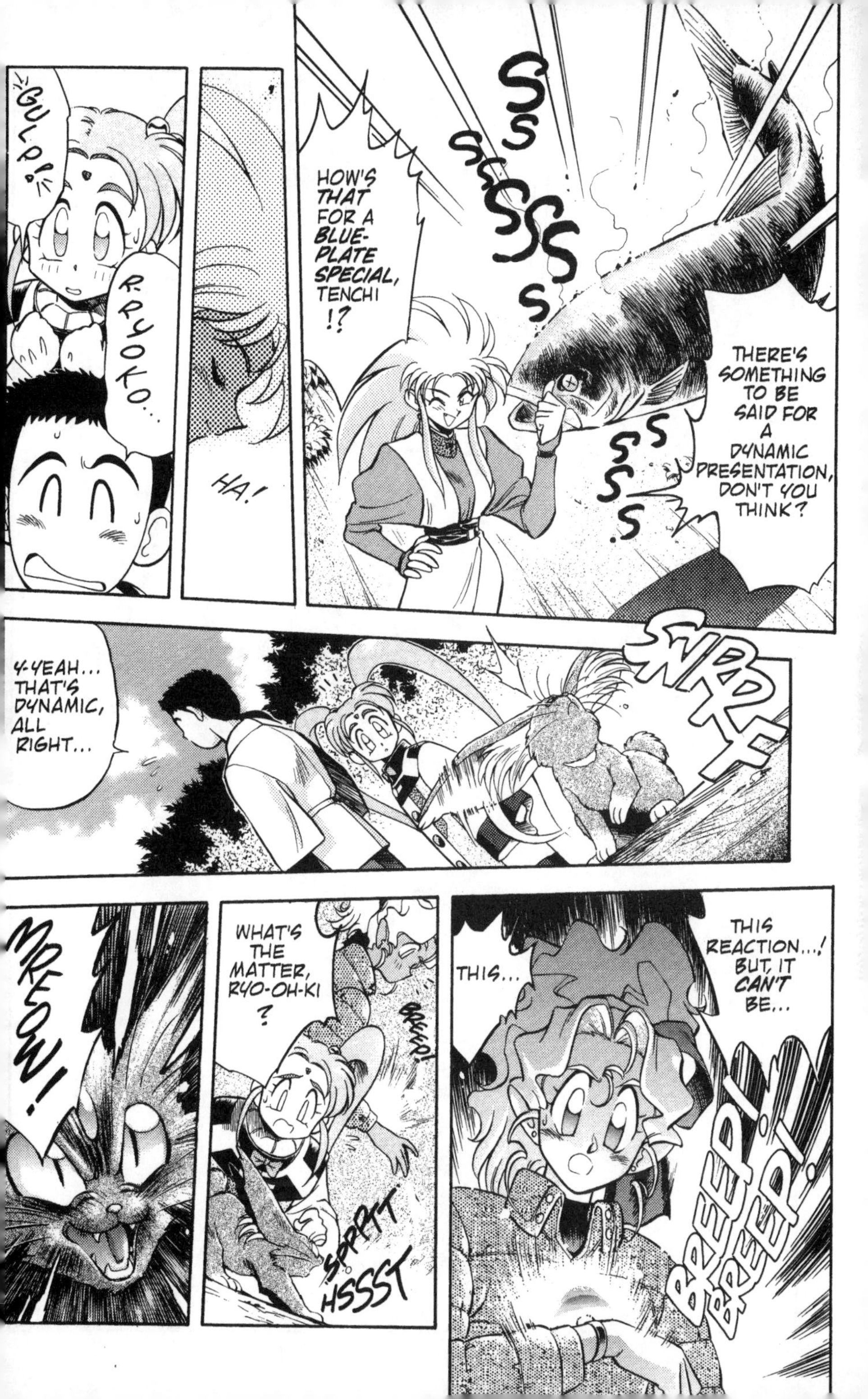
GULP!!
R-RYOKO...
HA!
HOW'S THAT FOR A BLUE-PLATE SPECIAL, TENCHI!?
SS SSSSSS
THERE'S SOMETHING TO BE SAID FOR A DYNAMIC PRESENTATION, DON'T YOU THINK?
SSSSS
Y-YEAH... THAT'S DYNAMIC, ALL RIGHT...
SNIFF
MREOW!
WHAT'S THE MATTER, RYO-OH-KI?
SPPPTT HSSST
THIS...
THIS REACTION...! BUT, IT CAN'T BE...
BREEP! BREEP!

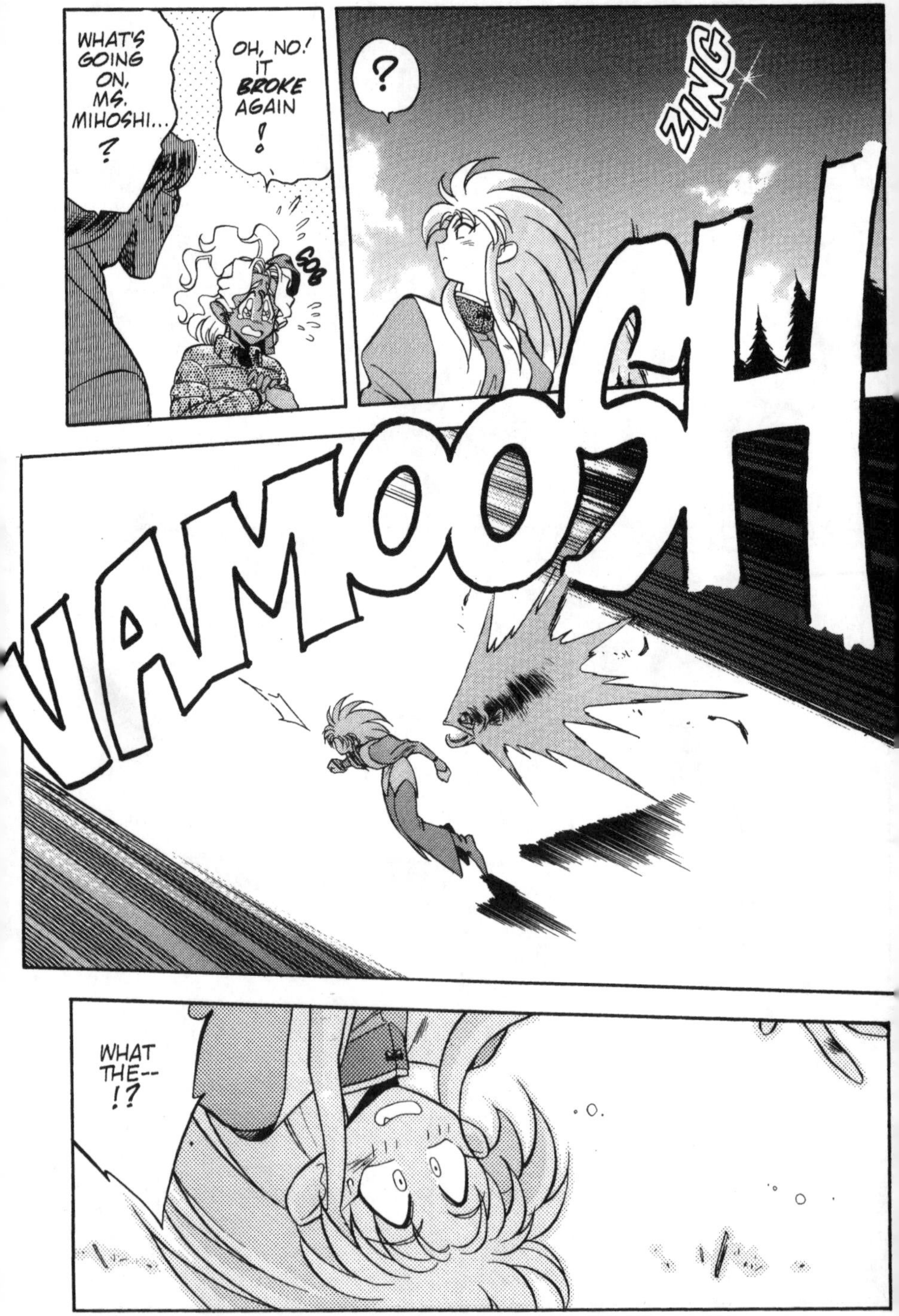

WHAT'S GOING ON, MS. MIHOSHI... ?
OH, NO! IT BROKE AGAIN!
GOB
?
ZING
VAMOOSH
WHAT THE-- !?

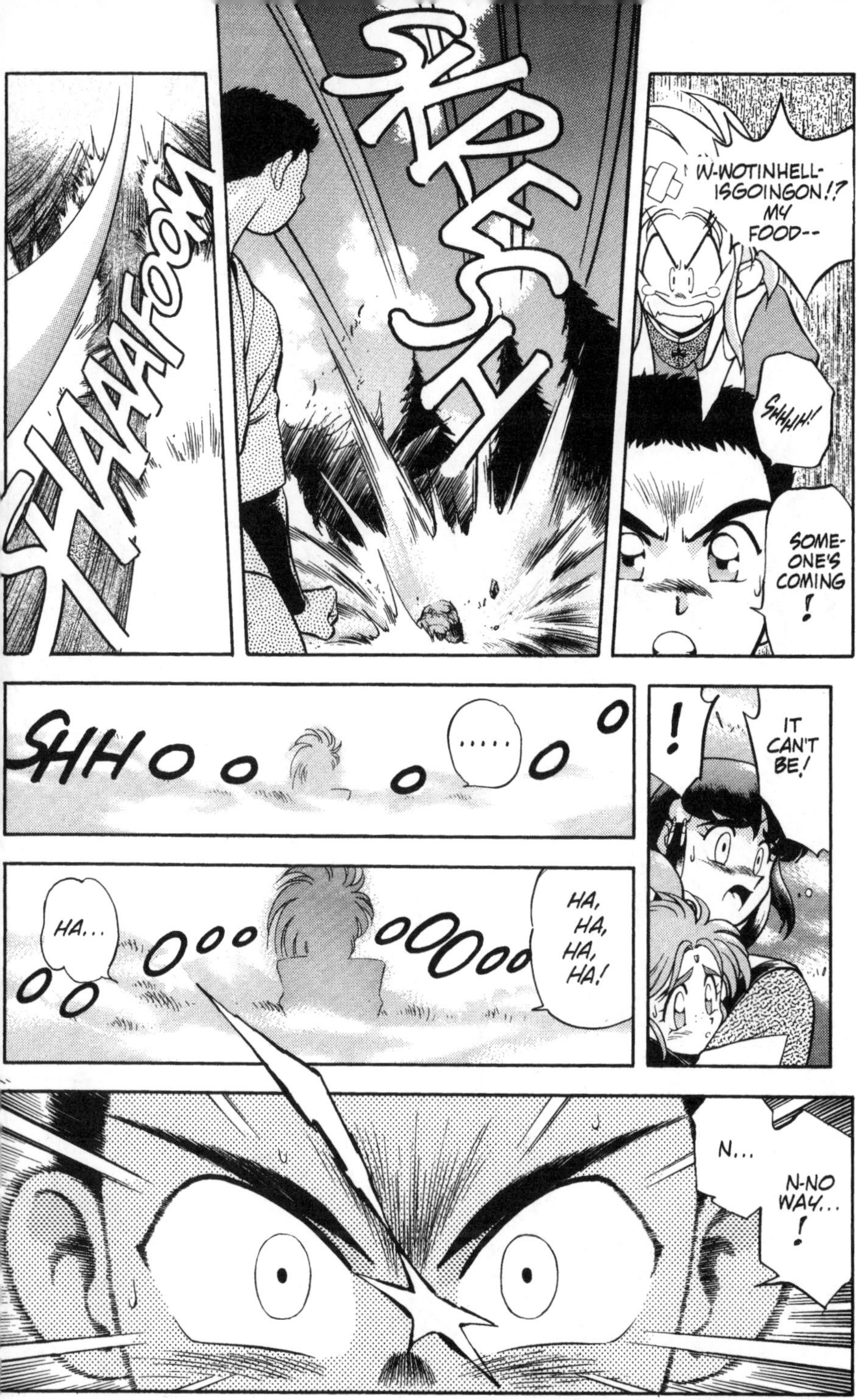

SHAAAFOOM
SKREESH
W-WOTINHELL-ISGOINGON!? MY FOOD--
SHHHH!
SOME-ONE'S COMING!
SHHOOOOOO
.....
IT CAN'T BE!
HA...
OOOOOOOOOOO
HA, HA, HA, HA!
N...
N-NO WAY...!

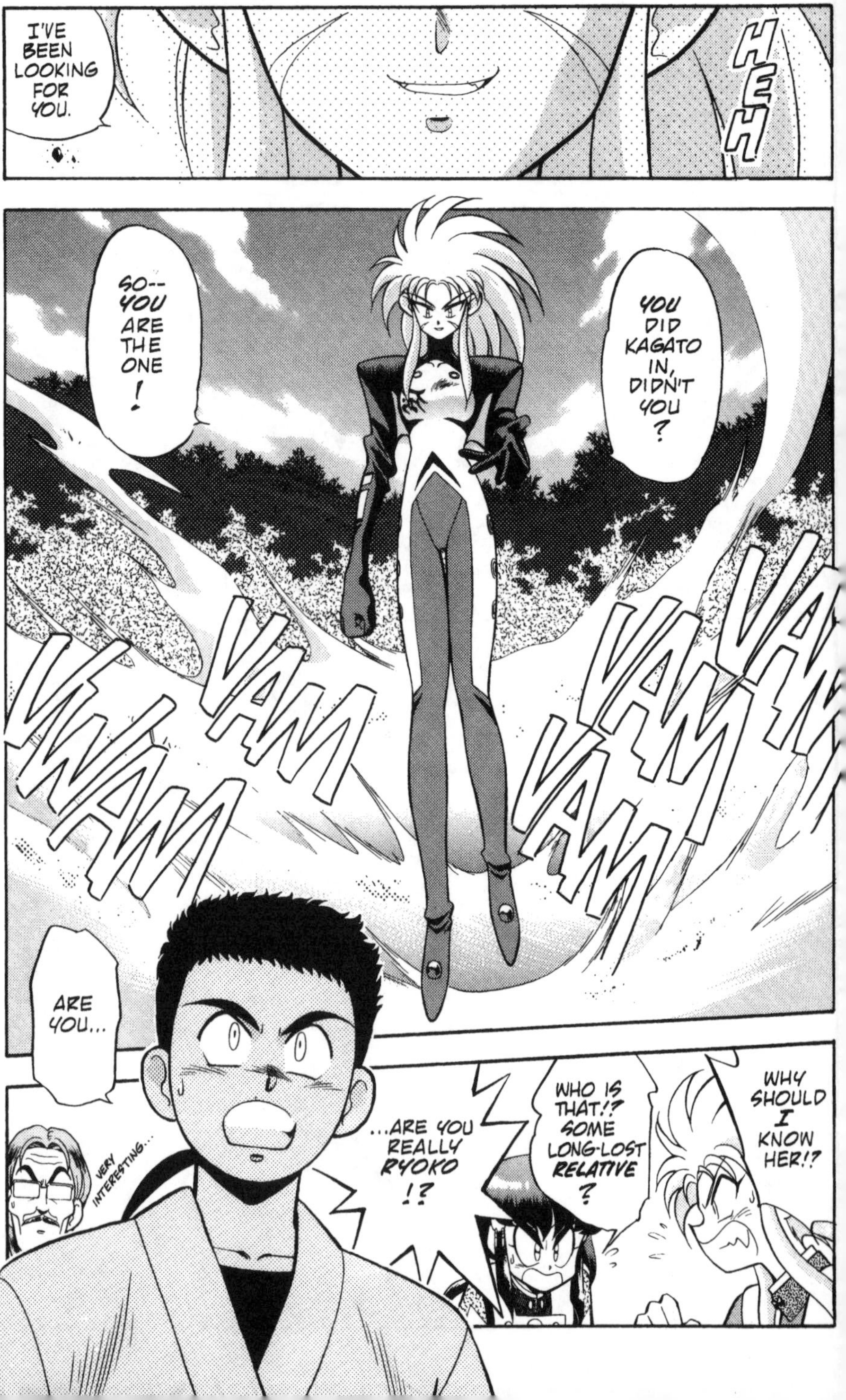
I'VE BEEN LOOKING FOR YOU.
HEH HEH
SO-- YOU ARE THE ONE!
YOU DID KAGATO IN, DIDN'T YOU?
VAM VWAM VAM
VAM VAM VAM VAM
ARE YOU...
VERY INTERESTING...
...ARE YOU REALLY RYOKO!?
WHO IS THAT!? SOME LONG-LOST RELATIVE?
WHY SHOULD I KNOW HER!?

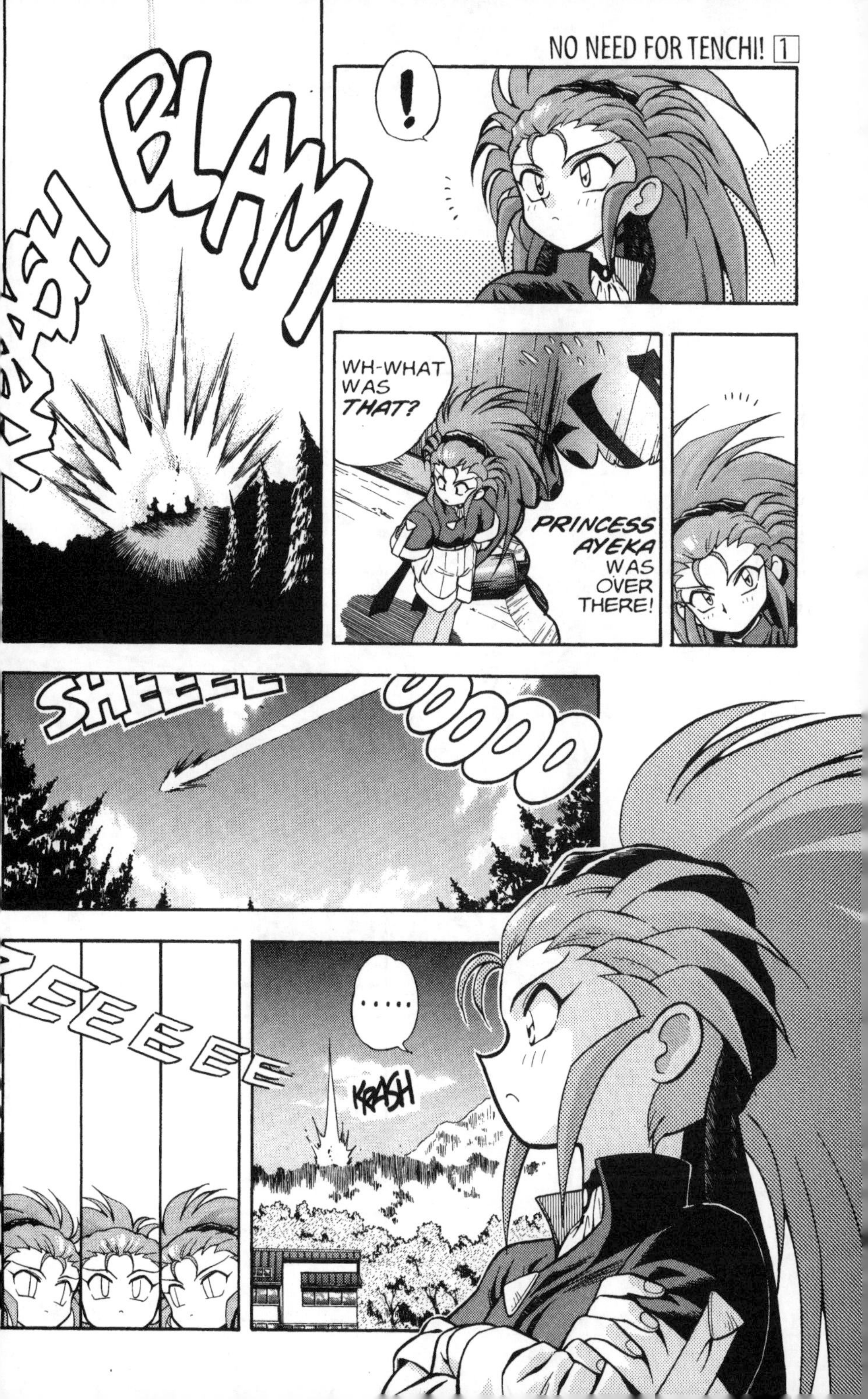
BLAM
!
WH-WHAT WAS THAT?
PRINCESS AYEKA WAS OVER THERE!
SHEEEE
OOOOO
EEEEEE
......
KRASH

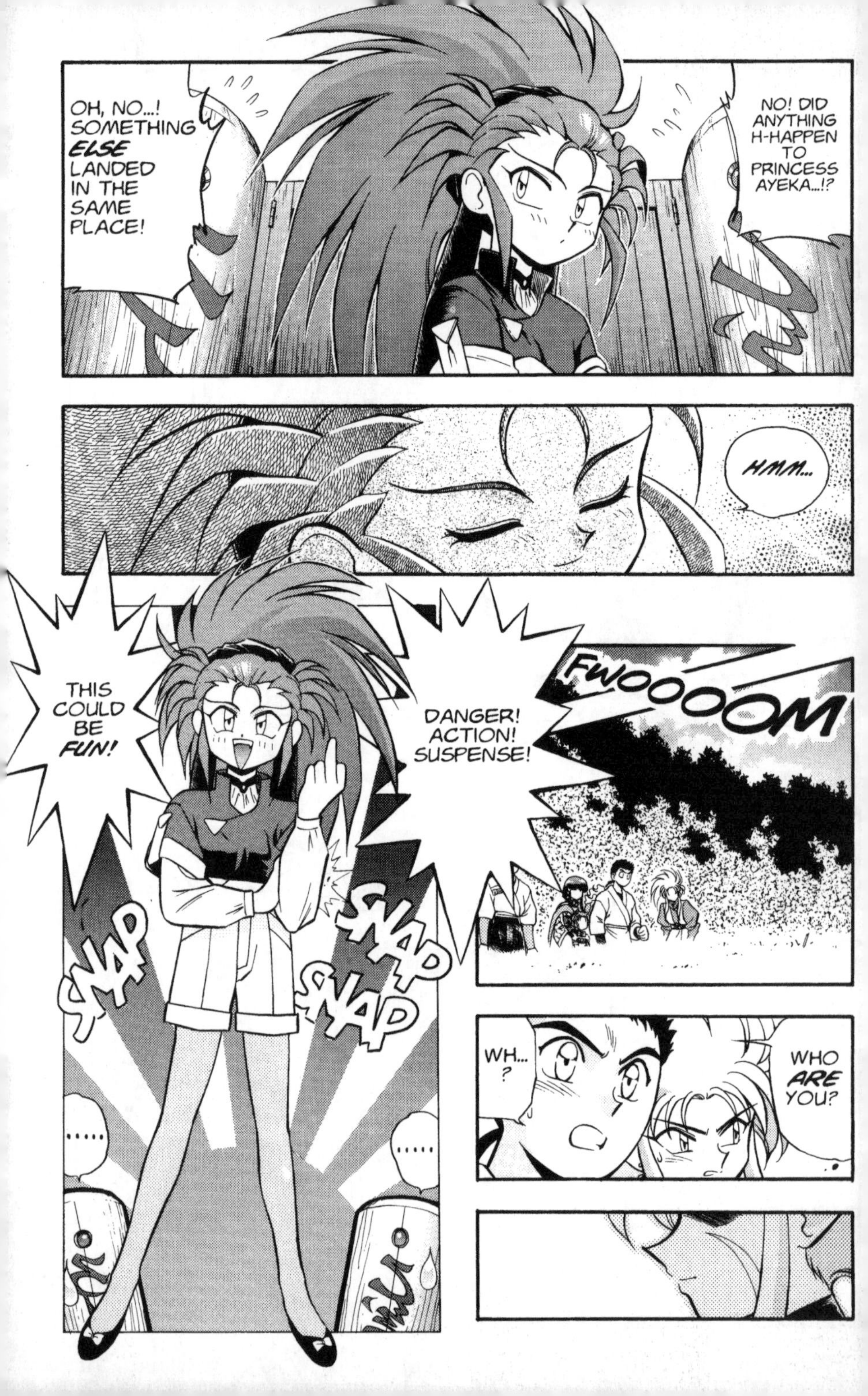
OH, NO...! SOMETHING ELSE LANDED IN THE SAME PLACE!
NO! DID ANYTHING H-HAPPEN TO PRINCESS AYEKA...!?
HMM...
THIS COULD BE FUN!
DANGER! ACTION! SUSPENSE!
SNAP
SNAP
SNAP
.....
.....
FWOOOOOM
WH...?
WHO ARE YOU?

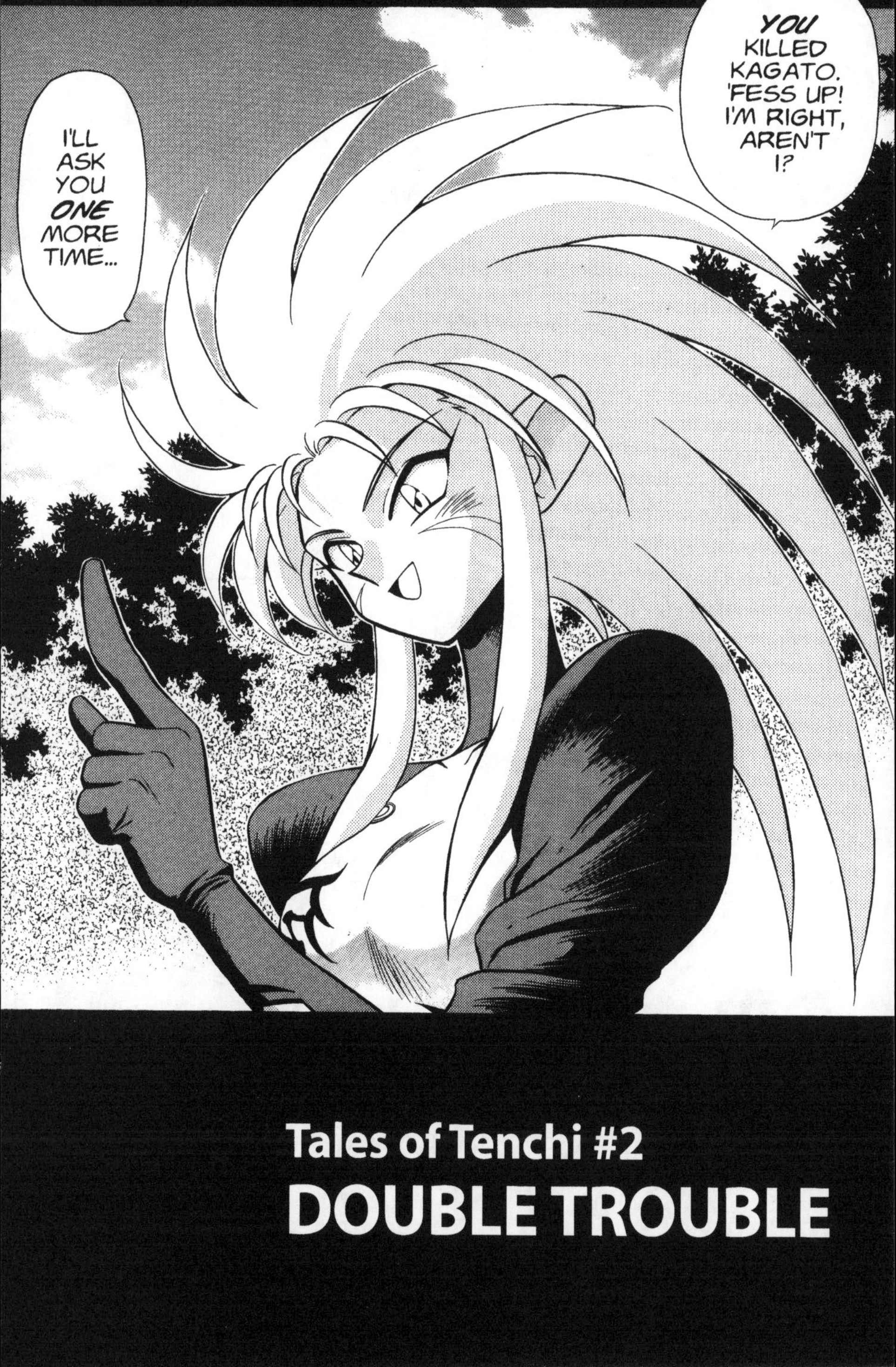
I'LL ASK YOU *ONE* MORE TIME...
YOU KILLED KAGATO. 'FESS UP! I'M RIGHT, AREN'T I?

Tales of Tenchi #2

DOUBLE TROUBLE

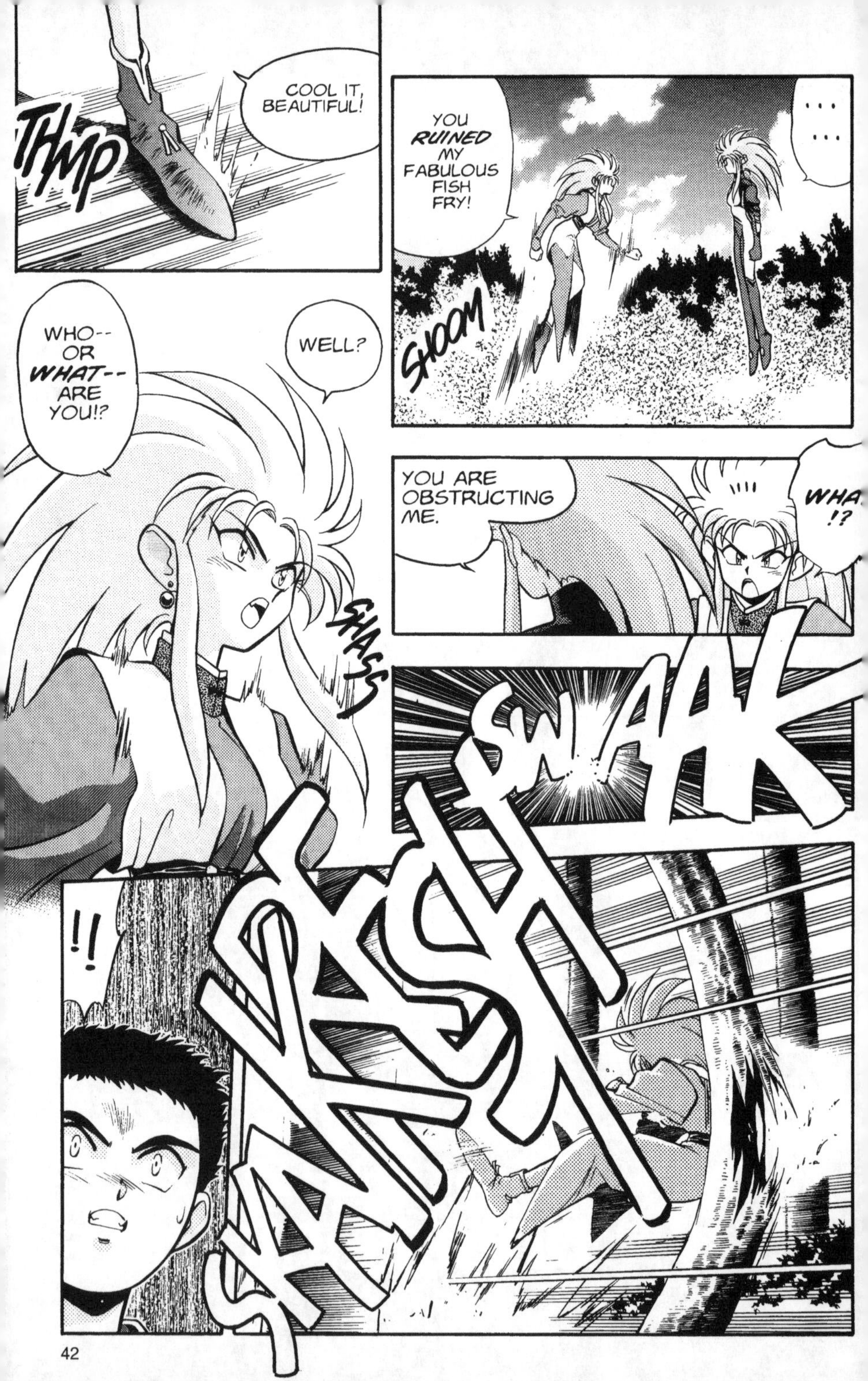
THMP
COOL IT, BEAUTIFUL!
YOU RUINED MY FABULOUS FISH FRY!
SHOOM
. . .
. . .
WHO-- OR WHAT-- ARE YOU!?
WELL?
GHASS
YOU ARE OBSTRUCTING ME.
WHA!?
SWAAK
!!
SKRASH

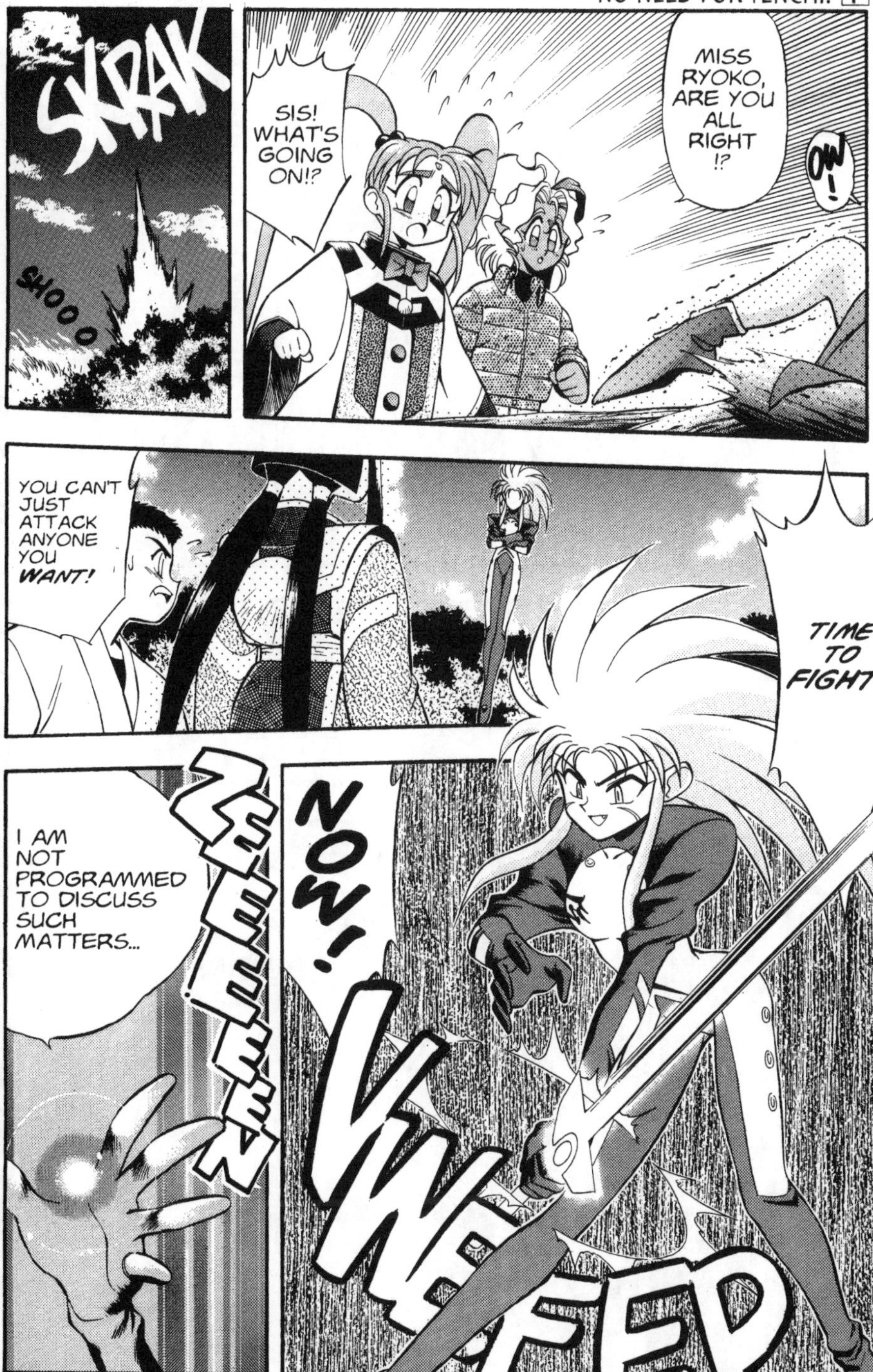
SKRAK
SHOOOO
SIS! WHAT'S GOING ON!?
MISS RYOKO, ARE YOU ALL RIGHT!?
OW!
YOU CAN'T JUST ATTACK ANYONE YOU ***WANT!***
TIME TO FIGHT!
I AM NOT PROGRAMMED TO DISCUSS SUCH MATTERS...
ZEEEEEEEN
NOW!
VWEEEP

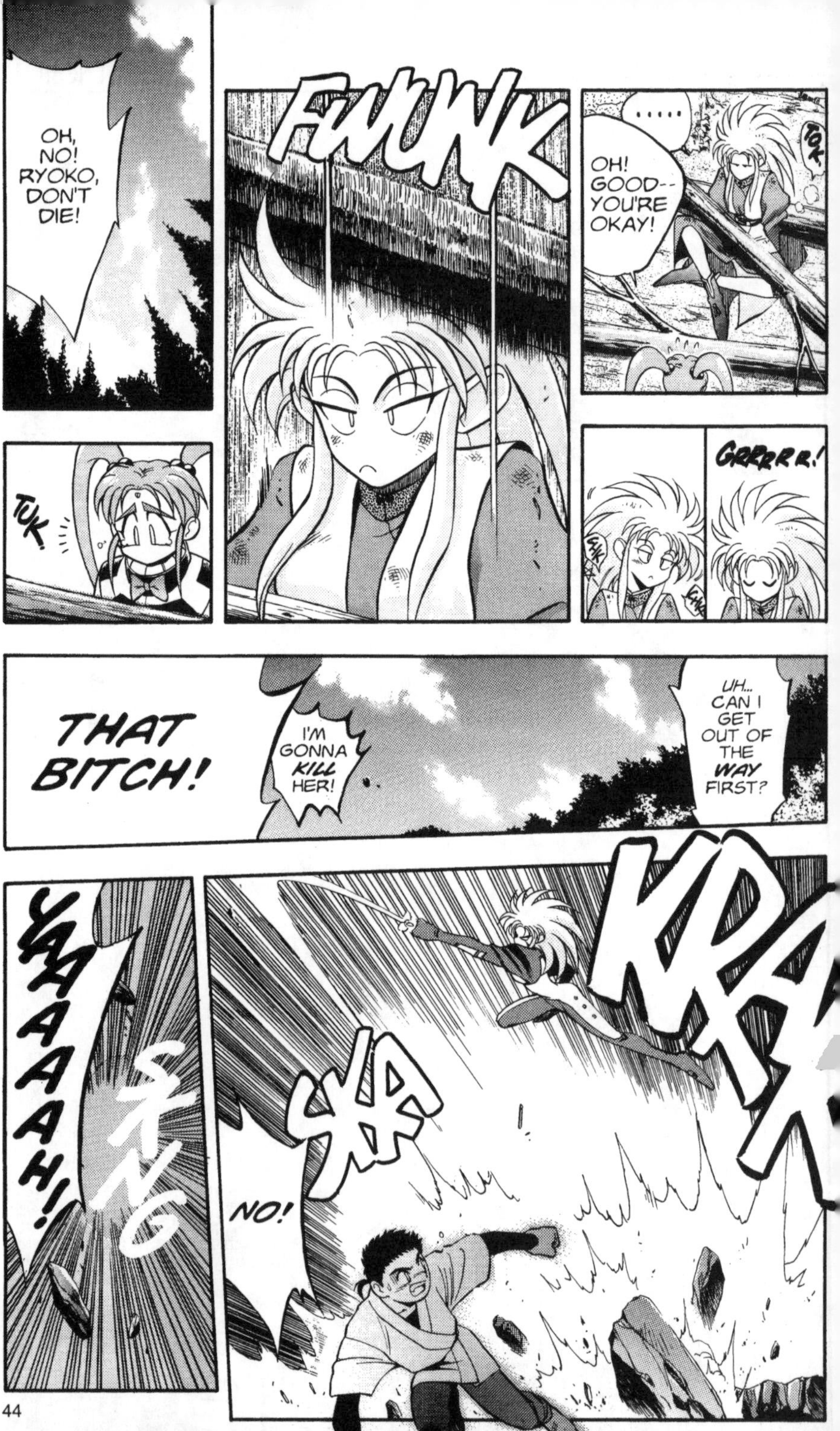
OH, NO! RYOKO, DON'T DIE!
FWUNK
.....
OH! GOOD--YOU'RE OKAY!
TOK
TUK!
GRRRRR!
THAT BITCH!
I'M GONNA KILL HER!
UH... CAN I GET OUT OF THE WAY FIRST?
YAAAAAAAH!
NO!

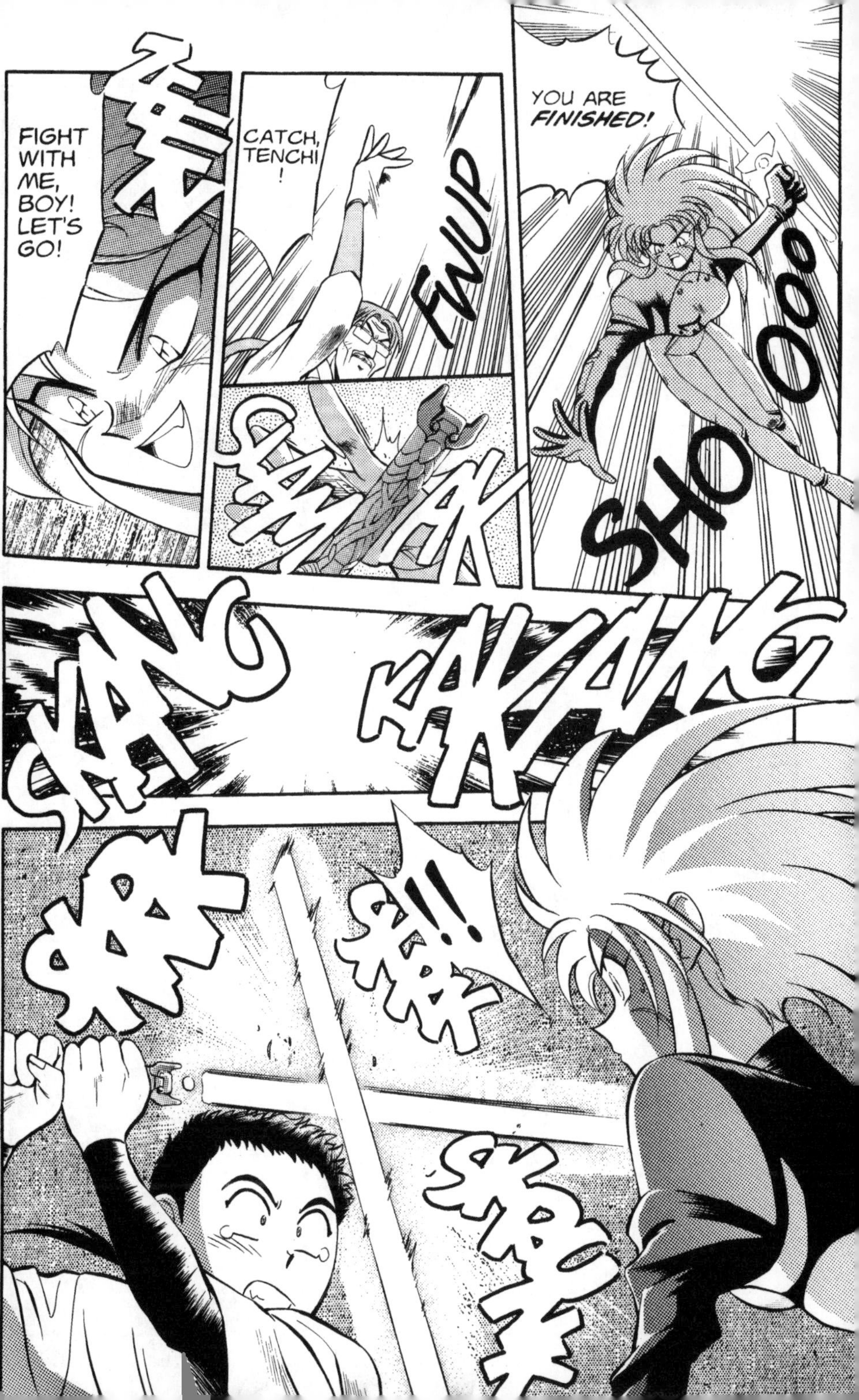
FIGHT WITH ME, BOY! LET'S GO!
CATCH, TENCHI!
FWUP
YOU ARE *FINISHED!*
SHOOOOO

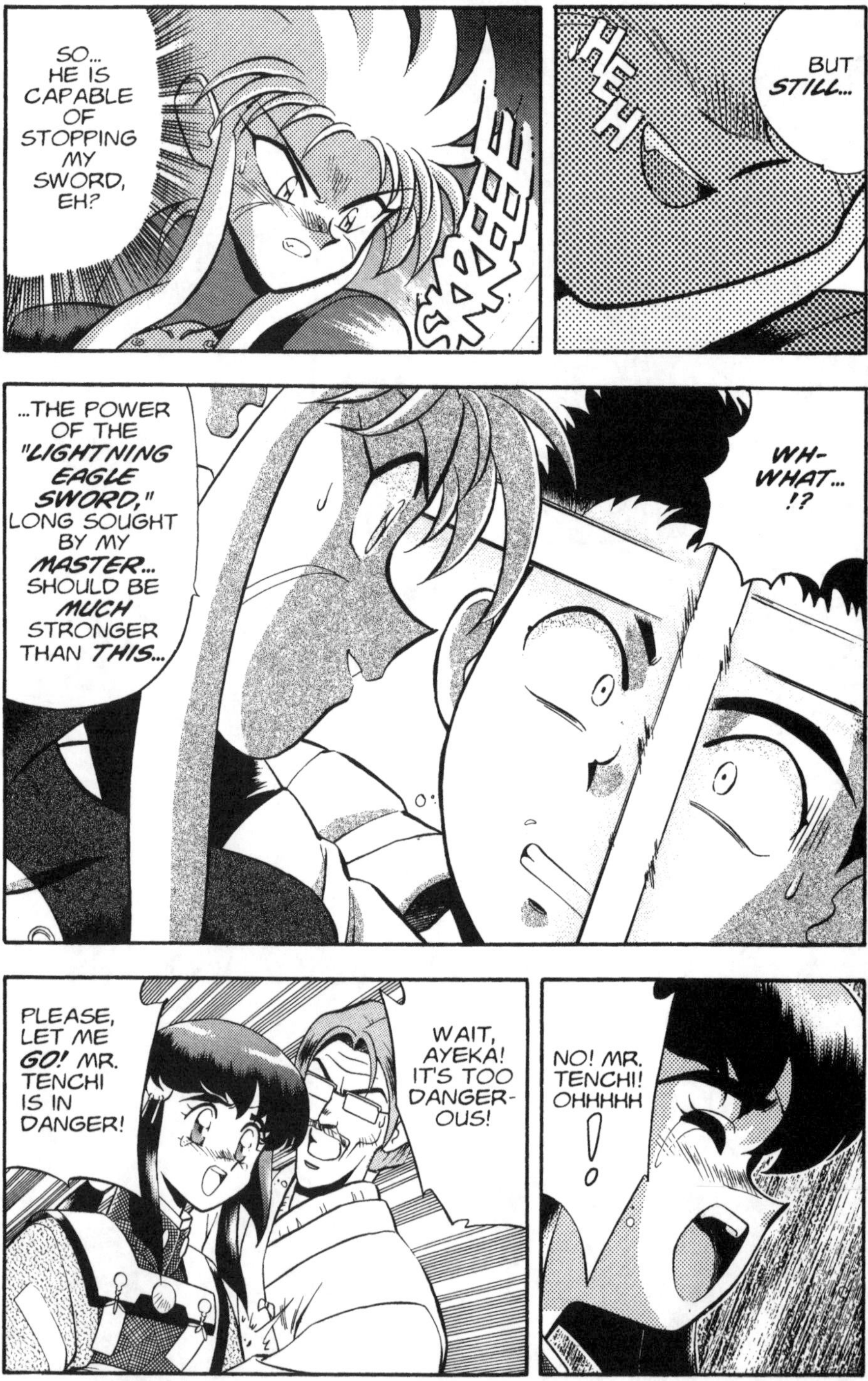
SO... HE IS CAPABLE OF STOPPING MY SWORD, EH?
SKREEEEE
HEH
BUT STILL...
...THE POWER OF THE "LIGHTNING EAGLE SWORD," LONG SOUGHT BY MY MASTER... SHOULD BE MUCH STRONGER THAN THIS...
WH-WHAT... !?
PLEASE, LET ME GO! MR. TENCHI IS IN DANGER!
WAIT, AYEKA! IT'S TOO DANGER-OUS!
NO! MR. TENCHI! OHHHHH !

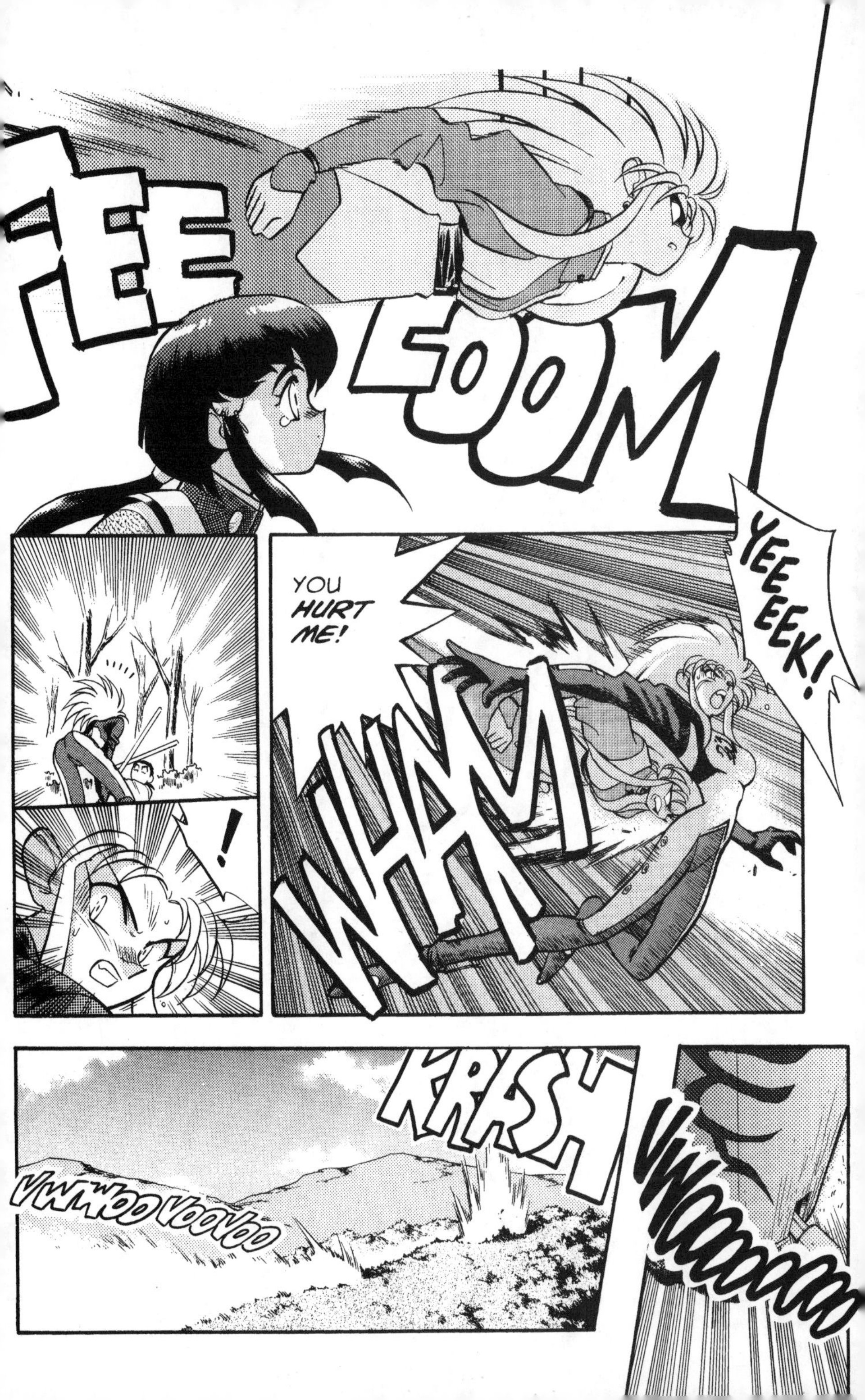
FEE
EOOM
!
YOU HURT ME!
WHAM
YEEEEK!
VWHOO VOOVOO
KRASH
VWOOOOOOOO

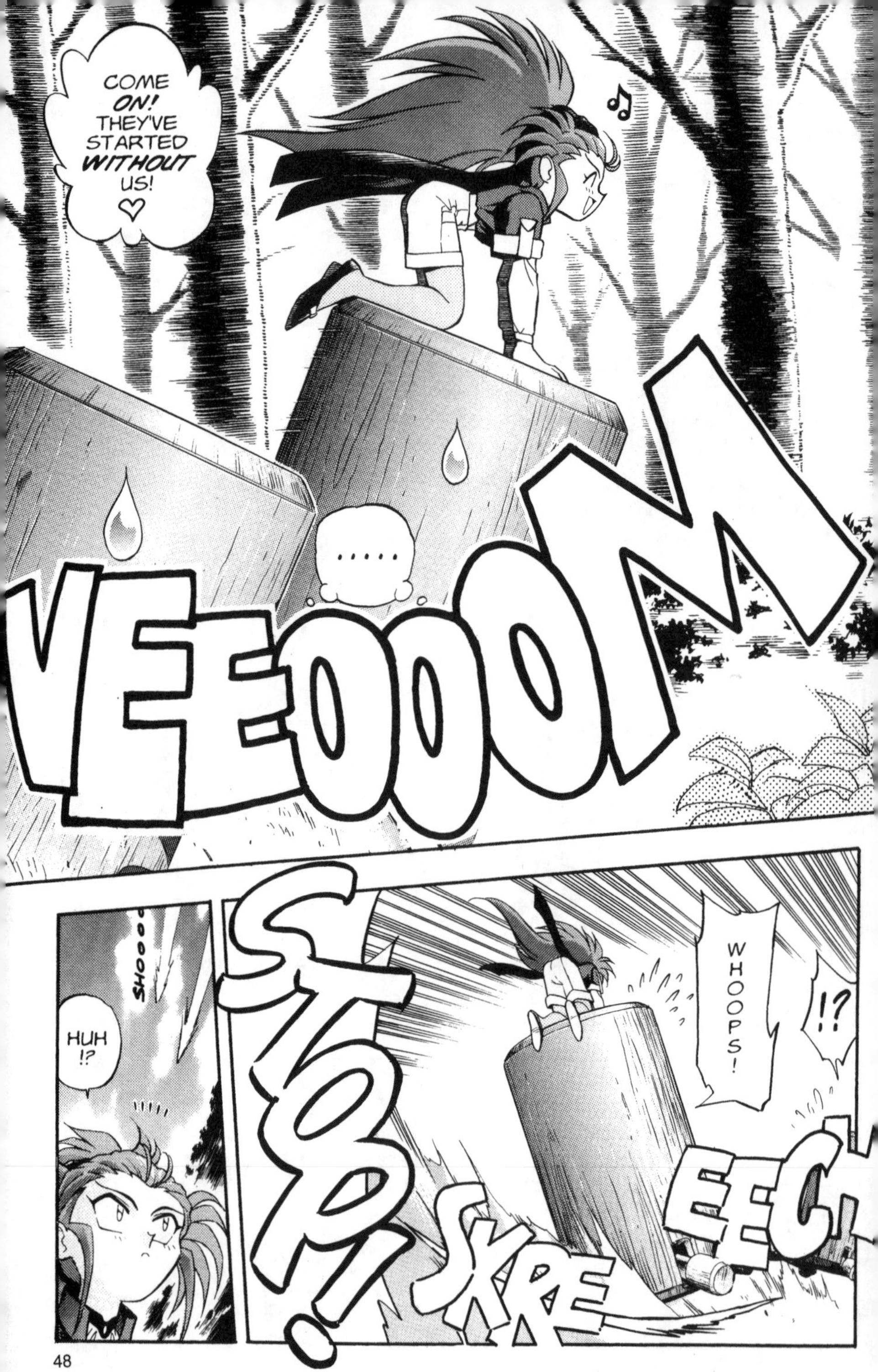
COME ON! THEY'VE STARTED WITHOUT US! ♡
♫
.....
VEEOOOOM
SHOOOO
HUH !?
!!!!
STOP!
WHOOPS!
!?
SKREEECH

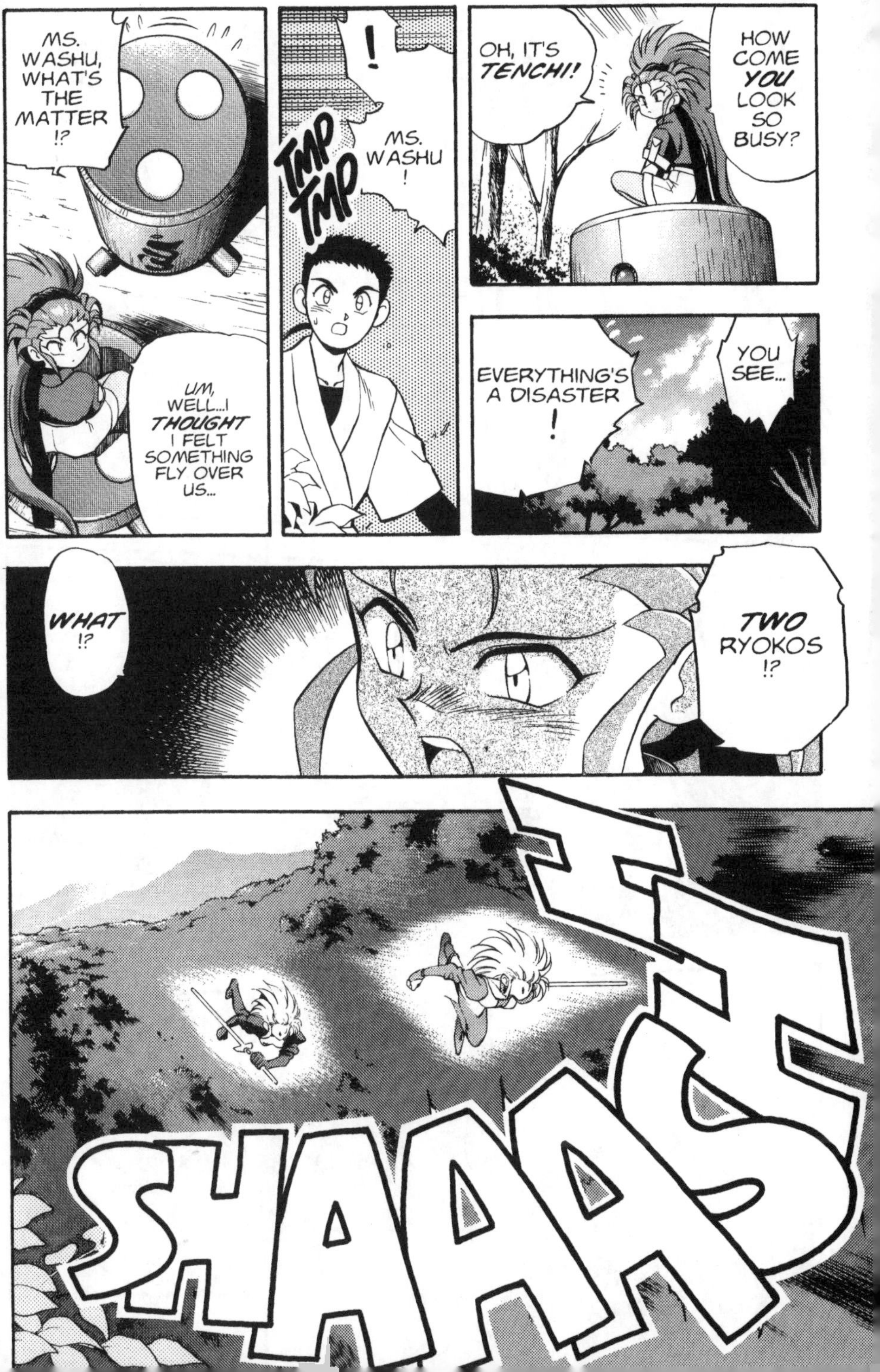
MS. WASHU, WHAT'S THE MATTER !?
UM, WELL...I THOUGHT I FELT SOMETHING FLY OVER US...
!
TMP TMP
MS. WASHU !
OH, IT'S TENCHI!
HOW COME YOU LOOK SO BUSY?
EVERYTHING'S A DISASTER !
YOU SEE...
WHAT !?
TWO RYOKOS !?
SHAAAS

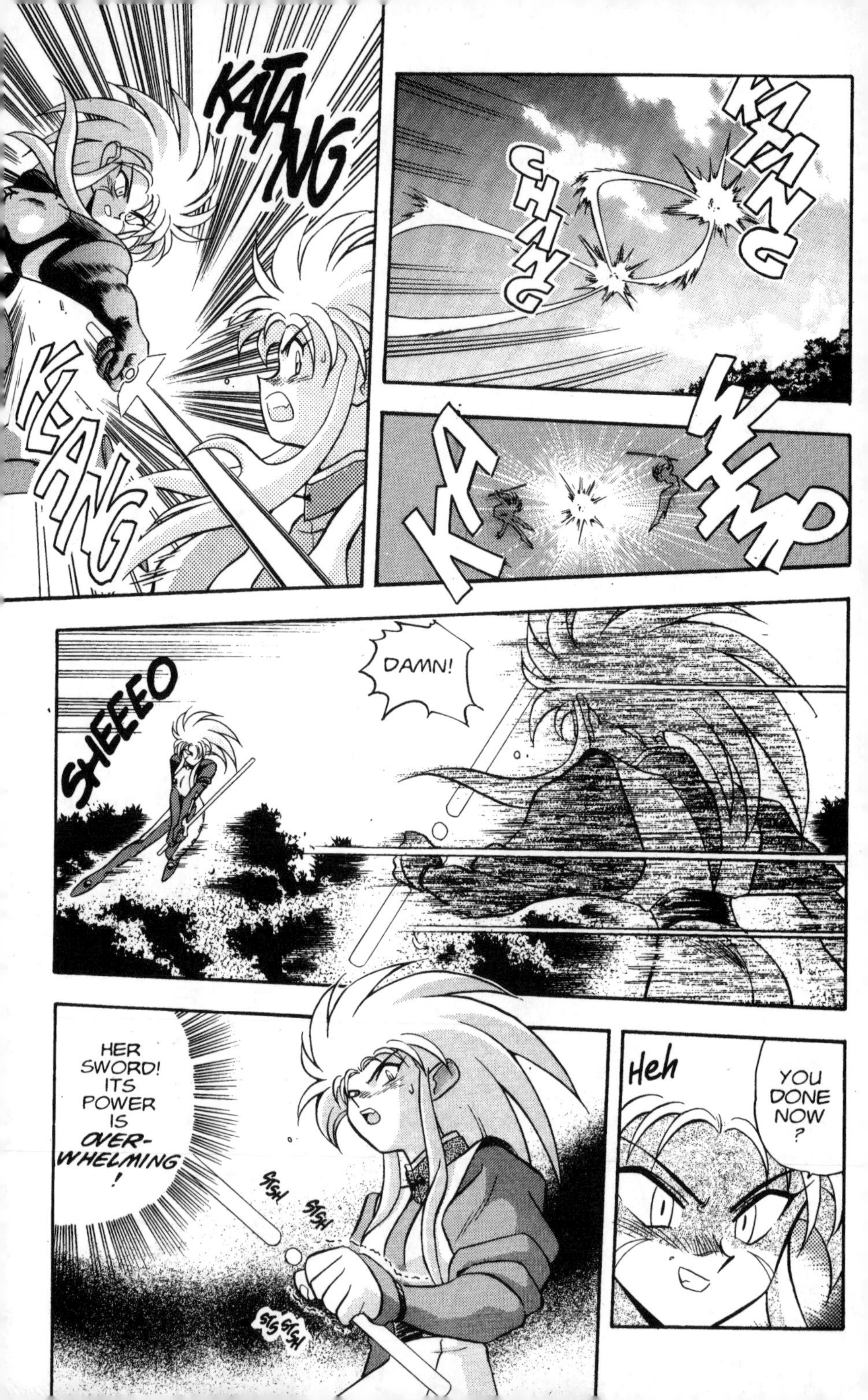
KATANG
KLANG
KATANG
CHANG
KA
WHMP
SHEEEO
DAMN!
HER SWORD! ITS POWER IS OVER-WHELMING!
SISH
SISH
SIS SISH
Heh
YOU DONE NOW?

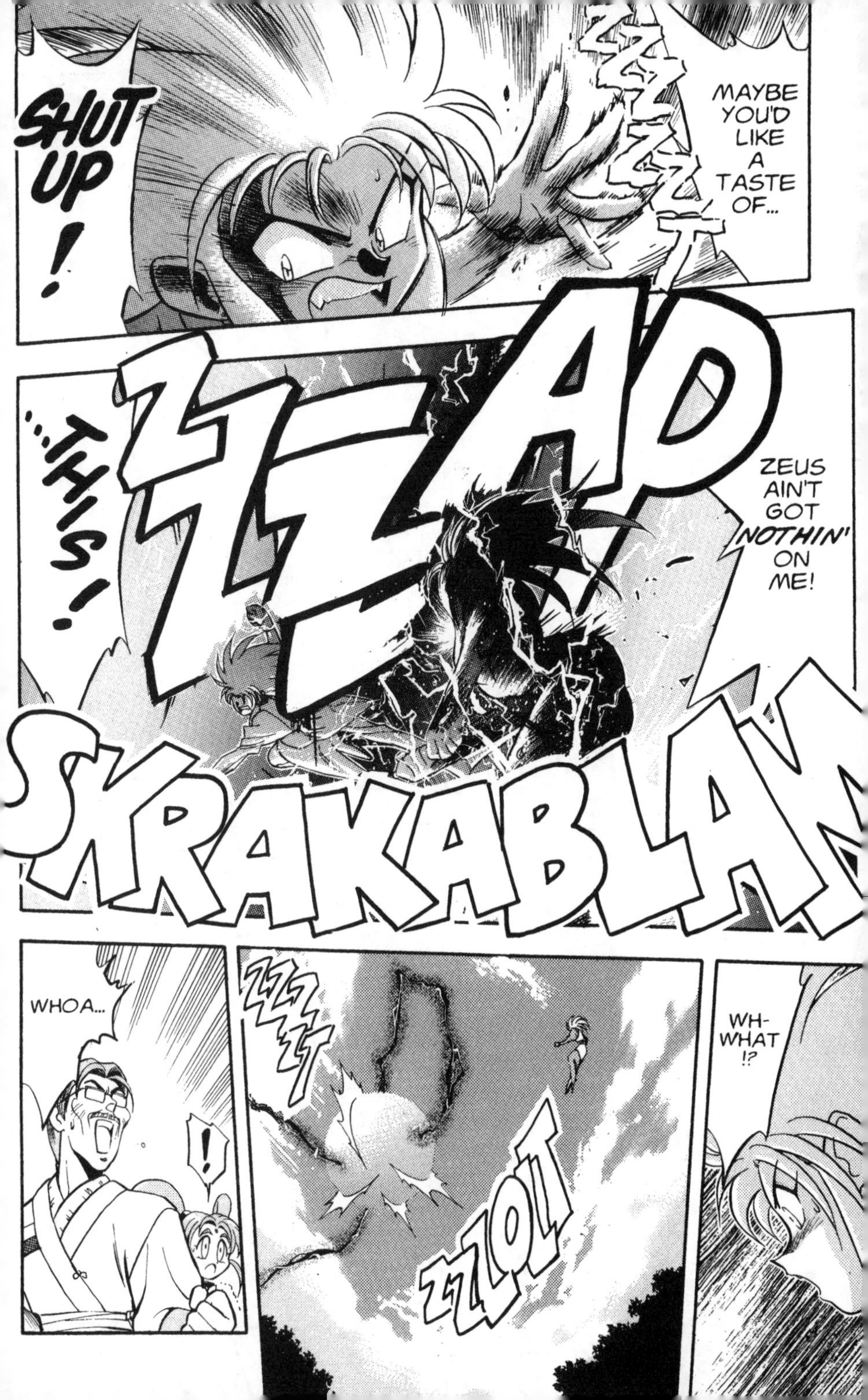
SHUT UP!
ZZZZT
MAYBE YOU'D LIKE A TASTE OF...
...THIS!!
ZZZAP
ZEUS AIN'T GOT NOTHIN' ON ME!
SKRAKABLAM
WHOA...
!
ZZZZT
ZZZOT
WH-WHAT!?

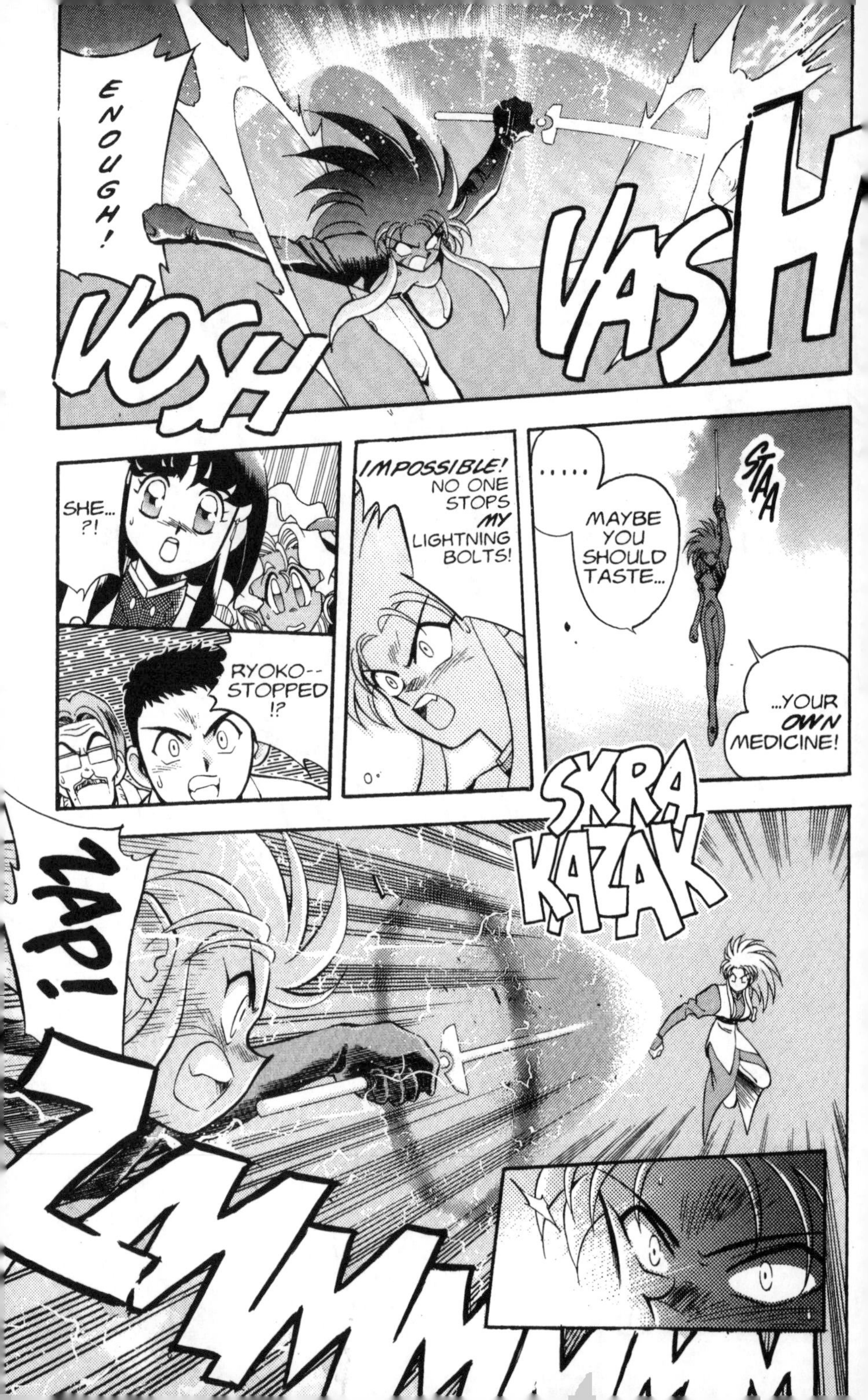
ENOUGH!
VOSH
VASH
SHE... ?!
RYOKO-- STOPPED !?
IMPOSSIBLE! NO ONE STOPS MY LIGHTNING BOLTS!
.....
MAYBE YOU SHOULD TASTE...
STAAA
...YOUR OWN MEDICINE!
SKRA KAZAK
ZAP!
ZZWMMMM

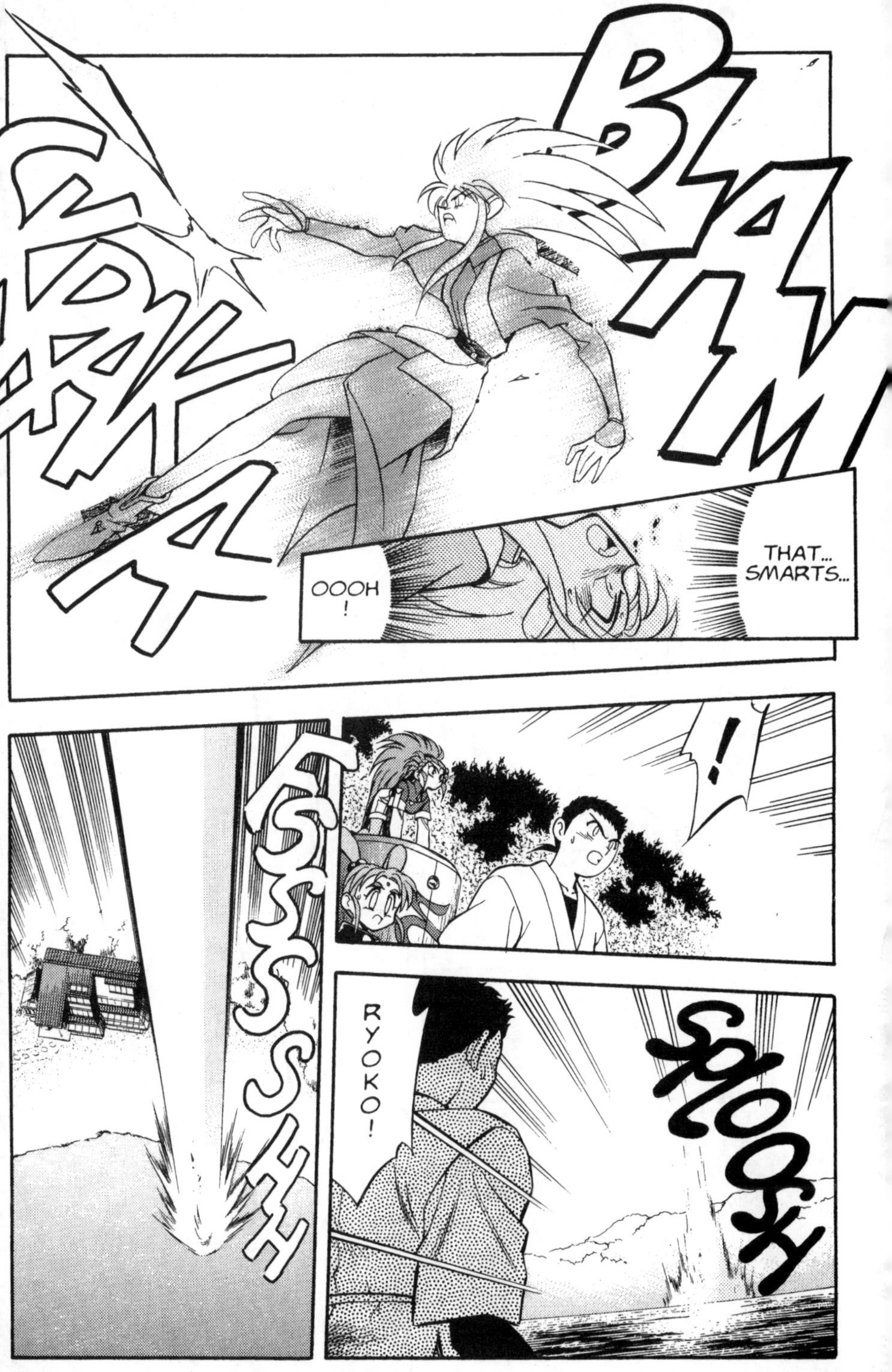
CHAKA
BLAAM
OOOH!
THAT... SMARTS...
FSSSSHH
!
RYOKO!
SPLOOSH

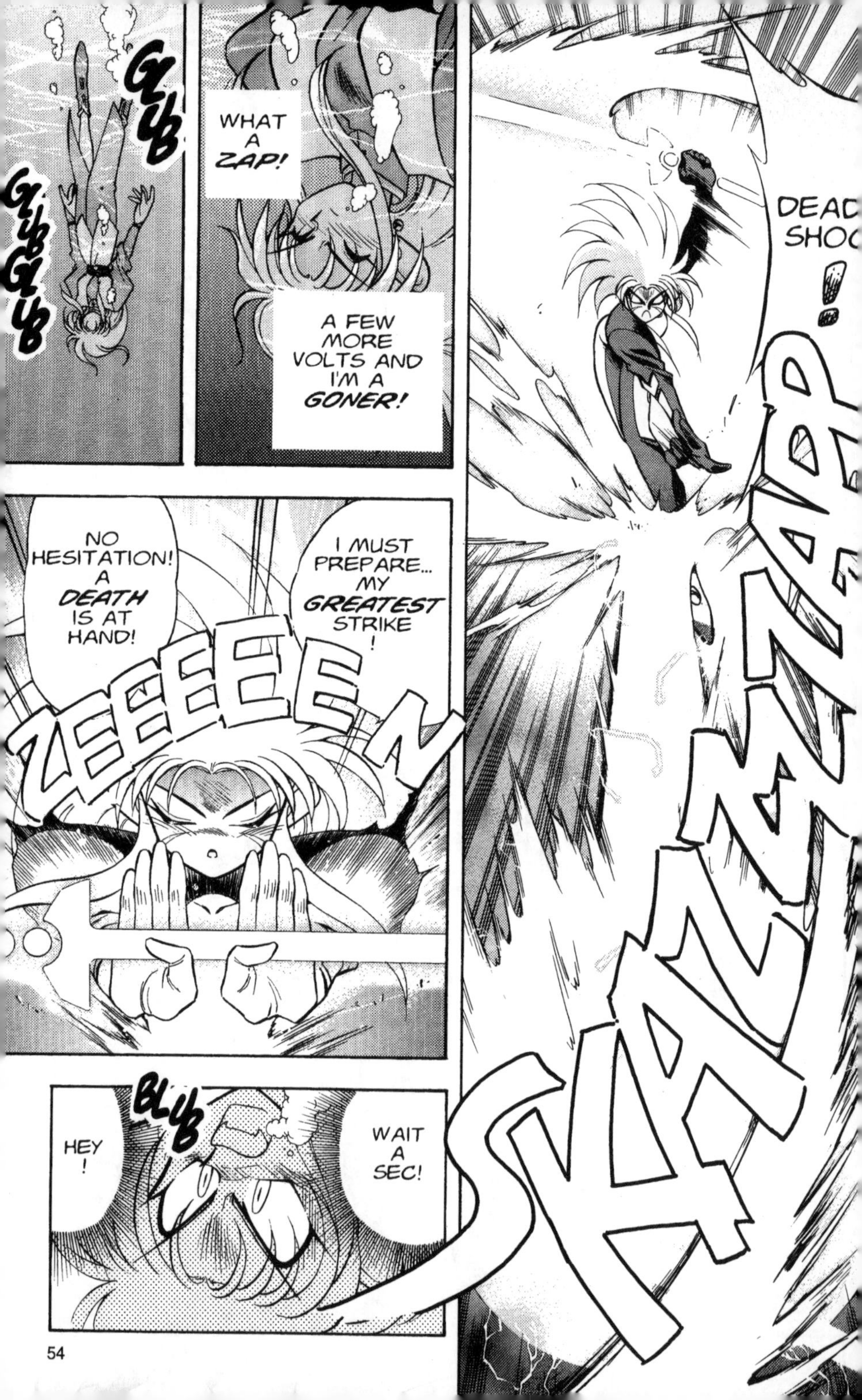
GLUB
GLUBGLUB
WHAT A ZAP!
A FEW MORE VOLTS AND I'M A GONER!
NO HESITATION! A DEATH IS AT HAND!
I MUST PREPARE... MY GREATEST STRIKE!
ZEEEEEN
HEY!
BLUB
WAIT A SEC!
DEAD SHOC!
SKAZZAPP

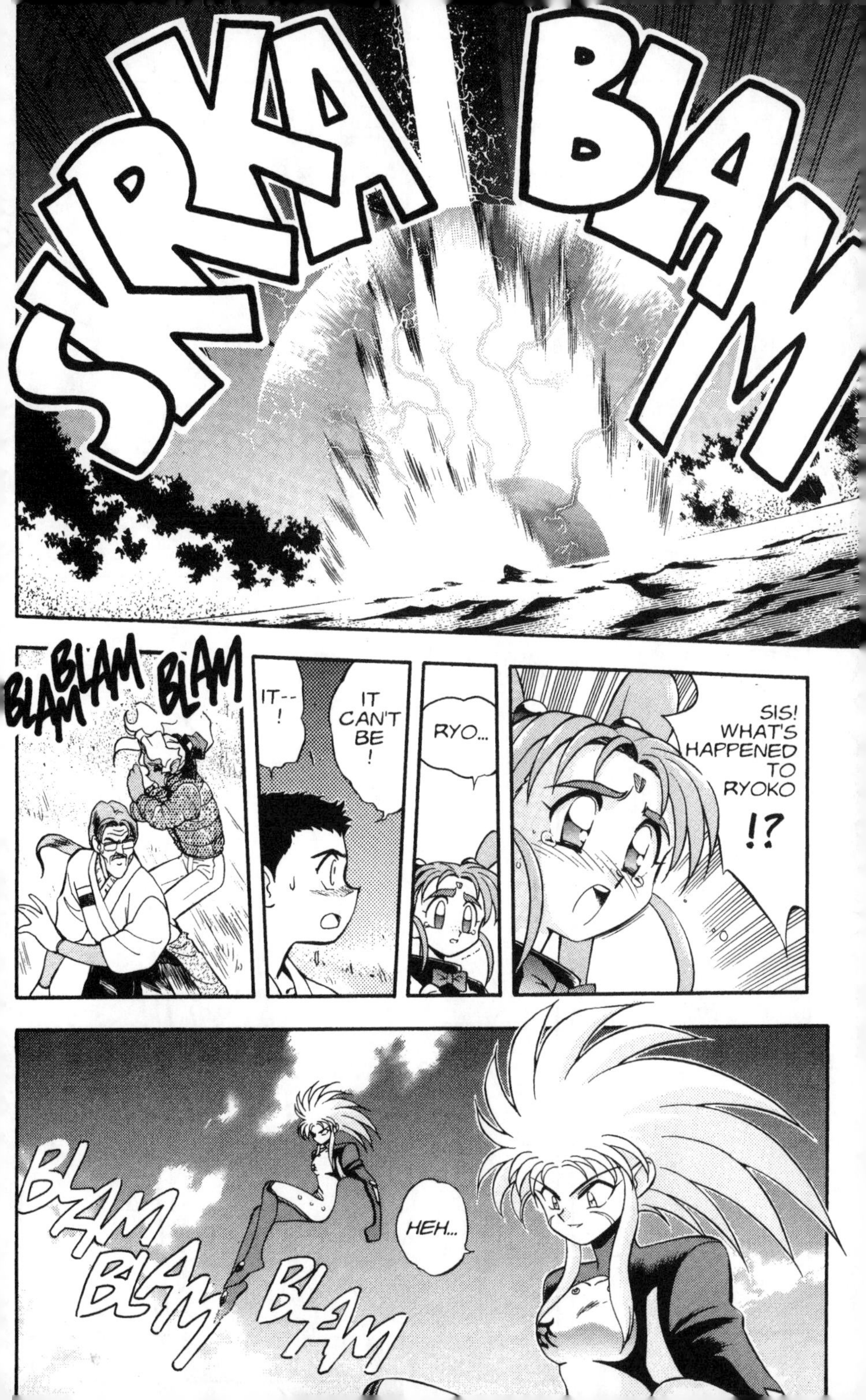
SKRKA!
BLAM
BLAM BLAM BLAM BLAM
IT--!
IT CAN'T BE!
RYO...
SIS! WHAT'S HAPPENED TO RYOKO !?
BLAM BLAM BLAM
HEH...

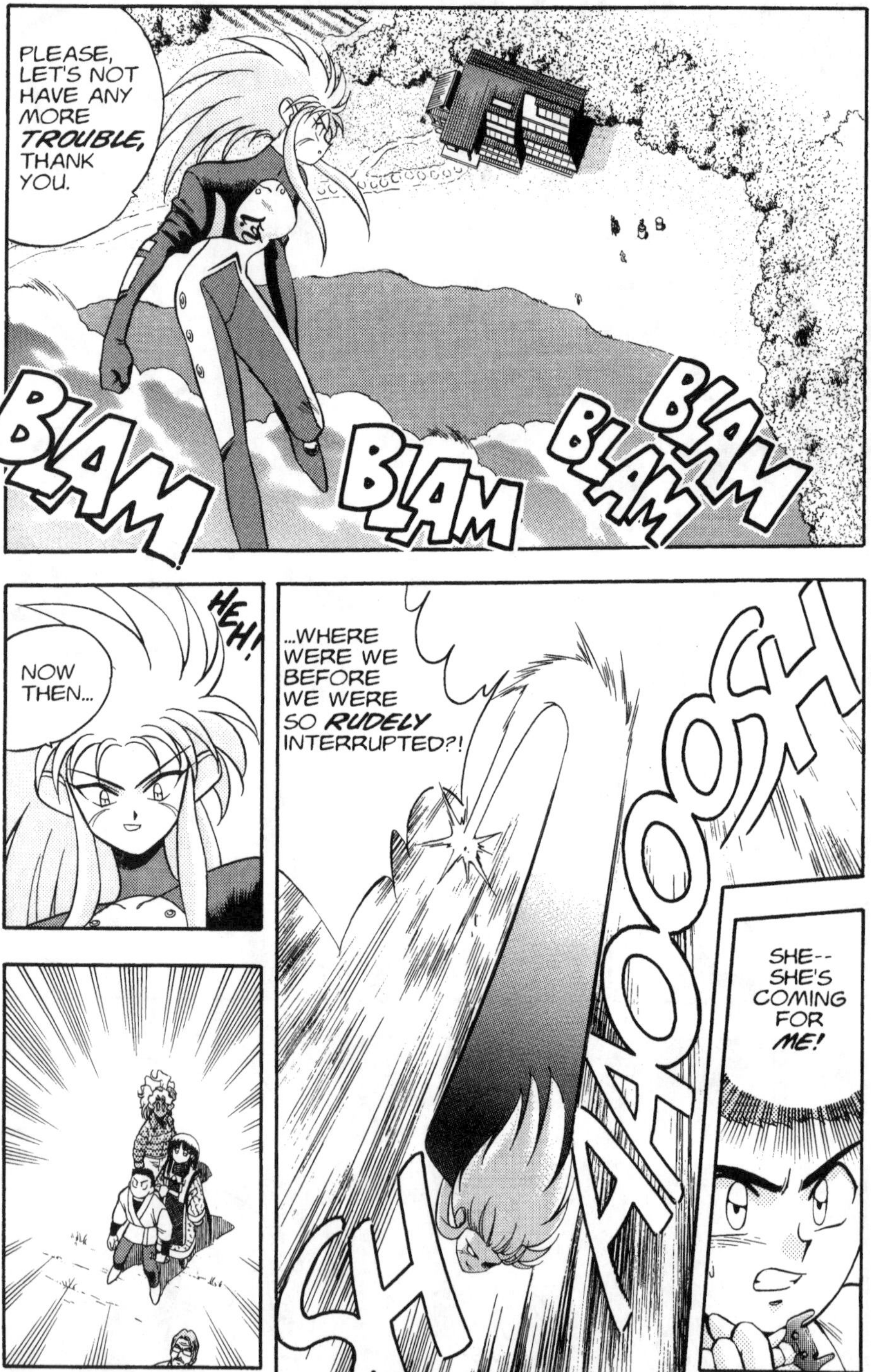
PLEASE, LET'S NOT HAVE ANY MORE TROUBLE, THANK YOU.
BLAM
BLAM
BLAM
BLAM
HEH!
NOW THEN...
...WHERE WERE WE BEFORE WE WERE SO RUDELY INTERRUPTED?!
SHWOOOSH
SHE-- SHE'S COMING FOR ME!

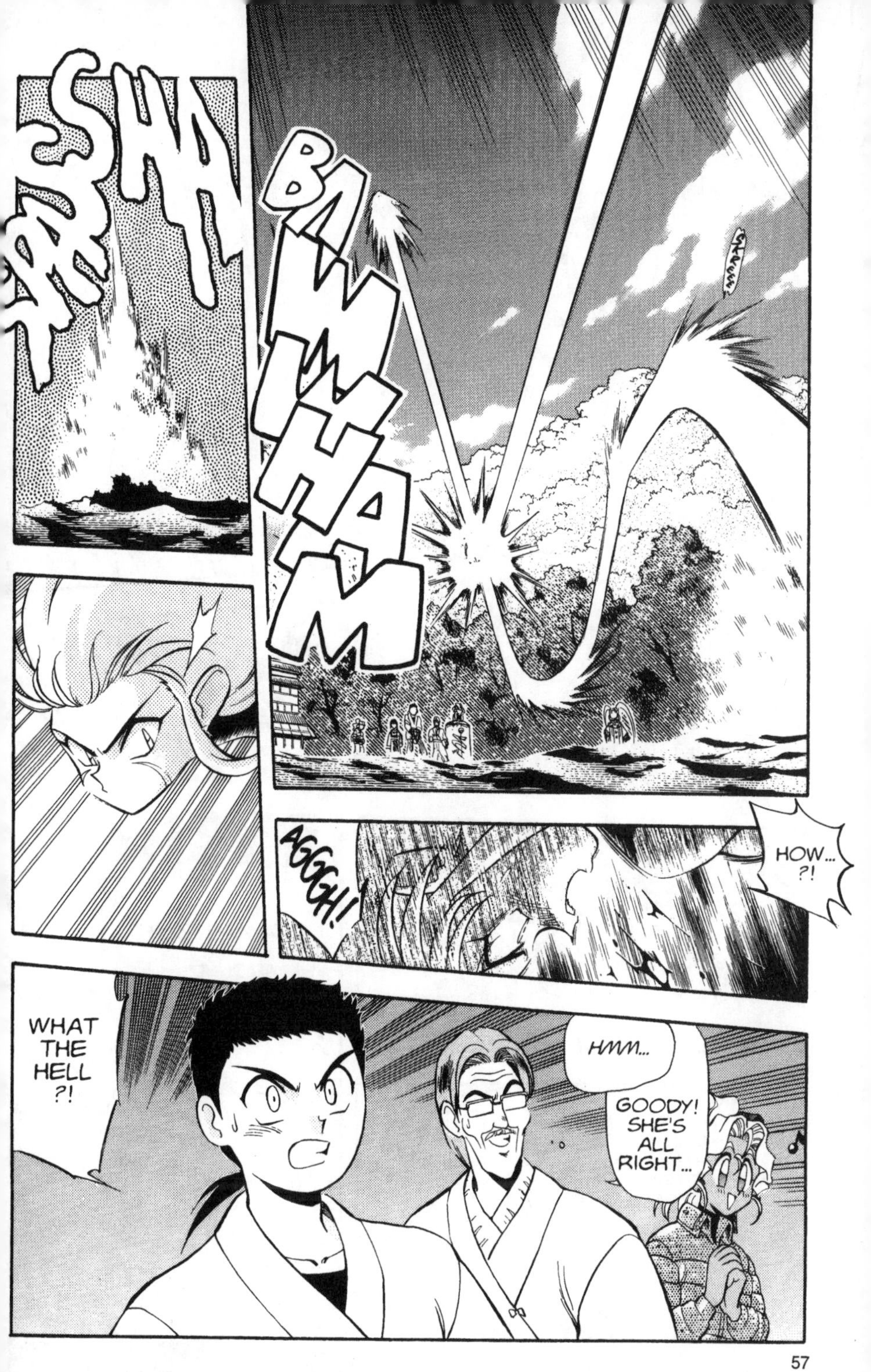
SHA
BAMMMHAMM
STREEE
AGGGH!
HOW... ?!
WHAT THE HELL ?!
HMM...
GOODY! SHE'S ALL RIGHT...

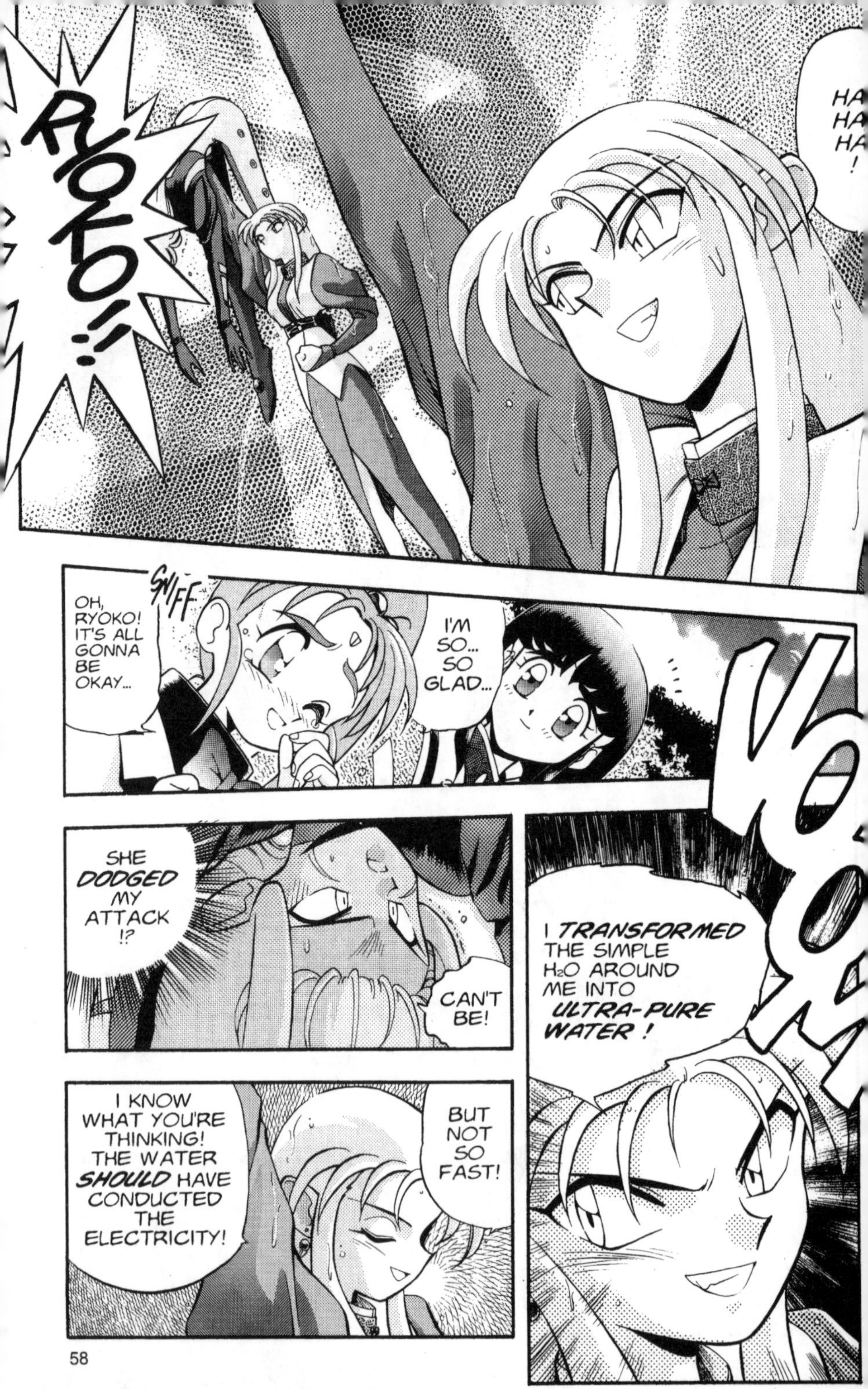
RYOKO!!!
HA HA HA!
SNIFF
OH, RYOKO! IT'S ALL GONNA BE OKAY...
I'M SO... SO GLAD...
SHE DODGED MY ATTACK!?
CAN'T BE!
I KNOW WHAT YOU'RE THINKING! THE WATER SHOULD HAVE CONDUCTED THE ELECTRICITY!
BUT NOT SO FAST!
I TRANSFORMED THE SIMPLE H_2O AROUND ME INTO ULTRA-PURE WATER!

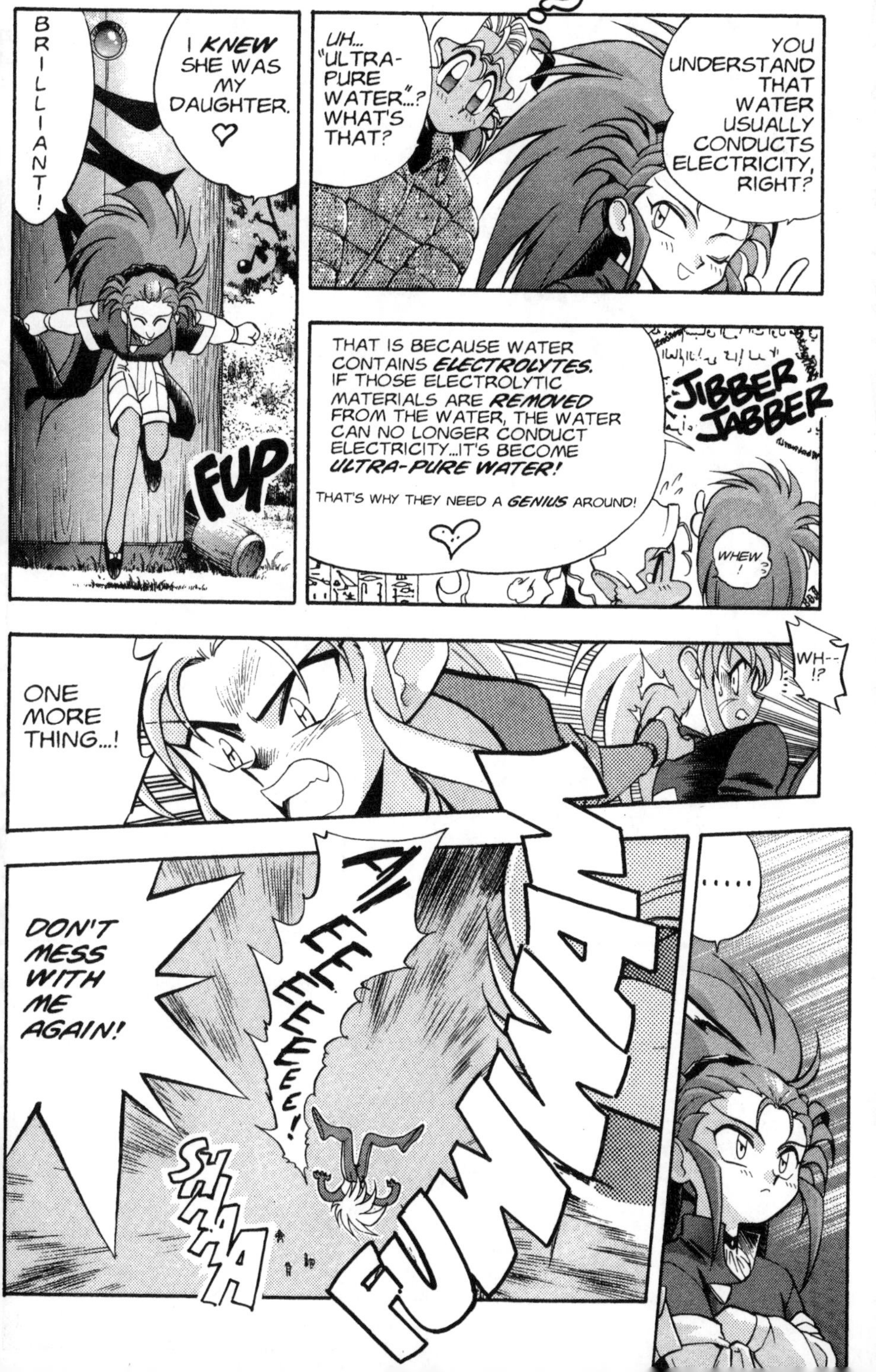
BRILLIANT!
I KNEW SHE WAS MY DAUGHTER. ♡
FUP
UH... "ULTRA-PURE WATER"...? WHAT'S THAT?
YOU UNDERSTAND THAT WATER USUALLY CONDUCTS ELECTRICITY, RIGHT?
THAT IS BECAUSE WATER CONTAINS ELECTROLYTES. IF THOSE ELECTROLYTIC MATERIALS ARE REMOVED FROM THE WATER, THE WATER CAN NO LONGER CONDUCT ELECTRICITY...IT'S BECOME ULTRA-PURE WATER!
THAT'S WHY THEY NEED A GENIUS AROUND! ♡
JIBBER JABBER
WHEW!
ONE MORE THING...!
WH--!?
DON'T MESS WITH ME AGAIN!
AIIEEEEEEEEE!
SHAAA
FUWAA
.....

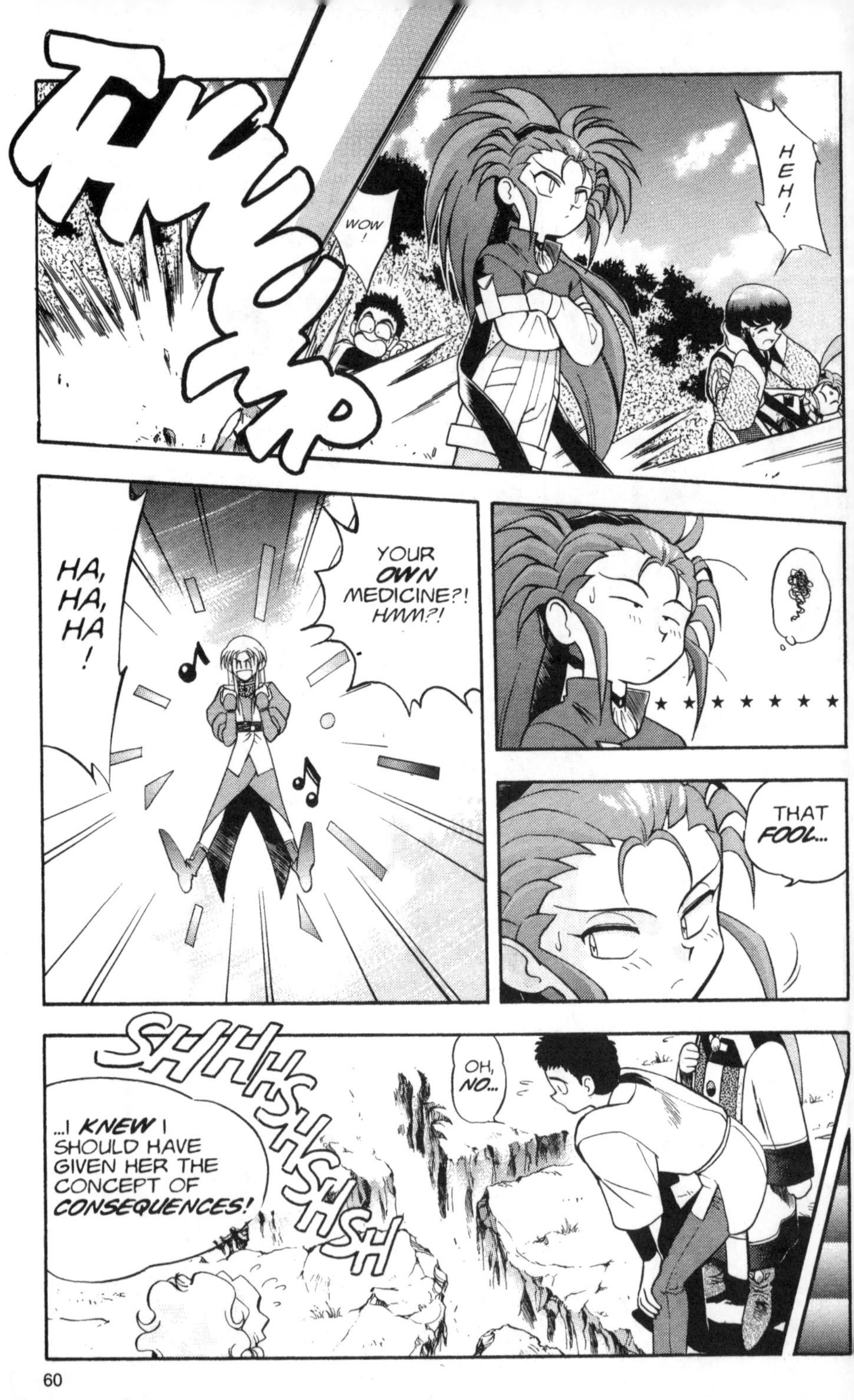
THUMP
WOW!
HEH!
HA, HA, HA!
YOUR *OWN* MEDICINE?! HMM?!
★★★★★★★
THAT *FOOL*...
SHHHSHSHSHSH
...I *KNEW* I SHOULD HAVE GIVEN HER THE CONCEPT OF *CONSEQUENCES!*
OH, *NO*...

WHAT'S UP?

SIGH

SHE'S SUDDENLY GOTTEN *VERY* QUIET.

hmm

HOW CAN SUCH A *CUTE GIRL* BE SO *AWFUL!*

I'LL SHOW YOU A THING CALLED A "MIRROR" LATER...

.....

NEVER MIND THESE IDIOTS-- WHO *ARE* YOU?

YOU'RE RYOKO'S *DOUBLE...*

WELL...

UM... MAY I ASK YOU *ONE THING* BEFORE I ANSWER YOUR QUESTION...?

IMPORTANT...?

IT'S VERY IMPORTANT. REALLY...

WELL...

ALL RIGHT, WHAT IS IT?

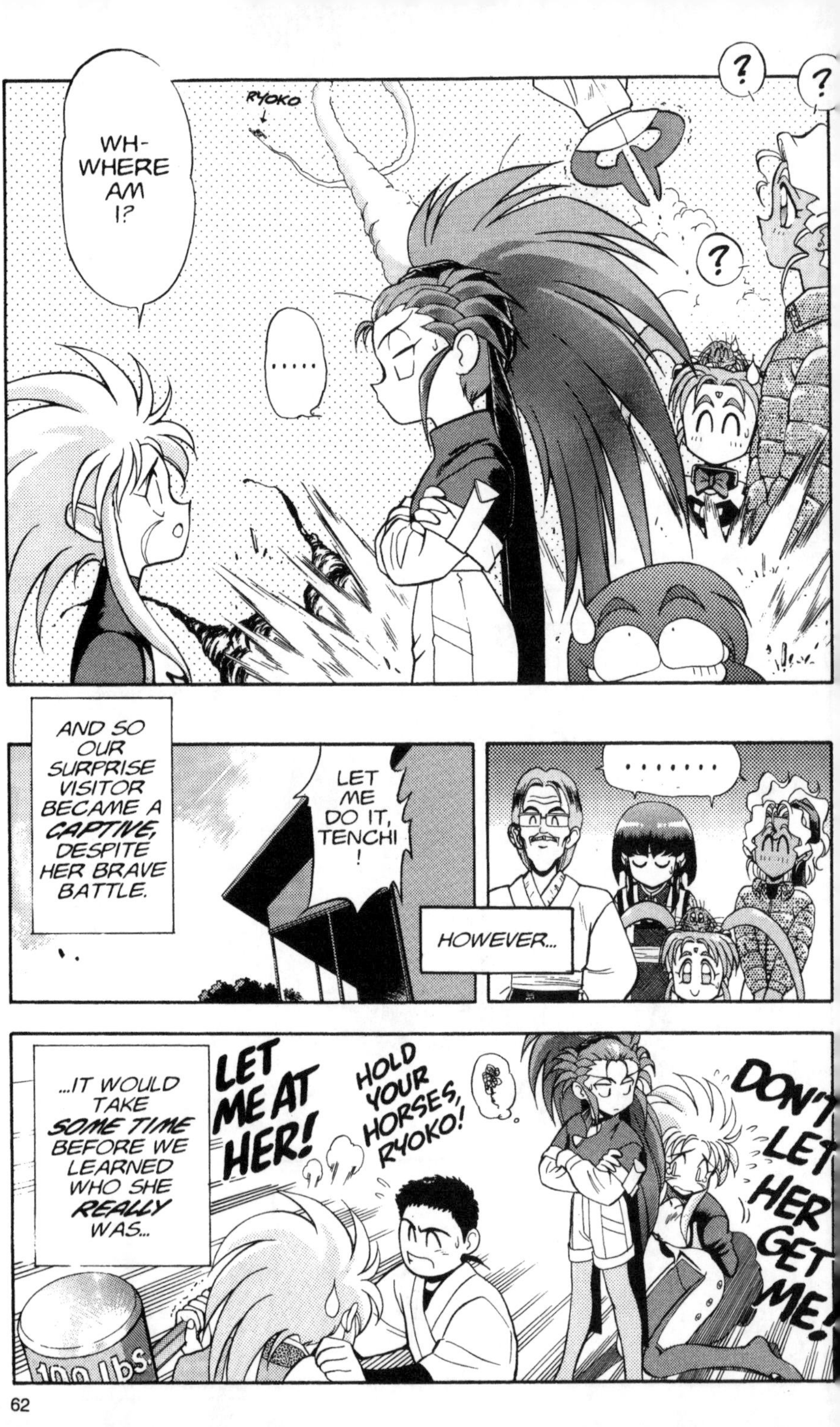
WH- WHERE AM I?
RYOKO
......
?
?
?
AND SO OUR SURPRISE VISITOR BECAME A CAPTIVE, DESPITE HER BRAVE BATTLE.
LET ME DO IT, TENCHI!
....
HOWEVER...
...IT WOULD TAKE SOME TIME BEFORE WE LEARNED WHO SHE REALLY WAS...
LET ME AT HER!
HOLD YOUR HORSES, RYOKO!
DON'T LET HER GET ME!
100 lbs.

Tales of Tenchi #3
UNDER OBSERVATION

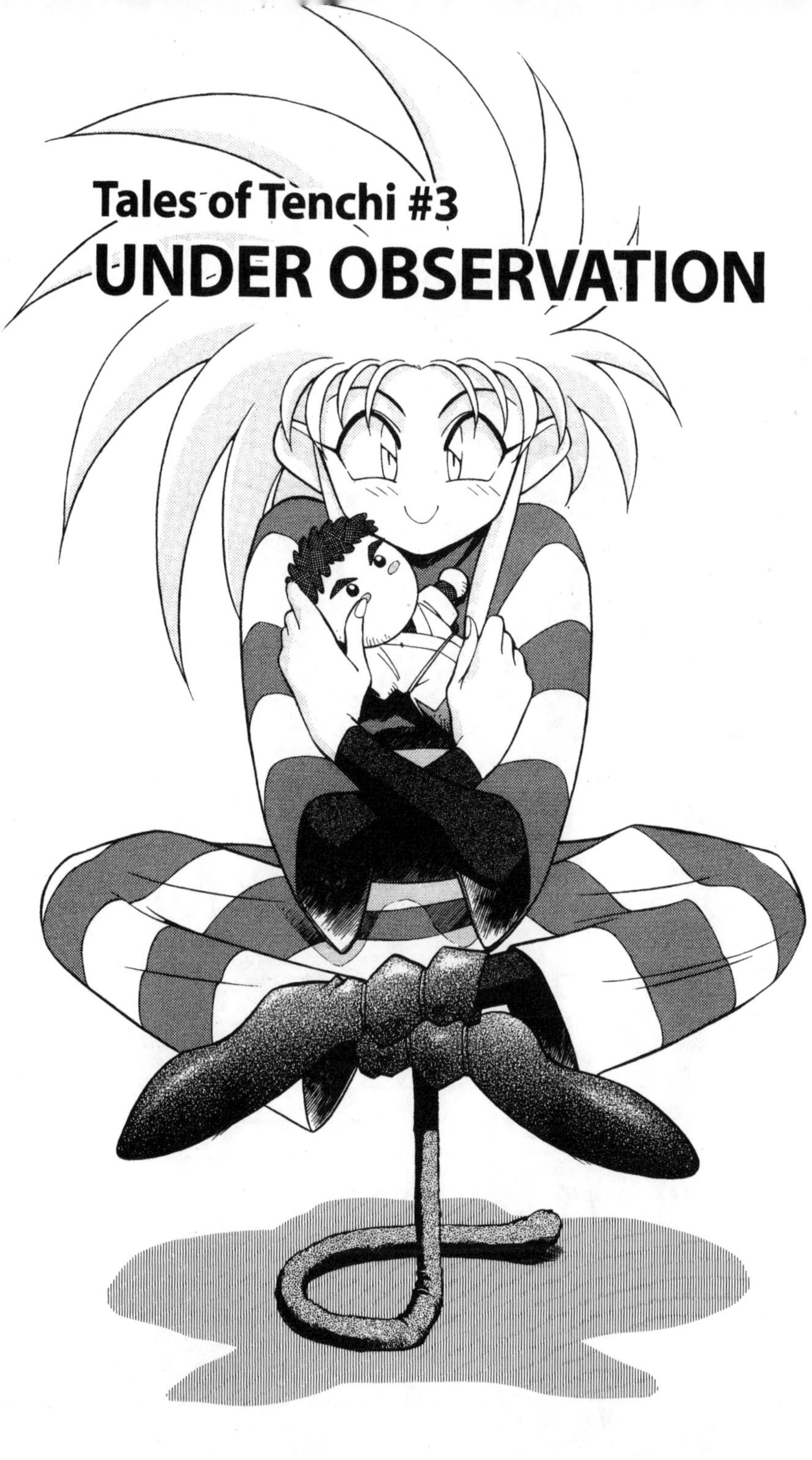

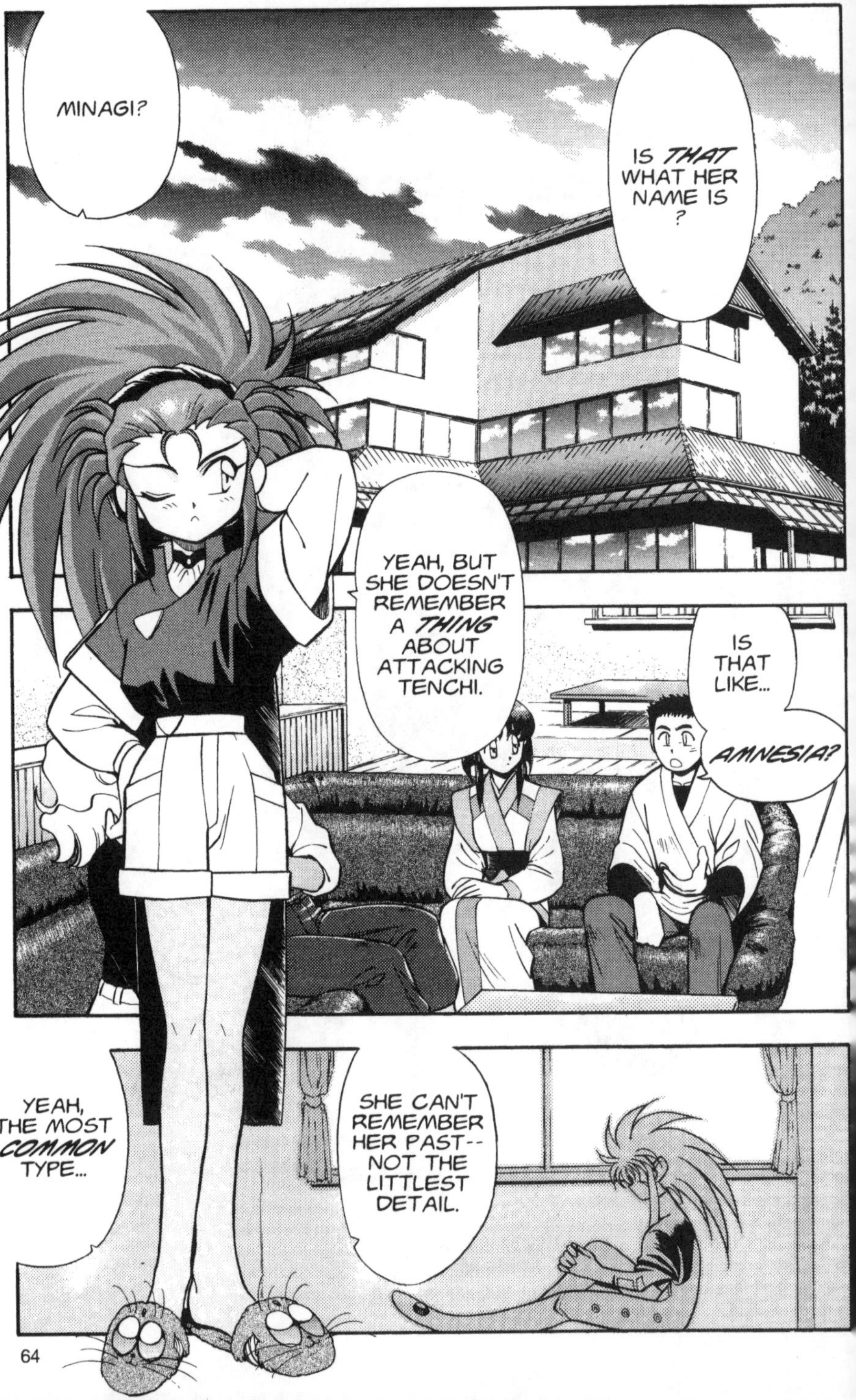
MINAGI?
IS THAT WHAT HER NAME IS ?
YEAH, BUT SHE DOESN'T REMEMBER A THING ABOUT ATTACKING TENCHI.
IS THAT LIKE... AMNESIA?
YEAH, THE MOST COMMON TYPE...
SHE CAN'T REMEMBER HER PAST-- NOT THE LITTLEST DETAIL.

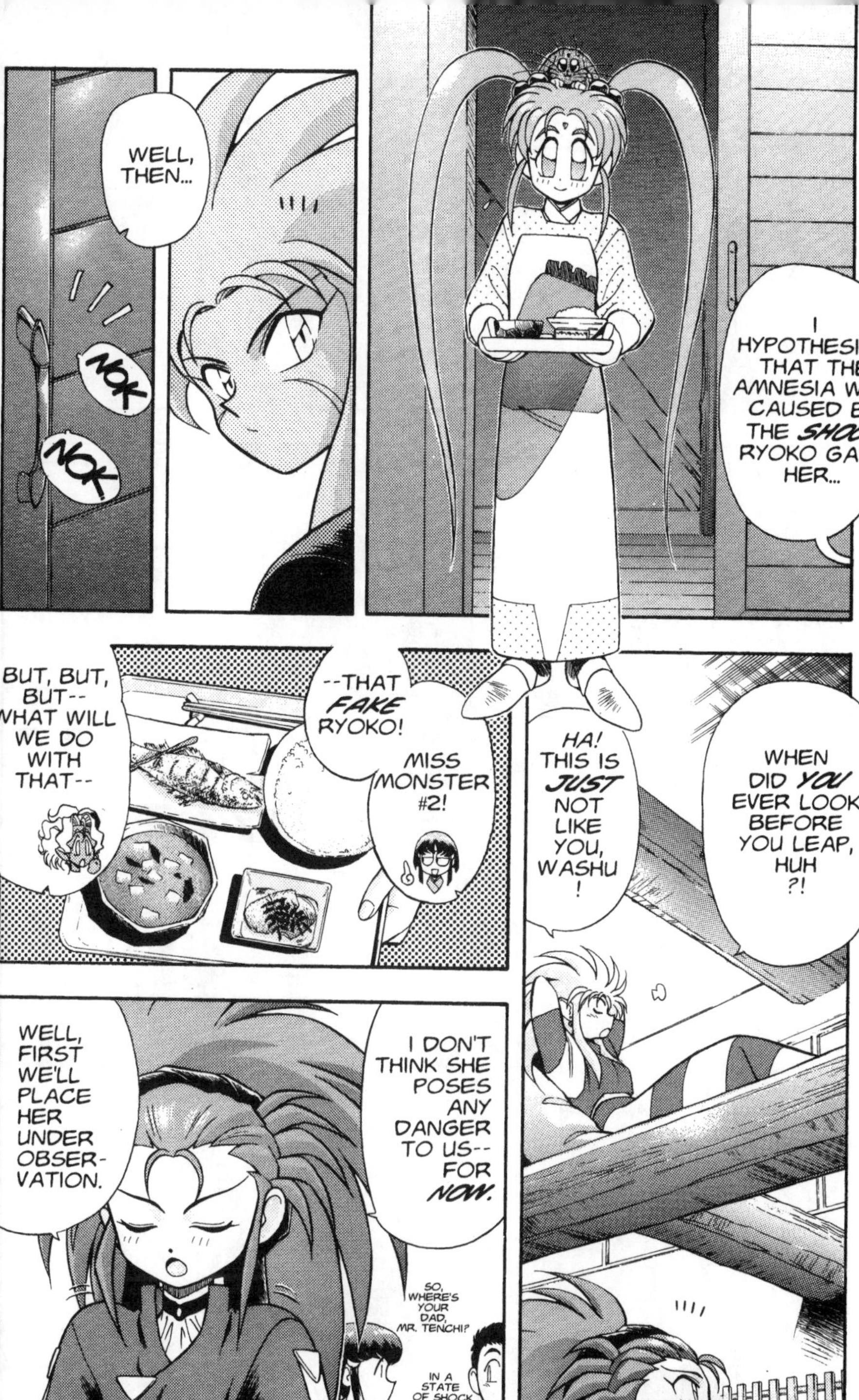
WELL, THEN...
NOK
NOK
I HYPOTHESIZE THAT THE AMNESIA WAS CAUSED BY THE *SHOCK* RYOKO GAVE HER...
BUT, BUT, BUT-- WHAT WILL WE DO WITH THAT--
--THAT *FAKE* RYOKO!
MISS MONSTER #2!
WELL, FIRST WE'LL PLACE HER UNDER OBSERVATION.
I DON'T THINK SHE POSES ANY DANGER TO US-- FOR *NOW.*
SO, WHERE'S YOUR DAD, MR. TENCHI?
IN A STATE OF SHOCK SOMEWHERE.
HA! THIS IS *JUST* NOT LIKE YOU, WASHU!
WHEN DID *YOU* EVER LOOK BEFORE YOU LEAP, HUH ?!

TUT
TUT
TUT...

DON'T YOU GO THINKING I'M JUST *ANY* MAD SCIENTIST!

WHAT KIND OF A MAD SCIENTIST ARE YOU?

AMNESIA IS A DELICATE STATE! I CAN'T SIMPLY GIVE A DIRECT SHOCK TO HER *HIPPOCAMPUS* OR GET RID OF HER *FRONTAL LOBE* OR DOWNLOAD HER *SYNAPSES* OR MASSAGE HER *MEDULLA OBLONGATA* OR....

OHH!

OHH!!

OHH!!

.....

SO WHAT ARE THOSE STRANGE TOOLS YOU'RE HOLDING?

OH! I FEEL SO SORRY FOR HER.

IT MUST BE HARD FOR HER NOT TO REMEMBER *ANYTHING* EXCEPT HER NAME... >SIGH<

I GUESS SHE WON'T EAT THE LOVELY MEAL SASAMI MADE.

TMPTMPTMP

FUFFF...

OH, *SASAMI...*

SPEAK OF THE DEVIL!

HOW IS SHE? SHE DIDN'T *EAT,* DID SHE?

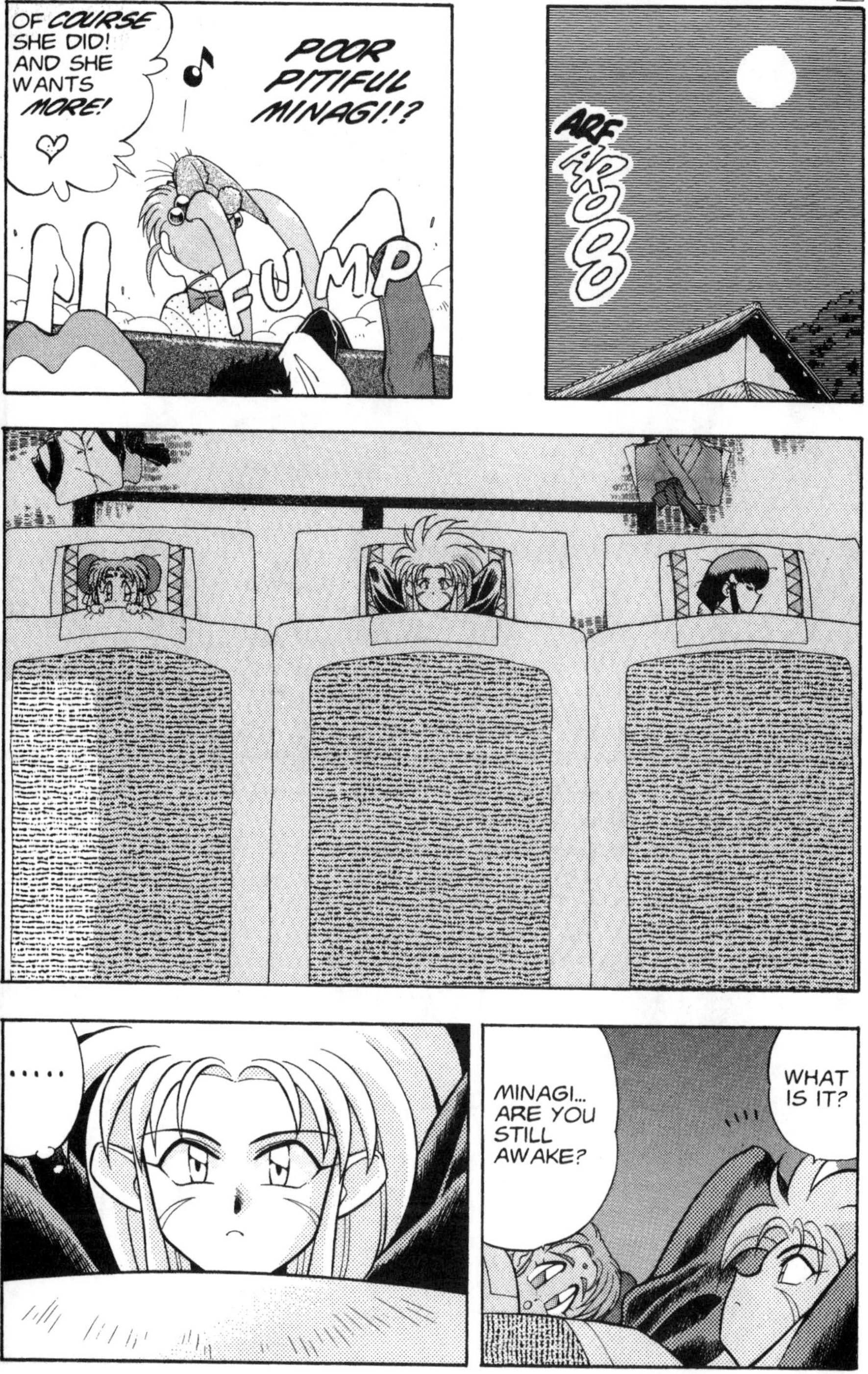
OF COURSE SHE DID! AND SHE WANTS MORE! ♡
POOR PITIFUL MINAGI!!?
FUMP
ARF
AROOO
.....
MINAGI... ARE YOU STILL AWAKE?
WHAT IS IT?

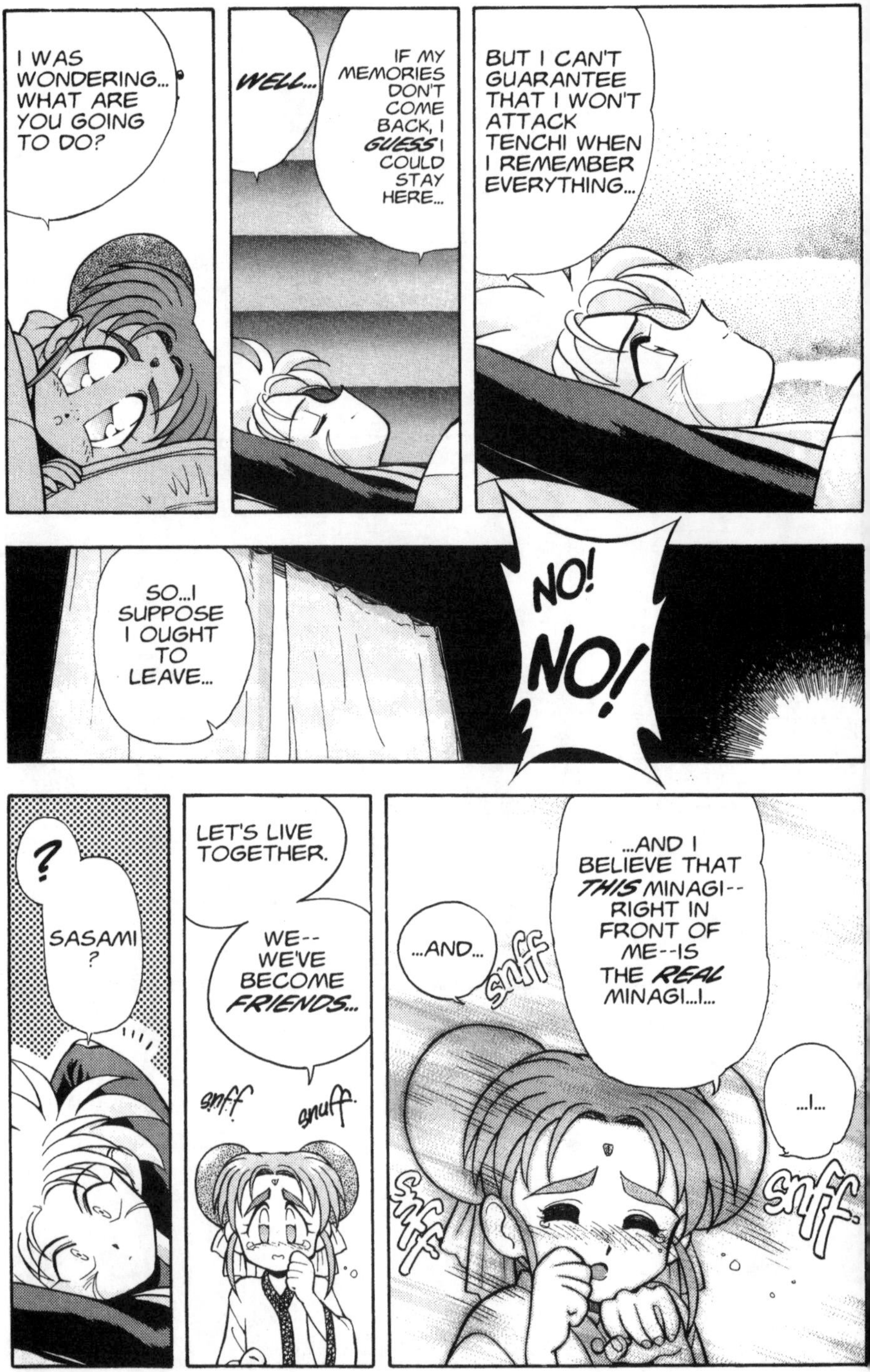
I WAS WONDERING... WHAT ARE YOU GOING TO DO?
WELL...
IF MY MEMORIES DON'T COME BACK, I GUESS I COULD STAY HERE...
BUT I CAN'T GUARANTEE THAT I WON'T ATTACK TENCHI WHEN I REMEMBER EVERYTHING...
SO...I SUPPOSE I OUGHT TO LEAVE...
NO! NO!
?
SASAMI?
LET'S LIVE TOGETHER.
WE--WE'VE BECOME FRIENDS...
snff
snuff
...AND...
snff
...AND I BELIEVE THAT THIS MINAGI--RIGHT IN FRONT OF ME--IS THE REAL MINAGI...I...
...I...
snff
snff

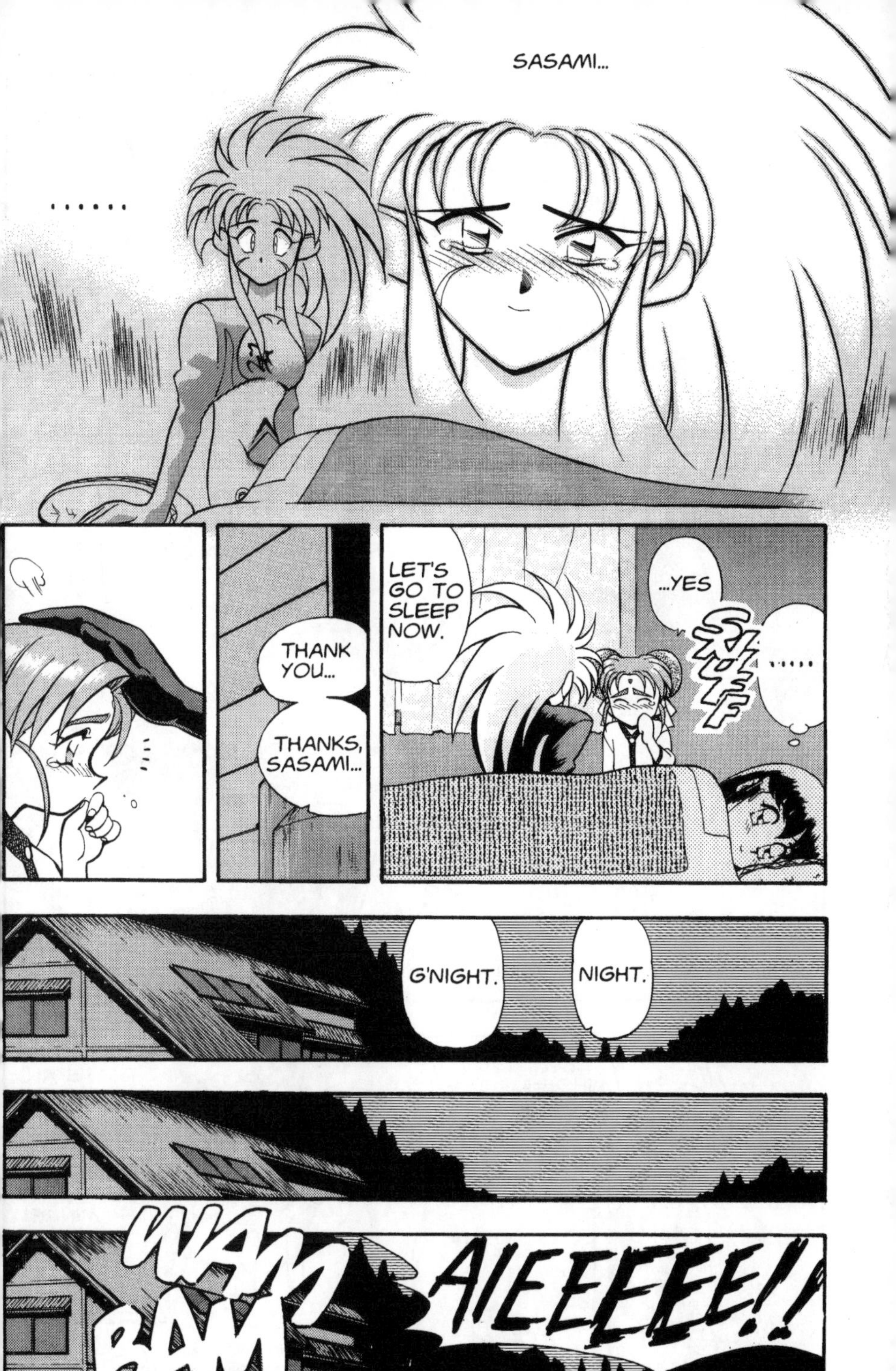
SASAMI...
......
THANK YOU...
THANKS, SASAMI...
LET'S GO TO SLEEP NOW.
...YES
SNIFF
.....
G'NIGHT.
NIGHT.
WAM
BAM
AIEEEEE!!

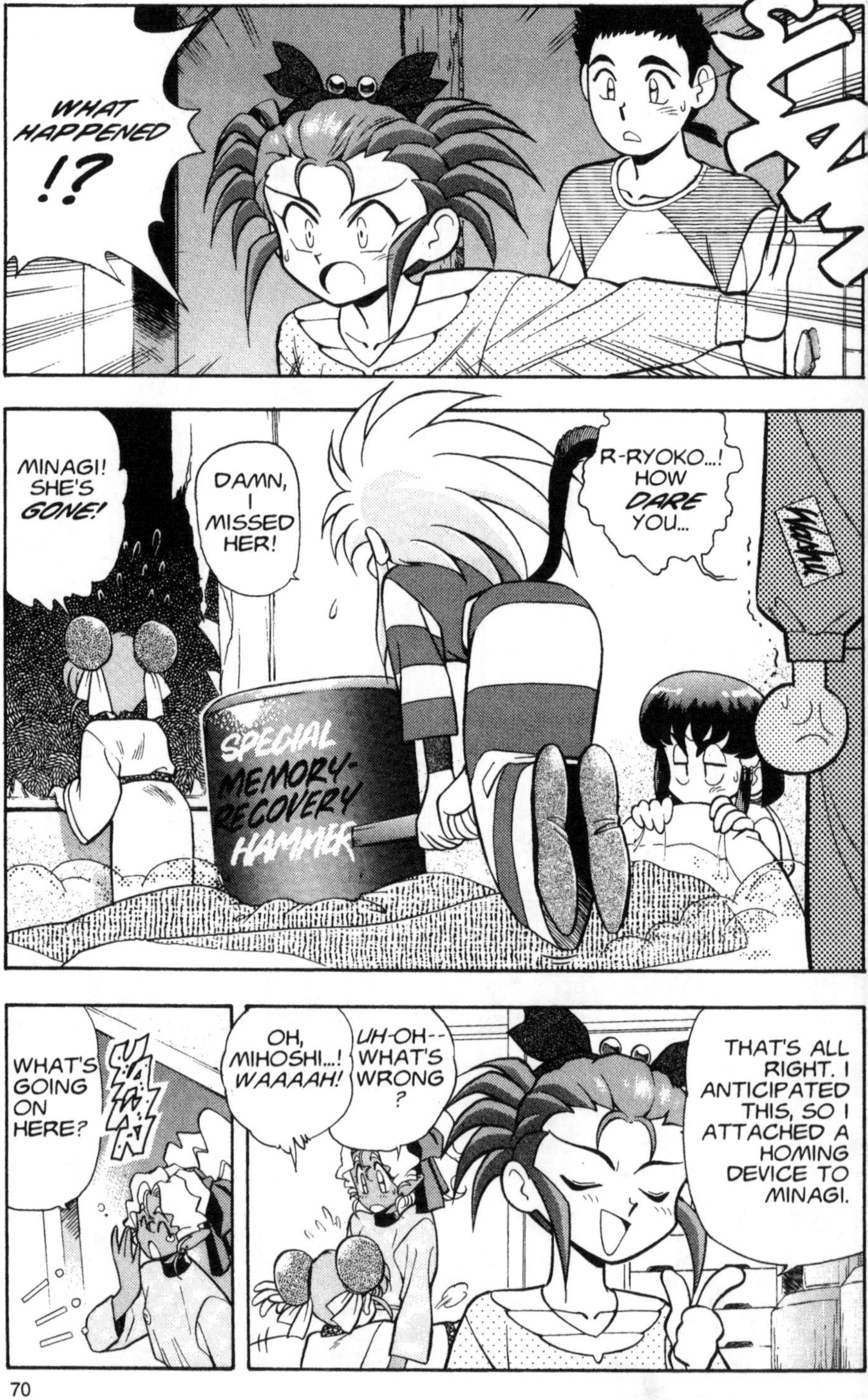
WHAT HAPPENED !?
MINAGI! SHE'S GONE!
DAMN, I MISSED HER!
R-RYOKO...! HOW DARE YOU...
SPECIAL MEMORY-RECOVERY HAMMER
WHAT'S GOING ON HERE?
OH, MIHOSHI...! WAAAAH!
UH-OH-- WHAT'S WRONG?
THAT'S ALL RIGHT. I ANTICIPATED THIS, SO I ATTACHED A HOMING DEVICE TO MINAGI.

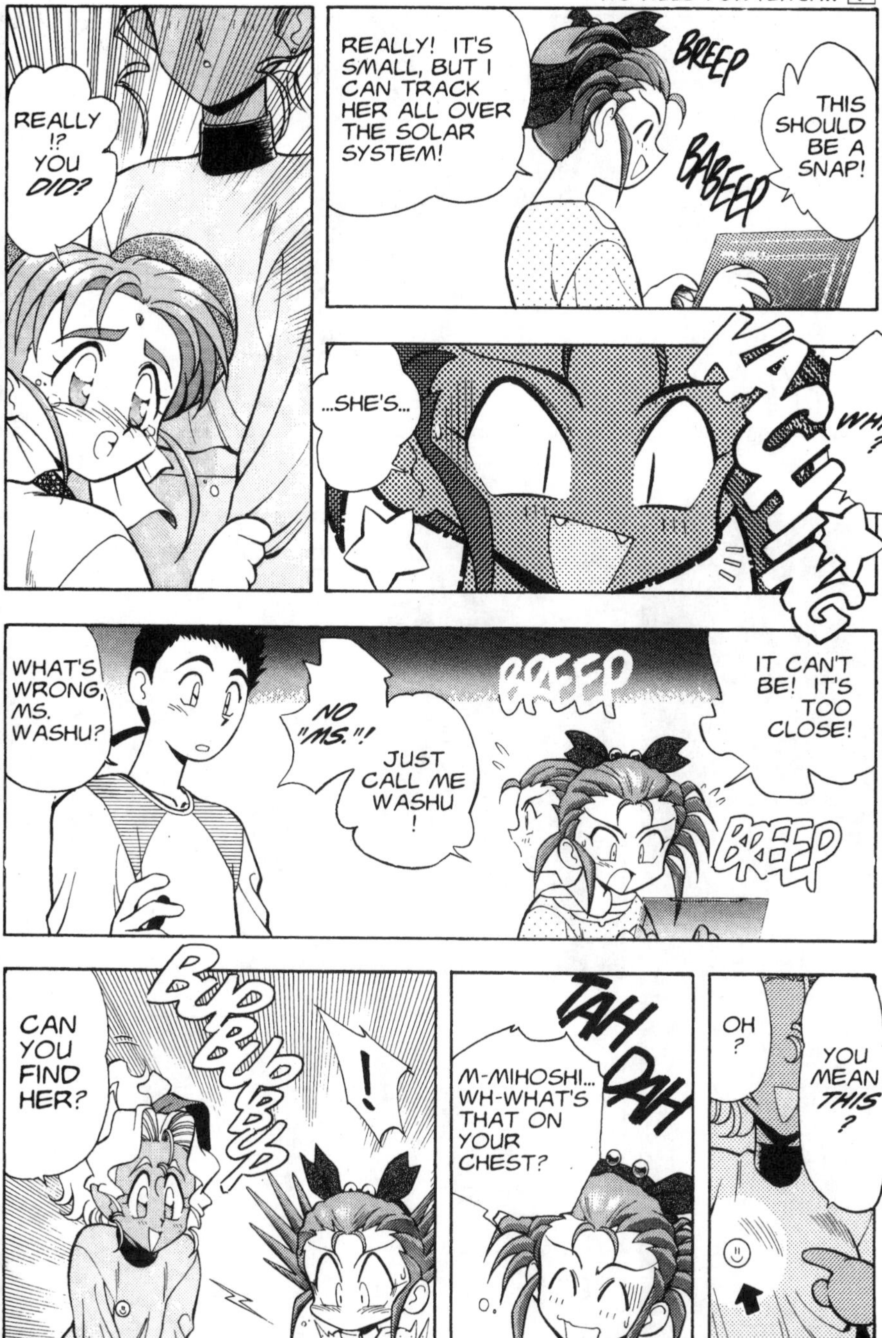
REALLY !? YOU *DID?*
REALLY! IT'S SMALL, BUT I CAN TRACK HER ALL OVER THE SOLAR SYSTEM!
BREEP
BABEEP
THIS SHOULD BE A SNAP!
...SHE'S...
KACHING
WHAT ?
WHAT'S WRONG, MS. WASHU?
NO "MS."! JUST CALL ME WASHU !
BREEP
IT CAN'T BE! IT'S TOO CLOSE!
BREEP
CAN YOU FIND HER?
BUBUBUBUP
!
M-MIHOSHI... WH-WHAT'S THAT ON YOUR CHEST?
TAH DAH
OH ?
YOU MEAN *THIS* ?

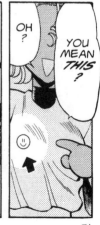

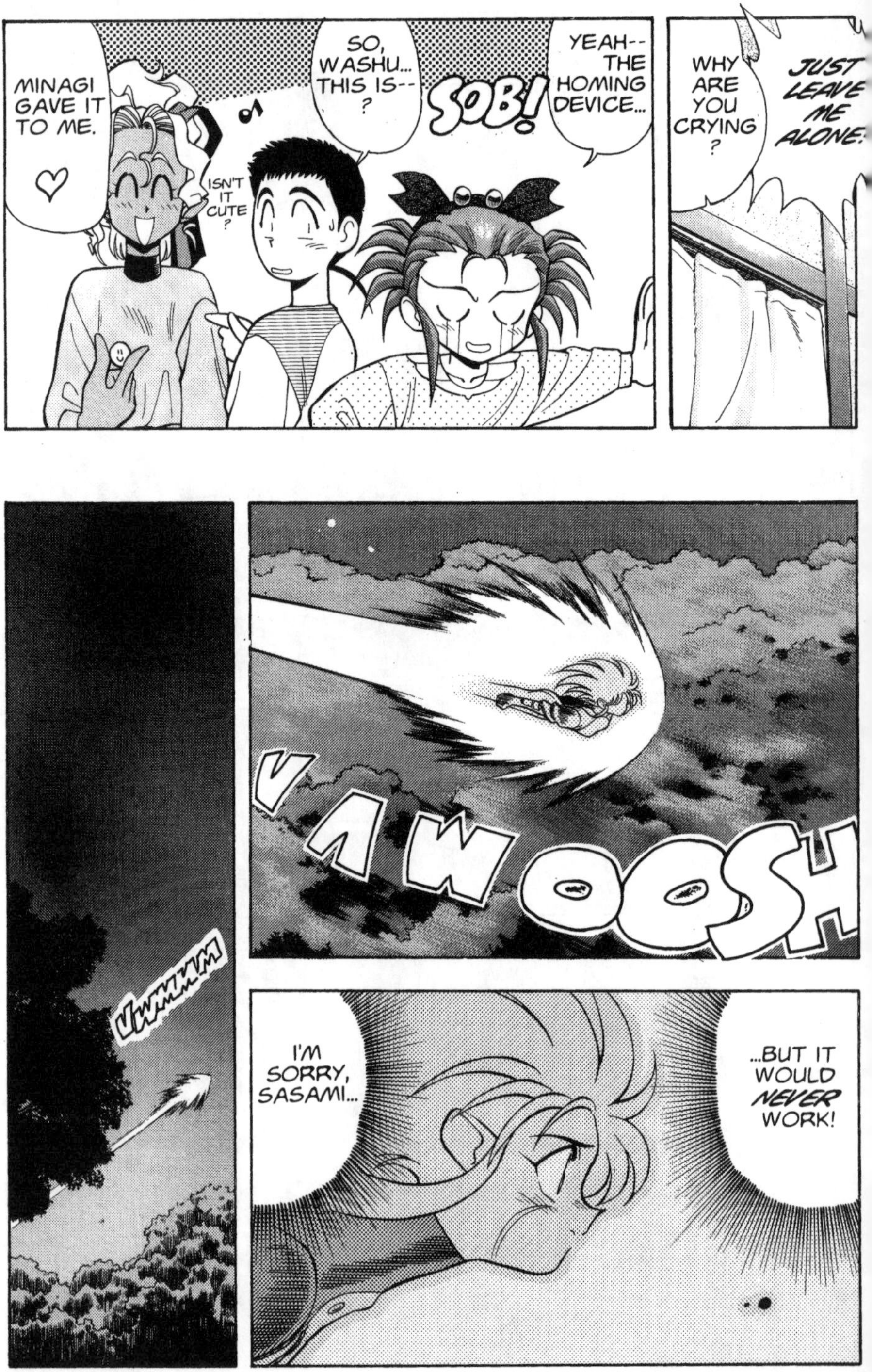
MINAGI GAVE IT TO ME.
ISN'T IT CUTE?
SO, WASHU... THIS IS--?
SOB!
YEAH--THE HOMING DEVICE...
WHY ARE YOU CRYING?
JUST LEAVE ME ALONE!
VWOOSH
UWMMMMM
I'M SORRY, SASAMI...
...BUT IT WOULD NEVER WORK!

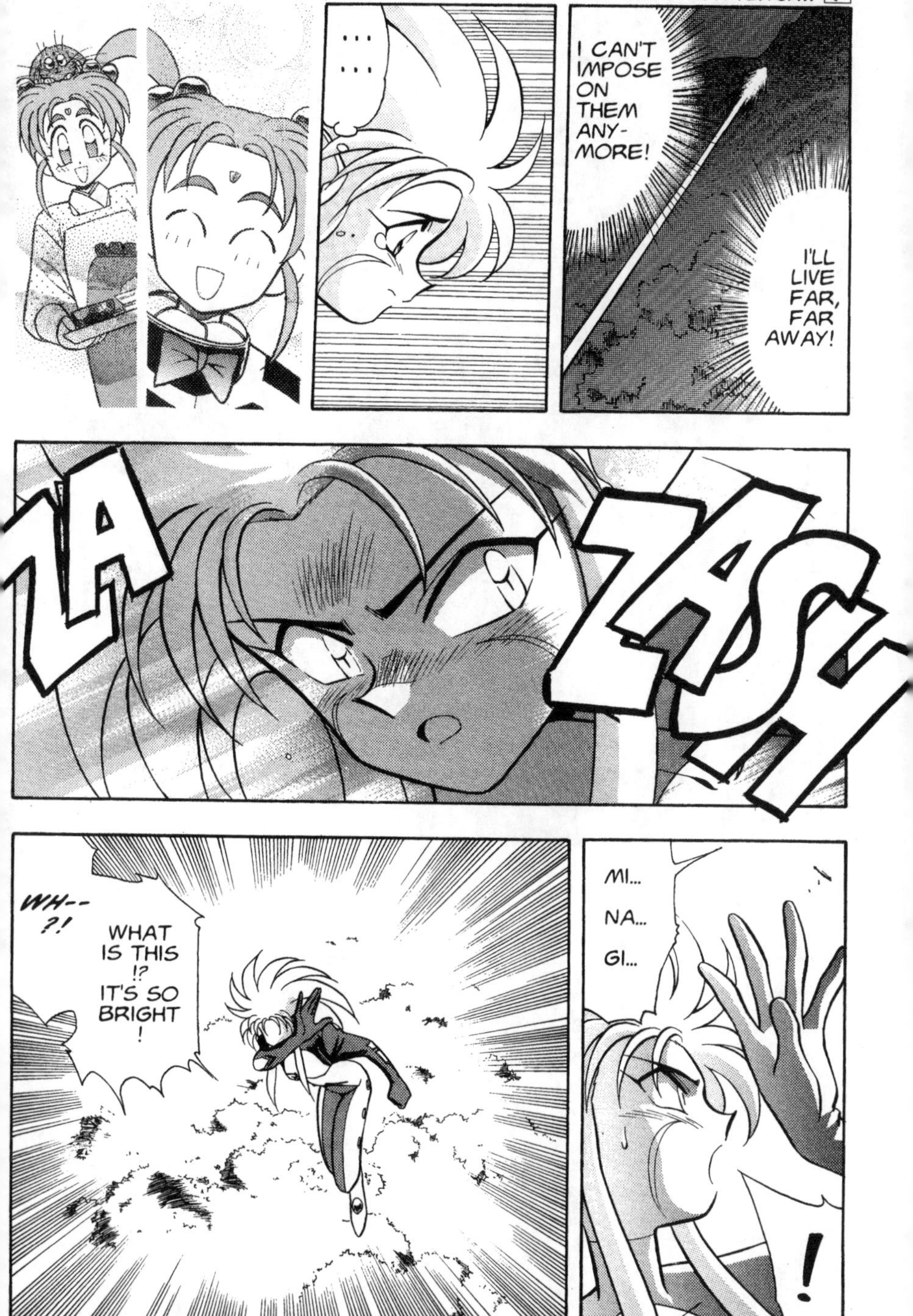
...
...
I CAN'T IMPOSE ON THEM ANY-MORE!
I'LL LIVE FAR, FAR AWAY!
ZA
ZASH
WH-- ?!
WHAT IS THIS !? IT'S SO BRIGHT !
MI... NA... GI...
!

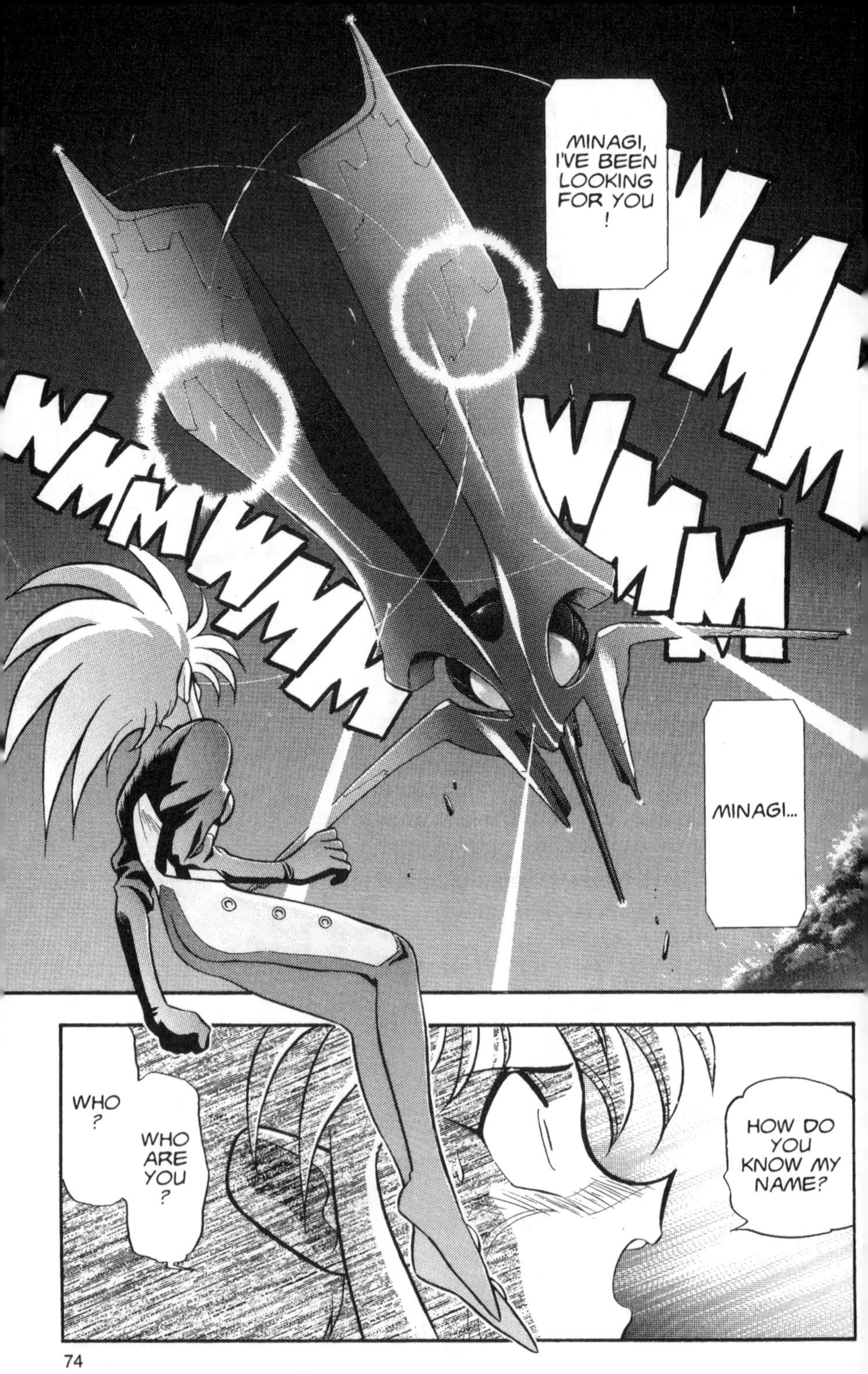
MINAGI, I'VE BEEN LOOKING FOR YOU!
WMMMMMMMMM
WMMMMMMM
MINAGI...
WHO?
WHO ARE YOU?
HOW DO YOU KNOW MY NAME?

MIHOSHI, COULD YOU PASS THE SOY SAUCE?

SURE! HERE IT IS! ♡

SASAMI?

CAN I HAVE SOME MORE?

CHATTER

CHATTER

FWIP

DINNER-TIME!

SO... WHAT'S WASHU UP TO?

SHE'S IN HER ROOM-- SHE'S UP TO SOME-THING.

C'MON, GIMME SOME MORE!

M-MY FACE

WHAT'S UP WITH HER?

SHE'S MAD 'CAUSE RYOKO DROVE MINAGI OFF.

CHMP

CHMP CHMP CHMP

I'M SORRY-- IT WAS ALL MY FAULT!

I'LL APOLOGIZE TO HER WHEN SHE GETS BACK.

TMP TMP

.....

YUM !

TEEHEE!

.....

OH, NO! I DROPPED THE SOY SAUCE !

AHAHAHAHA

KAKRIK

SHEEEOOOO

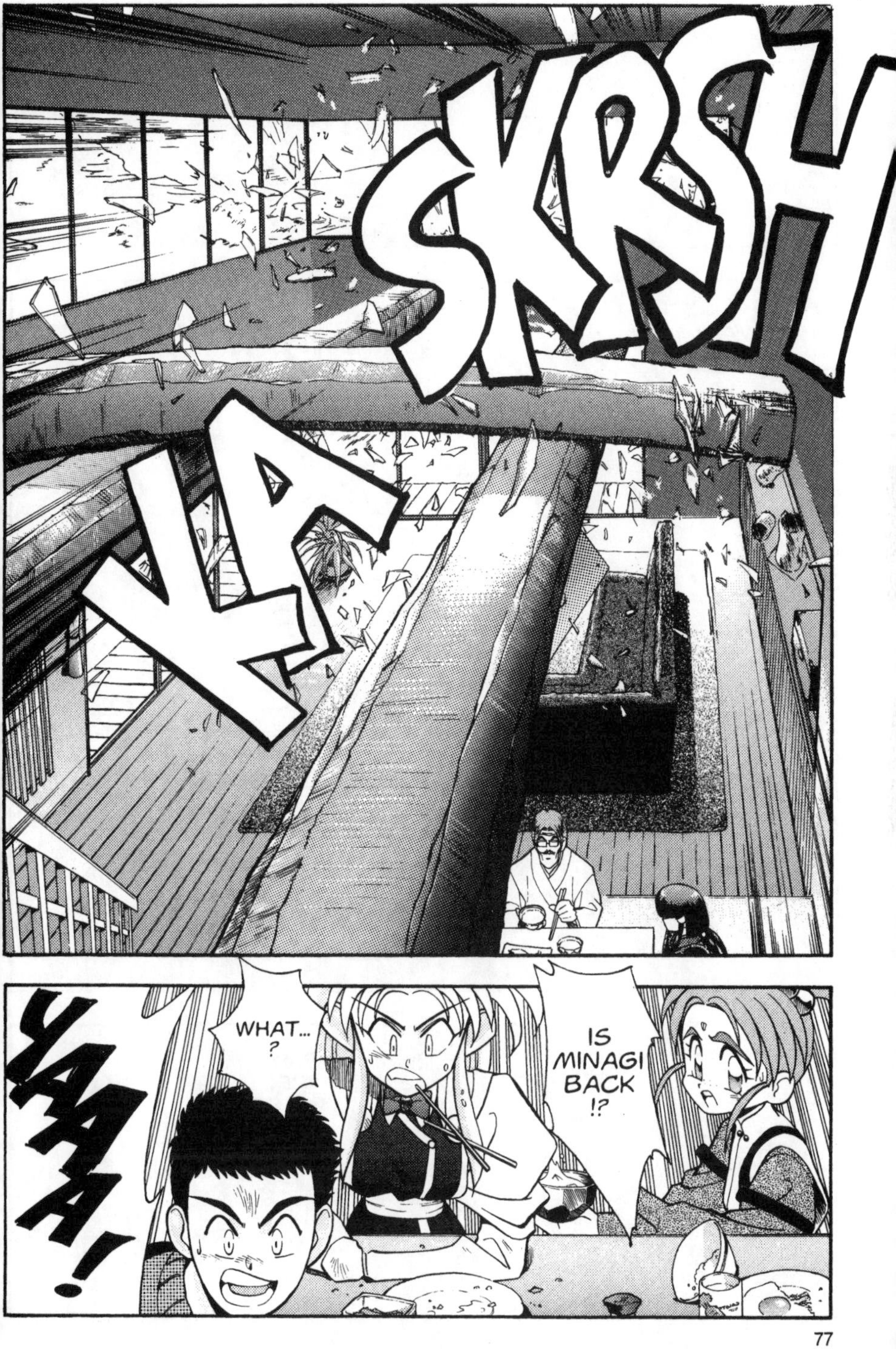
KA
SKRSH
YAAA!
WHAT... ?
IS MINAGI BACK !?

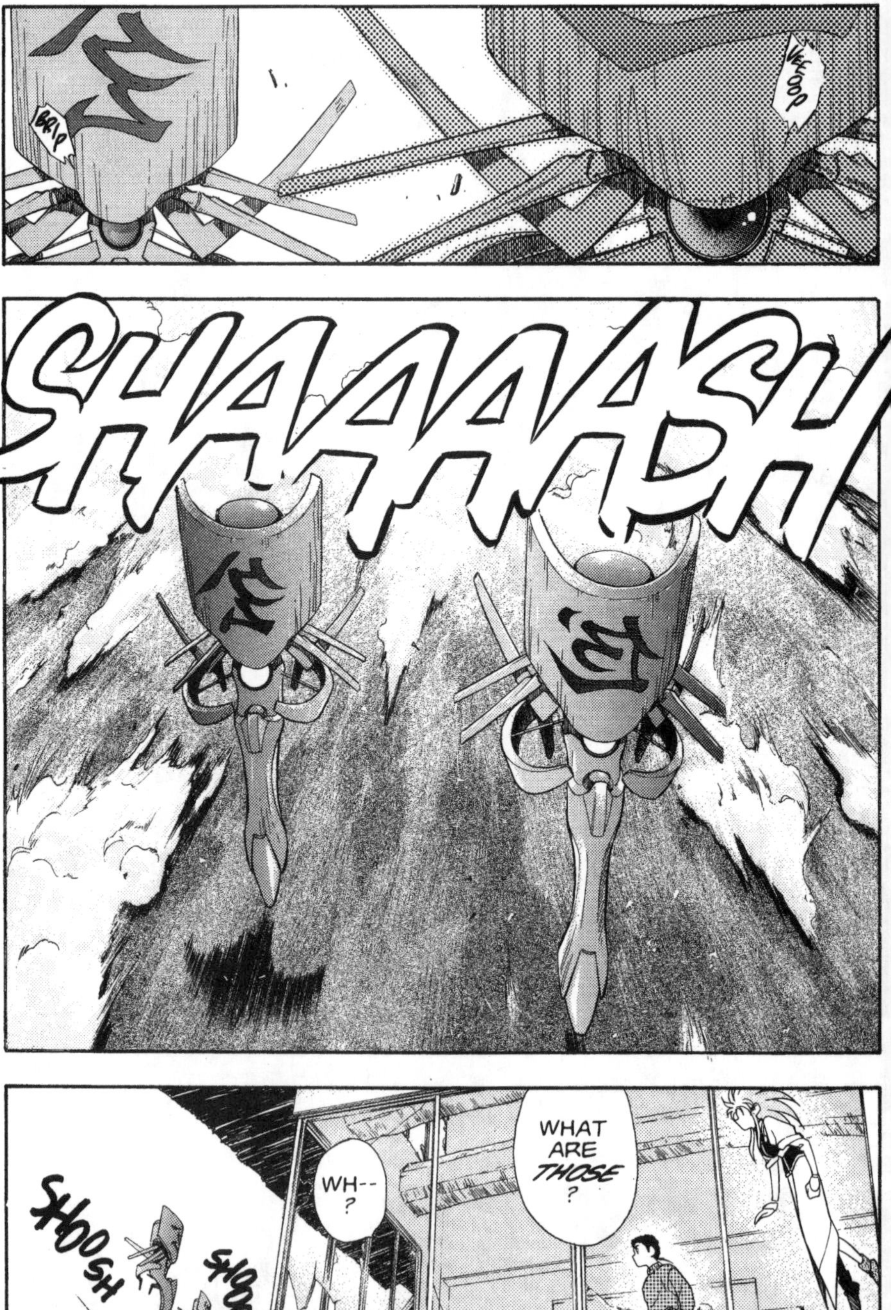
BRIP
SHAAAASH
SHOOSH
SHOOSH
WH--?
WHAT ARE *THOSE*?

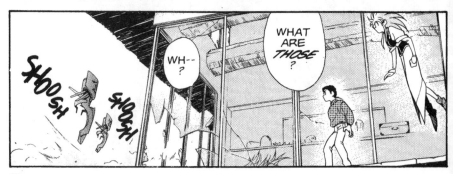

YOUNG MAN-- YES, YOU, OVER THERE!

CHMP CHMP

DON'T HIDE-- JUST SHOW YOURSELF!

WHAT !?

WHO'S HE TALKING TO?

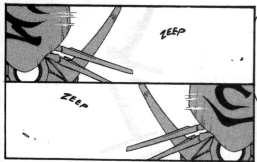

ZEEP

ZEEP

YOU'RE IN THE MIDDLE OF DINNER--

SHADDUP

--I'M SORRY TO INTERRUPT.

I WASN'T HIDING, EXACTLY...

SHUP SHUP SHUP

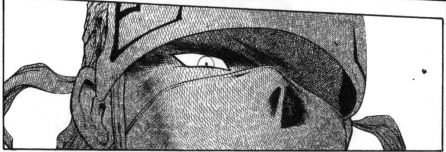

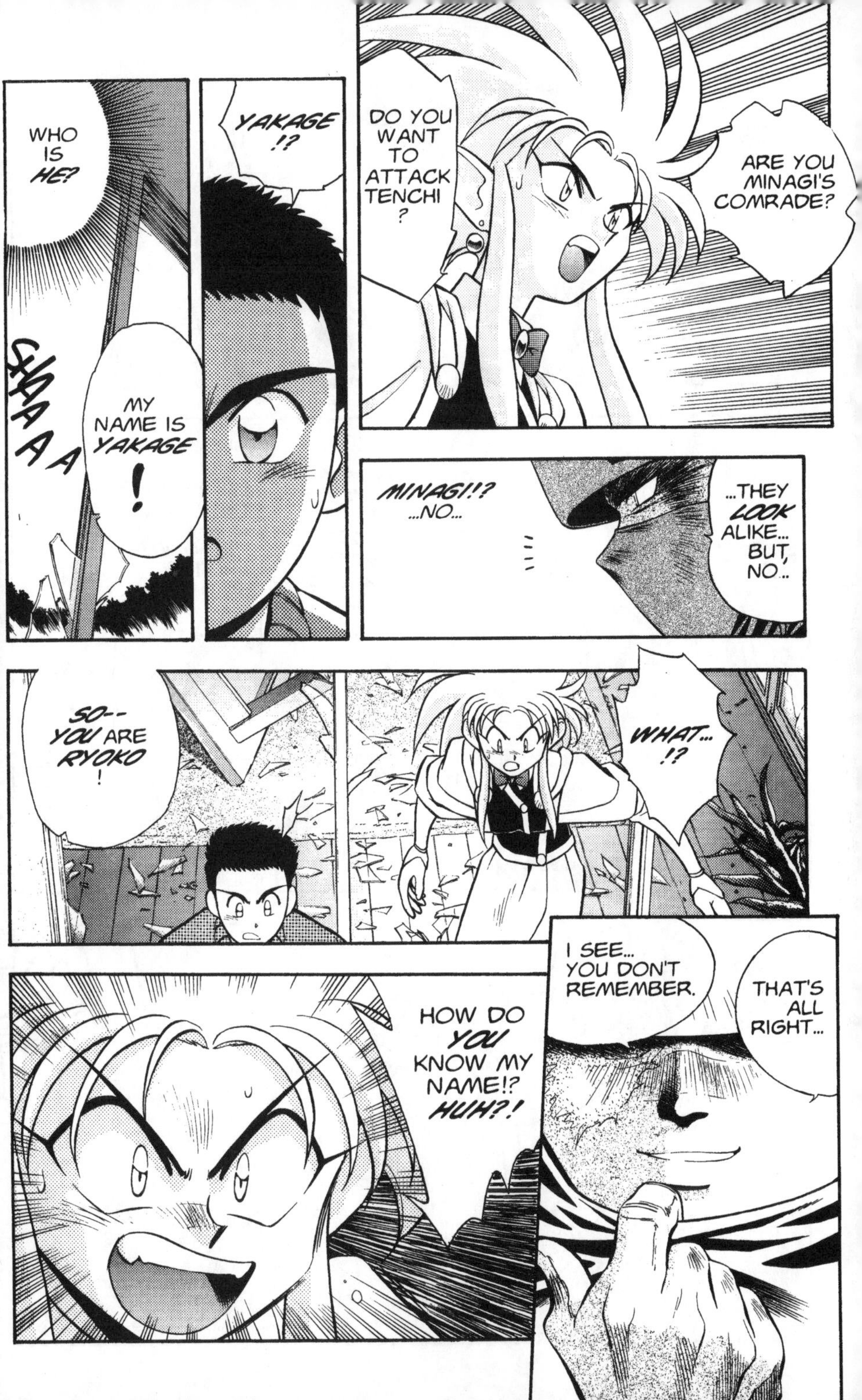
WHO IS HE?
SHAAAAA
YAKAGE !?
MY NAME IS YAKAGE !
DO YOU WANT TO ATTACK TENCHI ?
ARE YOU MINAGI'S COMRADE?
MINAGI!? ...NO...
...THEY LOOK ALIKE... BUT, NO...
SO-- YOU ARE RYOKO !
WHAT... !?
HOW DO YOU KNOW MY NAME!? HUH?!
I SEE... YOU DON'T REMEMBER.
THAT'S ALL RIGHT...

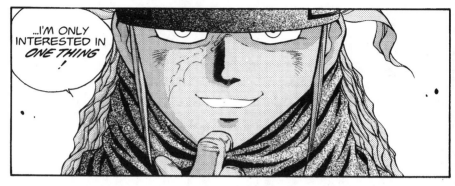

...I'M ONLY INTERESTED IN *ONE THING*!

BOY!

SHOW ME THE POWER OF *THE LIGHTNING EAGLE SWORD*!

MINAGI SAID THE SAME THING! THEN *THIS* IS WHO MINAGI WAS TALKING ABOUT!

WHY DO YOU WANT TO SEE IT!?

I DON'T HAVE TO ANSWER THAT...

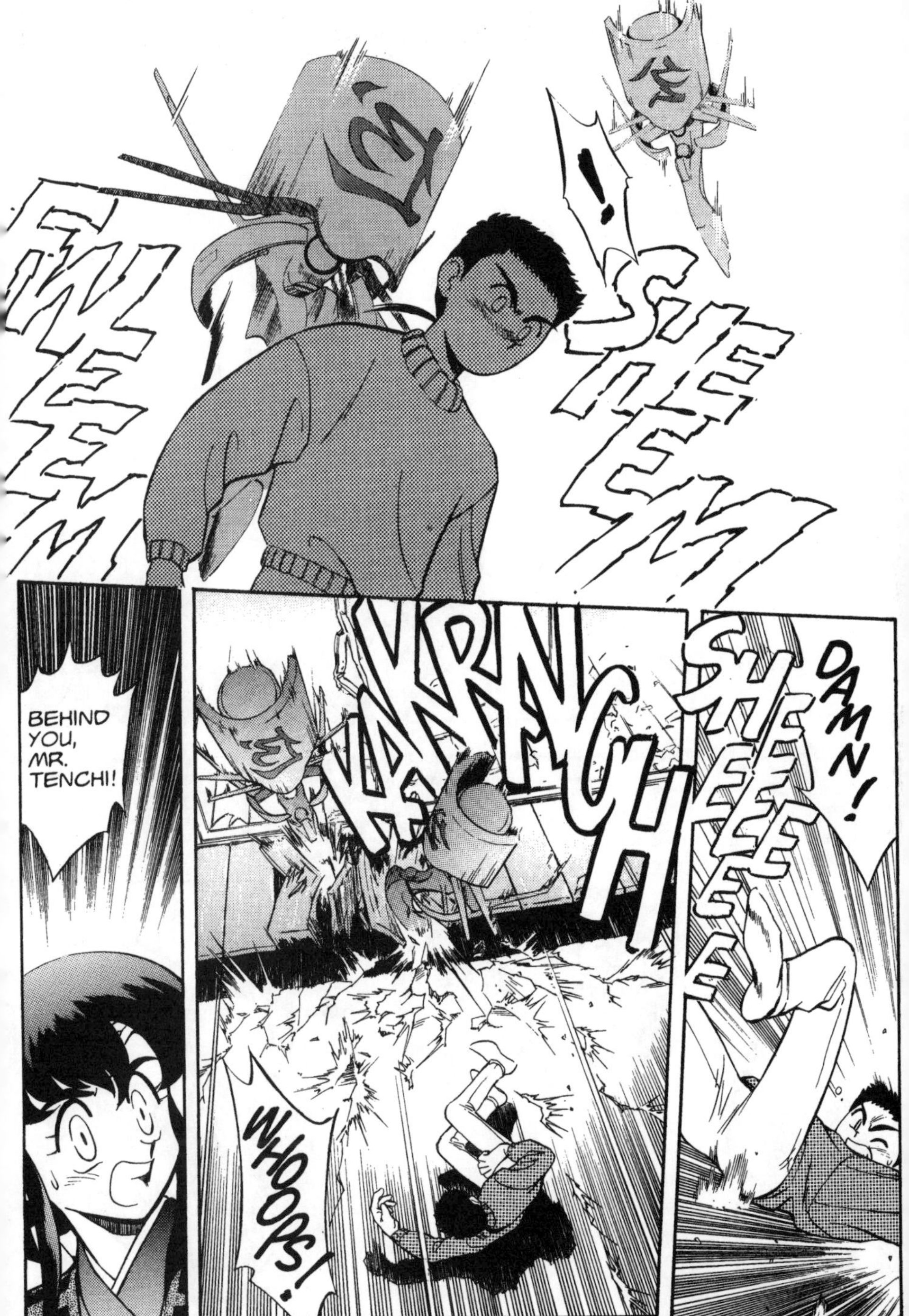
SHEEEM!
!
SHEEEM!
BEHIND YOU, MR. TENCHI!
KRANCH
WHOOPS!
SHEEEEEEE
DAMN!

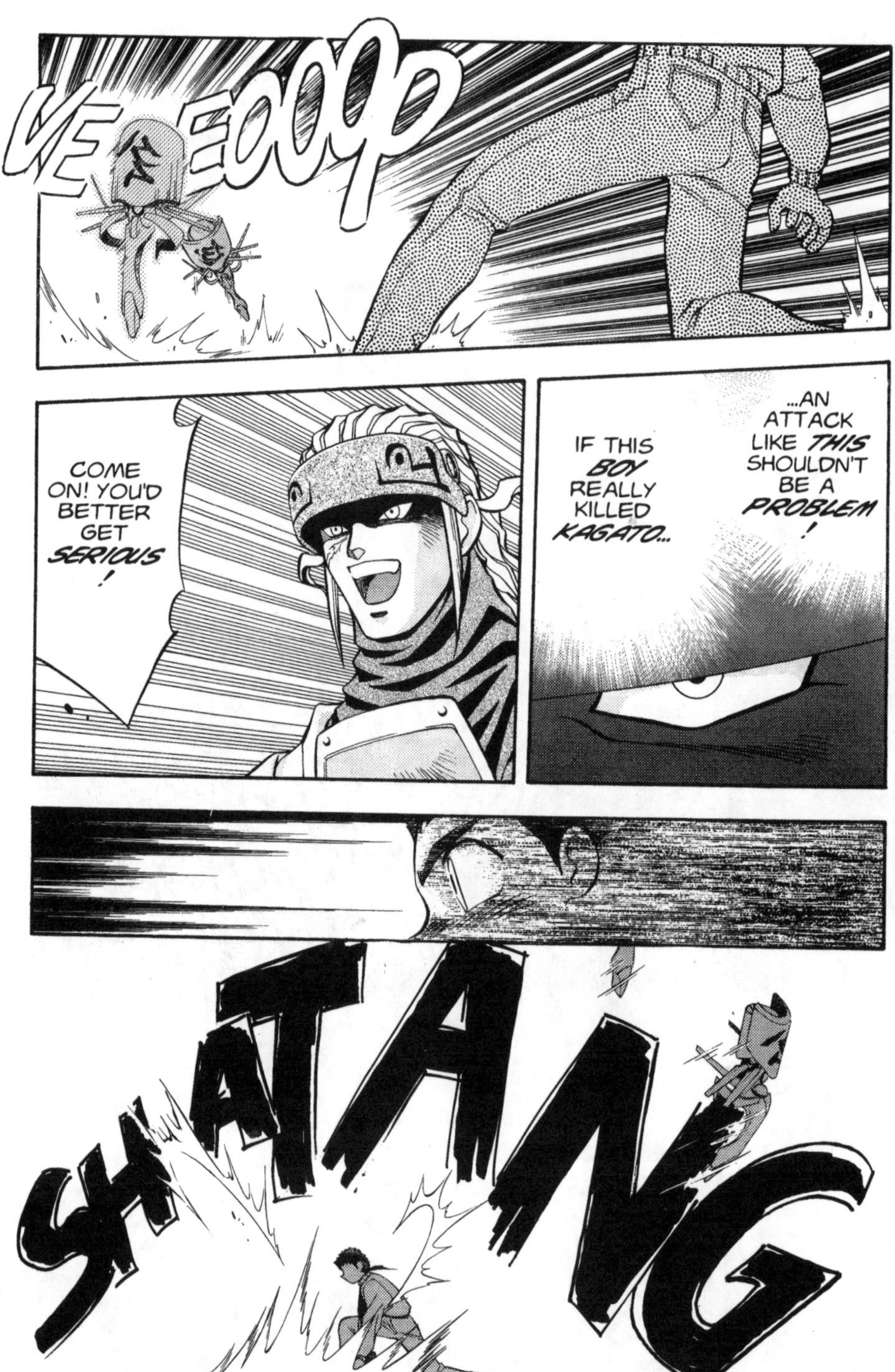
VEEOOOP
COME ON! YOU'D BETTER GET SERIOUS!
IF THIS BOY REALLY KILLED KAGATO...
...AN ATTACK LIKE THIS SHOULDN'T BE A PROBLEM!
SHATANG

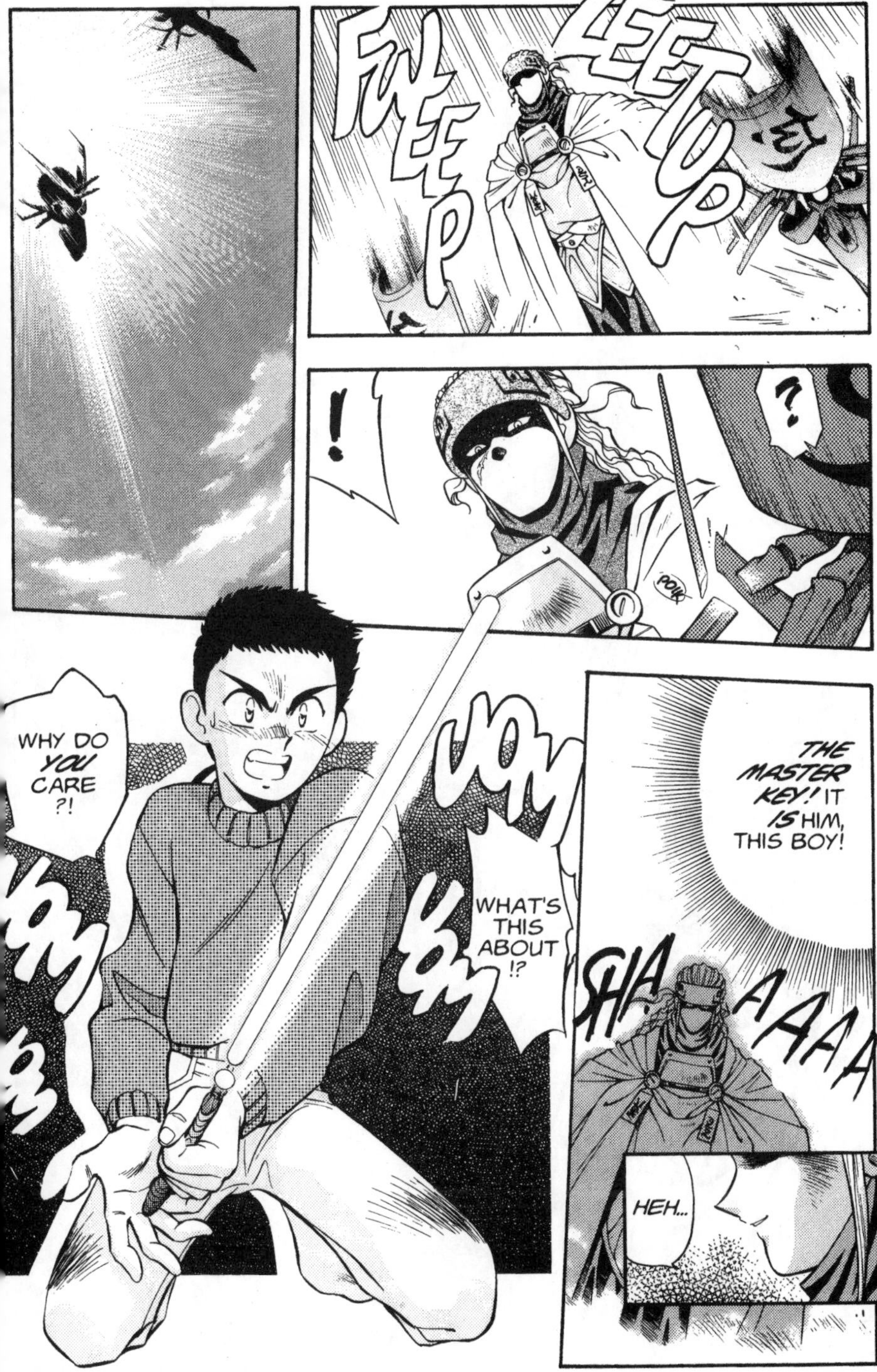
FULEEP
ZEETUP
!
?
POK
WHY DO *YOU* CARE ?!
VOM
VOM VOM
VOM VOM
WHAT'S THIS ABOUT !?
THE MASTER KEY! IT *IS* HIM, THIS BOY!
SHAAAAA
HEH...

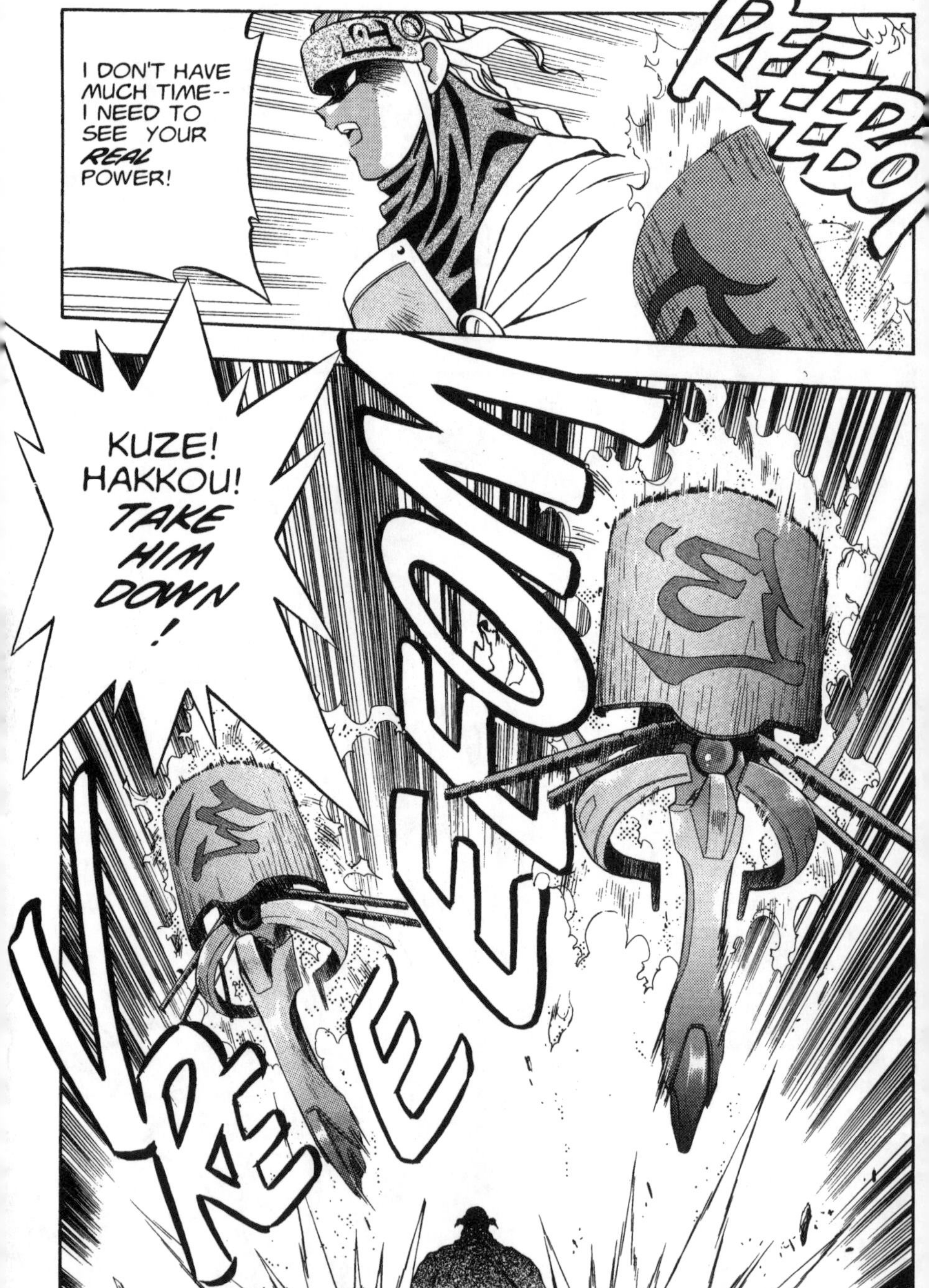
I DON'T HAVE MUCH TIME-- I NEED TO SEE YOUR *REAL* POWER!
REEEDOOM
KUZE! HAKKOU! *TAKE HIM DOWN!*
VREEEEOM

Tales of Tenchi #4
PLUNDER

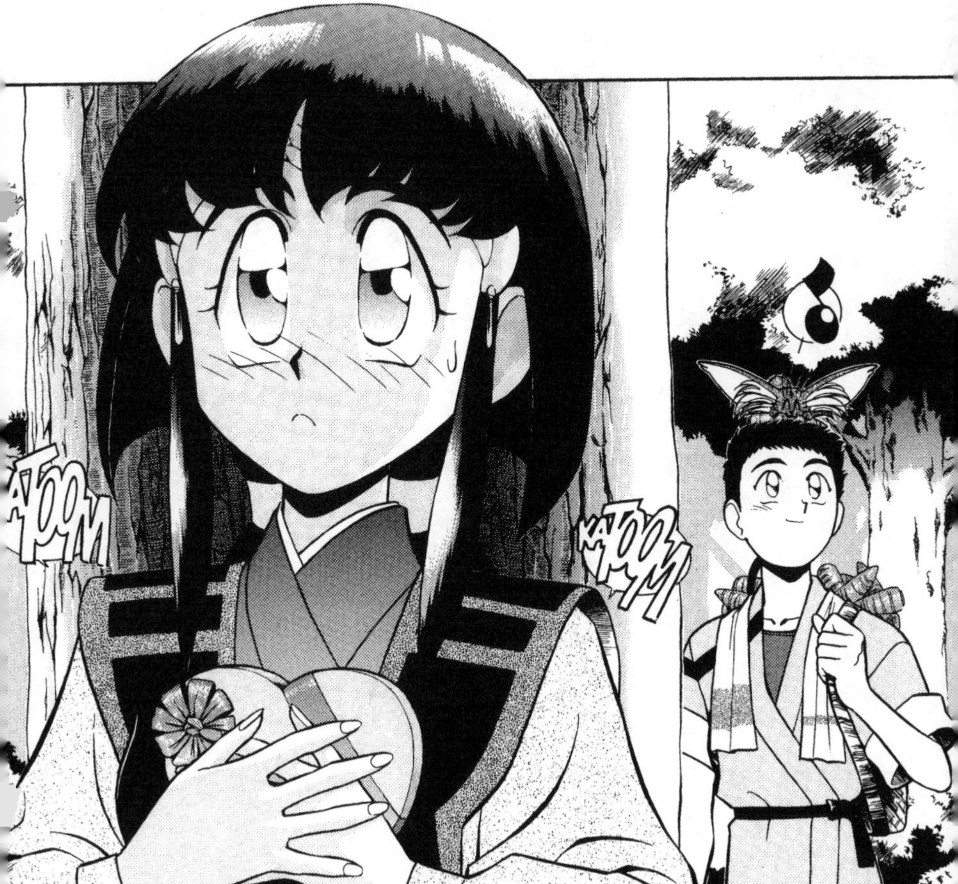
KATOOM
KATOOM

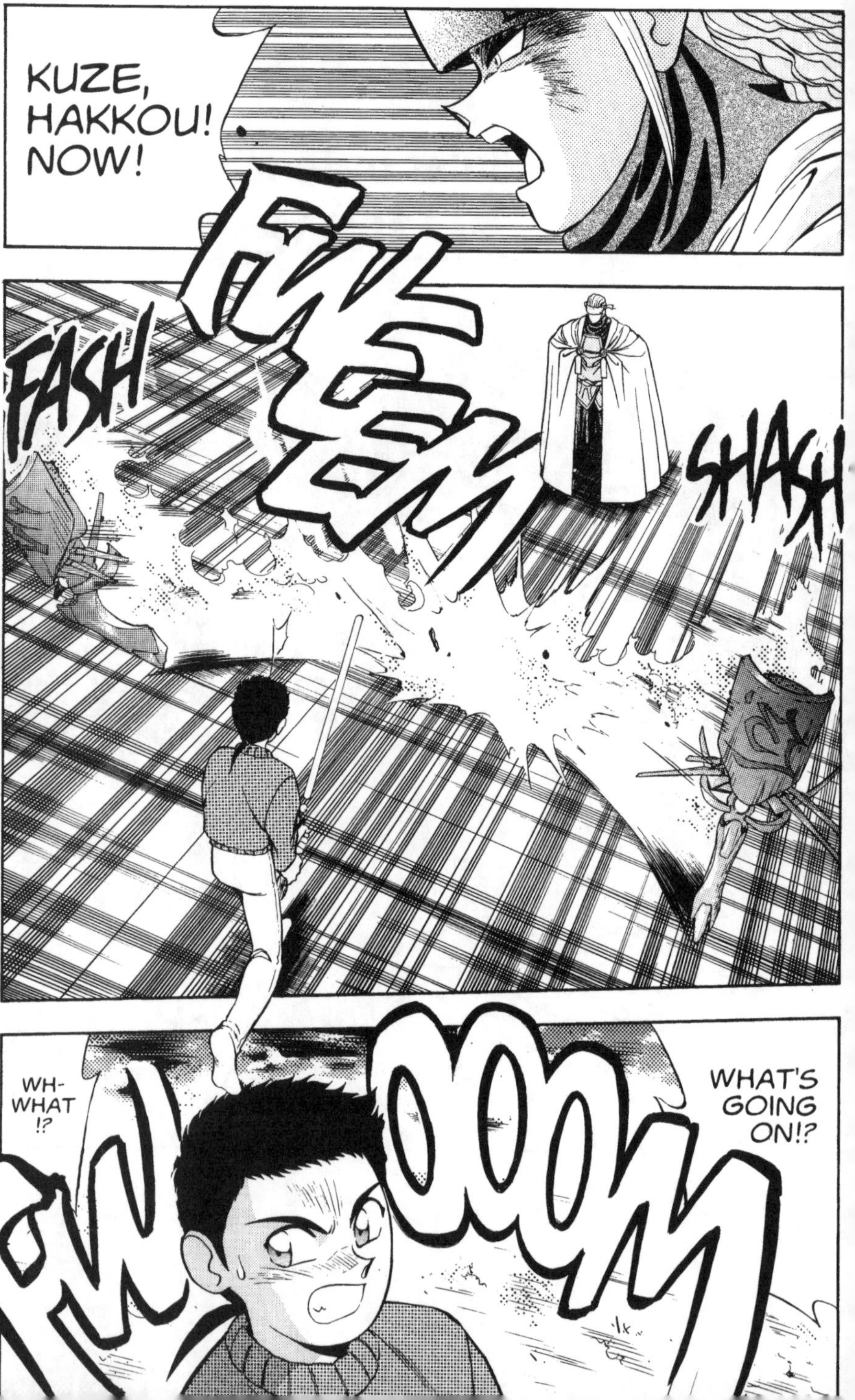
KUZE, HAKKOU! NOW!
FWEEM
FASH
SHASH
WH-WHAT!?
FWOOOOM
WHAT'S GOING ON!?

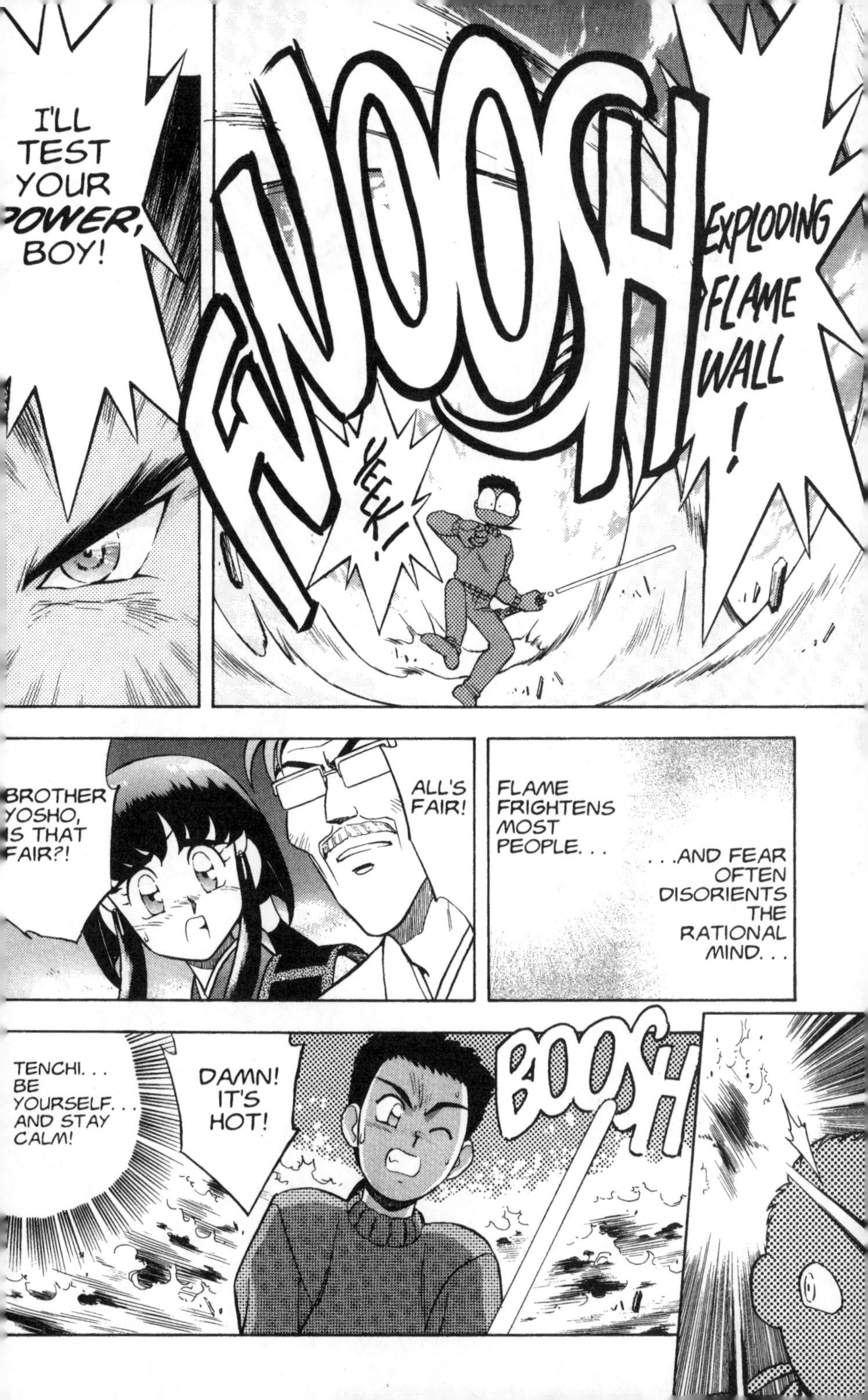
I'LL TEST YOUR POWER, BOY!
FWOOSH
EXPLODING FLAME WALL!
YEEK!
BROTHER YOSHO, IS THAT FAIR?!
ALL'S FAIR!
FLAME FRIGHTENS MOST PEOPLE...
...AND FEAR OFTEN DISORIENTS THE RATIONAL MIND...
TENCHI... BE YOURSELF... AND STAY CALM!
DAMN! IT'S HOT!
BOOSH

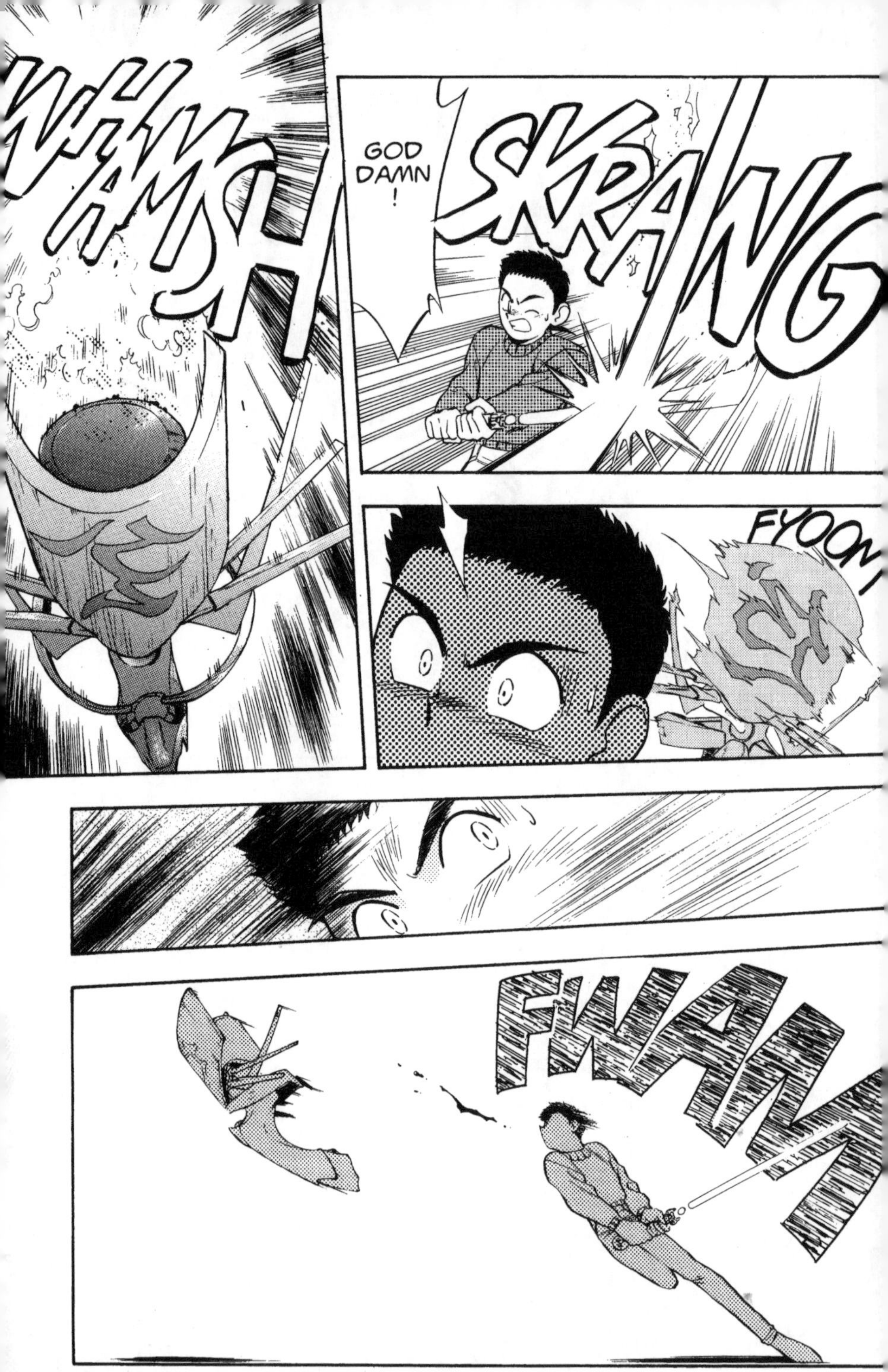
WHAM
SH
GOD DAMN !
SKRANG
FYOON
FWAN

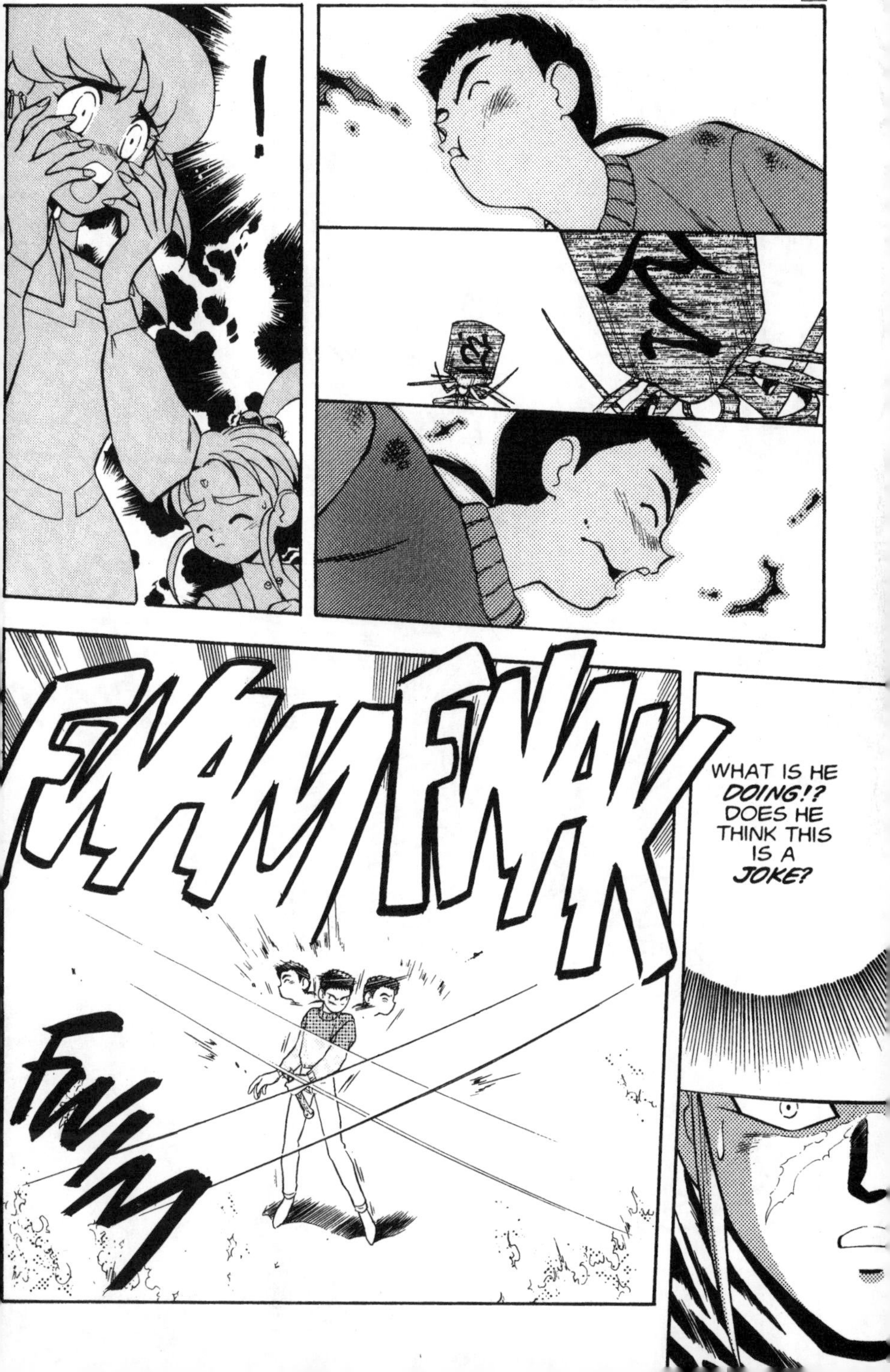
!
FWAMFWAK
FWIM
WHAT IS HE *DOING!?* DOES HE THINK THIS IS A *JOKE?*

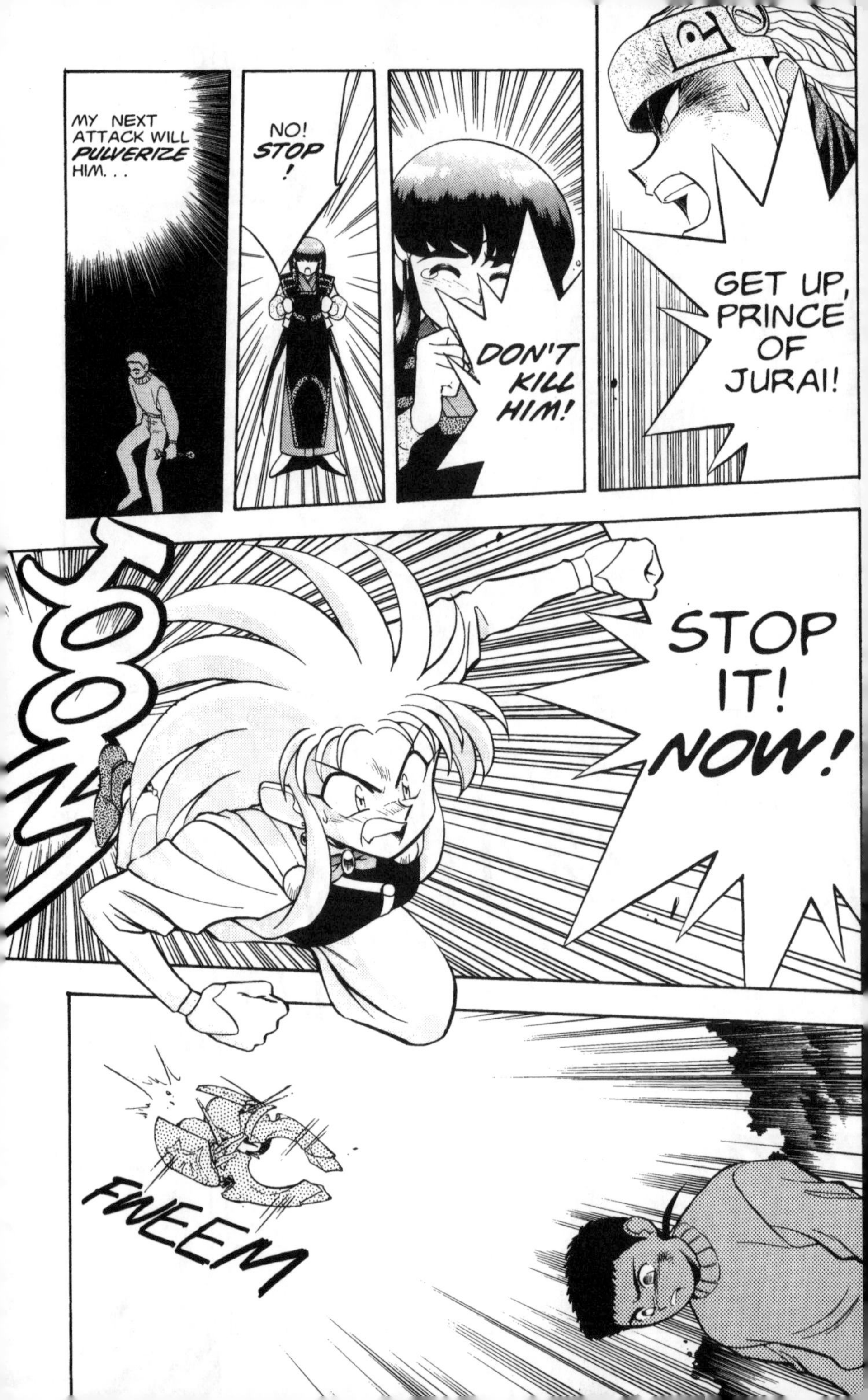
MY NEXT ATTACK WILL PULVERIZE HIM. . .
NO! STOP!
DON'T KILL HIM!
GET UP, PRINCE OF JURAI!
WOOOT
STOP IT! NOW!
FWEEM

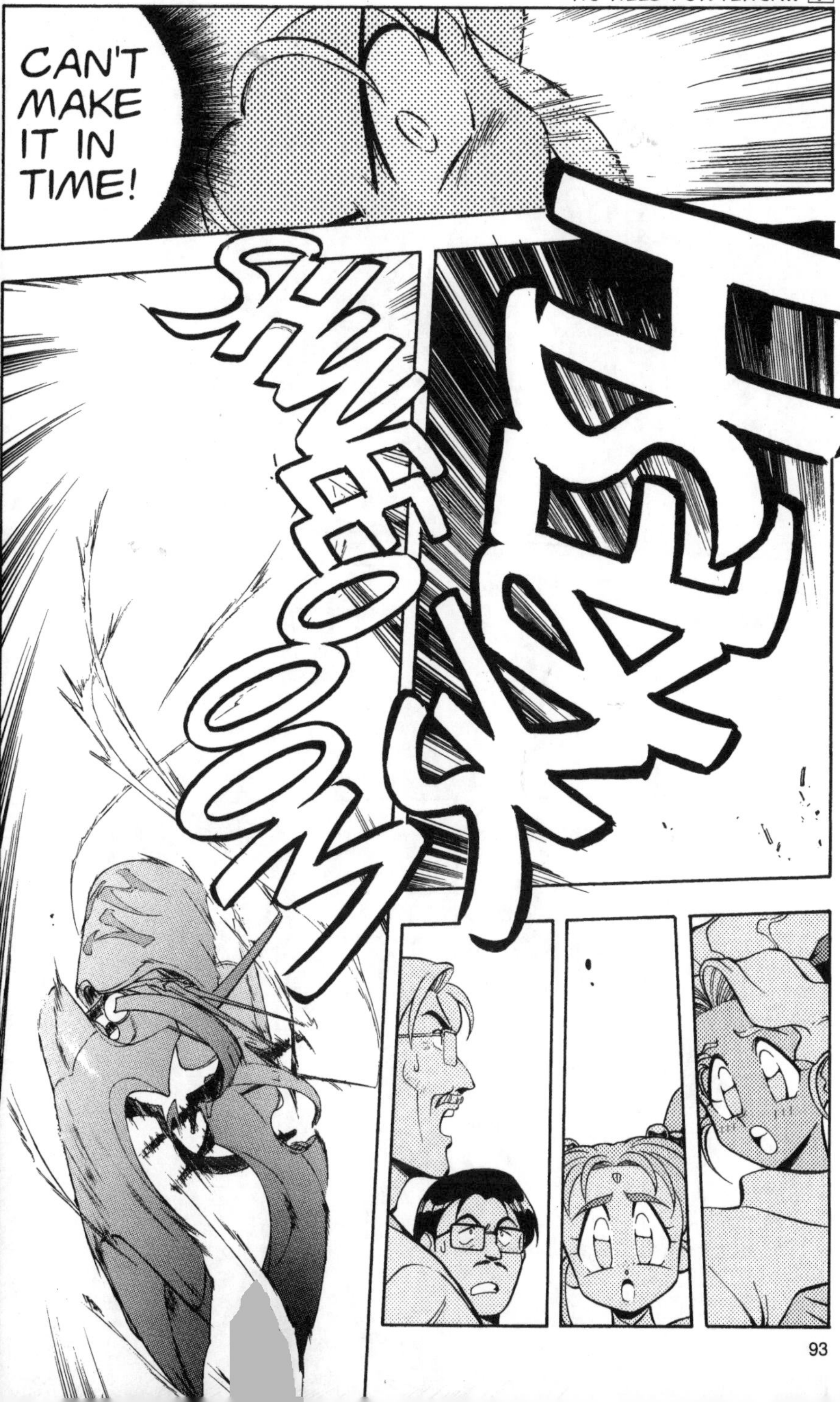
CAN'T MAKE IT IN TIME!
SHWEEOOOM

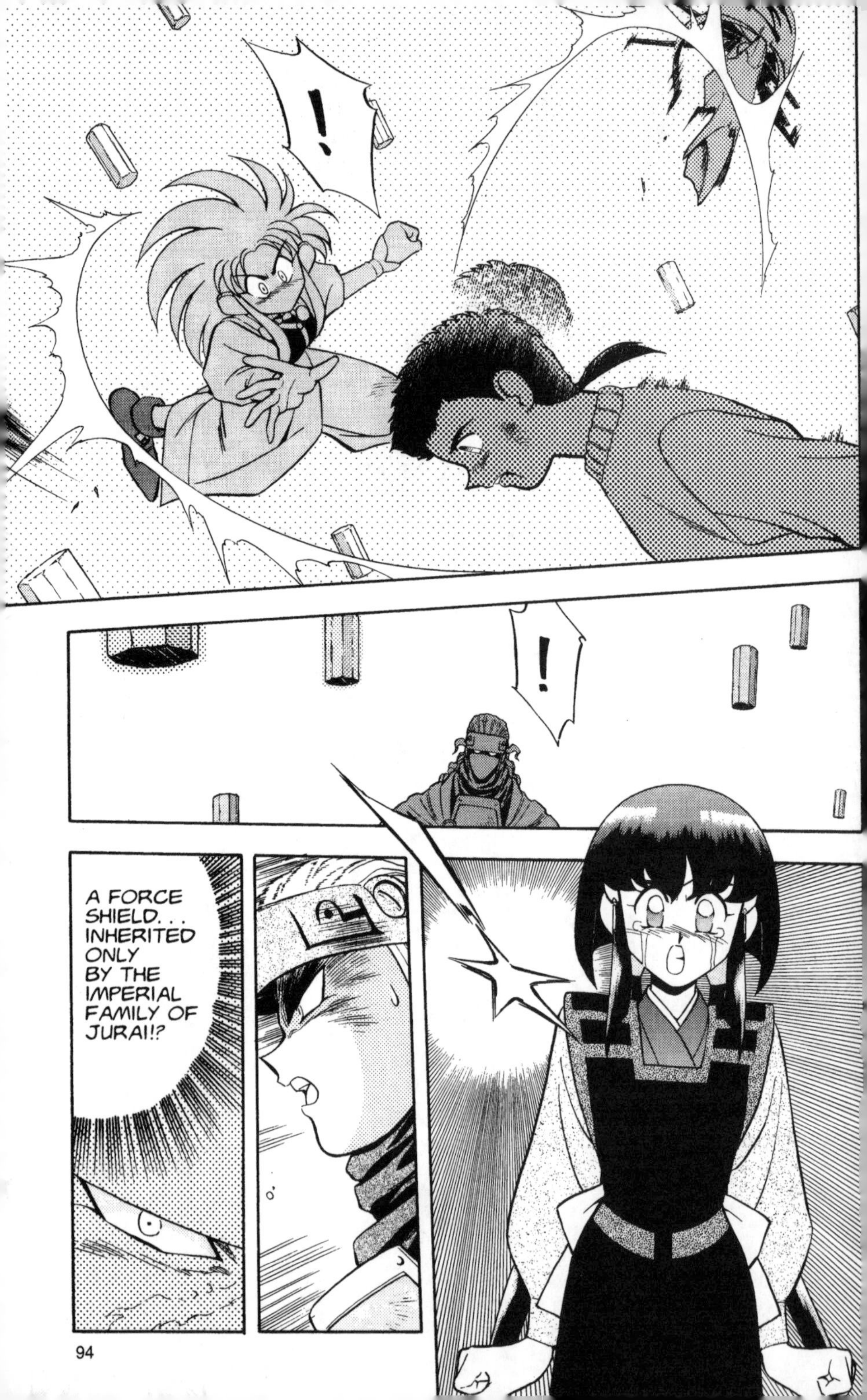
!
!
A FORCE SHIELD... INHERITED ONLY BY THE IMPERIAL FAMILY OF JURAI!?

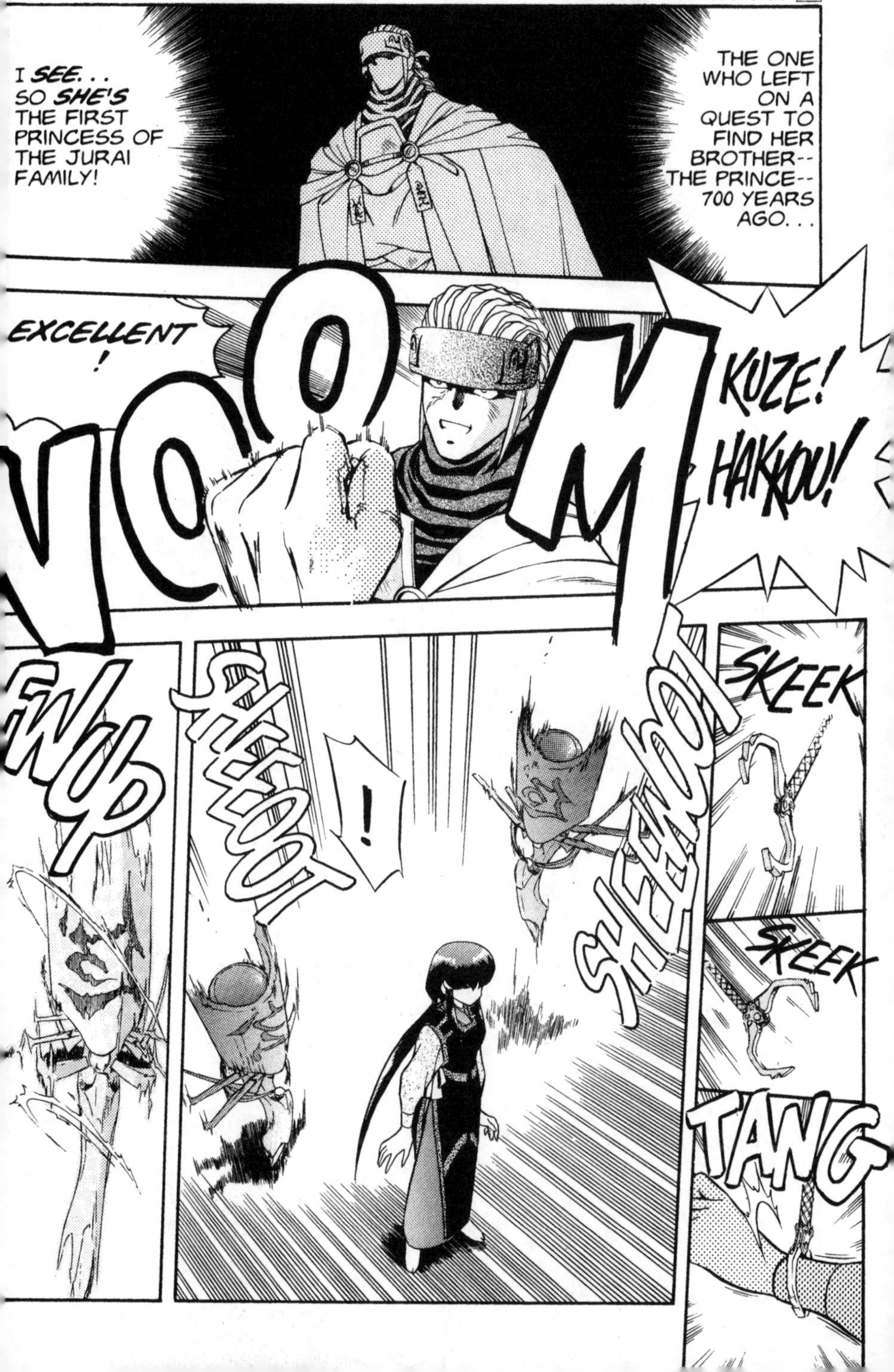
I SEE... SO SHE'S THE FIRST PRINCESS OF THE JURAI FAMILY!
THE ONE WHO LEFT ON A QUEST TO FIND HER BROTHER-- THE PRINCE-- 700 YEARS AGO...
EXCELLENT!
VOOM
KUZE! HAKKOU!
FWUP
SHEEOOT
!
SHEEWOOT
SKEEK
SKEEK
TANG

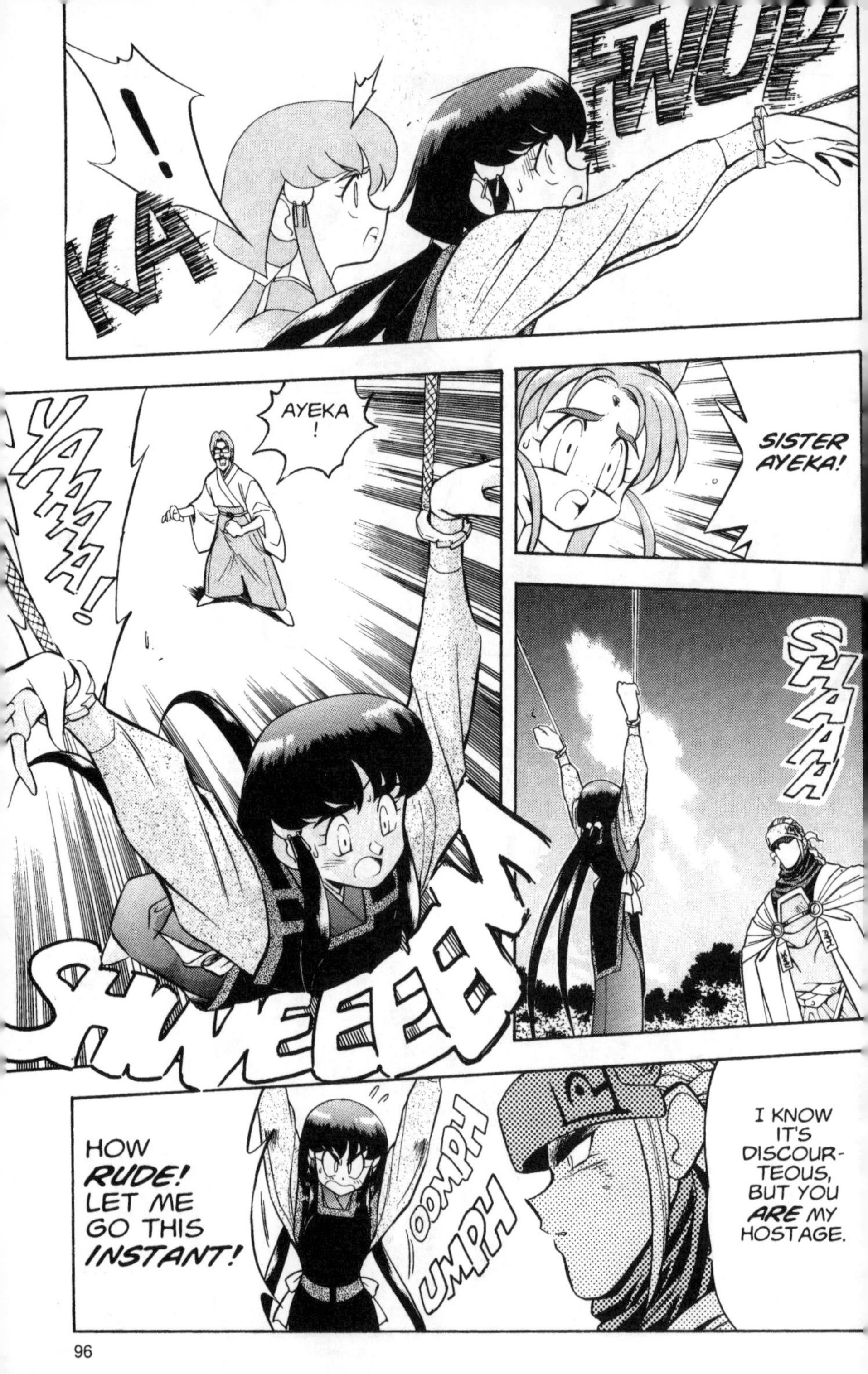

!
KA
FWUP
YAAAAA!
AYEKA!
SISTER AYEKA!
SHAAAA
SHWEEEE
HOW RUDE! LET ME GO THIS INSTANT!
UMPH OOMPH
I KNOW IT'S DISCOURTEOUS, BUT YOU ARE MY HOSTAGE.

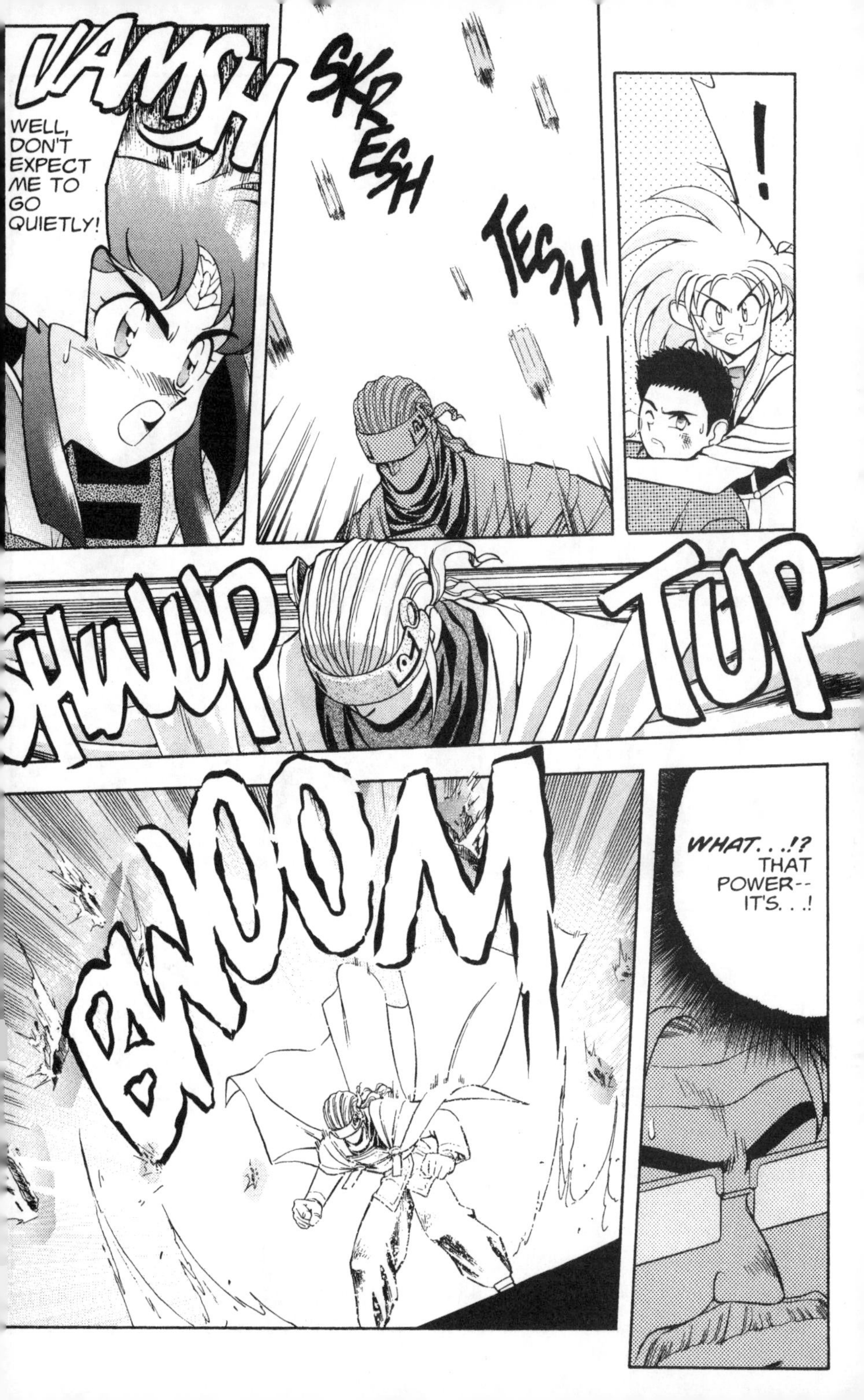
VAMSH
WELL, DON'T EXPECT ME TO GO QUIETLY!
SKRESH
TESH
!
SHUUP
TUP
BAOOM
WHAT. . .!? THAT POWER-- IT'S. . .!

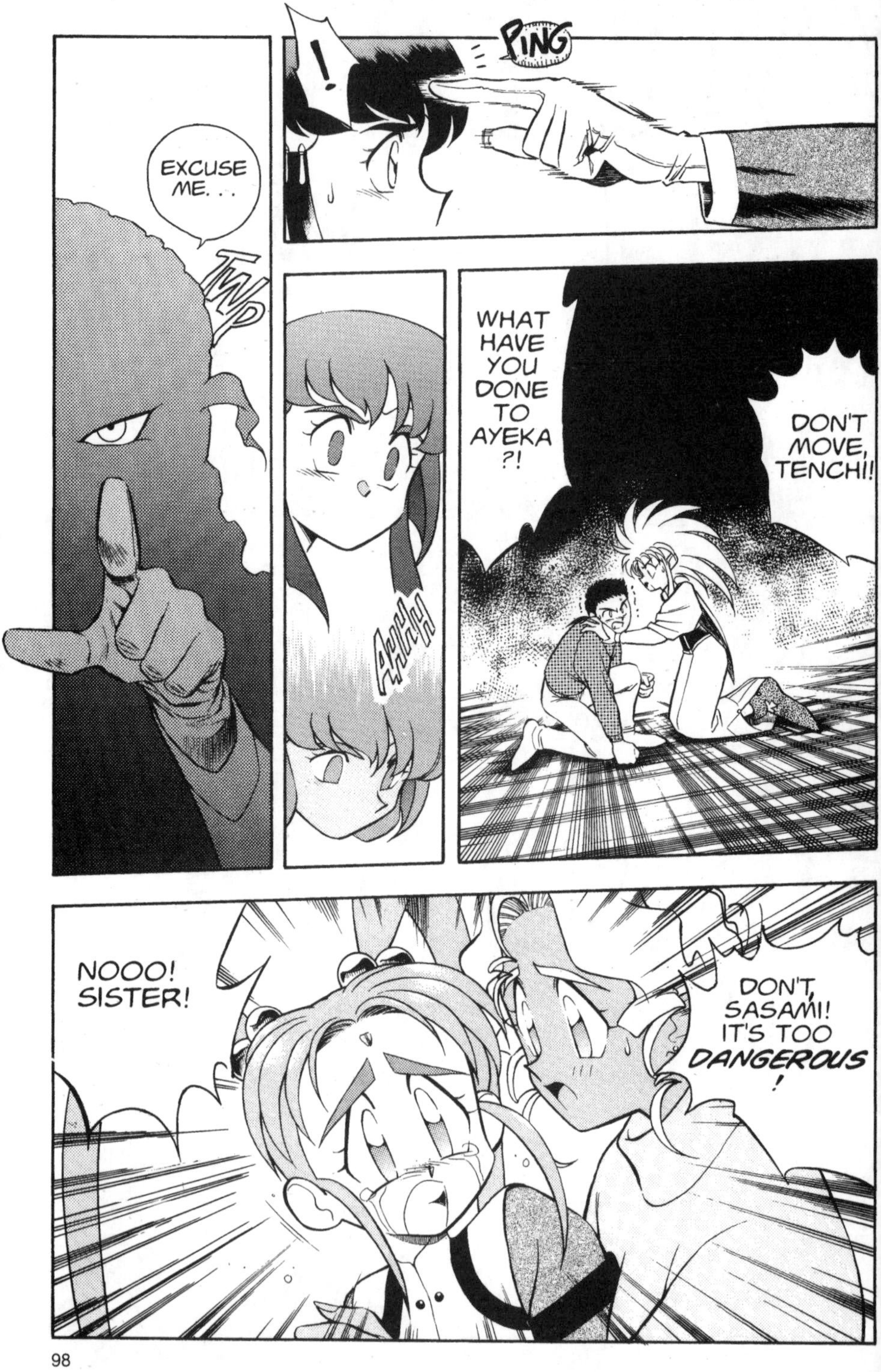
EXCUSE ME. . .
TWP
!
PING
AHHH
WHAT HAVE YOU DONE TO AYEKA ?!
DON'T MOVE, TENCHI!!
NOOO! SISTER!
DON'T, SASAMI! IT'S TOO *DANGEROUS* !

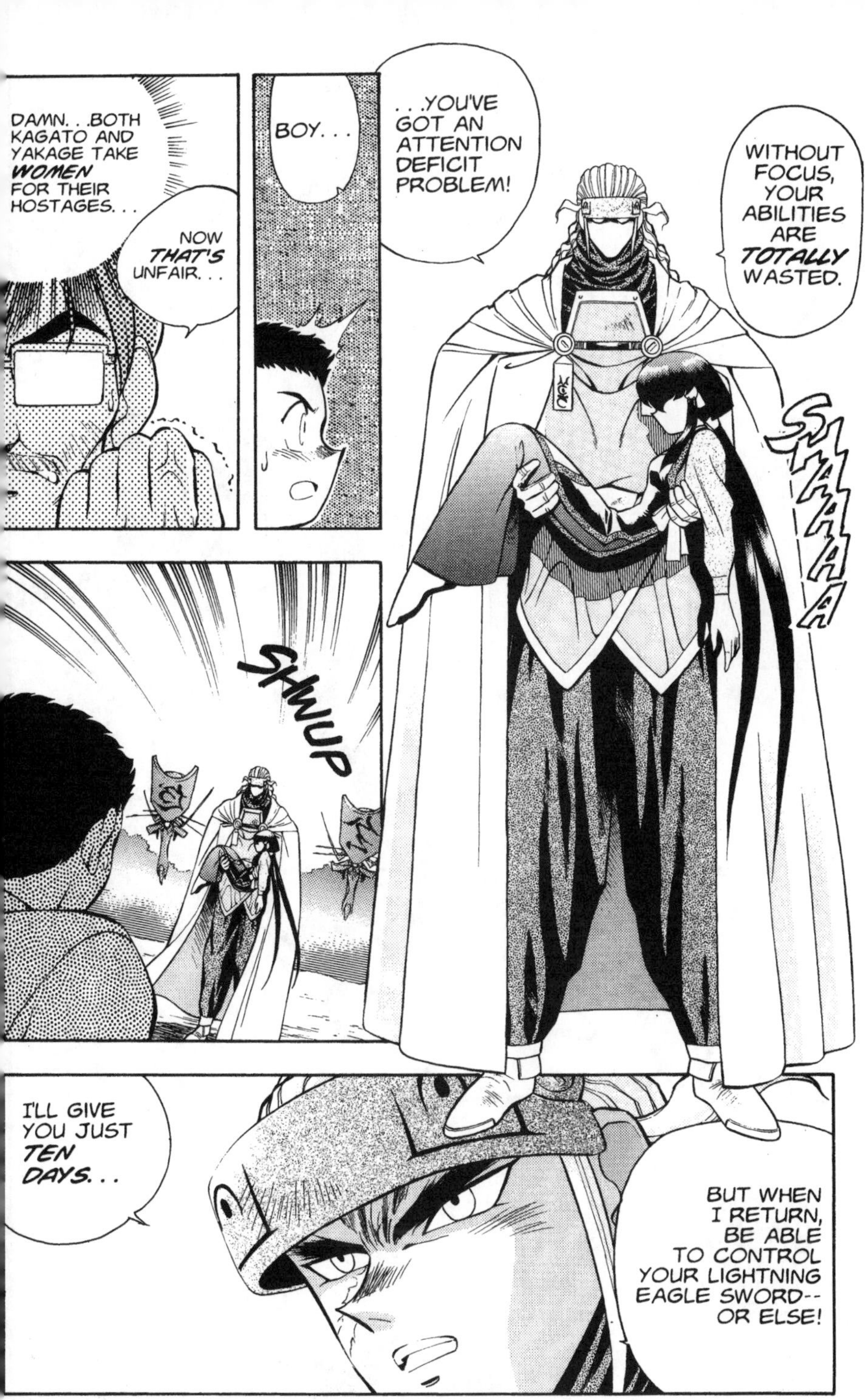
DAMN. . .BOTH KAGATO AND YAKAGE TAKE ***WOMEN*** FOR THEIR HOSTAGES. . .
NOW ***THAT'S*** UNFAIR. . .
BOY. . .
. . .YOU'VE GOT AN ATTENTION DEFICIT PROBLEM!
WITHOUT FOCUS, YOUR ABILITIES ARE ***TOTALLY*** WASTED.
SHAAAA
SHWUP
I'LL GIVE YOU JUST ***TEN DAYS. . .***
BUT WHEN I RETURN, BE ABLE TO CONTROL YOUR LIGHTNING EAGLE SWORD-- OR ELSE!

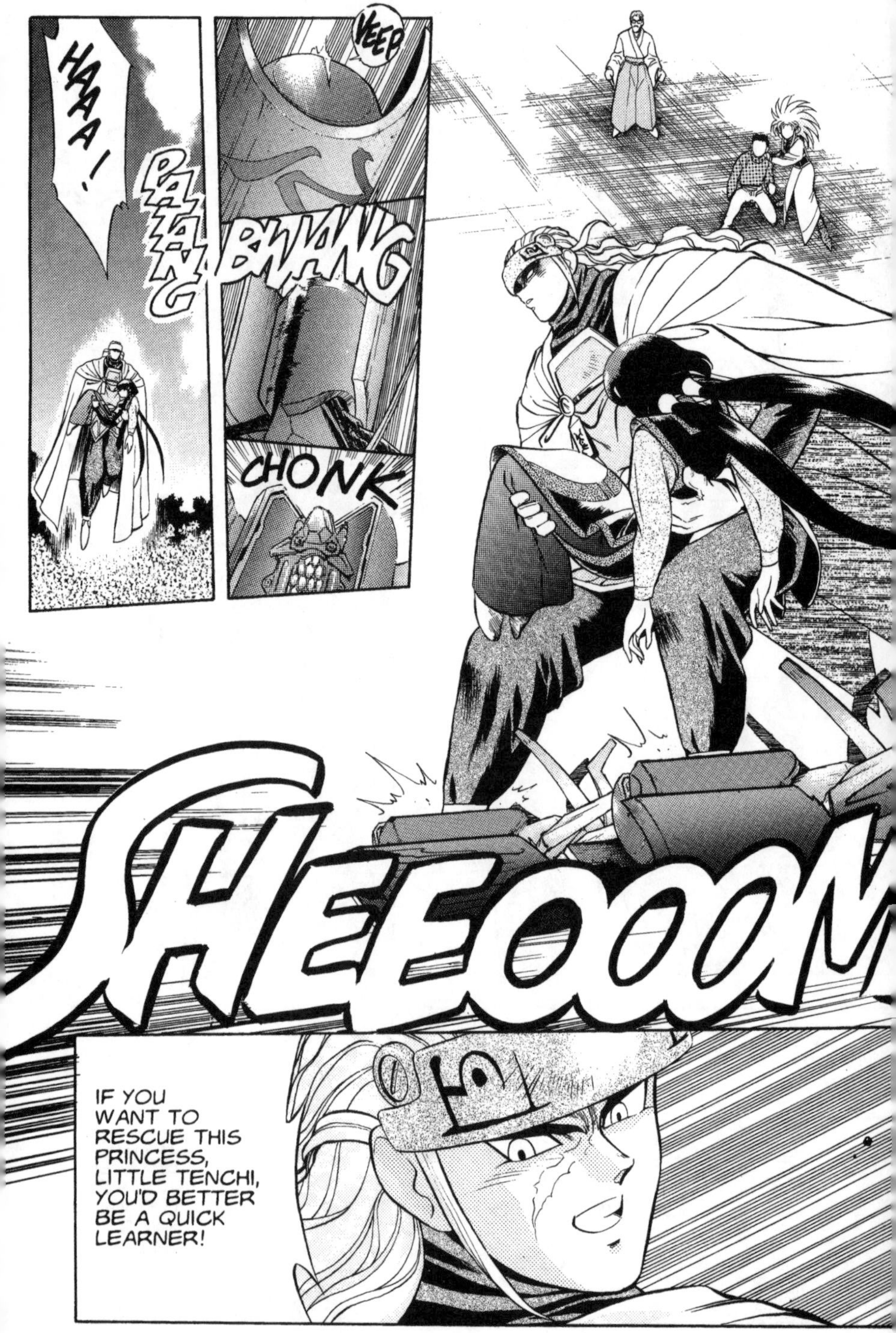
HAAAA!
PAPANG
VEEP
BWANG
CHONK
SHEOOOM
IF YOU WANT TO RESCUE THIS PRINCESS, LITTLE TENCHI, YOU'D BETTER BE A QUICK LEARNER!

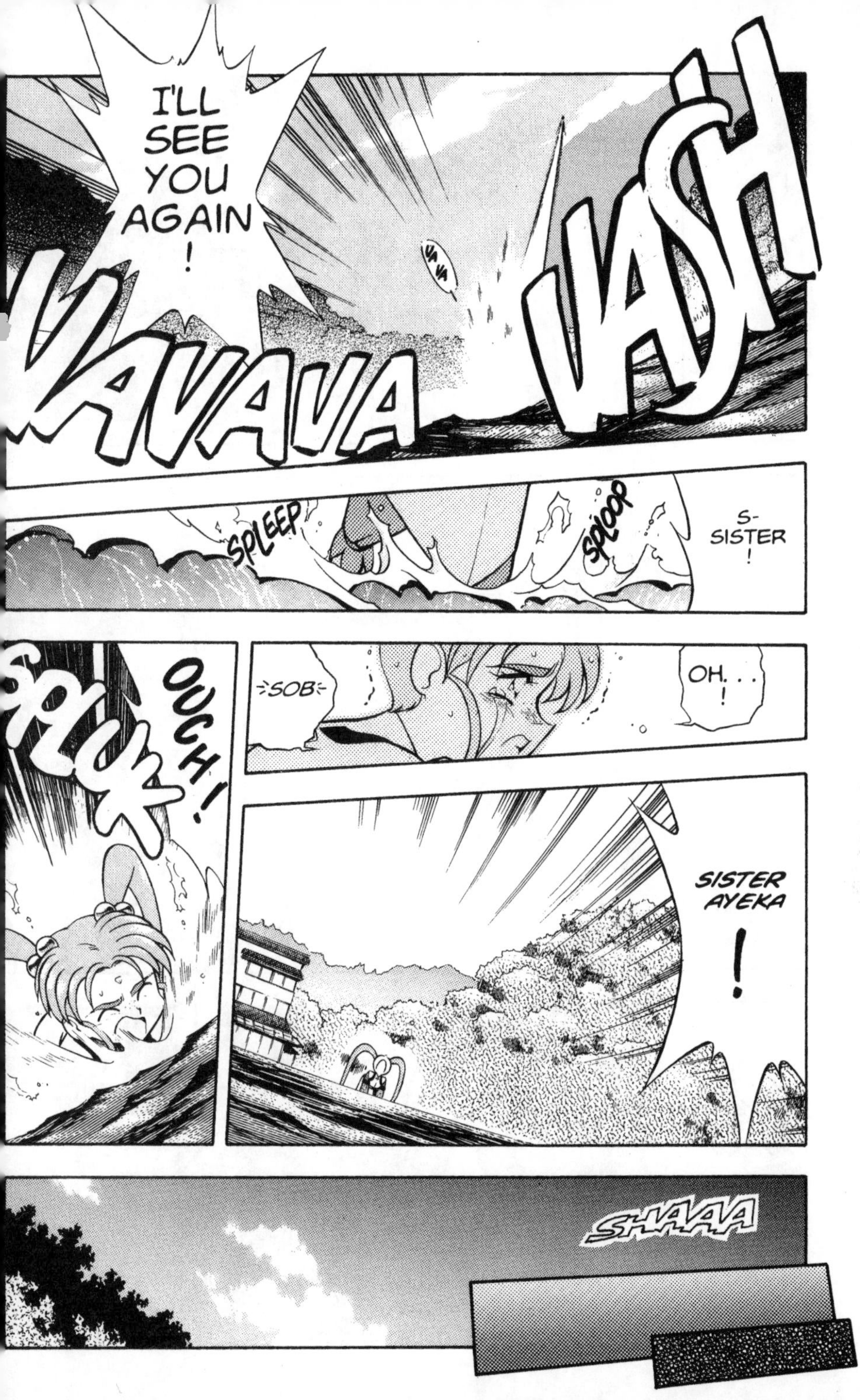
I'LL SEE YOU AGAIN!
VAVAVA
VASH
SPLEEP
SPLOOP
S-SISTER!
OUCH!!
SOB
OH...!
SISTER AYEKA!
SHAAAA

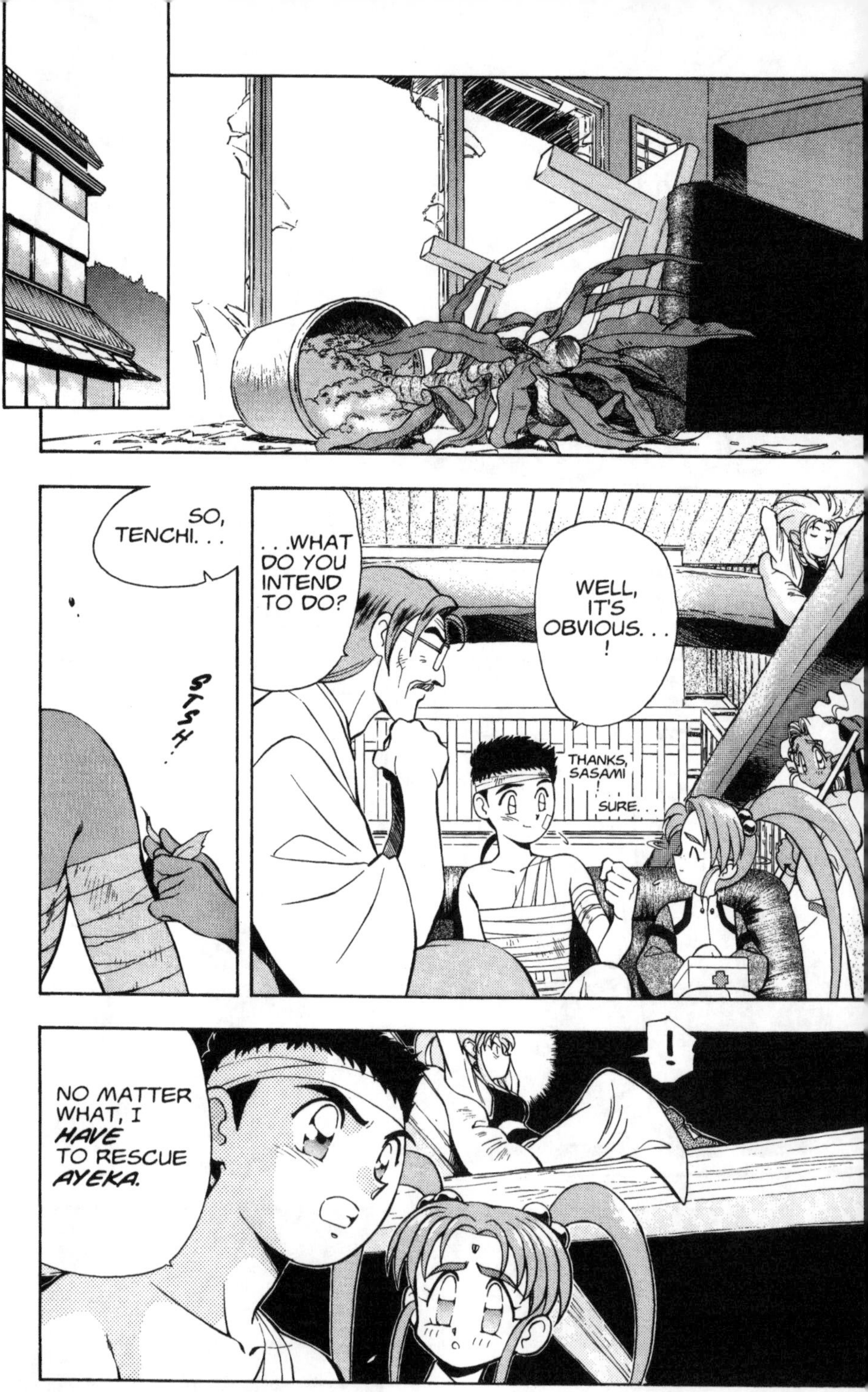
SO, TENCHI. . .
. . .WHAT DO YOU INTEND TO DO?
WELL, IT'S OBVIOUS. . . !
THANKS, SASAMI!
SURE. . .
NO MATTER WHAT, I *HAVE* TO RESCUE *AYEKA.*
!

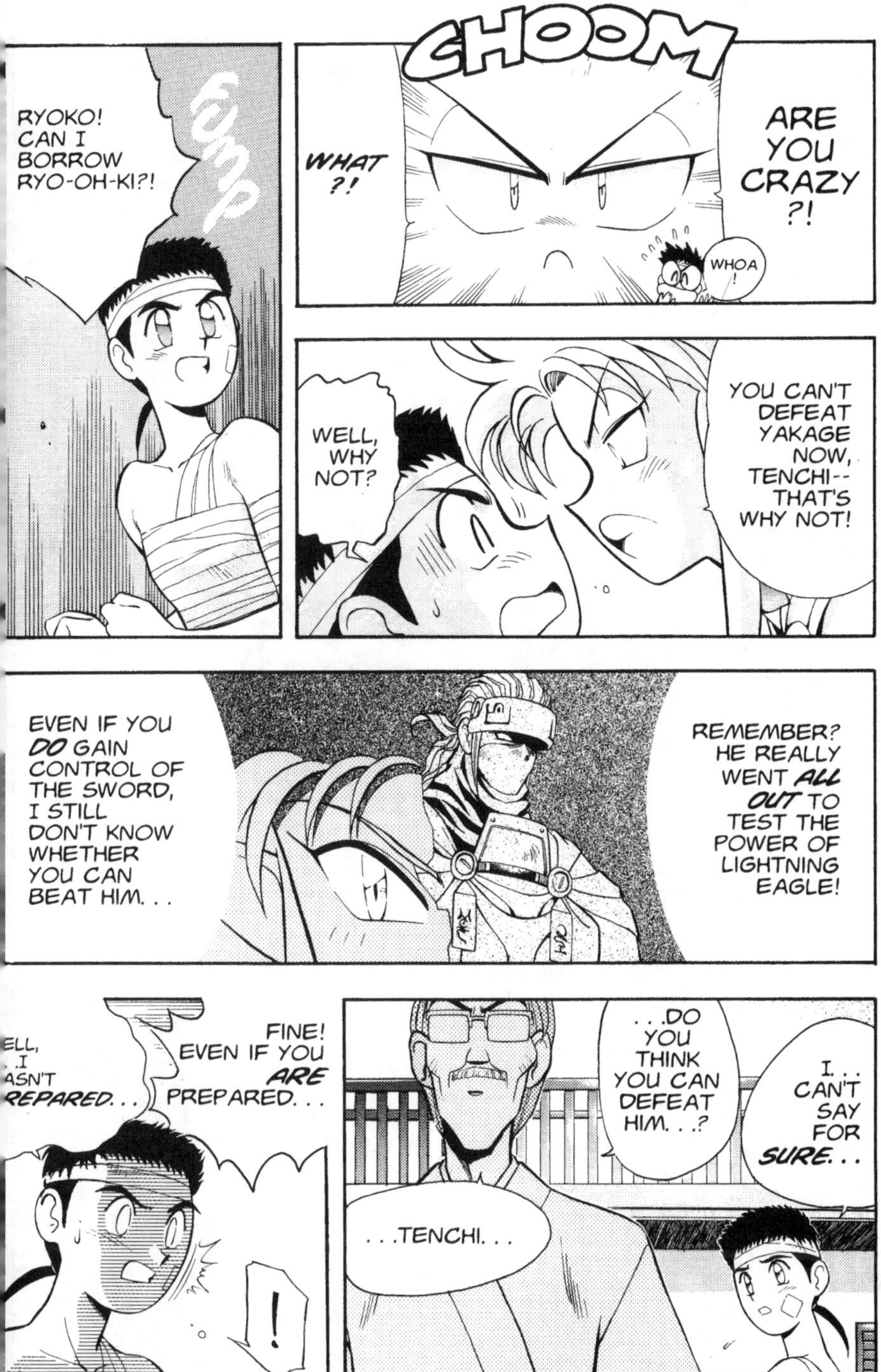
RYOKO! CAN I BORROW RYO-OH-KI?!
FOMP
CHOOM
WHAT?!
ARE YOU CRAZY?!
WHOA!
WELL, WHY NOT?
YOU CAN'T DEFEAT YAKAGE NOW, TENCHI-- THAT'S WHY NOT!
EVEN IF YOU DO GAIN CONTROL OF THE SWORD, I STILL DON'T KNOW WHETHER YOU CAN BEAT HIM. . .
REMEMBER? HE REALLY WENT ALL OUT TO TEST THE POWER OF LIGHTNING EAGLE!
ELL, . .I ASN'T REPARED. . .
FINE! EVEN IF YOU ARE PREPARED. . .
!
. . .TENCHI. . .
. . .DO YOU THINK YOU CAN DEFEAT HIM. . .?
I. . . CAN'T SAY FOR SURE. . .

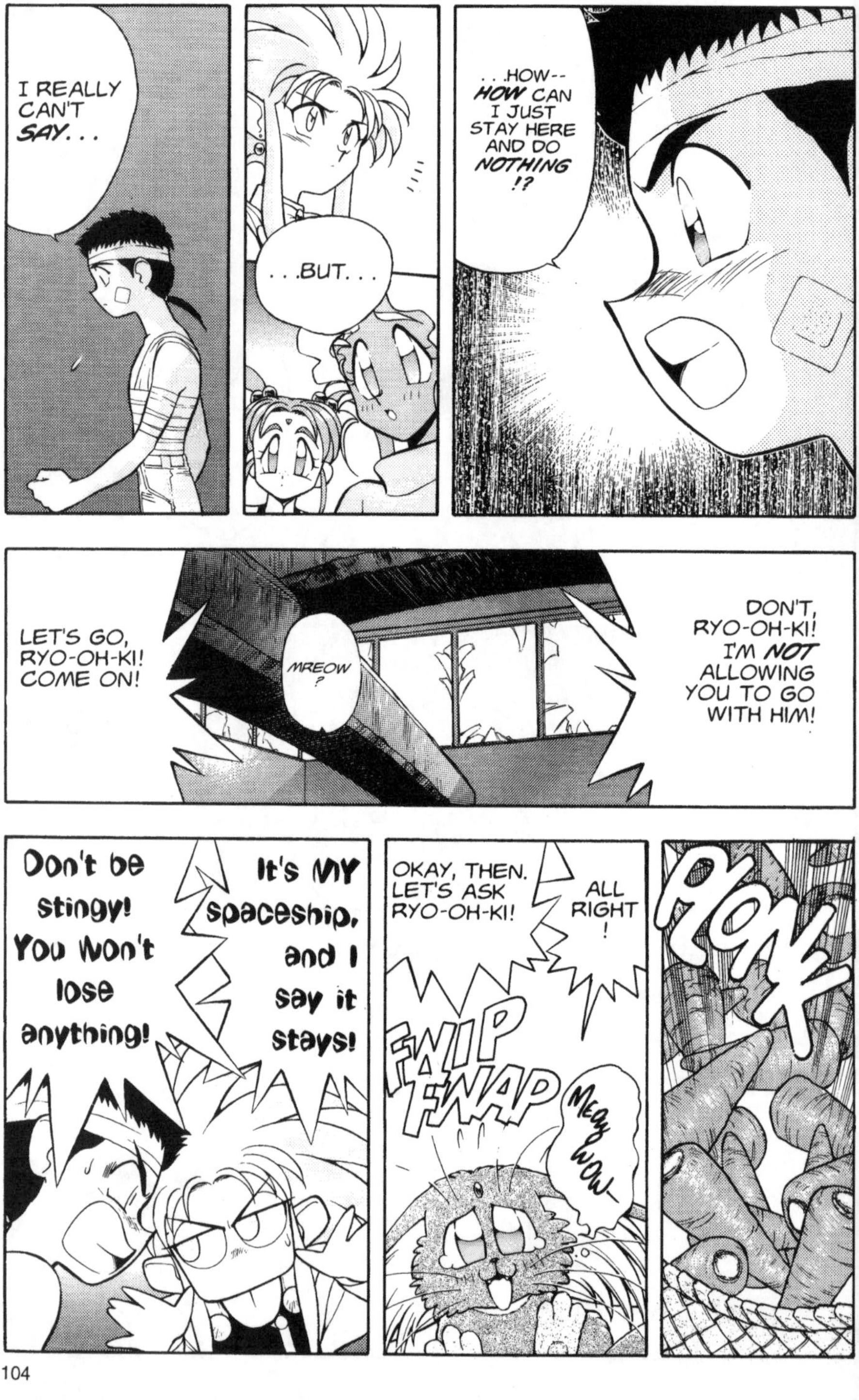
I REALLY CAN'T SAY...
...BUT...
...HOW-- HOW CAN I JUST STAY HERE AND DO NOTHING!?
LET'S GO, RYO-OH-KI! COME ON!
MREOW?
DON'T, RYO-OH-KI! I'M NOT ALLOWING YOU TO GO WITH HIM!
Don't be stingy! You won't lose anything!
It's MY spaceship, and I say it stays!
OKAY, THEN. LET'S ASK RYO-OH-KI!
ALL RIGHT!
FWIP FWAP
MEOW WOW~
PLONK

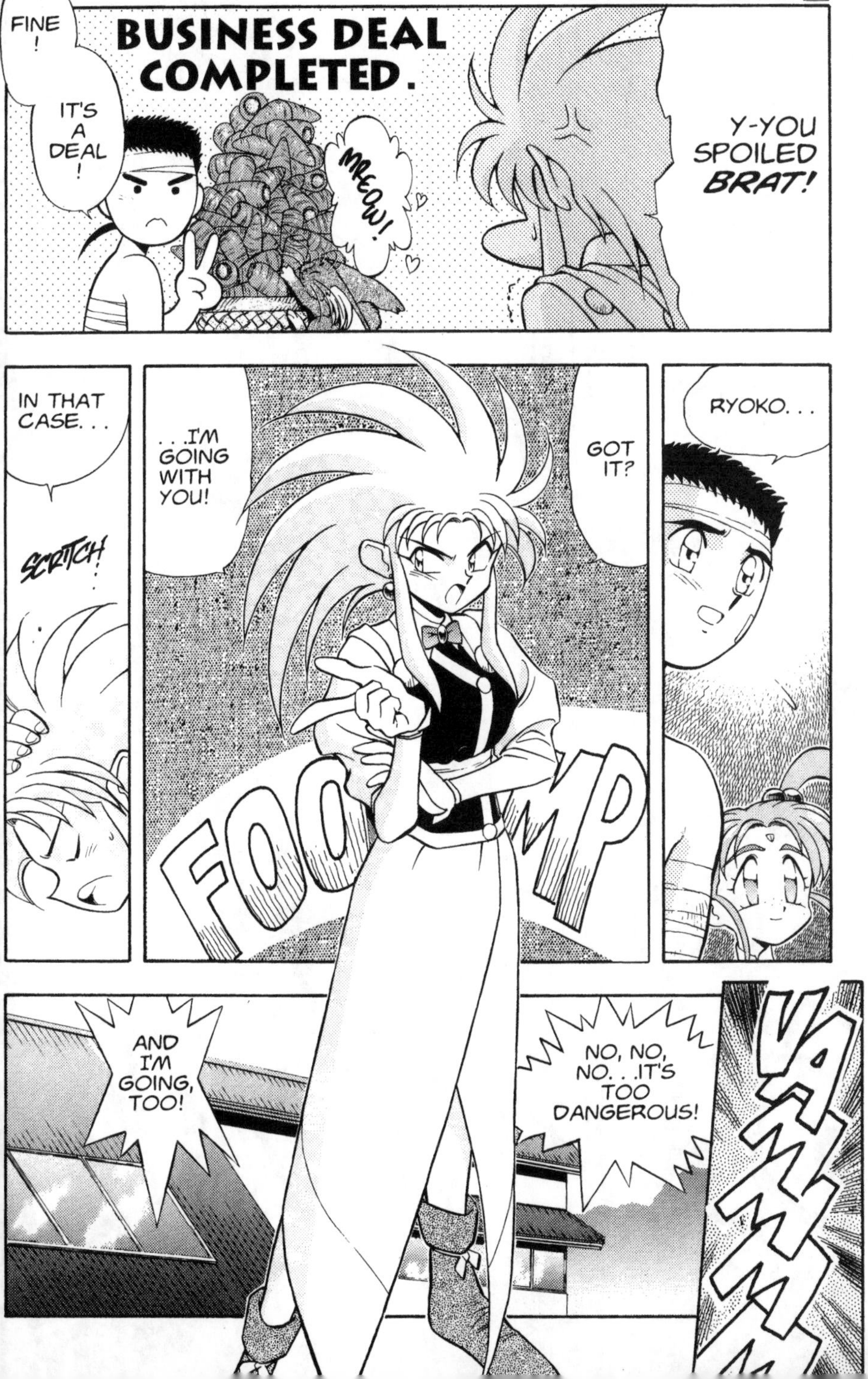
FINE!
IT'S A DEAL!
BUSINESS DEAL COMPLETED.
MREOW!
Y-YOU SPOILED BRAT!
IN THAT CASE...
SCRITCH!
...I'M GOING WITH YOU!
GOT IT?
FOO
MP
RYOKO...
AND I'M GOING, TOO!
NO, NO, NO...IT'S TOO DANGEROUS!
VAMMMM

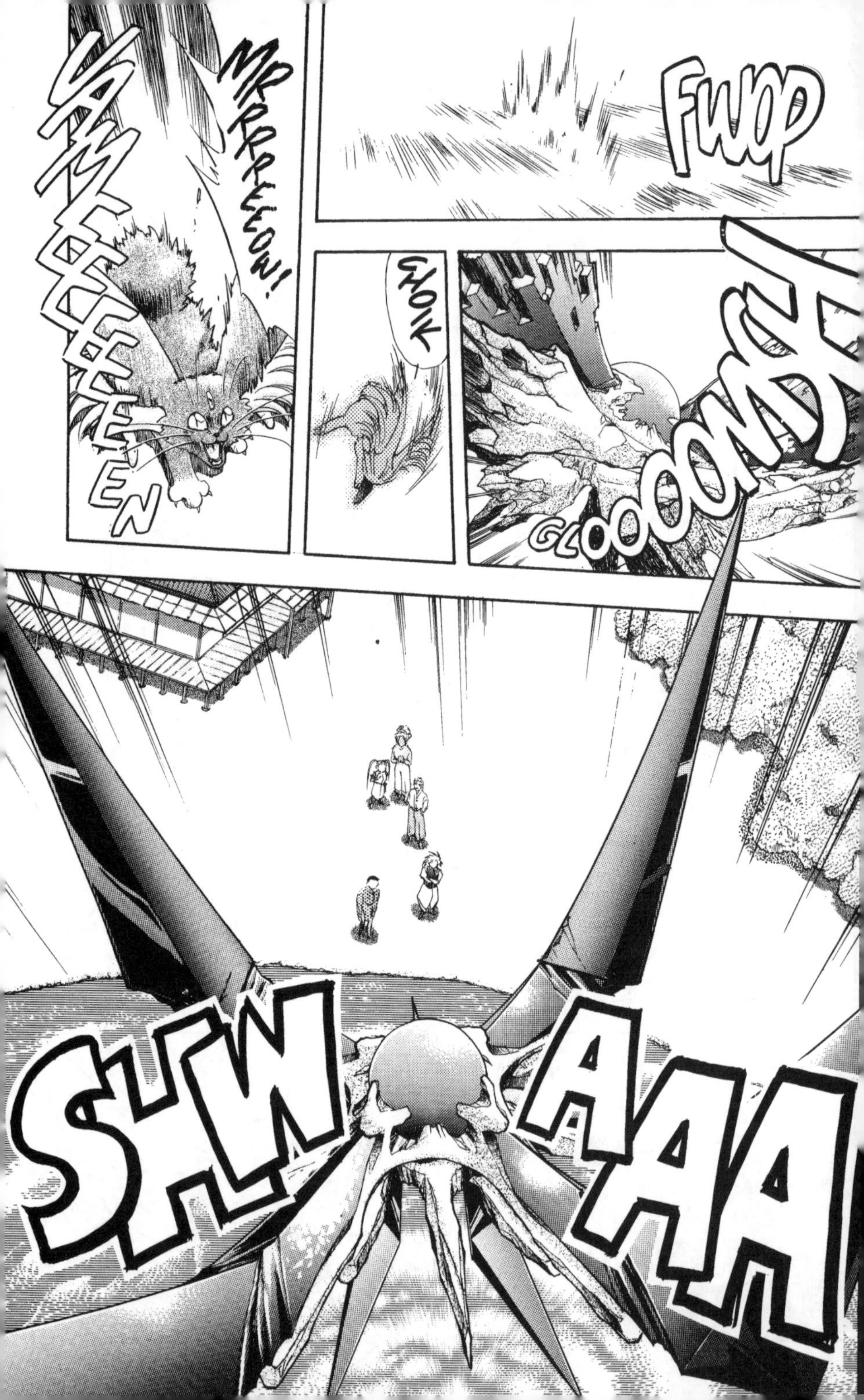

MRRRREEOW!
FWOP
GLOIK
GLOOOOMSH
SHW
AAAA

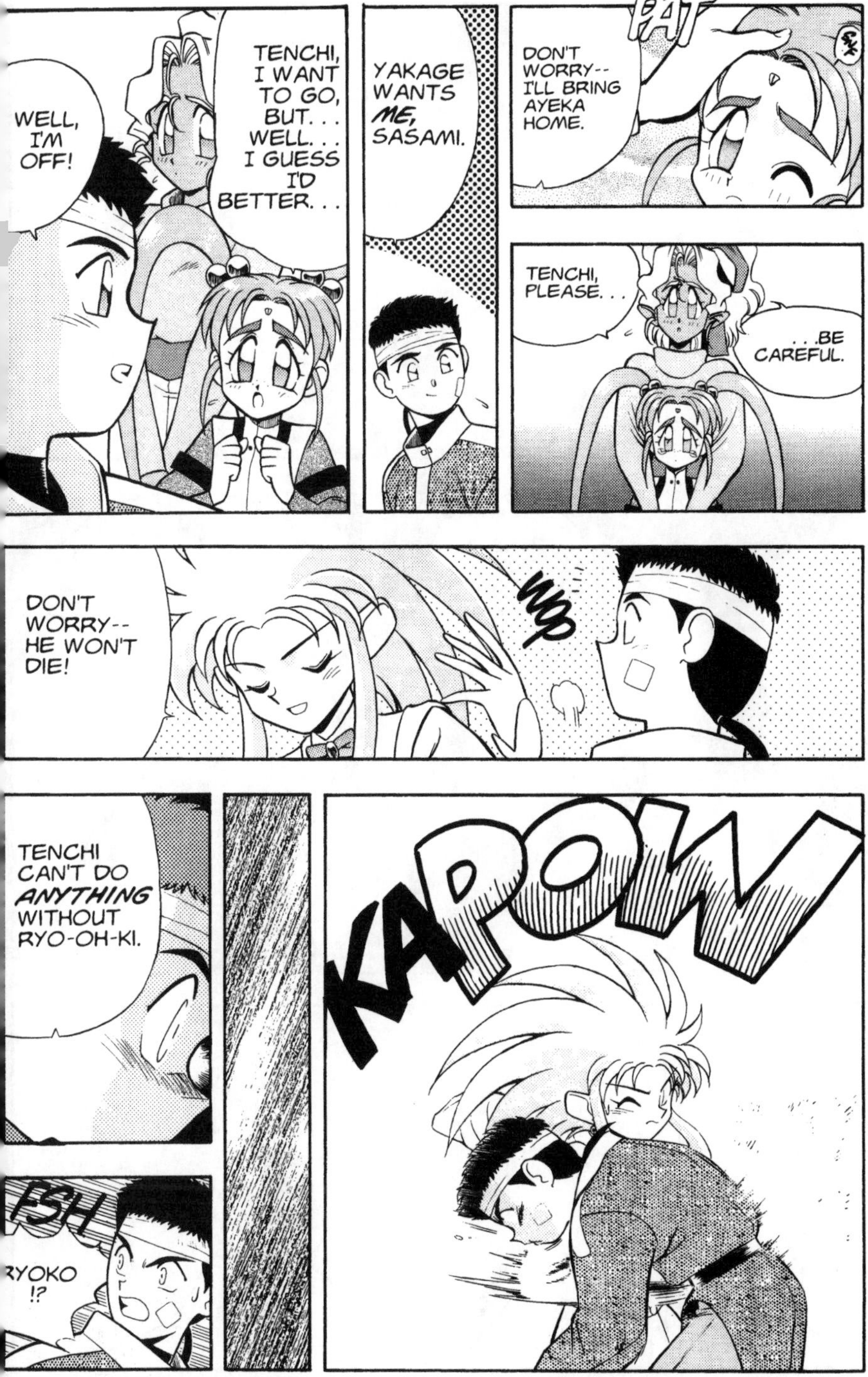
WELL, I'M OFF!
TENCHI, I WANT TO GO, BUT. . . WELL. . . I GUESS I'D BETTER. . .
YAKAGE WANTS *ME,* SASAMI.
PAT
DON'T WORRY-- I'LL BRING AYEKA HOME.
TENCHI, PLEASE. . .
. . .BE CAREFUL.
DON'T WORRY-- HE WON'T DIE!
WOP
TENCHI CAN'T DO *ANYTHING* WITHOUT RYO-OH-KI.
RYOKO !?
KAPOW

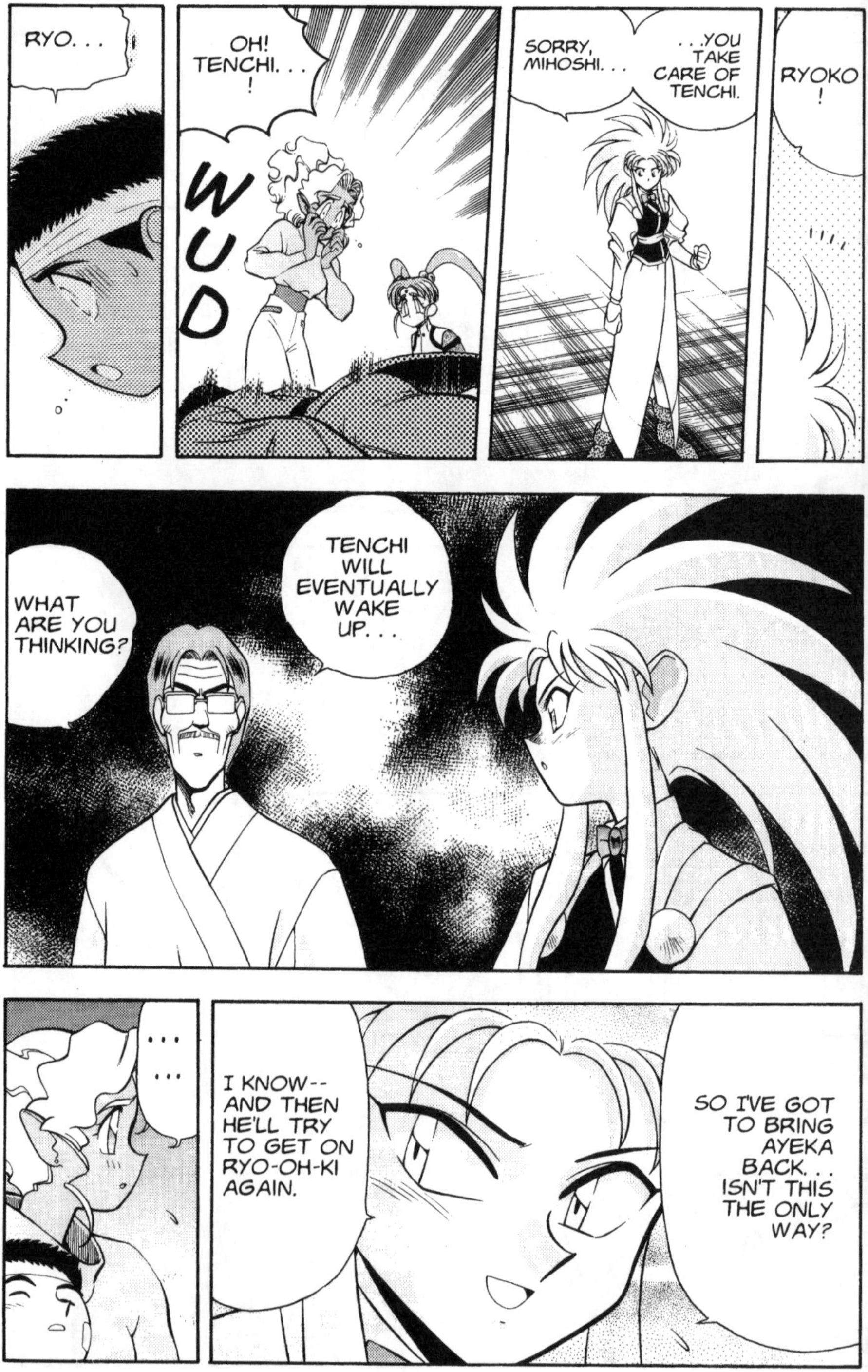
RYO. . .
OH! TENCHI. . . !
WUD
SORRY, MIHOSHI. . .
. . .YOU TAKE CARE OF TENCHI.
RYOKO !
WHAT ARE YOU THINKING?
TENCHI WILL EVENTUALLY WAKE UP. . .
. . .
. . .
I KNOW-- AND THEN HE'LL TRY TO GET ON RYO-OH-KI AGAIN.
SO I'VE GOT TO BRING AYEKA BACK. . . ISN'T THIS THE ONLY WAY?

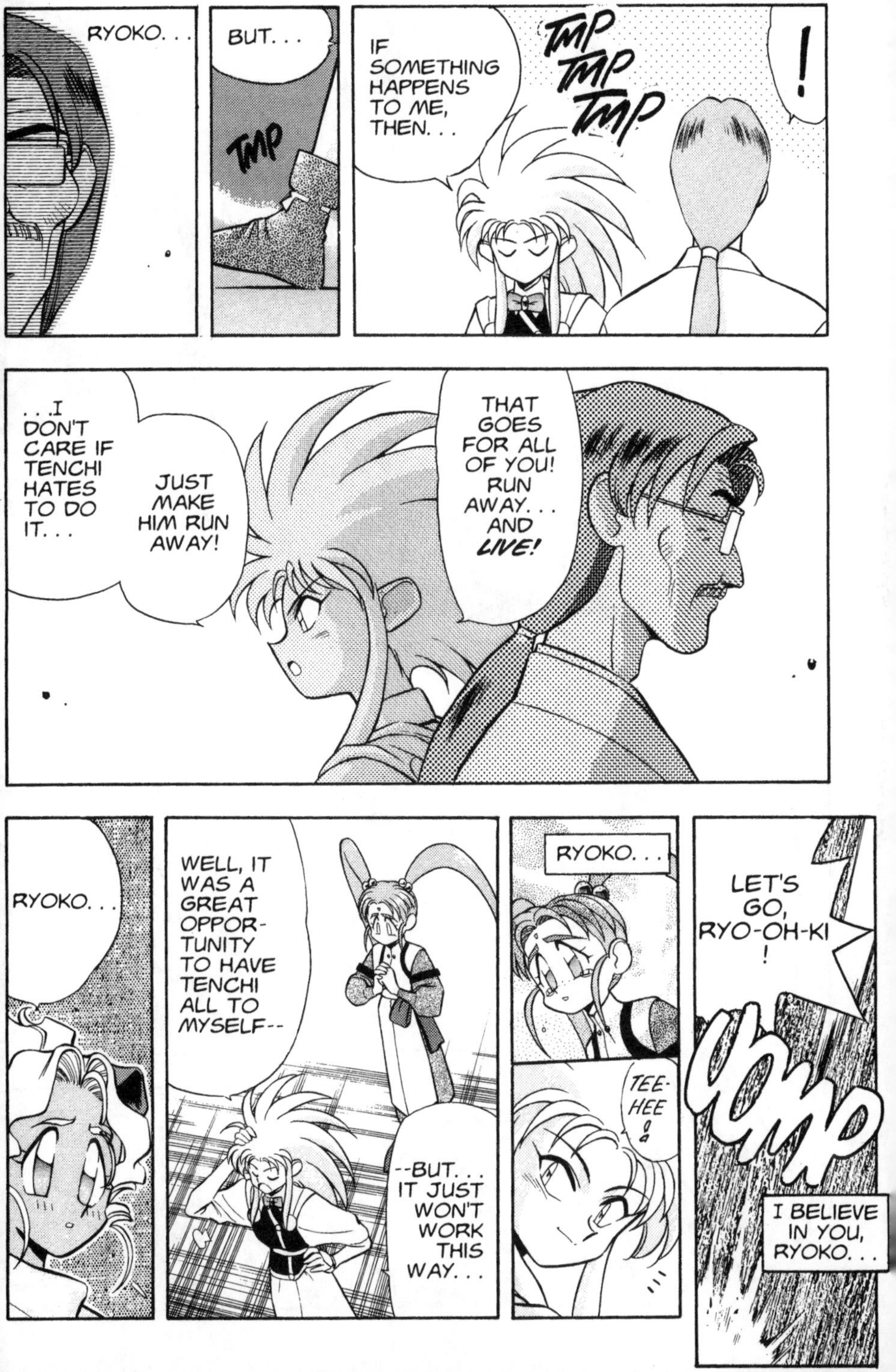
RYOKO. . .
BUT. . .
TMP
IF SOMETHING HAPPENS TO ME, THEN. . .
TMP TMP TMP
!
. . .I DON'T CARE IF TENCHI HATES TO DO IT. . .
JUST MAKE HIM RUN AWAY!
THAT GOES FOR ALL OF YOU! RUN AWAY. . . AND LIVE!
RYOKO. . .
WELL, IT WAS A GREAT OPPOR-TUNITY TO HAVE TENCHI ALL TO MYSELF--
--BUT. . . IT JUST WON'T WORK THIS WAY. . .
RYOKO. . .
TEE-HEE
LET'S GO, RYO-OH-KI!
I BELIEVE IN YOU, RYOKO. . .

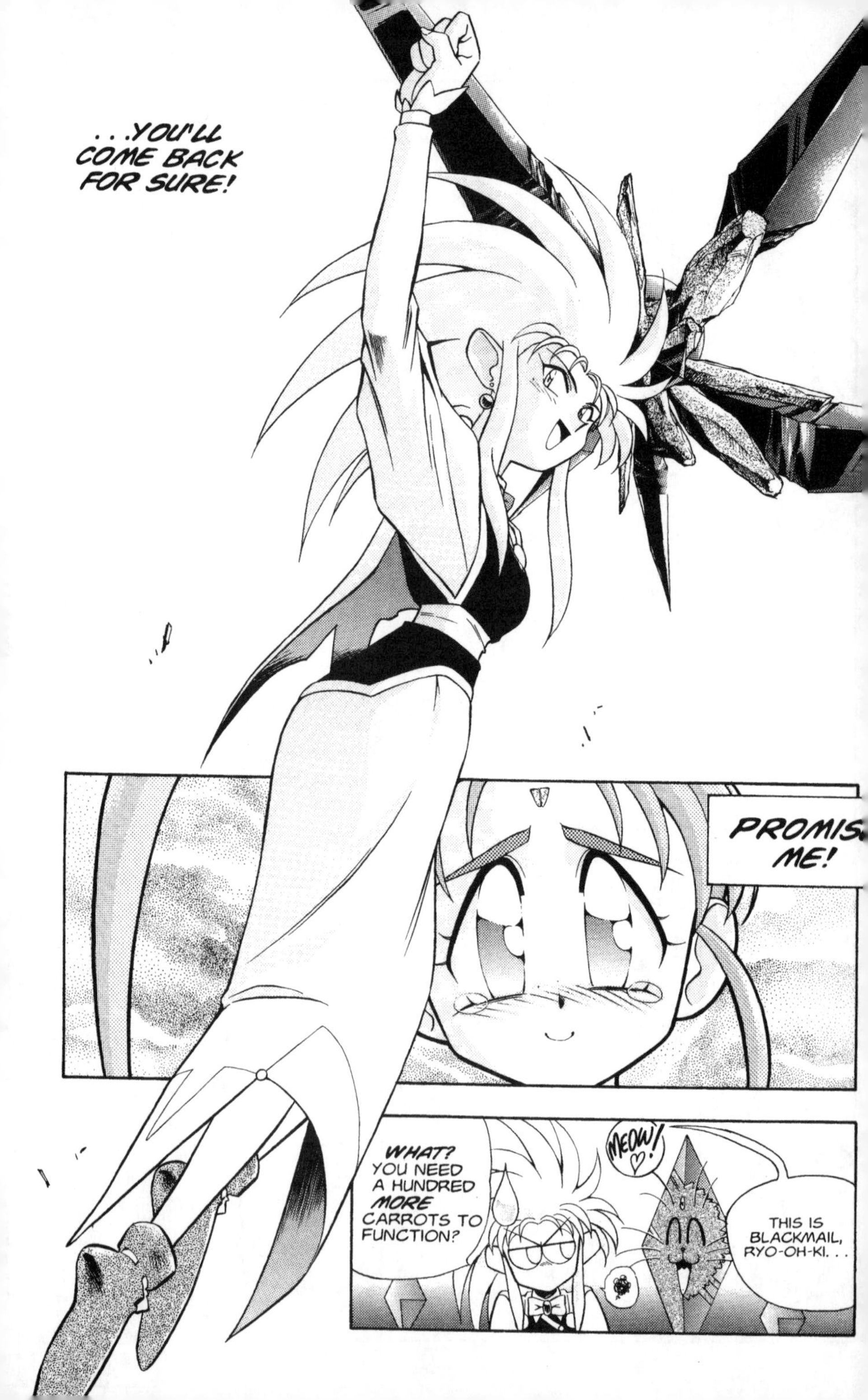
...YOU'LL COME BACK FOR SURE!
PROMIS
ME!
WHAT? YOU NEED A HUNDRED MORE CARROTS TO FUNCTION?
MEOW! ♡
THIS IS BLACKMAIL, RYO-OH-KI...

Tales of Tenchi #5

PRACTICE MAKES PERFECT

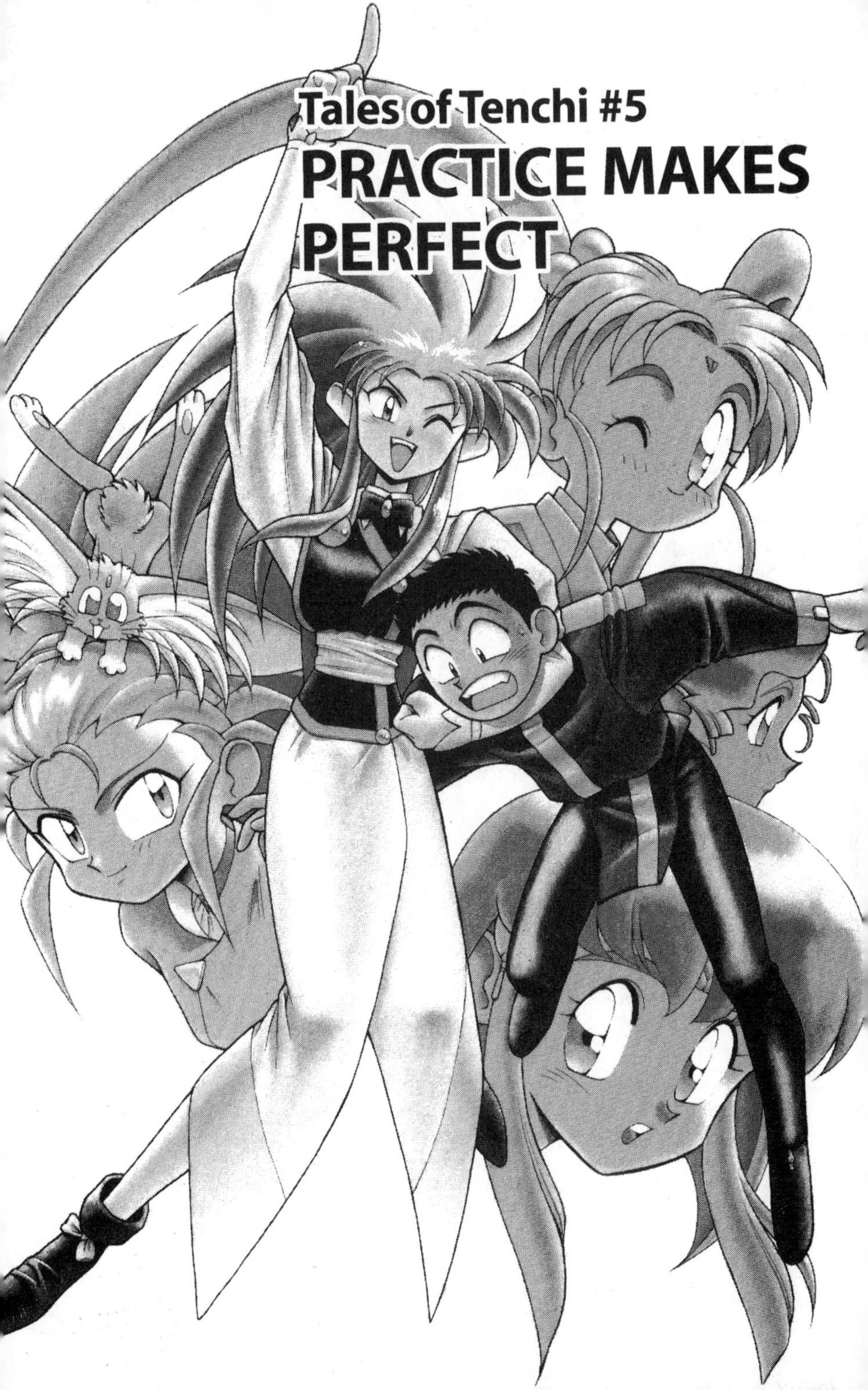

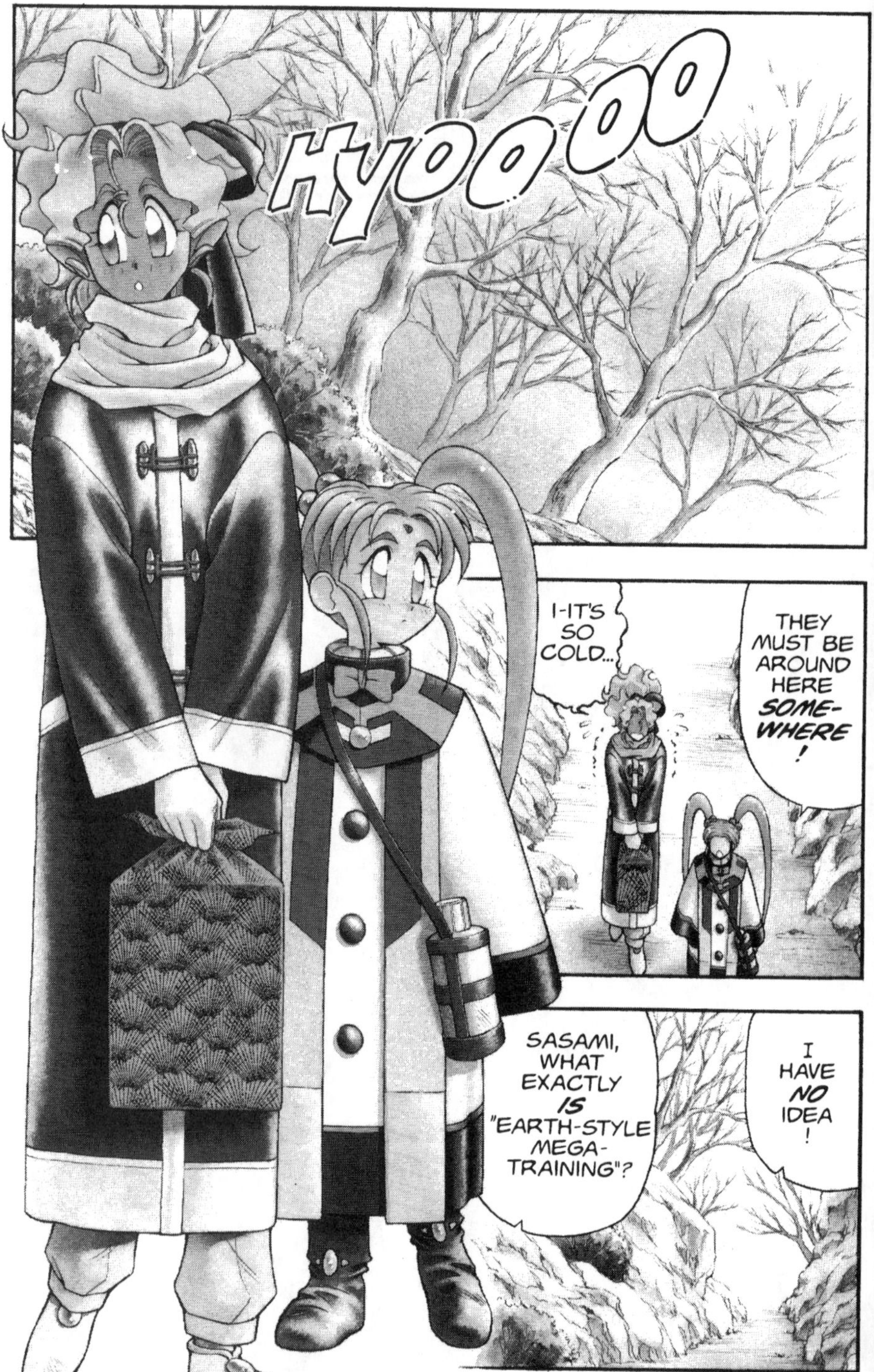
HYOOOOO
I-IT'S SO COLD...
THEY MUST BE AROUND HERE **SOME-WHERE**!
SASAMI, WHAT EXACTLY ***IS*** "EARTH-STYLE MEGA-TRAINING"?
I HAVE ***NO*** IDEA!

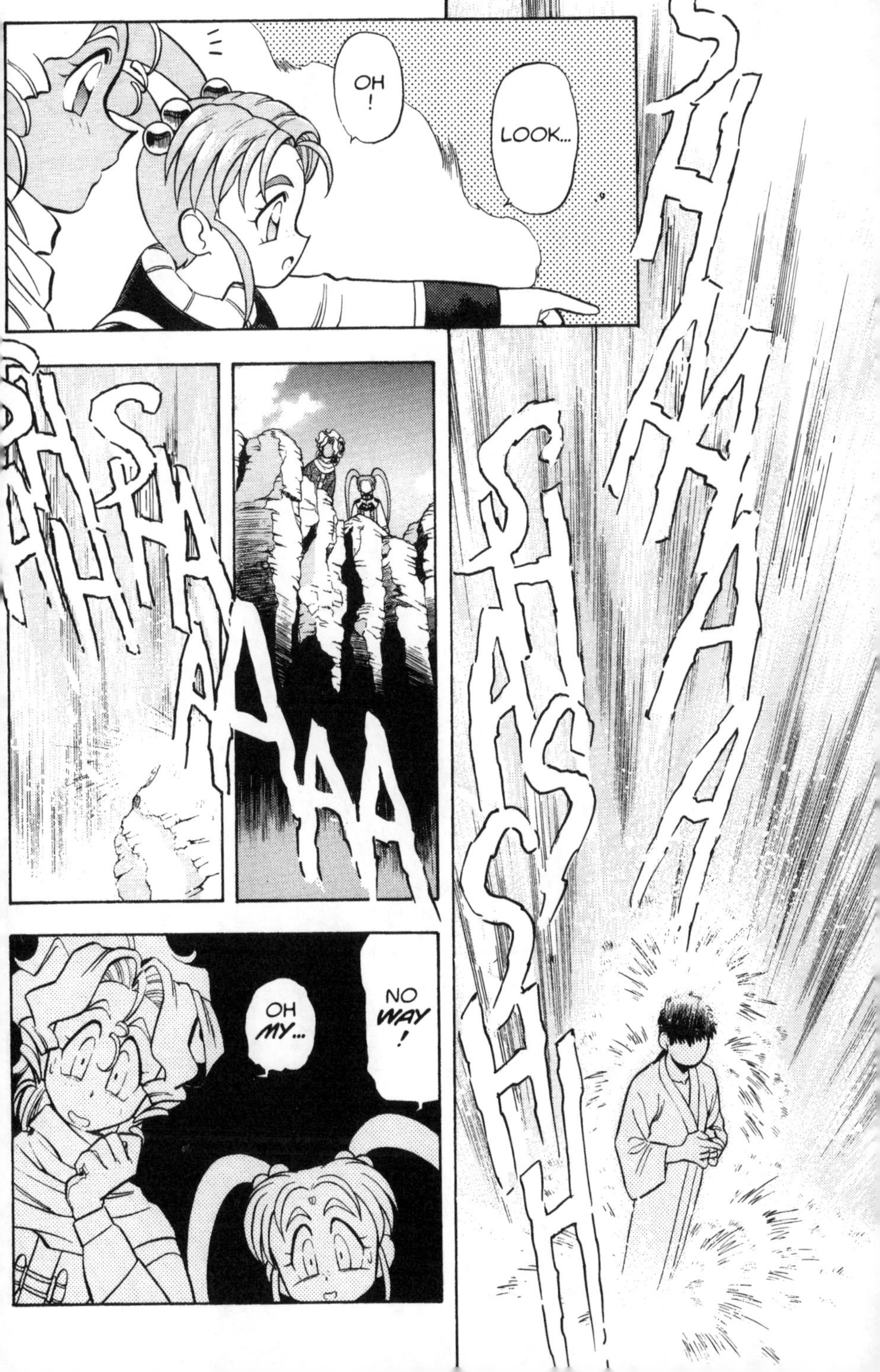
OH!
LOOK...
OH MY...
NO WAY!

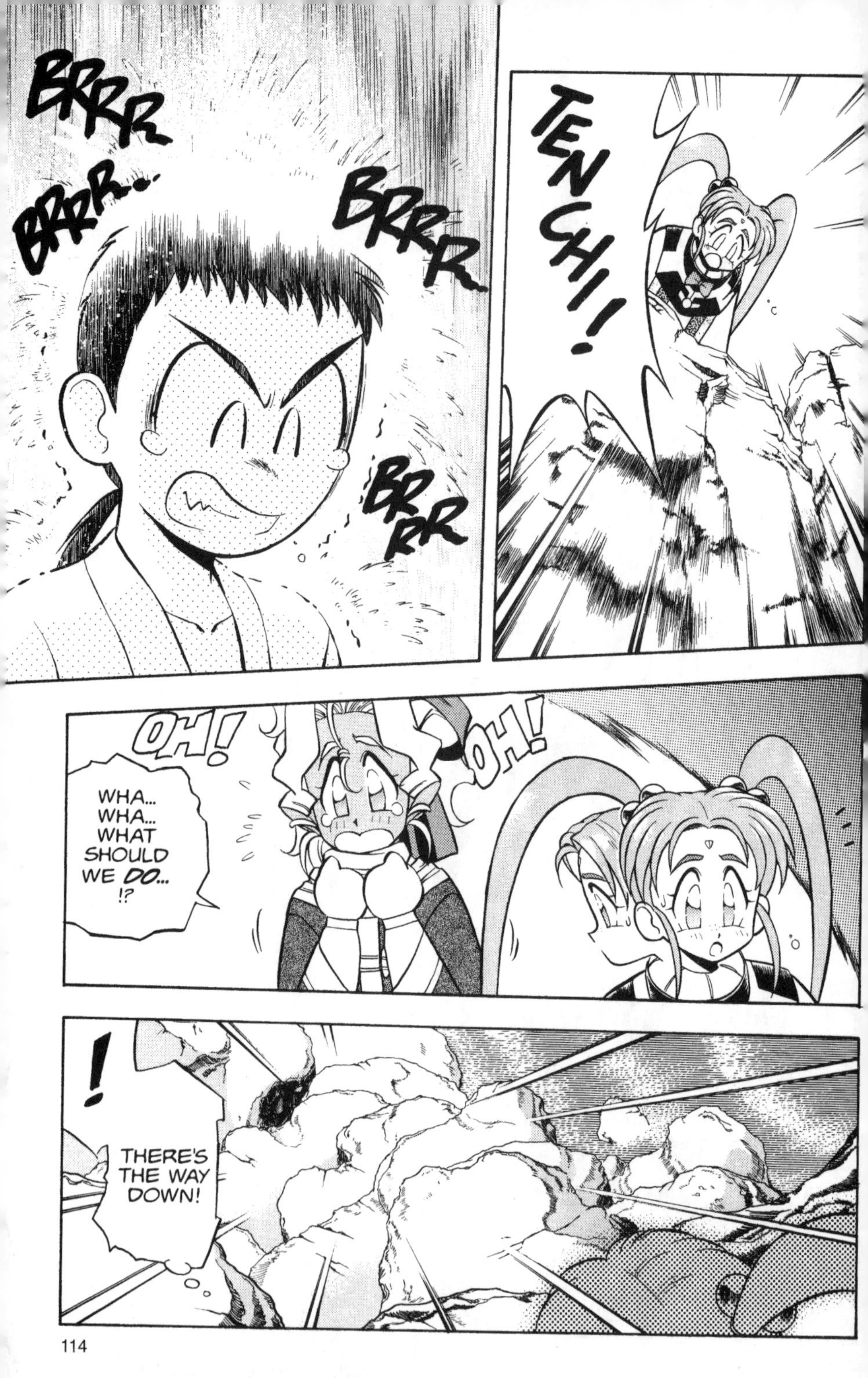
BRRRR
BRRR...
BRRRR
BRRR
TENCHI!!
OH!
OH!
WHA... WHA... WHAT SHOULD WE DO... !?
!
THERE'S THE WAY DOWN!

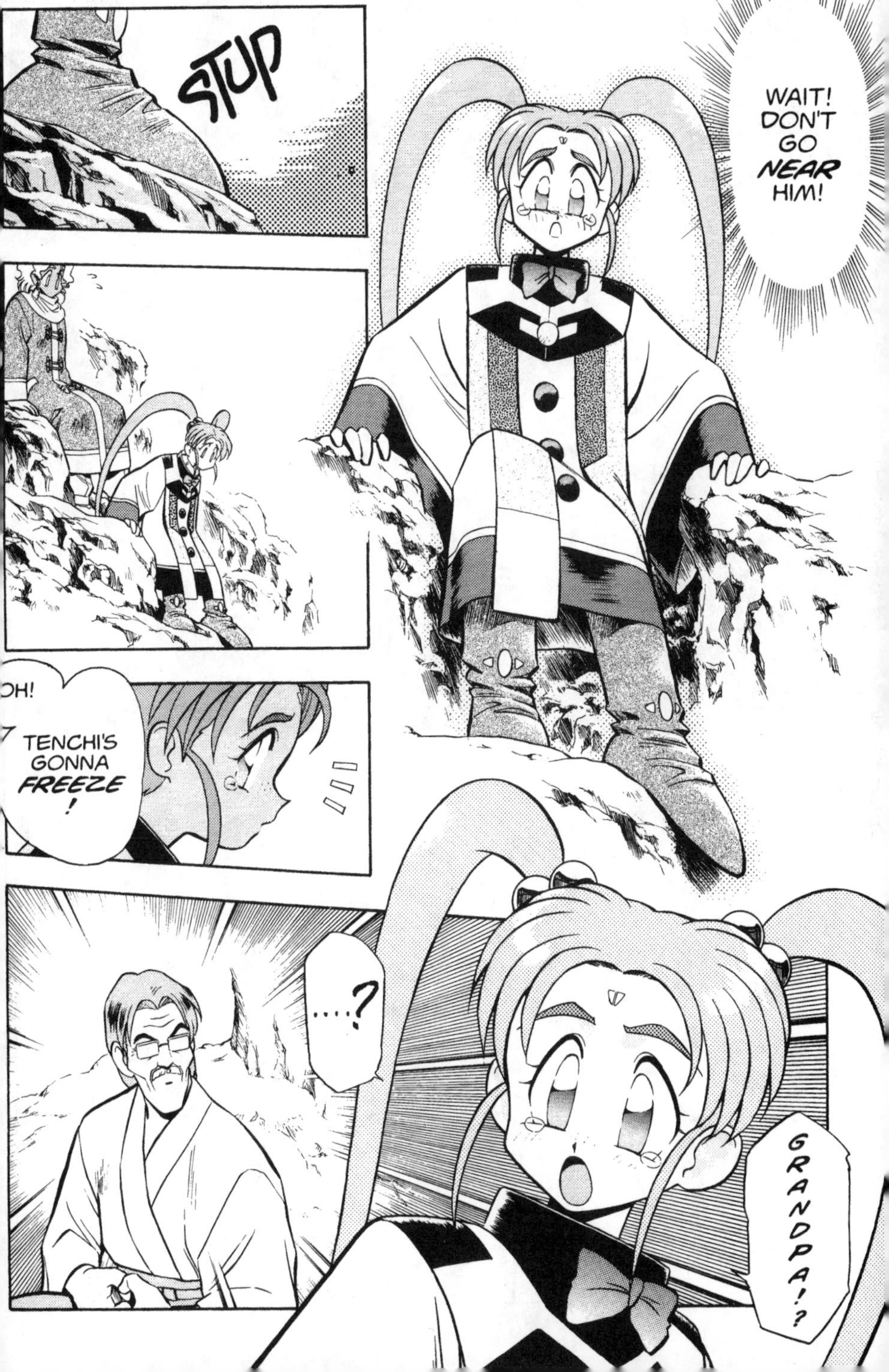
STUP
OH!
TENCHI'S GONNA FREEZE!
WAIT! DON'T GO NEAR HIM!
....?
GRANDPA!?

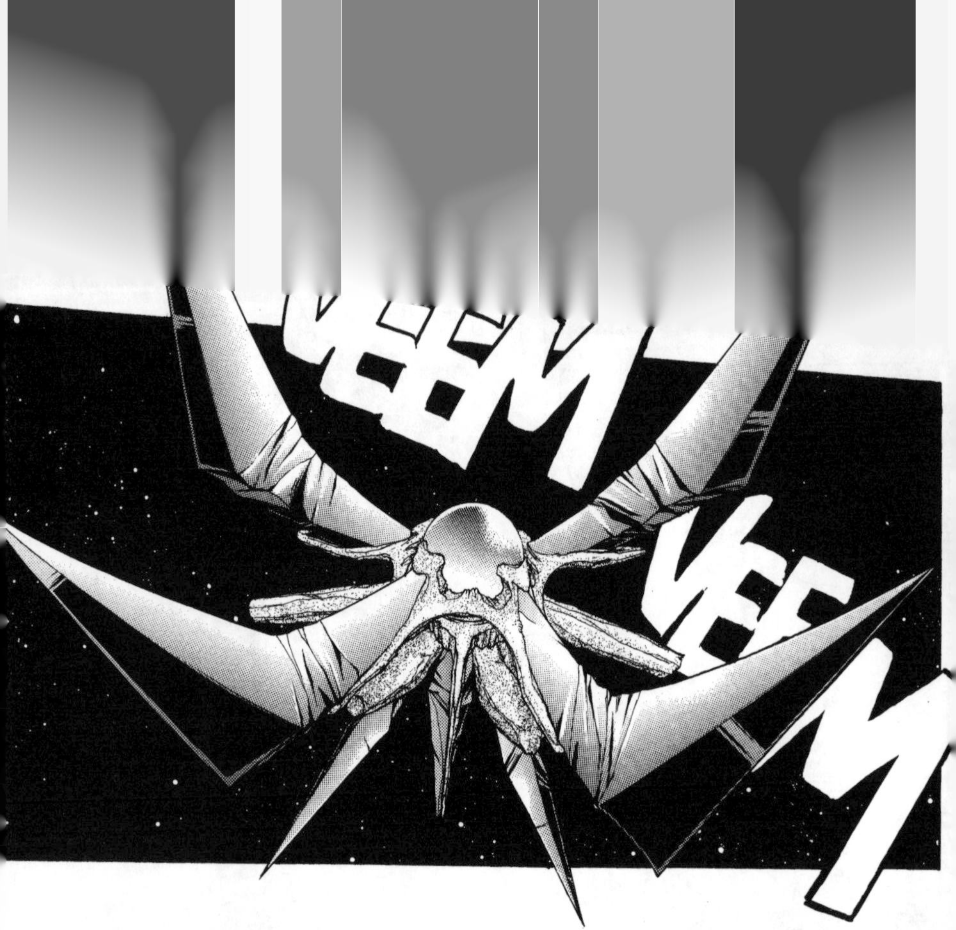
VEEM
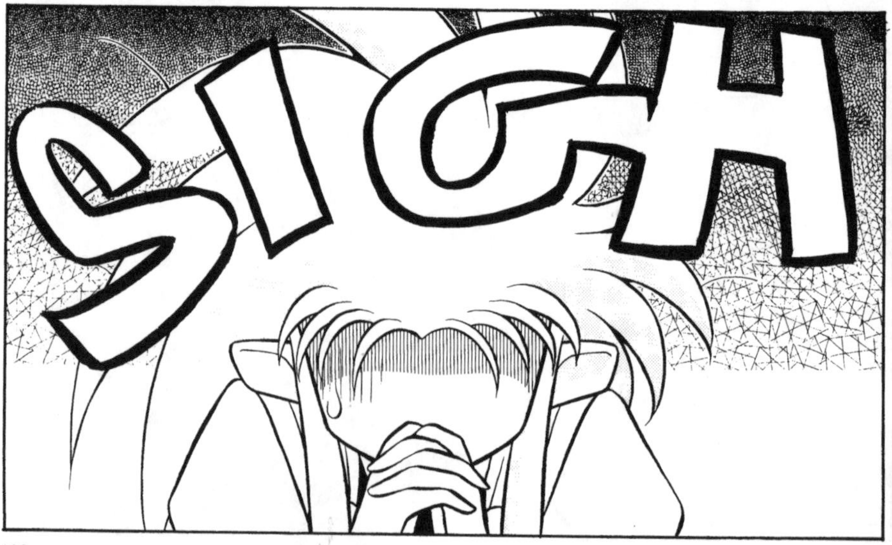
SIGH

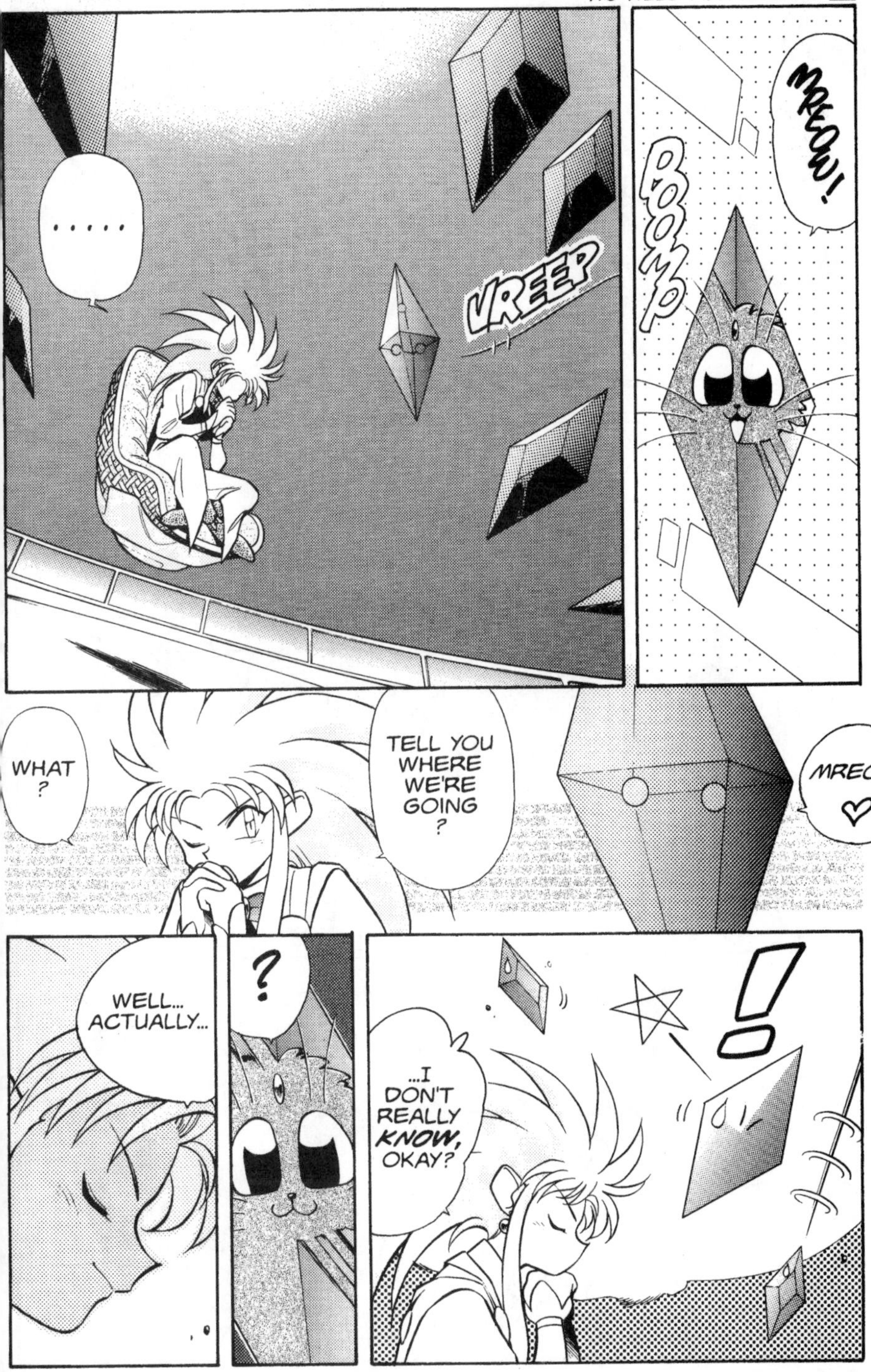
.....
VREEP
BOOMP
MREOW!
WHAT?
TELL YOU WHERE WE'RE GOING?
MREOW ♡
WELL... ACTUALLY...
?
...I DON'T REALLY *KNOW,* OKAY?
!

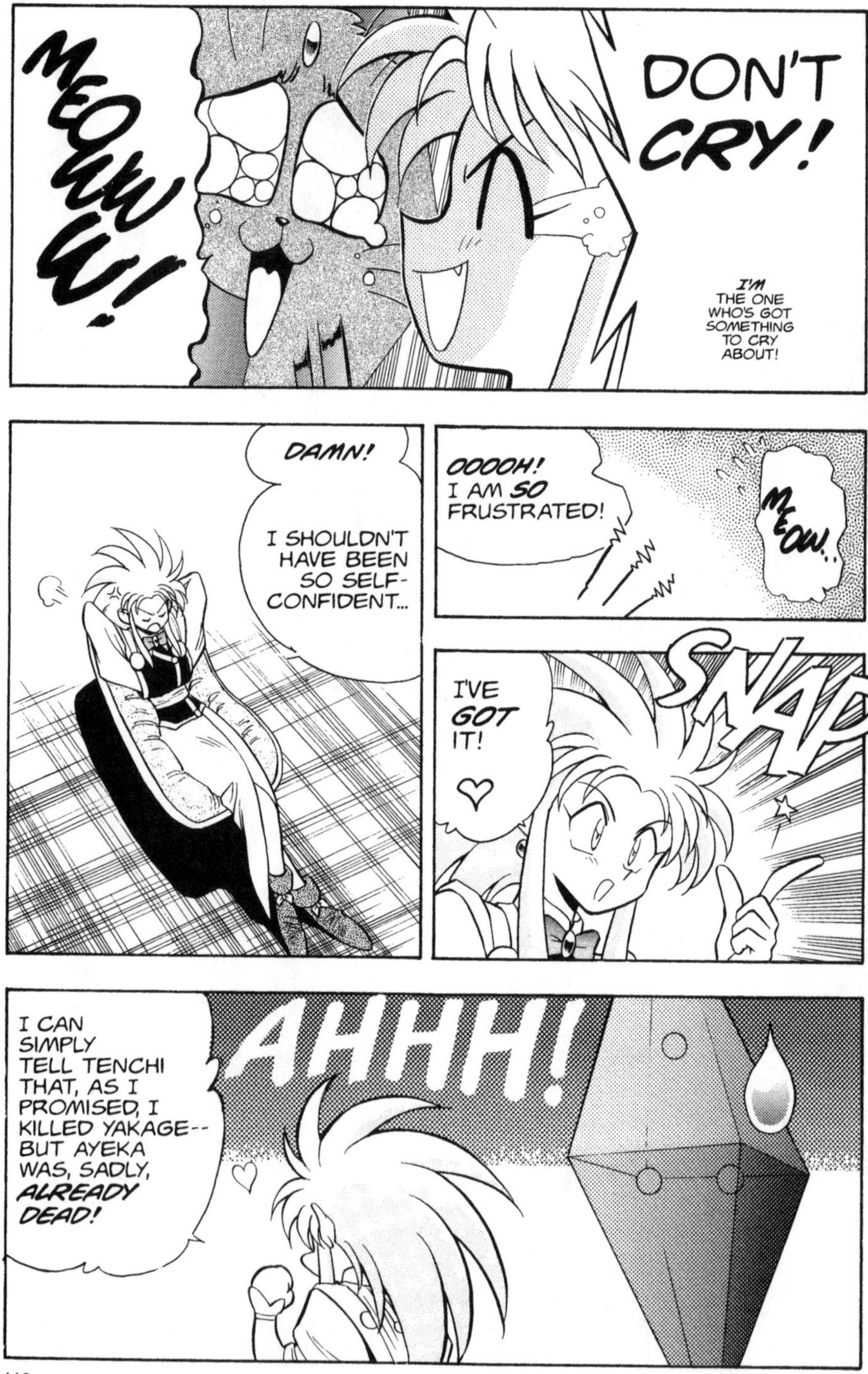
MEOWWWW!
DON'T CRY!
I'M THE ONE WHO'S GOT SOMETHING TO CRY ABOUT!
DAMN!
I SHOULDN'T HAVE BEEN SO SELF-CONFIDENT...
OOOOH! I AM SO FRUSTRATED!
MEOW...
I'VE GOT IT!
SNAP
I CAN SIMPLY TELL TENCHI THAT, AS I PROMISED, I KILLED YAKAGE--BUT AYEKA WAS, SADLY, ALREADY DEAD!
AHHH!

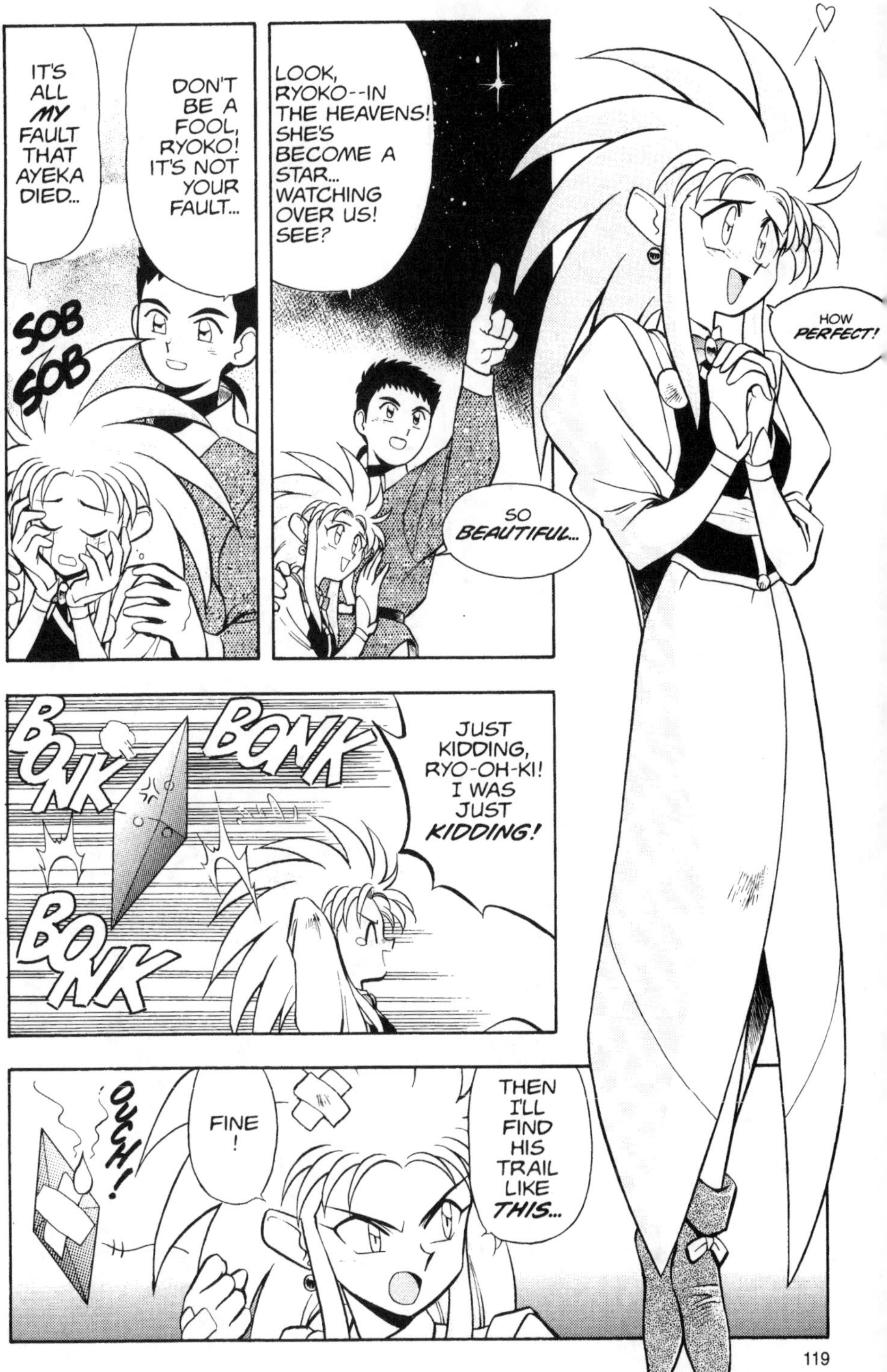
IT'S ALL MY FAULT THAT AYEKA DIED...
SOB SOB
DON'T BE A FOOL, RYOKO! IT'S NOT YOUR FAULT...
LOOK, RYOKO--IN THE HEAVENS! SHE'S BECOME A STAR... WATCHING OVER US! SEE?
SO BEAUTIFUL...
HOW PERFECT!
BONK
BONK
BONK
JUST KIDDING, RYO-OH-KI! I WAS JUST KIDDING!
OUCH!
FINE!
THEN I'LL FIND HIS TRAIL LIKE THIS...

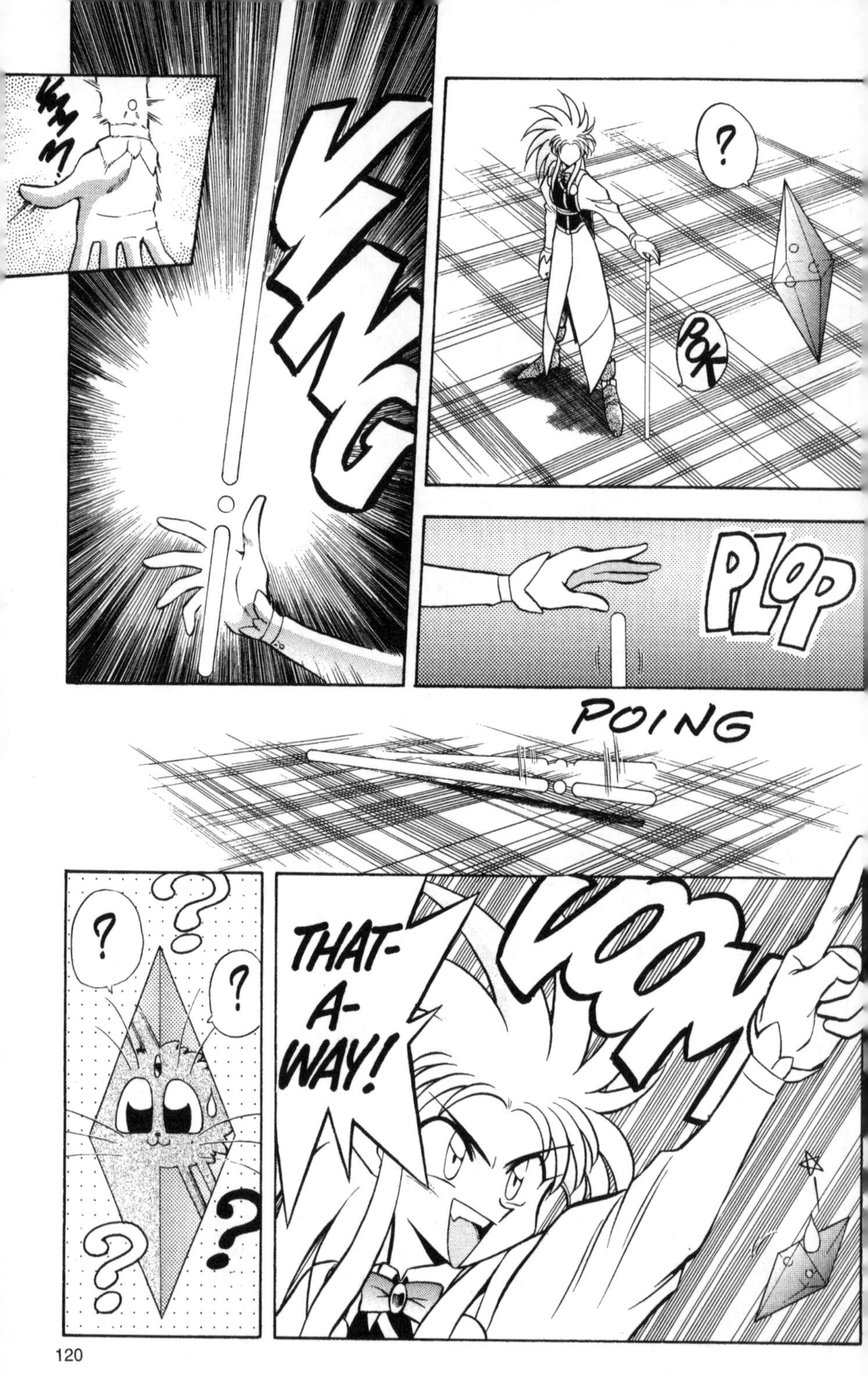
SHING
?
POK
PLOP
POING
?
?
THAT-A-WAY!

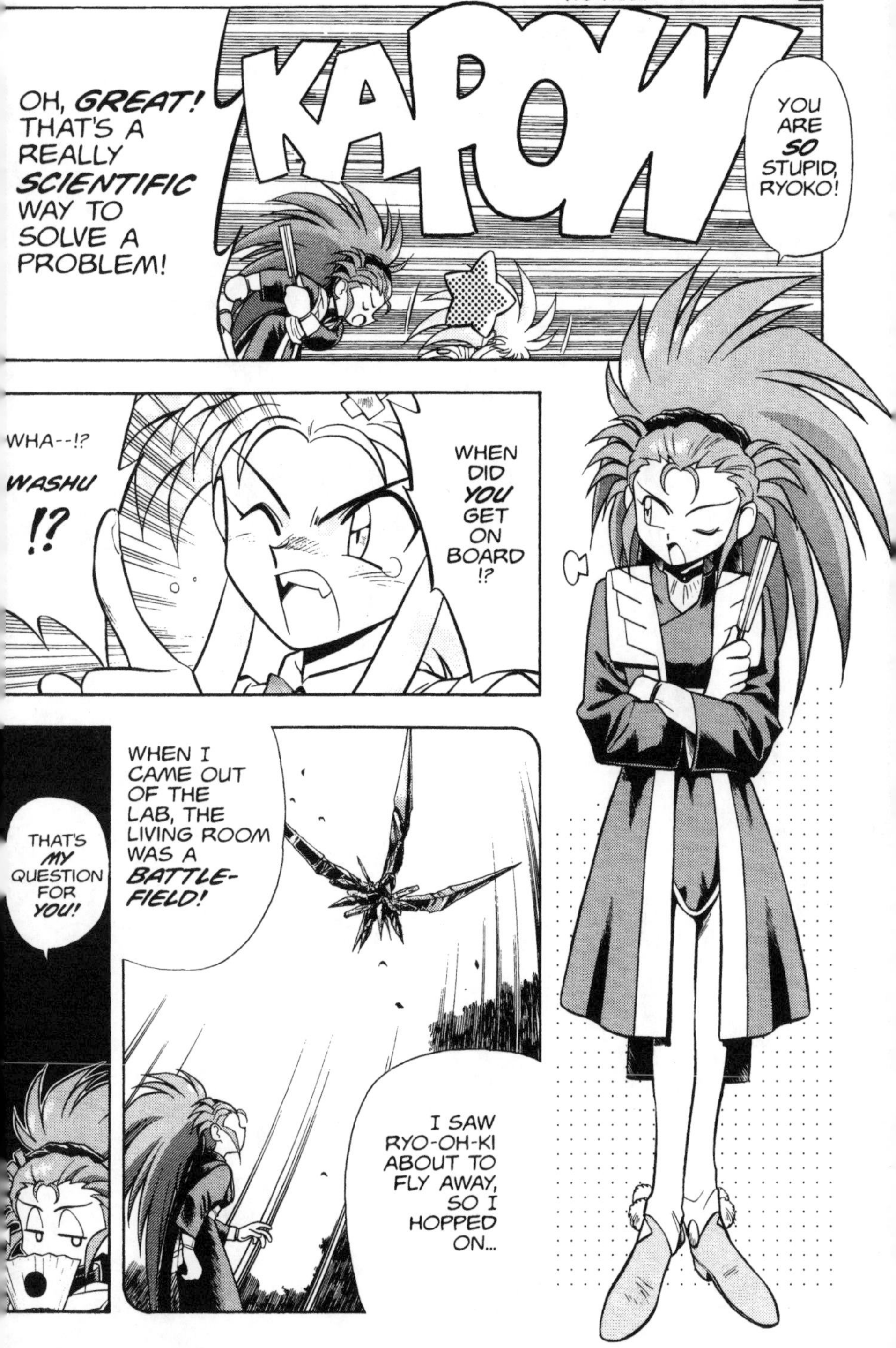
OH, GREAT! THAT'S A REALLY SCIENTIFIC WAY TO SOLVE A PROBLEM!
KAPOW
YOU ARE SO STUPID, RYOKO!
WHA--!?
WASHU !?
WHEN DID YOU GET ON BOARD !?
THAT'S MY QUESTION FOR YOU!
WHEN I CAME OUT OF THE LAB, THE LIVING ROOM WAS A BATTLE-FIELD!
I SAW RYO-OH-KI ABOUT TO FLY AWAY, SO I HOPPED ON...

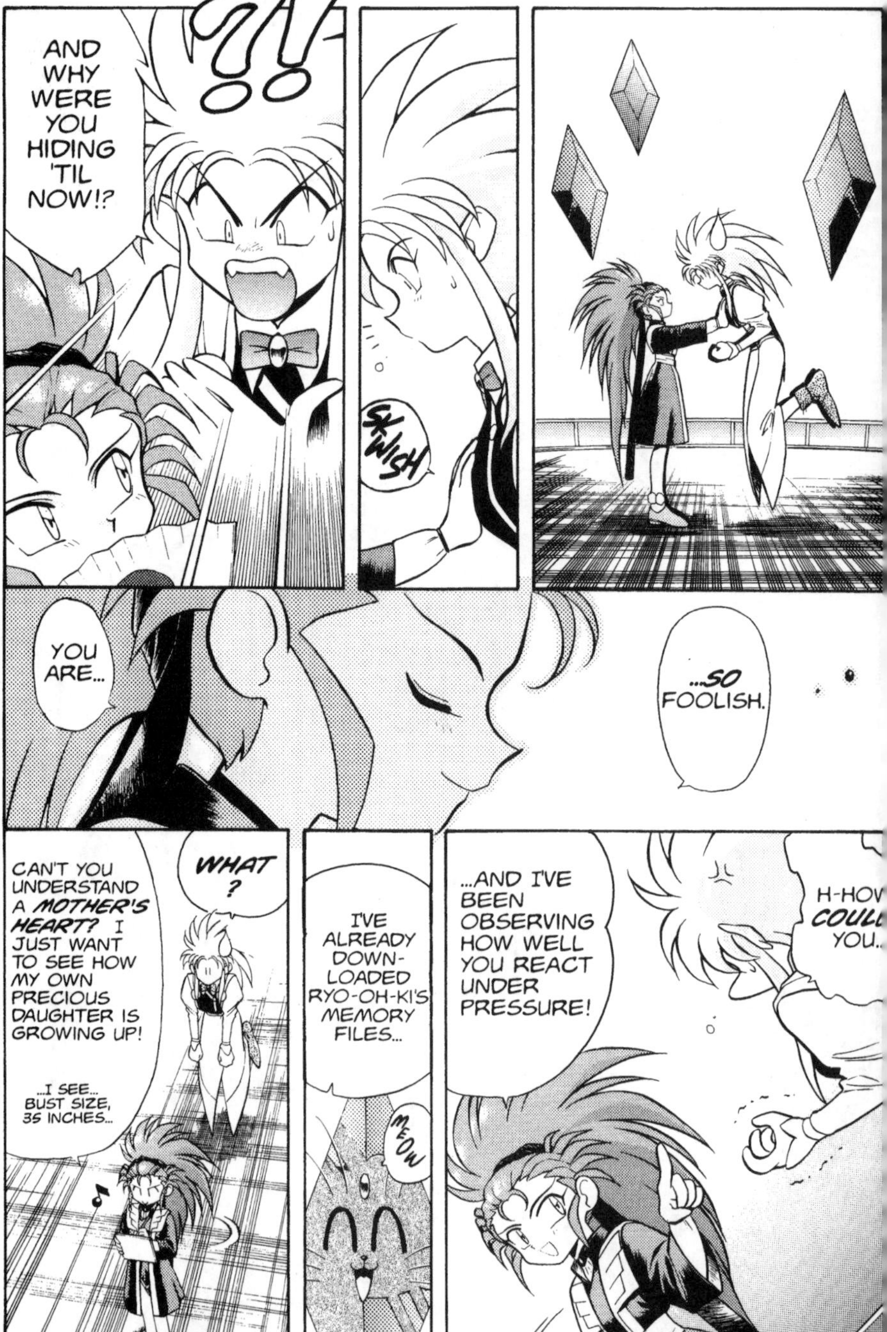
AND WHY WERE YOU HIDING 'TIL NOW!?
?!
SKWISH
YOU ARE...
...SO FOOLISH.
CAN'T YOU UNDERSTAND A MOTHER'S HEART? I JUST WANT TO SEE HOW MY OWN PRECIOUS DAUGHTER IS GROWING UP!
WHAT?
...I SEE... BUST SIZE, 35 INCHES...
I'VE ALREADY DOWN-LOADED RYO-OH-KI'S MEMORY FILES...
MEOW
...AND I'VE BEEN OBSERVING HOW WELL YOU REACT UNDER PRESSURE!
H-HOW COULD YOU...

IT'S NOT PRETTY!

YOU CAN'T EVEN DETECT WHERE YOUR *ENEMY* IS-- MUCH LESS RESCUE AYEKA!

I WEEP FOR YOU...?

GRRRRR

WELL THEN...

ARE YOU TELLING ME *YOU* KNOW WHERE HE IS?

YOU MUSTN'T UNDER- ESTIMATE AN ULTRAGENIUS SCIENTIST WITH THE *BEST* BRAIN IN THIS UNIVERSE!

AH HA!

URGH.

OH!

OF COURSE!

YOU *DO*...?

RYO-OH-KI!

SMELL THIS! GET A GOOD WHIFF!

MREOW?

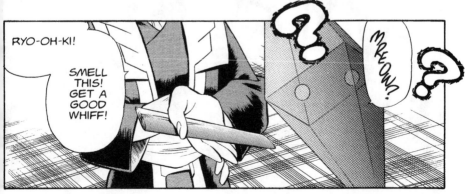

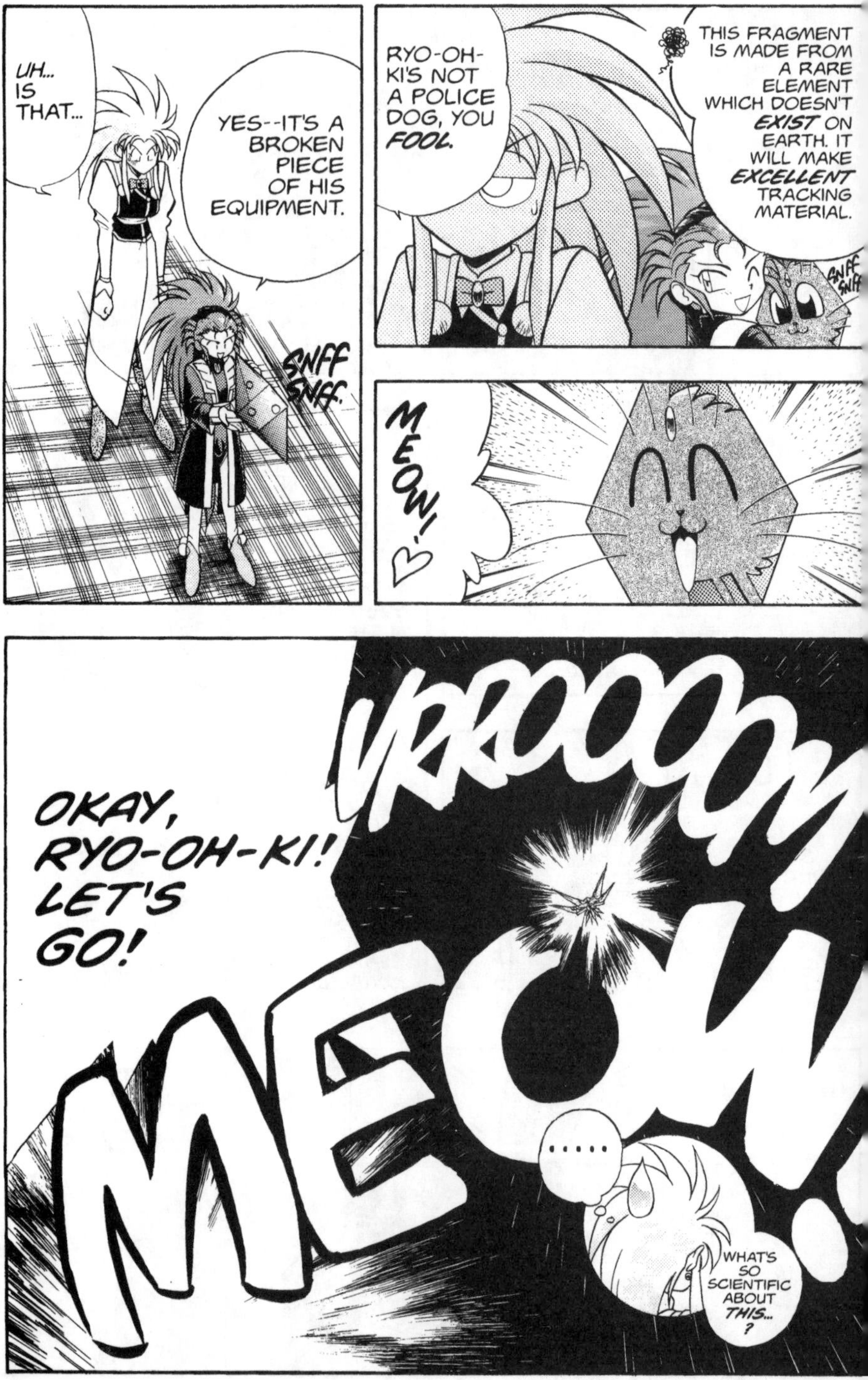
UH... IS THAT...
YES--IT'S A BROKEN PIECE OF HIS EQUIPMENT.
SNFF SNFF.
RYO-OH-KI'S NOT A POLICE DOG, YOU FOOL.
THIS FRAGMENT IS MADE FROM A RARE ELEMENT WHICH DOESN'T EXIST ON EARTH. IT WILL MAKE EXCELLENT TRACKING MATERIAL.
SNFF SNFF
MEOW!
OKAY, RYO-OH-KI! LET'S GO!
VRROOOM
MEOW...
.....
WHAT'S SO SCIENTIFIC ABOUT THIS...?

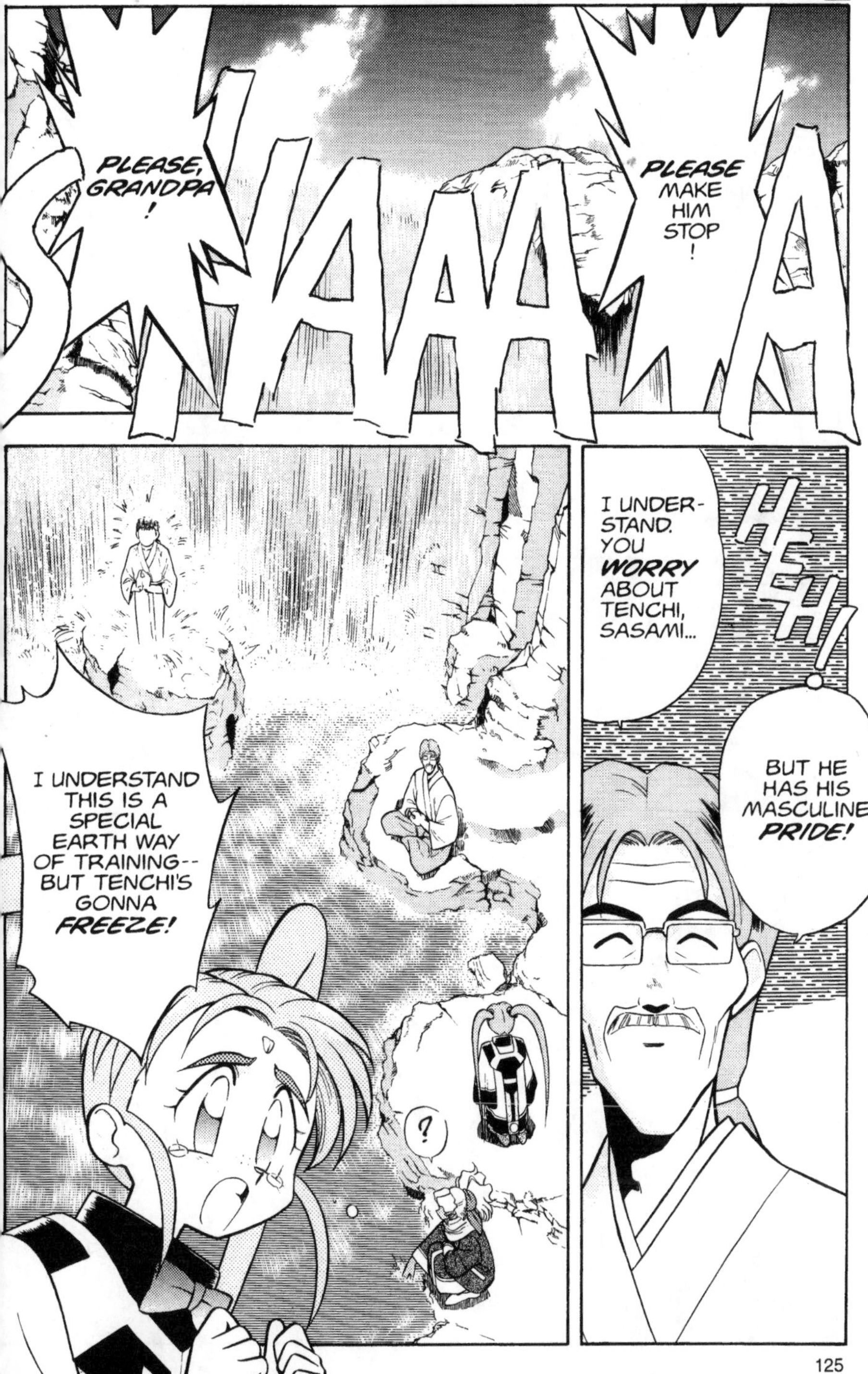
PLEASE, GRANDPA!
SHAAAA
PLEASE MAKE HIM STOP!
I UNDERSTAND THIS IS A SPECIAL EARTH WAY OF TRAINING--BUT TENCHI'S GONNA FREEZE!
?
I UNDERSTAND. YOU WORRY ABOUT TENCHI, SASAMI...
HEH!
BUT HE HAS HIS MASCULINE PRIDE!

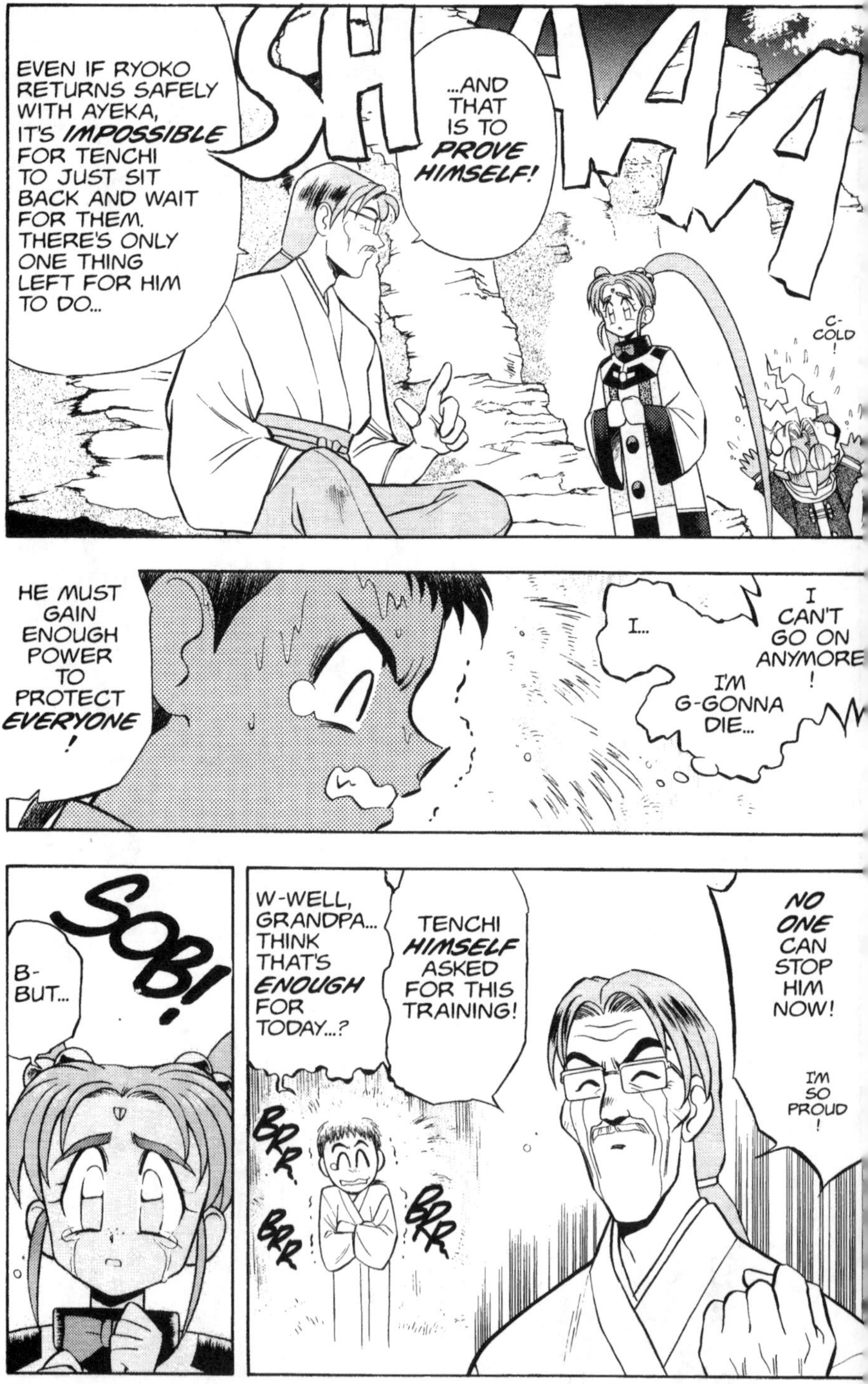
EVEN IF RYOKO RETURNS SAFELY WITH AYEKA, IT'S *IMPOSSIBLE* FOR TENCHI TO JUST SIT BACK AND WAIT FOR THEM. THERE'S ONLY ONE THING LEFT FOR HIM TO DO...
...AND THAT IS TO *PROVE HIMSELF!*
SHAAA
C-COLD!
HE MUST GAIN ENOUGH POWER TO PROTECT *EVERYONE!*
I...
I CAN'T GO ON ANYMORE!
I'M G-GONNA DIE...
SOB!
B-BUT...
W-WELL, GRANDPA... THINK THAT'S *ENOUGH* FOR TODAY...?
TENCHI *HIMSELF* ASKED FOR THIS TRAINING!
NO ONE CAN STOP HIM NOW!
I'M SO PROUD!
BRR
BRR
BRRR

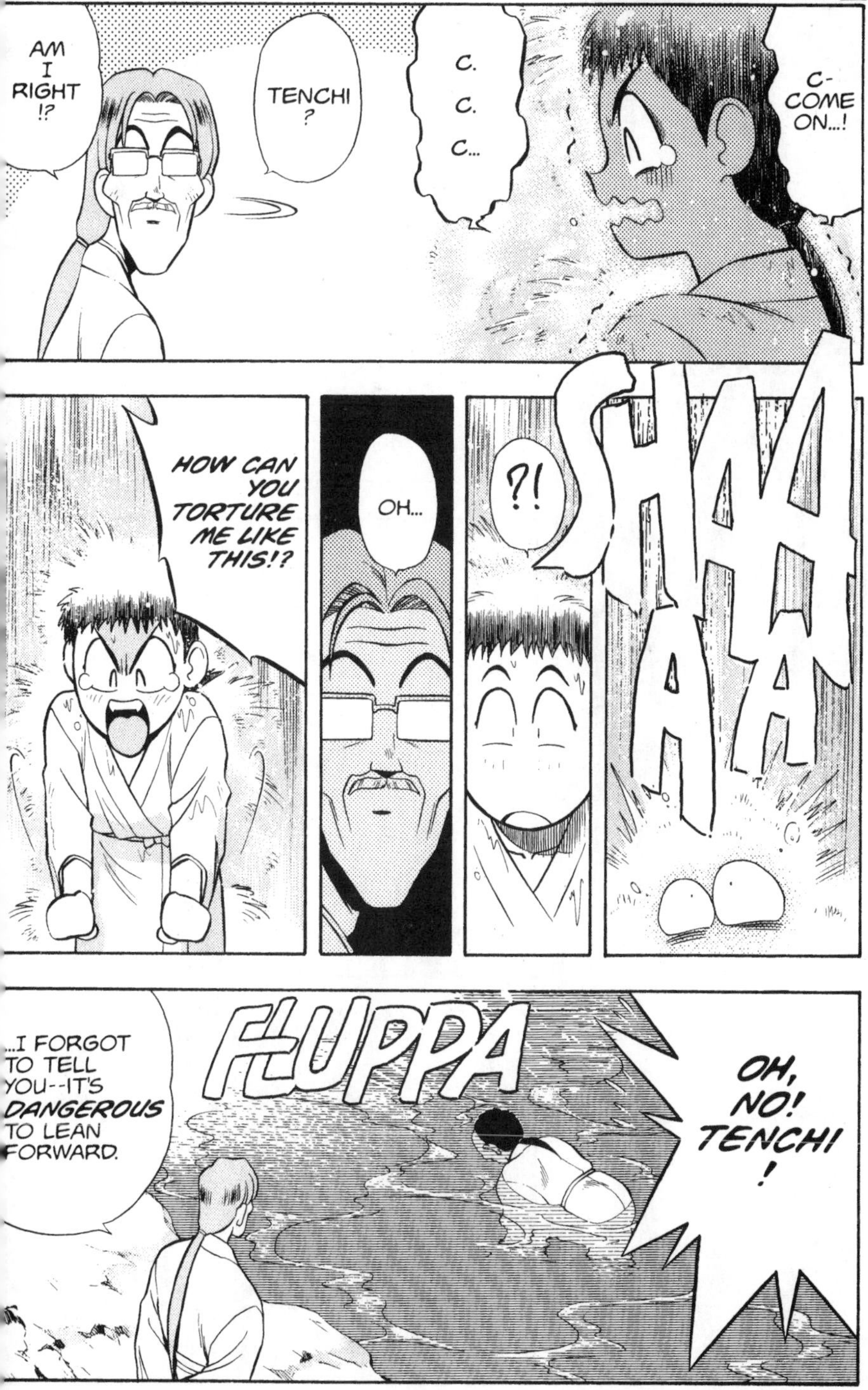
AM I RIGHT !?
TENCHI ?
C. C. C...
C- COME ON...!
HOW CAN YOU TORTURE ME LIKE THIS!?
OH...
?!
SHAAAA
...I FORGOT TO TELL YOU--IT'S DANGEROUS TO LEAN FORWARD.
FLUPPA
OH, NO! TENCHI !

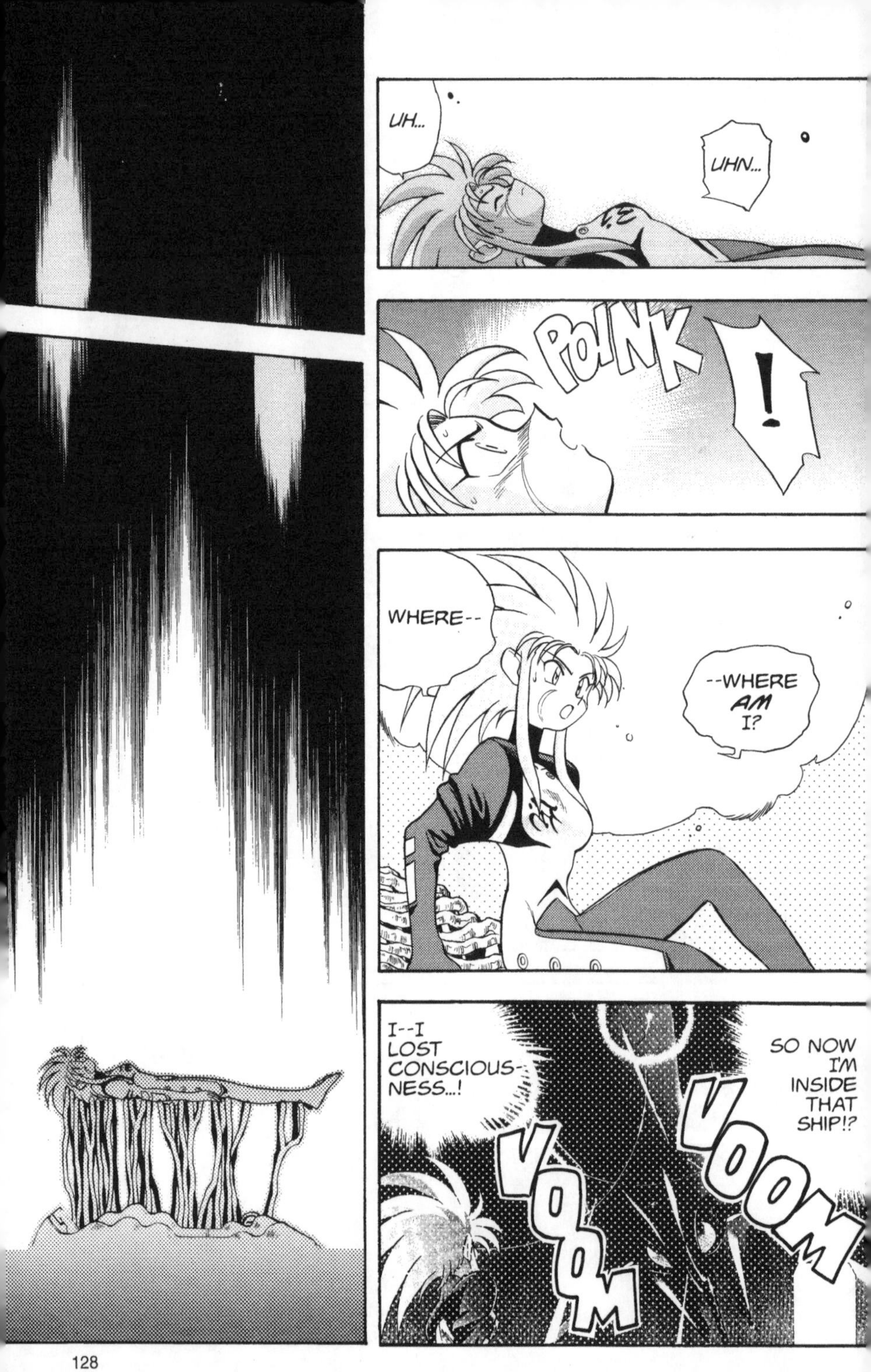
UH...
UHN...
POINK
!
WHERE--
--WHERE AM I?
I--I LOST CONSCIOUS-NESS...!
SO NOW I'M INSIDE THAT SHIP!?
VOOM
VOOM

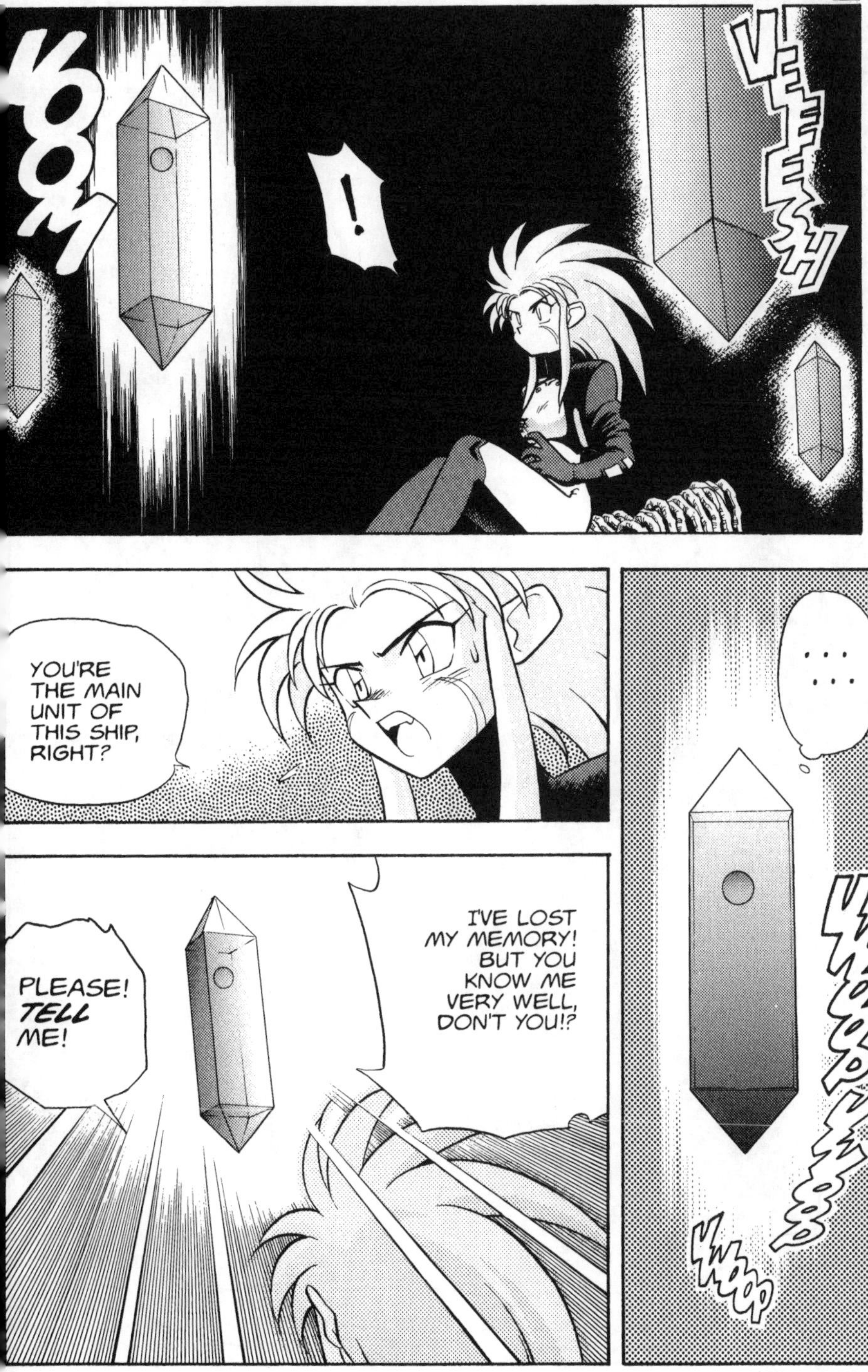
VOOM
!
VEEESH
YOU'RE THE MAIN UNIT OF THIS SHIP, RIGHT?
PLEASE! TELL ME!
I'VE LOST MY MEMORY! BUT YOU KNOW ME VERY WELL, DON'T YOU!?
......
VWOOP VWOOP
VWOOP

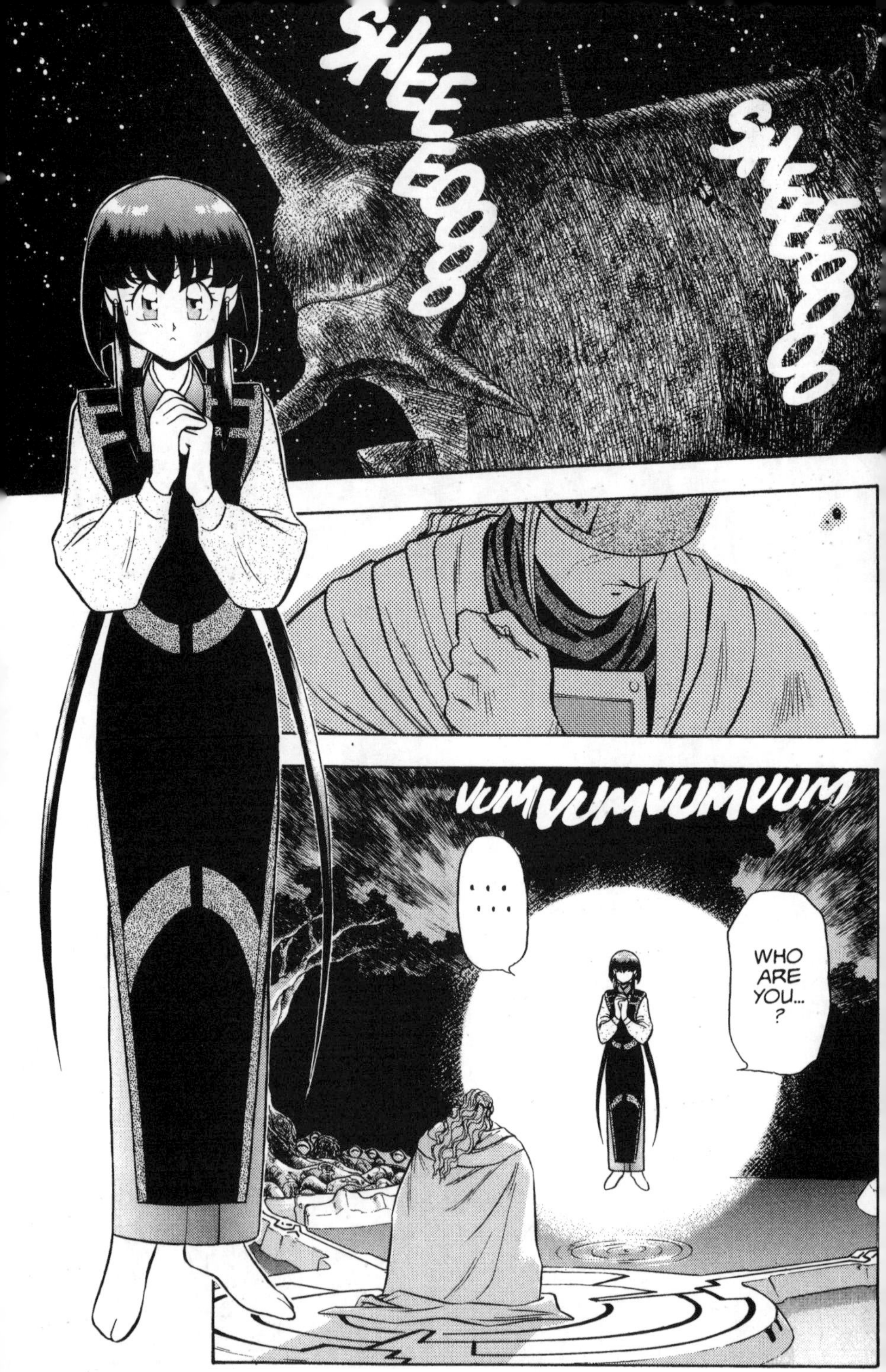
SHEEOOO
SHEEOOOO
VUM VUM VUM VUM
. . .
. . .
WHO ARE YOU... ?

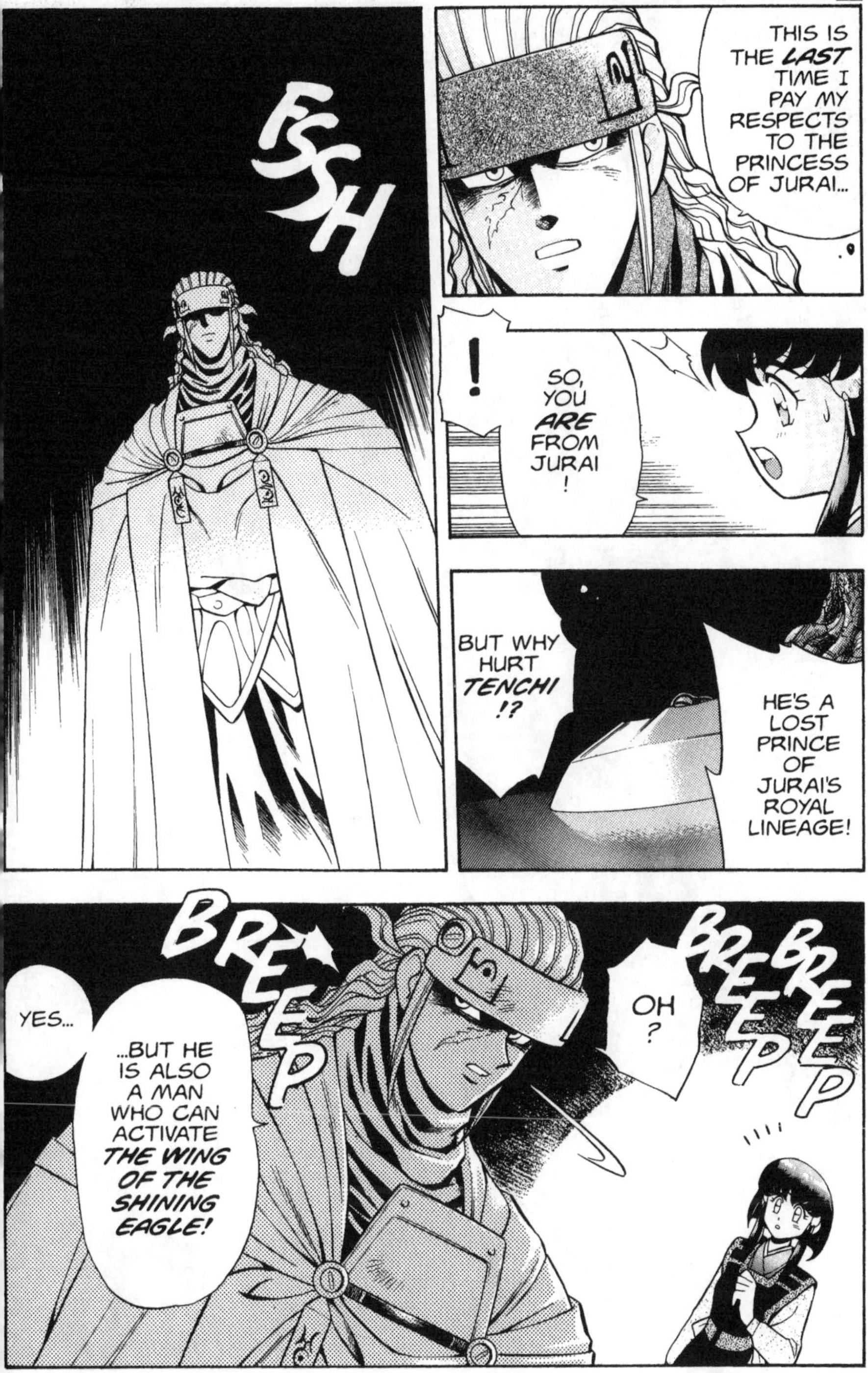
FSSH
THIS IS THE *LAST* TIME I PAY MY RESPECTS TO THE PRINCESS OF JURAI...
!
SO, YOU *ARE* FROM JURAI!
BUT WHY HURT *TENCHI* !?
HE'S A LOST PRINCE OF JURAI'S ROYAL LINEAGE!
BREEP
YES...
...BUT HE IS ALSO A MAN WHO CAN ACTIVATE ***THE WING OF THE SHINING EAGLE!***
OH?
BREEP BREEP

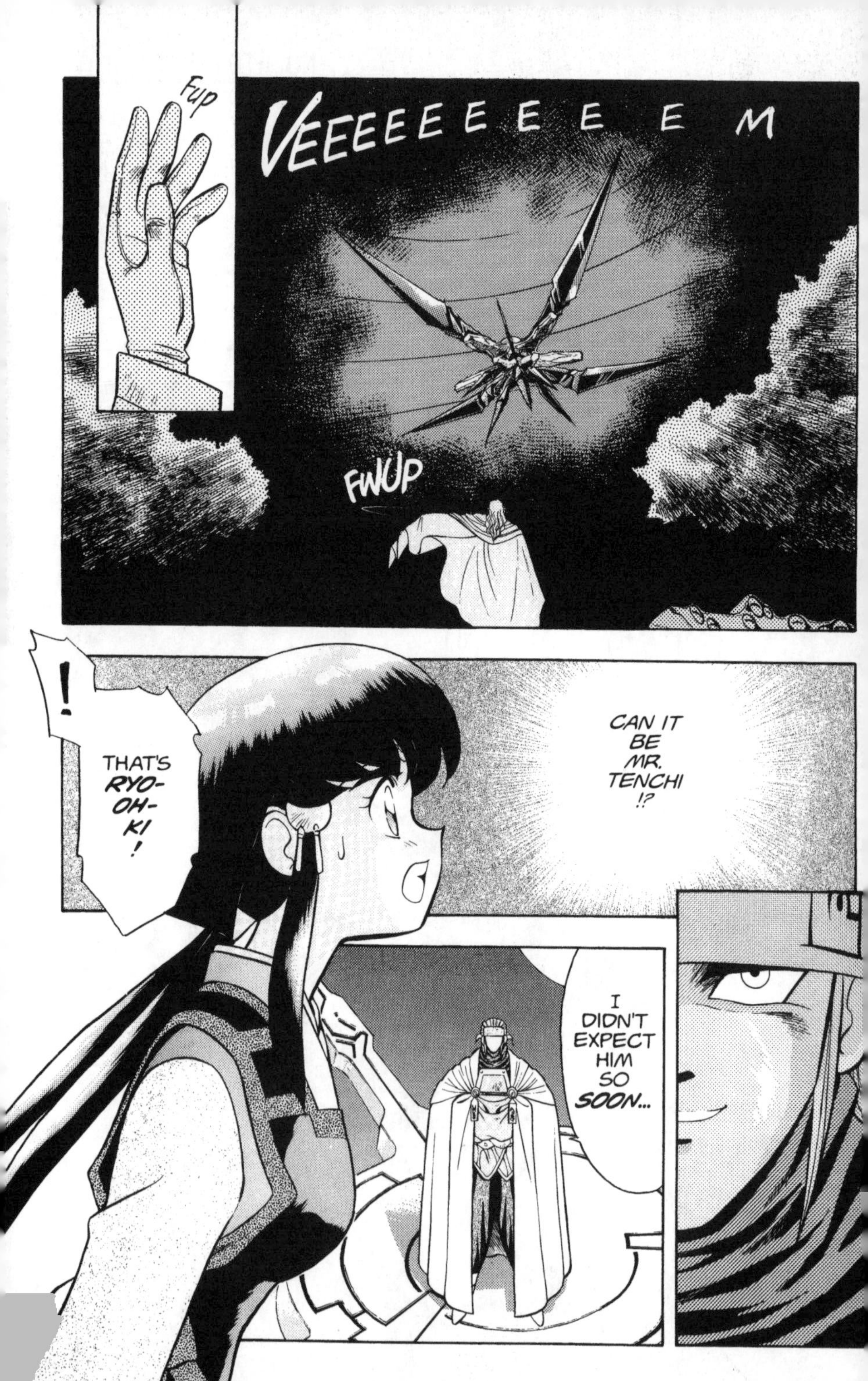
Fup
VEEEEEEEEEM
FWUP
!
THAT'S RYO-OH-KI!
CAN IT BE MR. TENCHI !?
I DIDN'T EXPECT HIM SO SOON...

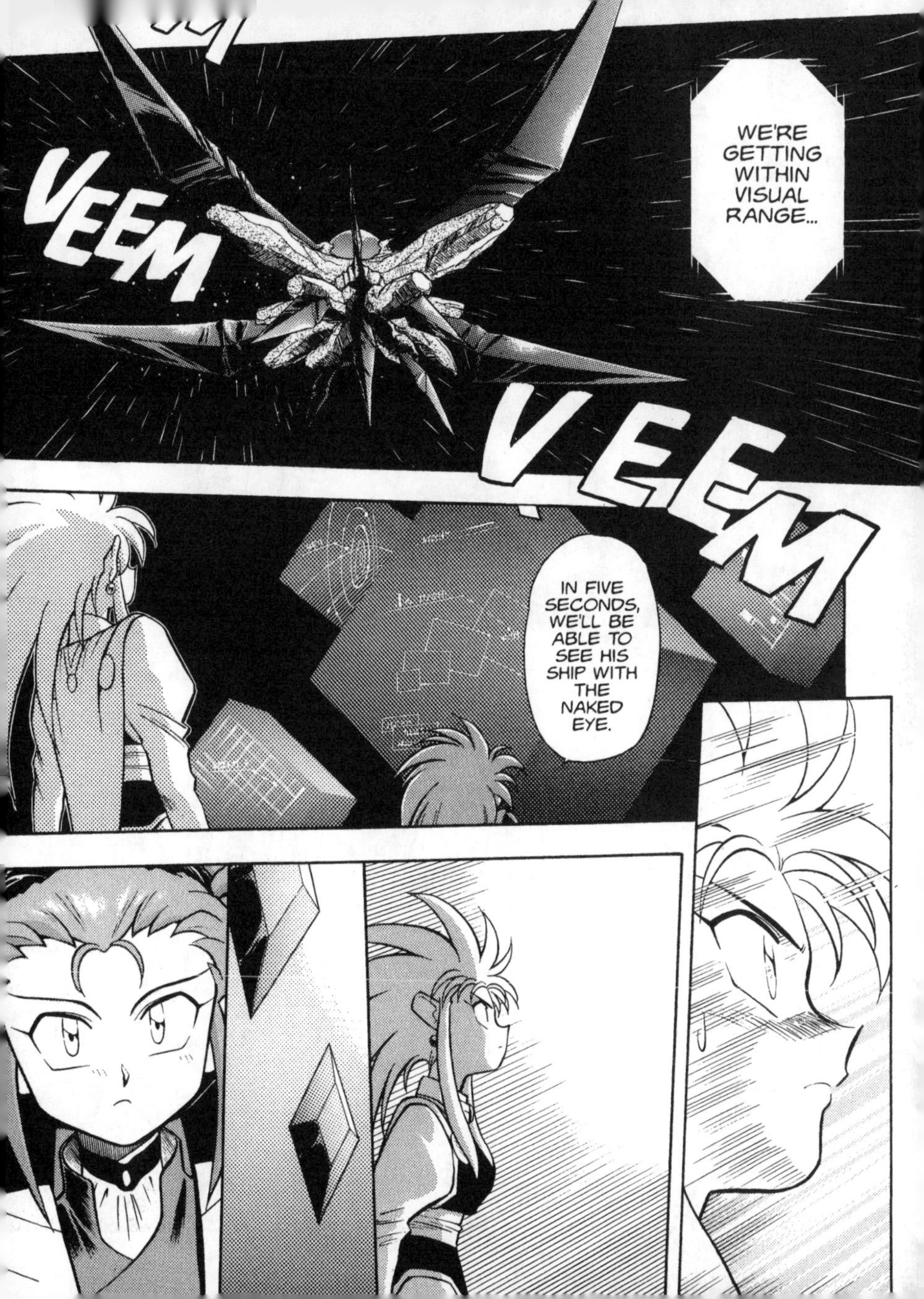
VEEM
WE'RE GETTING WITHIN VISUAL RANGE...
VEEM
IN FIVE SECONDS, WE'LL BE ABLE TO SEE HIS SHIP WITH THE NAKED EYE.

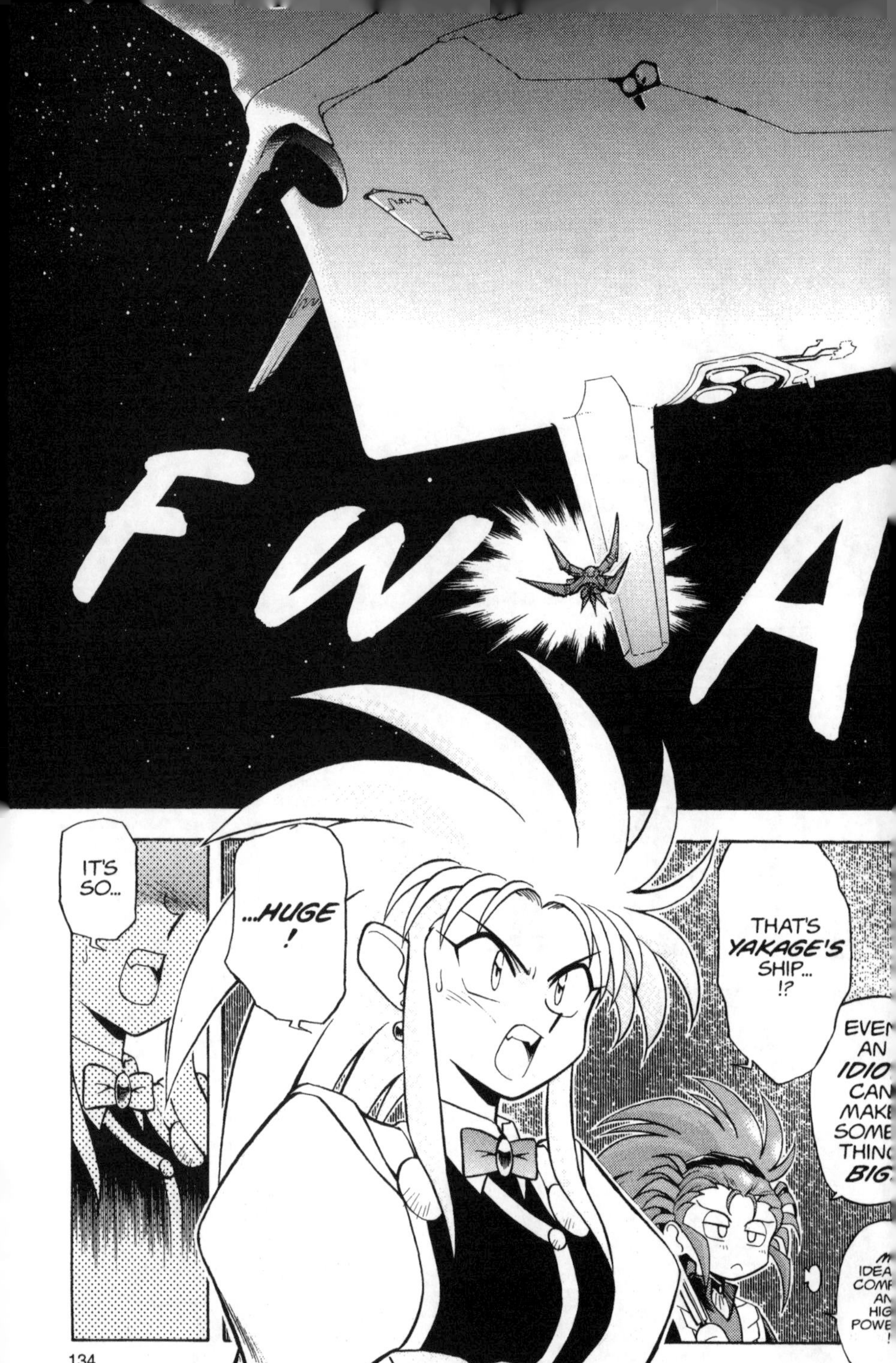
FWA
IT'S SO...
...HUGE!
THAT'S YAKAGE'S SHIP...!?
EVEN AN IDIO CAN MAKE SOME THIN BIG

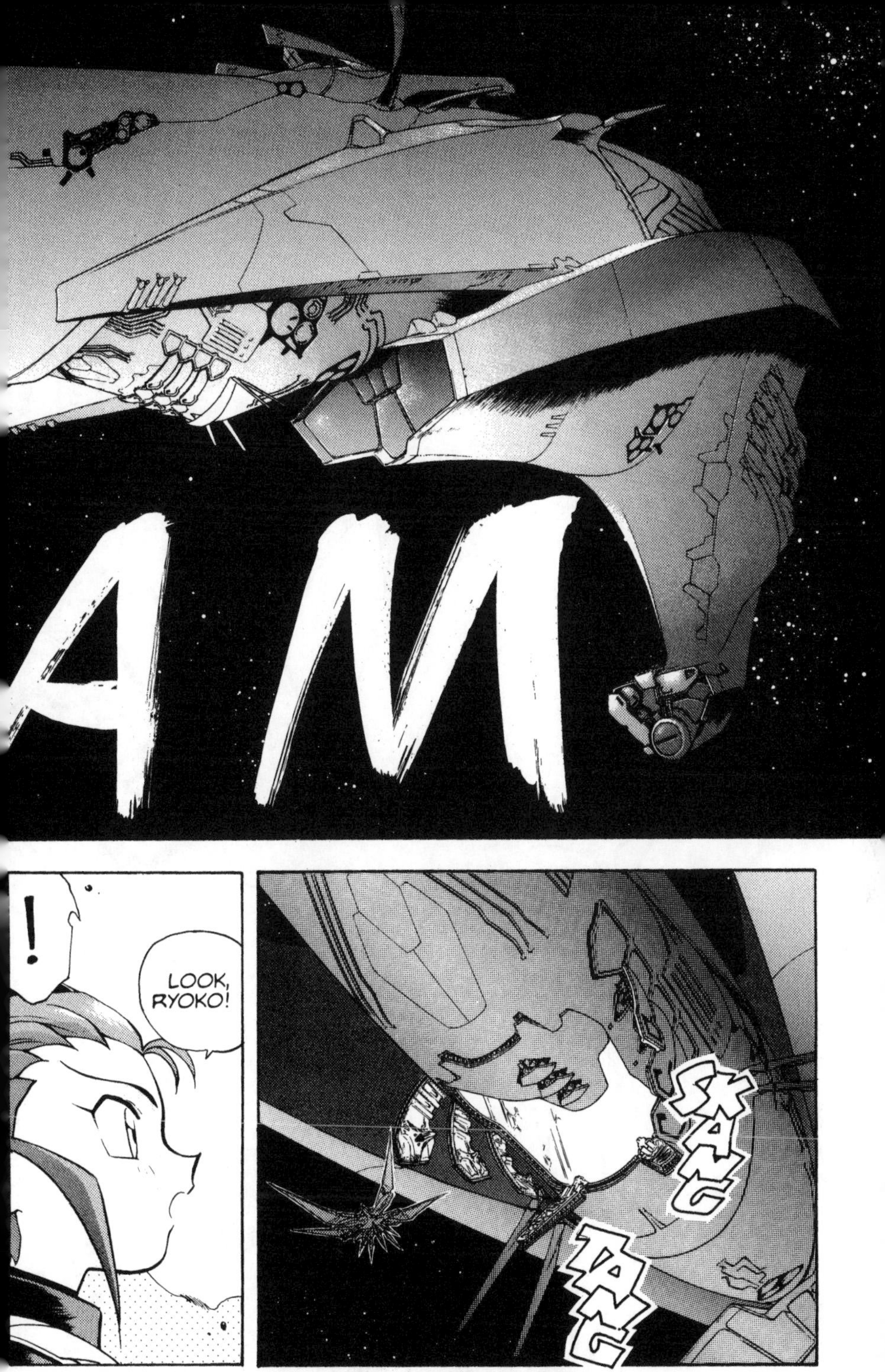
AM
!
LOOK, RYOKO!
SKANG
TANG

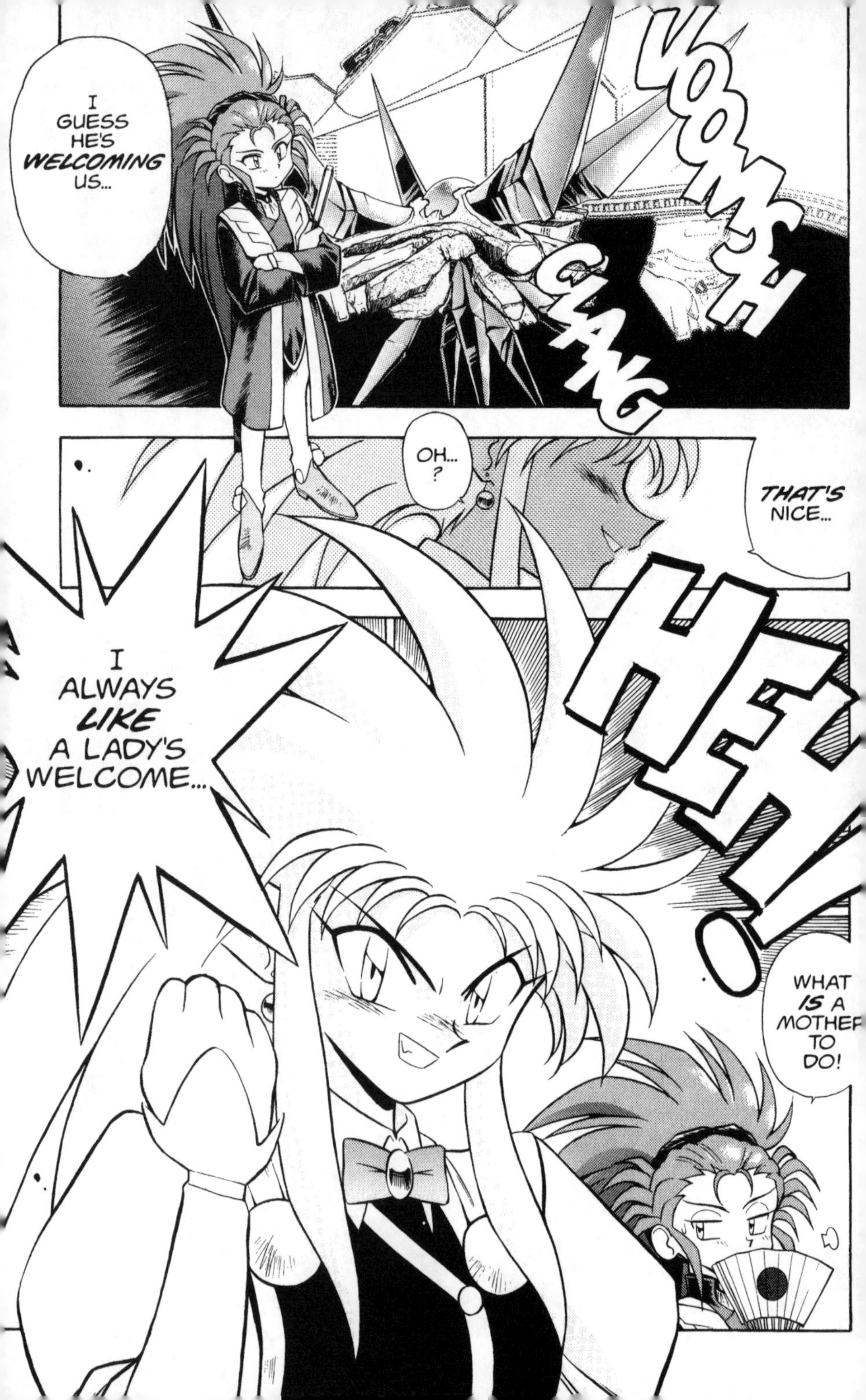
I GUESS HE'S WELCOMING US...
VOOOMSH
CLANG
OH... ?
THAT'S NICE...
I ALWAYS LIKE A LADY'S WELCOME...
HEH!!
WHAT IS A MOTHER TO DO!

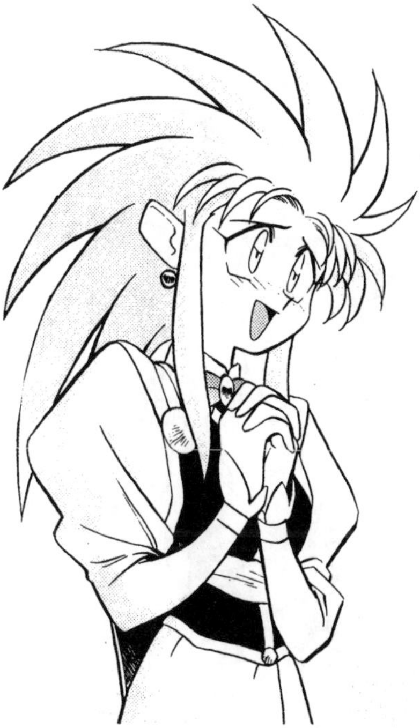

the heart-warming theater of life:

The Cast of No Need for Tenchi!

part 1: Ryoko

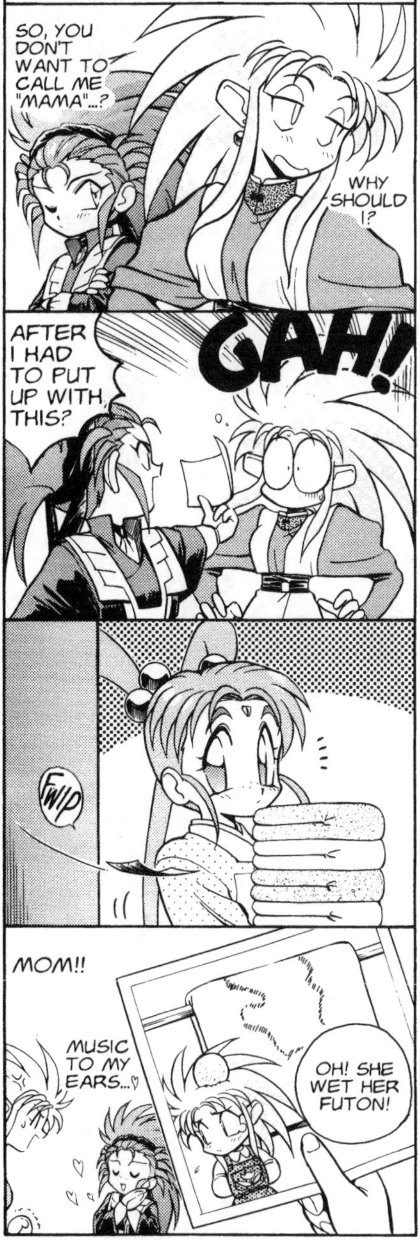

SO, YOU DON'T WANT TO CALL ME "MAMA"...?
WHY SHOULD I!?
AFTER I HAD TO PUT UP WITH THIS?
GAH!
FWIP
MOM!!
MUSIC TO MY EARS...♡
OH! SHE WET HER FUTON!

the heart-warming theater of life:

The Cast of No Need for Tenchi

part 2: Tenchi

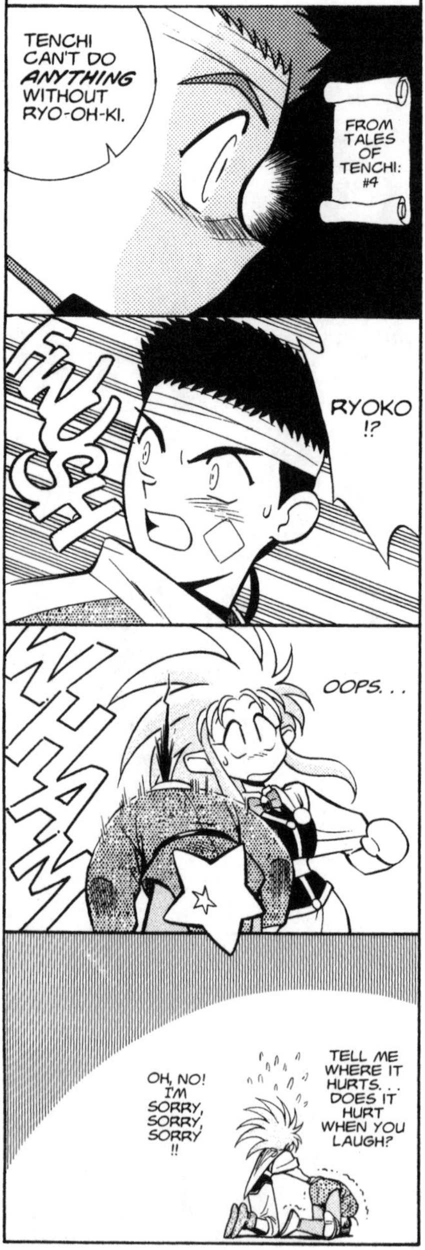
TENCHI CAN'T DO *ANYTHING* WITHOUT RYO-OH-KI.
FROM TALES OF TENCHI: #4
RYOKO !?
WHAM
OOPS. . .
OH, NO! I'M SORRY, SORRY, SORRY !!
TELL ME WHERE IT HURTS. . . DOES IT HURT WHEN YOU LAUGH?

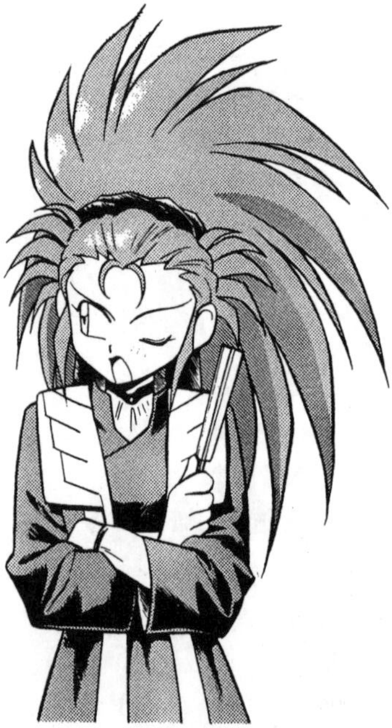

Tales of Tenchi #6

A GOOD SCOLDING

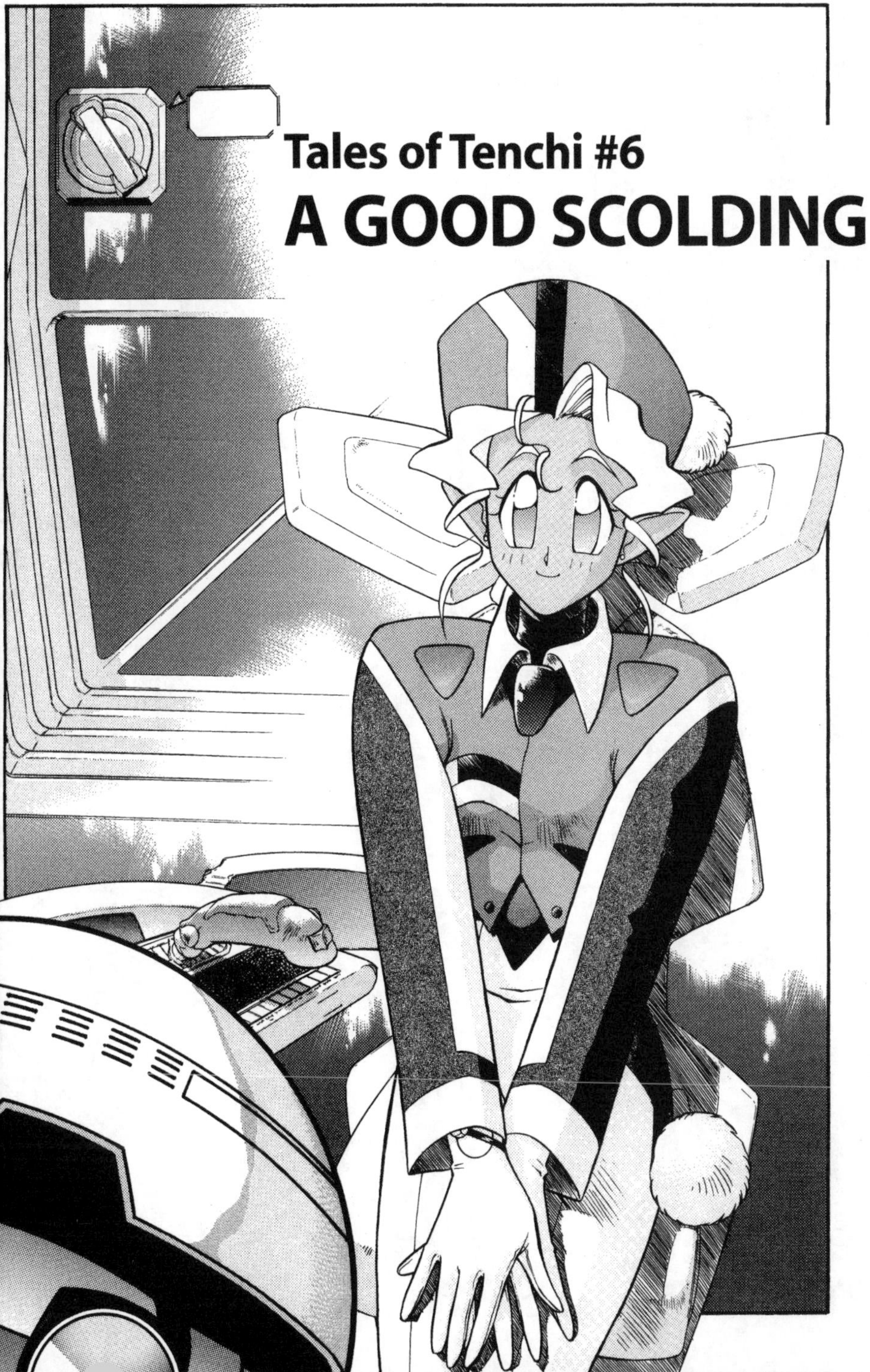

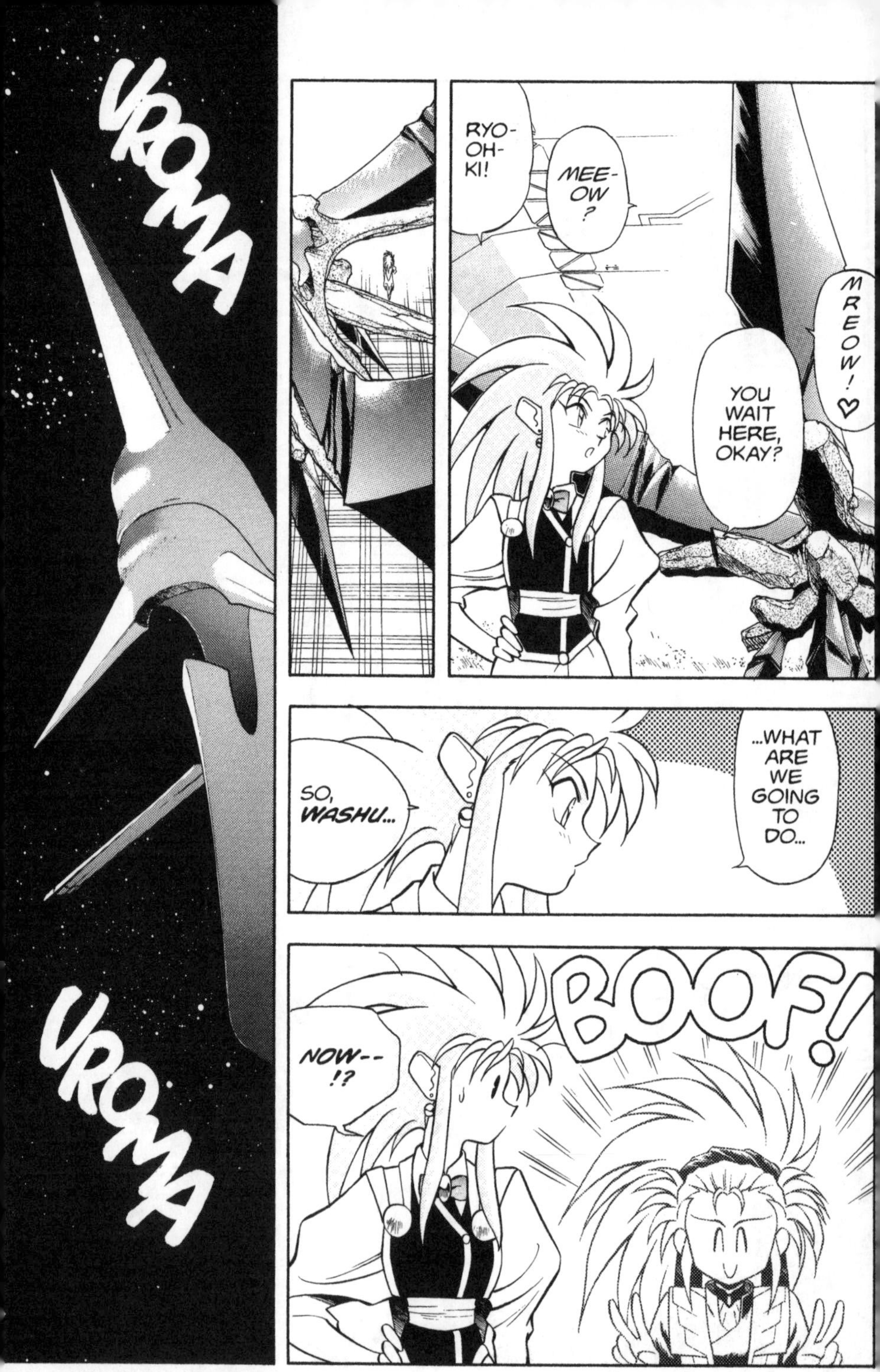
VROMA
VROMA
RYO-OH-KI!
MEE-OW?
YOU WAIT HERE, OKAY?
MREOW! ♥
SO, WASHU...
...WHAT ARE WE GOING TO DO...
NOW--!?
BOOF!

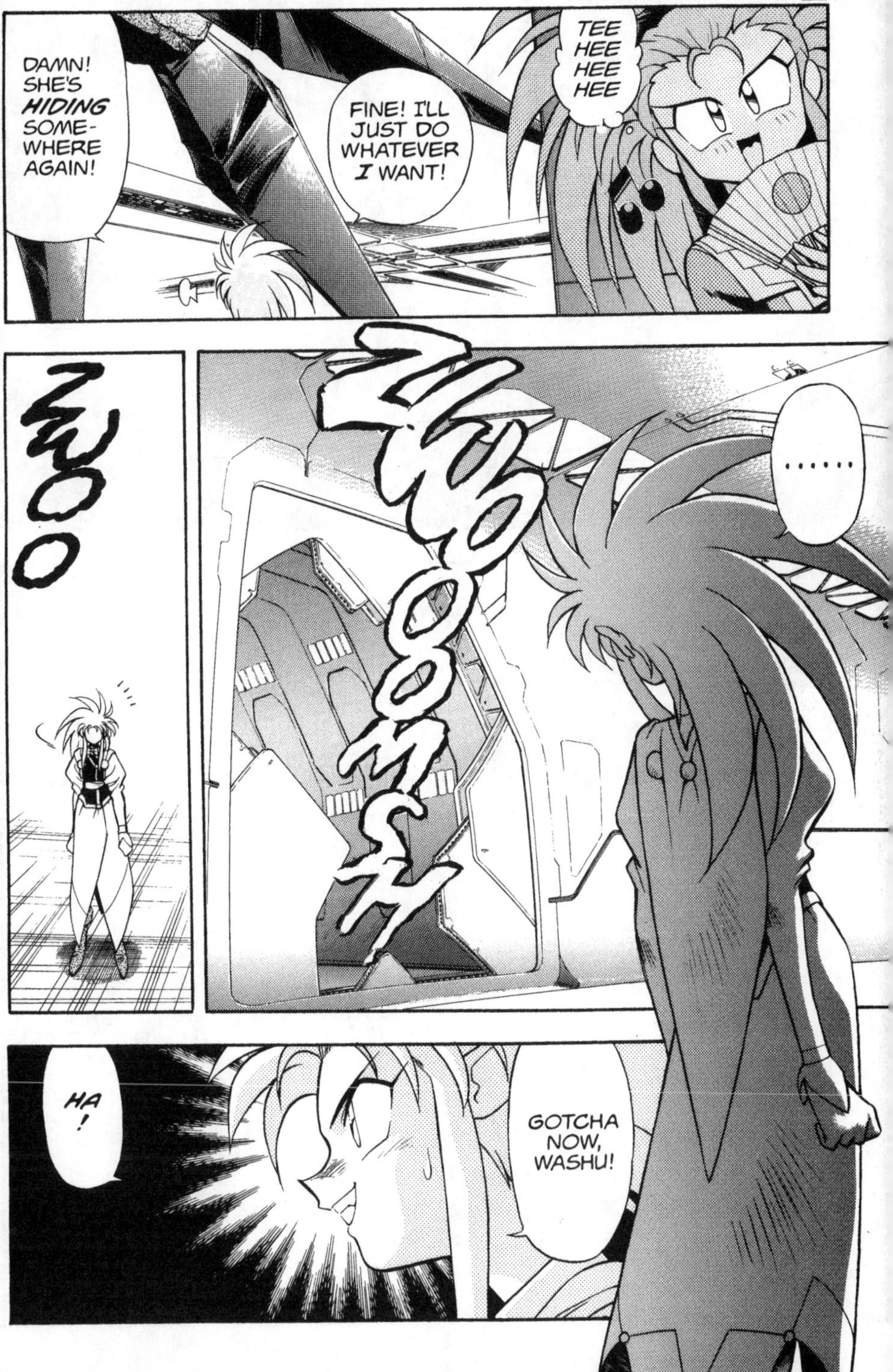
DAMN! SHE'S *HIDING* SOMEWHERE AGAIN!
FINE! I'LL JUST DO WHATEVER *I* WANT!
TEE HEE HEE HEE
ZWOO
ZWOOOOMSH
......
HA!
GOTCHA NOW, WASHU!

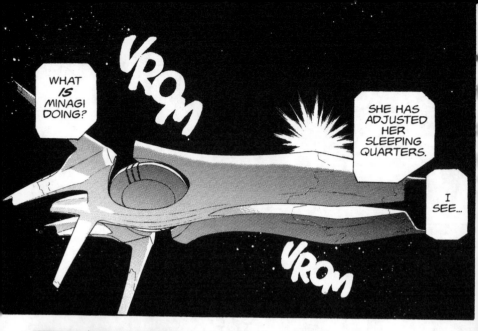

WHAT *IS* MINAGI DOING?

SHE HAS ADJUSTED HER SLEEPING QUARTERS.

I SEE...

VROM

VROM

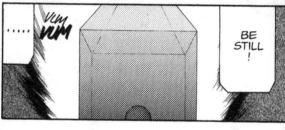

..... VLM NM

BE STILL !

BY THE WAY, MAIN UNIT...

OUR MASTER HAS BEEN TRYING TO CONTACT US. IS IT ALL RIGHT TO KEEP IGNORING HIM?

BUT...I DON'T UNDER-STAND!

MINAGI IS A CYBER-MARIONETTE, CREATED FOR OUR MASTER!

SHE SHOULDN'T JUST REMAIN IN THE AMNESIA STAGE!

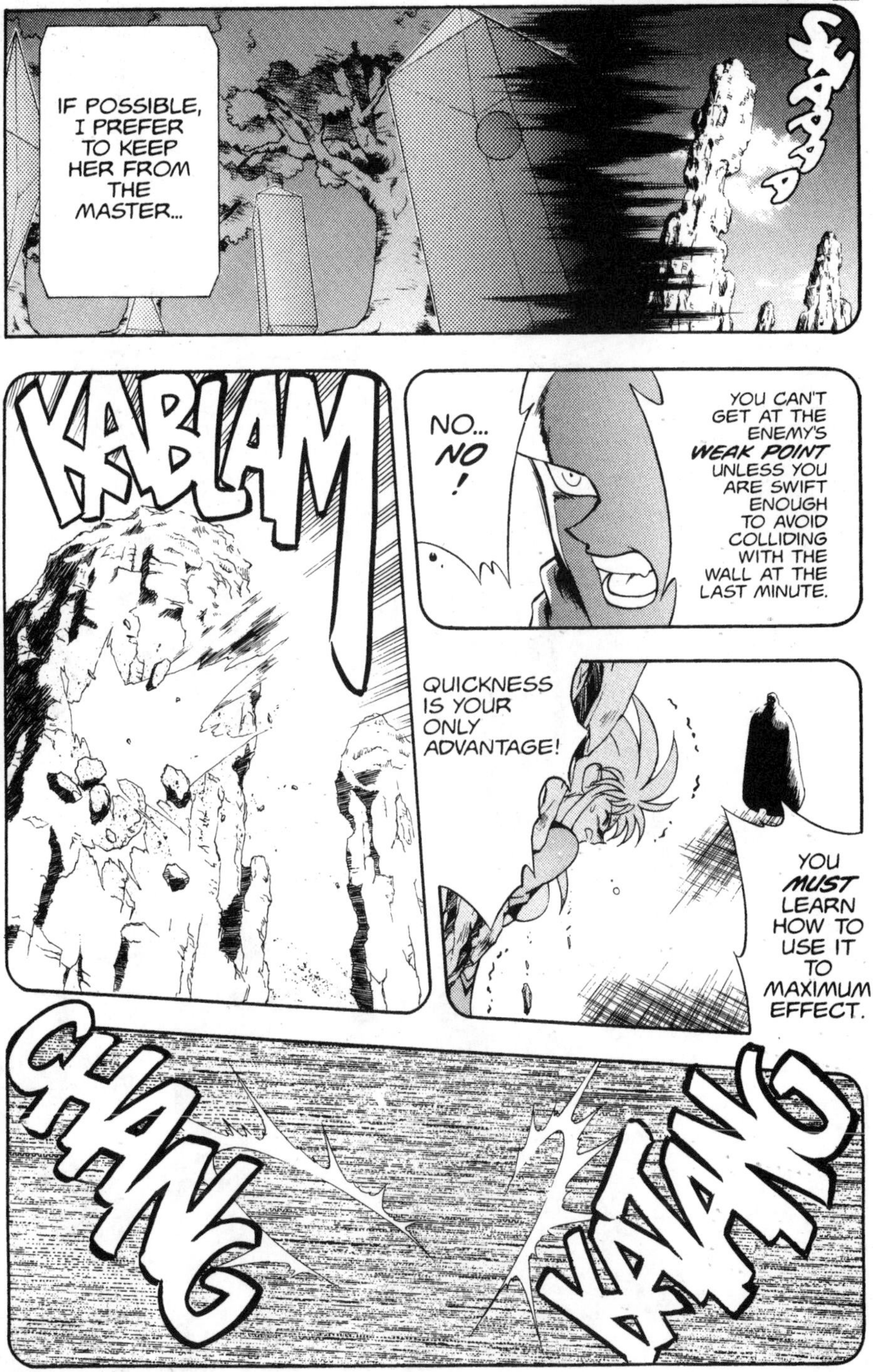
IF POSSIBLE, I PREFER TO KEEP HER FROM THE MASTER...
SHAPPA
KABLAM
NO... NO!
YOU CAN'T GET AT THE ENEMY'S WEAK POINT UNLESS YOU ARE SWIFT ENOUGH TO AVOID COLLIDING WITH THE WALL AT THE LAST MINUTE.
QUICKNESS IS YOUR ONLY ADVANTAGE!
YOU MUST LEARN HOW TO USE IT TO MAXIMUM EFFECT.
CHANG
KYANG

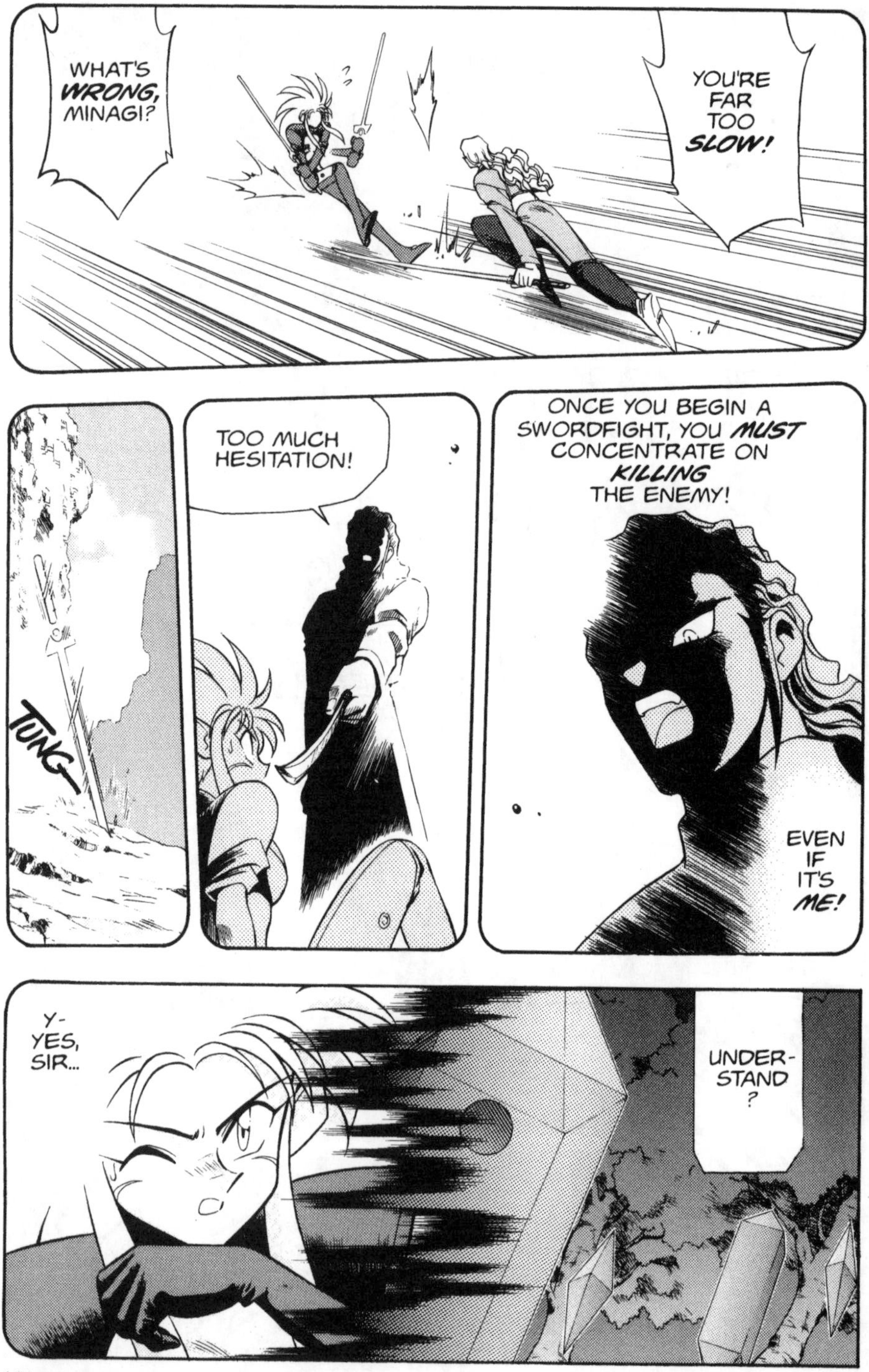
WHAT'S WRONG, MINAGI?
YOU'RE FAR TOO SLOW!
TUNG
TOO MUCH HESITATION!
ONCE YOU BEGIN A SWORDFIGHT, YOU MUST CONCENTRATE ON KILLING THE ENEMY!
EVEN IF IT'S ME!
Y-YES, SIR...
UNDER-STAND?

SHE'S BEEN THROUGH ENOUGH *HARDSHIP.* I THINK IT'S BETTER *NOT* TO GIVE HER MEMORIES BACK...

B-BUT... BRO-THER...

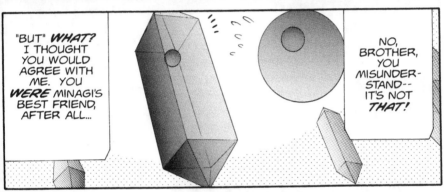

"BUT" *WHAT?* I THOUGHT YOU WOULD AGREE WITH ME. YOU *WERE* MINAGI'S BEST FRIEND, AFTER ALL...

NO, BROTHER, YOU MISUNDER-STAND-- IT'S NOT *THAT!*

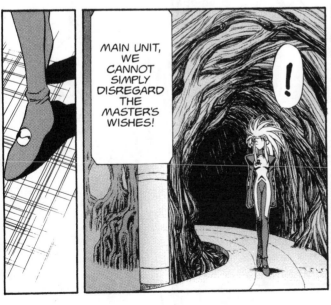

MAIN UNIT, WE CANNOT SIMPLY DISREGARD THE MASTER'S WISHES!

!

IT'S *HERESY!* DON'T YOU *REMEM-BER...?*

VREEEEEP

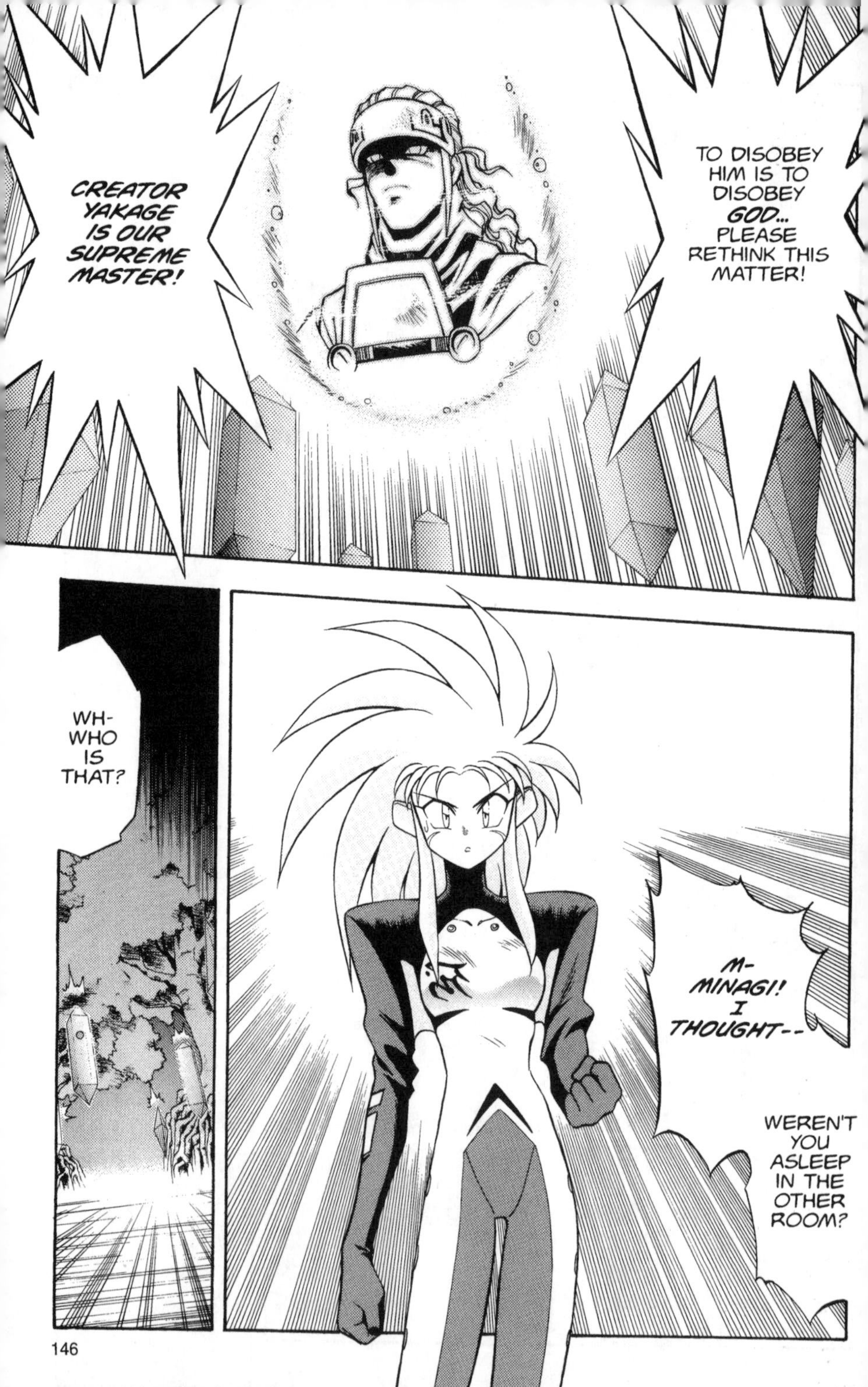
CREATOR YAKAGE IS OUR SUPREME MASTER!
TO DISOBEY HIM IS TO DISOBEY GOD... PLEASE RETHINK THIS MATTER!
WH-WHO IS THAT?
M-MINAGI! I THOUGHT--
WEREN'T YOU ASLEEP IN THE OTHER ROOM?

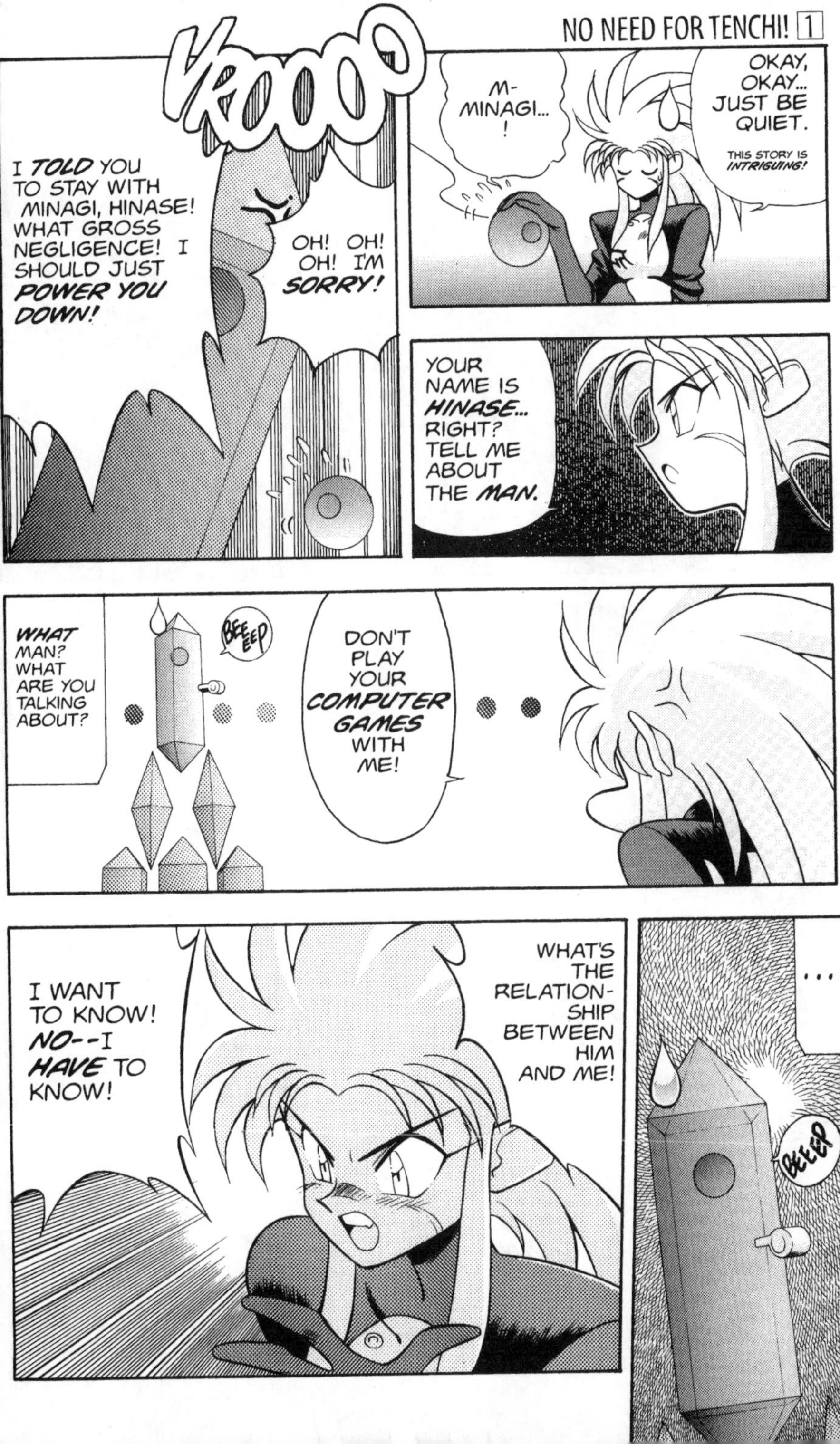
VROOOO
I TOLD YOU TO STAY WITH MINAGI, HINASE! WHAT GROSS NEGLIGENCE! I SHOULD JUST POWER YOU DOWN!
OH! OH! OH! I'M SORRY!
M-MINAGI... !
OKAY, OKAY... JUST BE QUIET.
THIS STORY IS INTRIGUING!
YOUR NAME IS HINASE... RIGHT? TELL ME ABOUT THE MAN.
WHAT MAN? WHAT ARE YOU TALKING ABOUT?
BEEEEP
DON'T PLAY YOUR COMPUTER GAMES WITH ME!
I WANT TO KNOW! NO--I HAVE TO KNOW!
WHAT'S THE RELATIONSHIP BETWEEN HIM AND ME!
.....
BEEEP

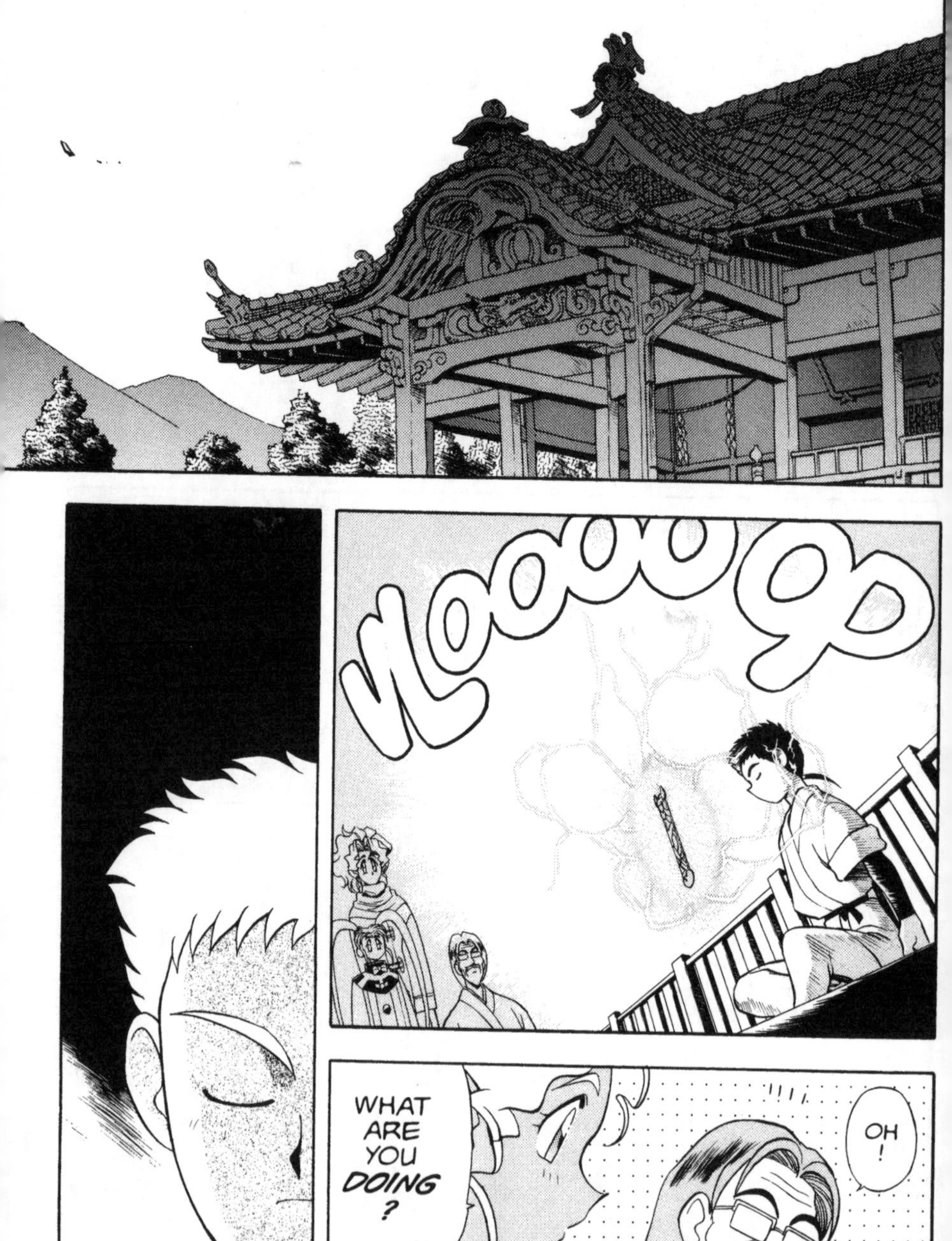
WOOOOP
WHAT ARE YOU *DOING*?
!!!
OH!

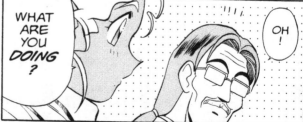

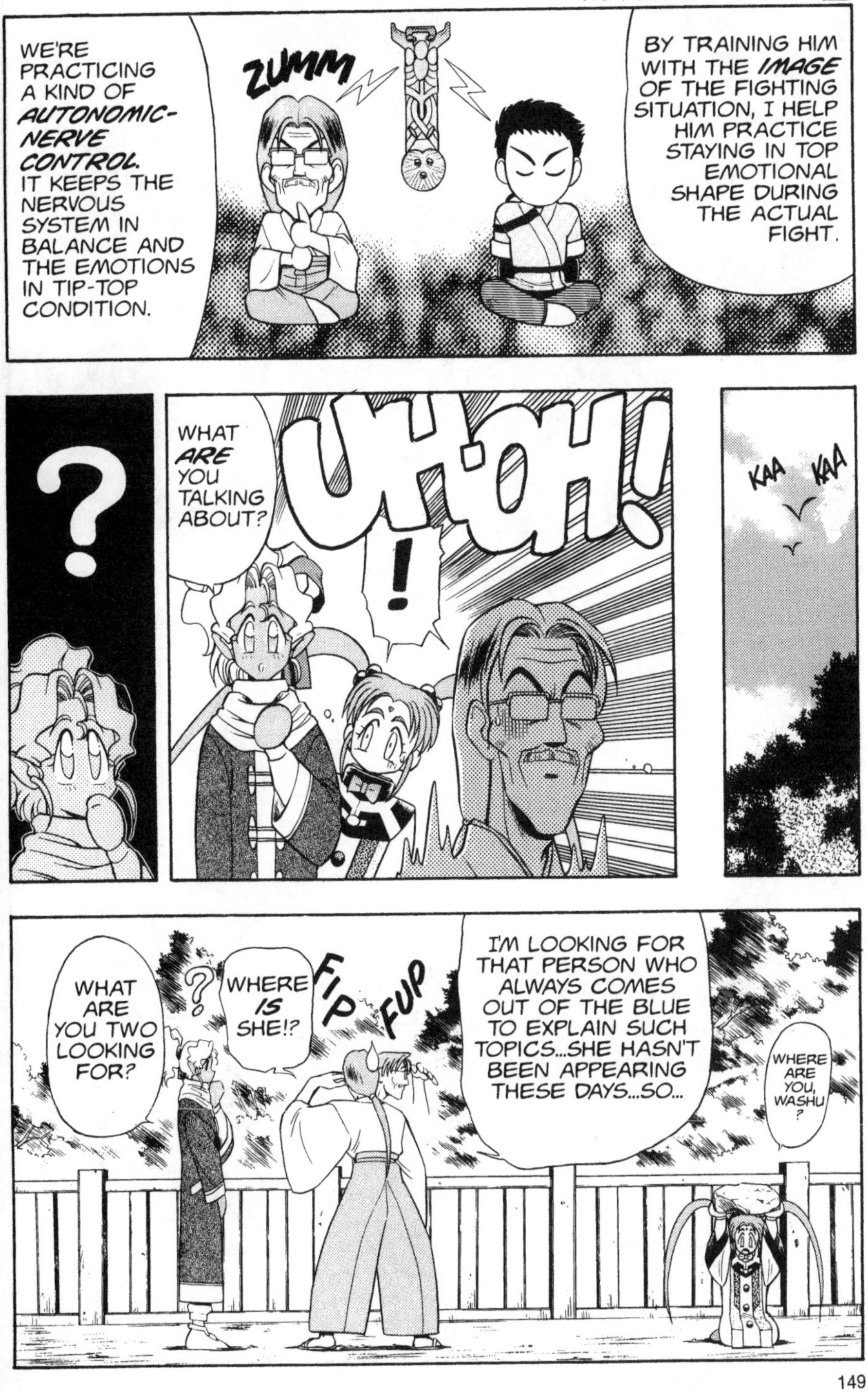
WE'RE PRACTICING A KIND OF AUTONOMIC-NERVE CONTROL. IT KEEPS THE NERVOUS SYSTEM IN BALANCE AND THE EMOTIONS IN TIP-TOP CONDITION.
ZUMM
BY TRAINING HIM WITH THE IMAGE OF THE FIGHTING SITUATION, I HELP HIM PRACTICE STAYING IN TOP EMOTIONAL SHAPE DURING THE ACTUAL FIGHT.
?
WHAT ARE YOU TALKING ABOUT?
UH-OH!
!
KAA KAA
WHAT ARE YOU TWO LOOKING FOR?
?
WHERE IS SHE!?
FIP FUP
I'M LOOKING FOR THAT PERSON WHO ALWAYS COMES OUT OF THE BLUE TO EXPLAIN SUCH TOPICS...SHE HASN'T BEEN APPEARING THESE DAYS...SO...
WHERE ARE YOU, WASHU?

WELL, IT'S UP TO *ME* THEN, I GUESS!

AHEM!

IT'S IMPORTANT TO KEEP A CALM HEAD DURING ANY FIGHT, BUT *TENCHI* IS NOT CAPABLE OF HANDLING SUCH INTENSE EMOTIONS.

USUALLY, PEOPLE MAINTAIN *BETA-WAVES* IN THEIR BRAIN DURING AN ALTERCATION, BUT TENCHI NEEDS TO INTENTIONALLY CREATE *ALPHA-WAVES* DURING A FIGHT.

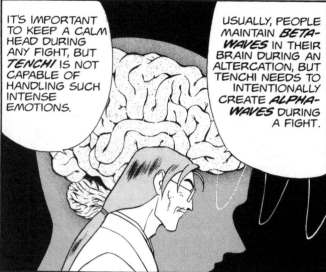

TENCHI! YOU *MUST* MASTER THIS!

uff

uff

uff

DAMN THAT WOODEN TOY!

THIS GUY→

uff

FWIP

FWUP

uff

WHERE'S IT COMING FROM *NEXT...?*

150

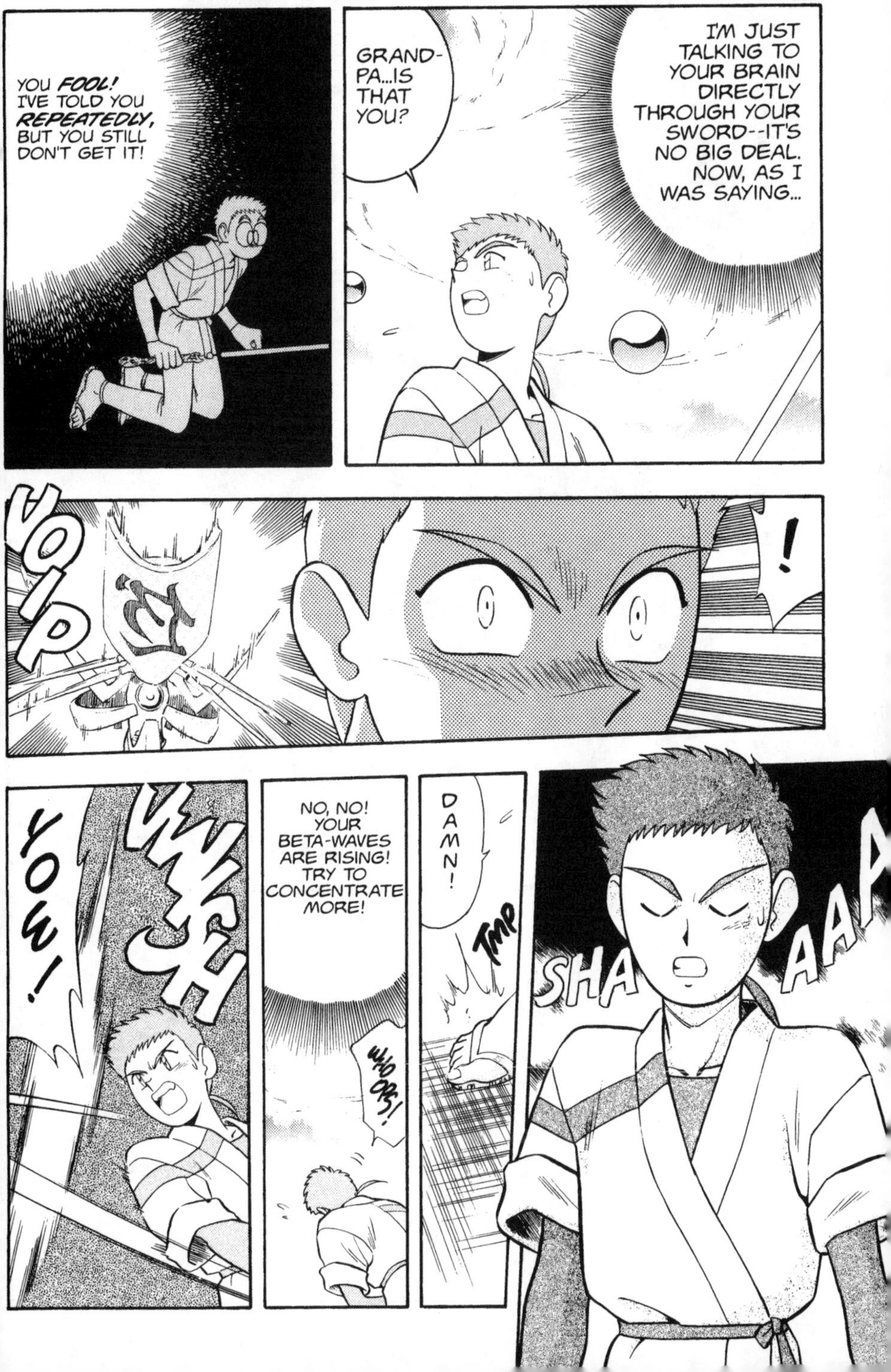
YOU FOOL! I'VE TOLD YOU REPEATEDLY, BUT YOU STILL DON'T GET IT!
GRAND-PA...IS THAT YOU?
I'M JUST TALKING TO YOUR BRAIN DIRECTLY THROUGH YOUR SWORD--IT'S NO BIG DEAL. NOW, AS I WAS SAYING...
VOIP
!
YOW!
NO, NO! YOUR BETA-WAVES ARE RISING! TRY TO CONCENTRATE MORE!
WHOOPS!
DAMN!
TMP
SHAAAA

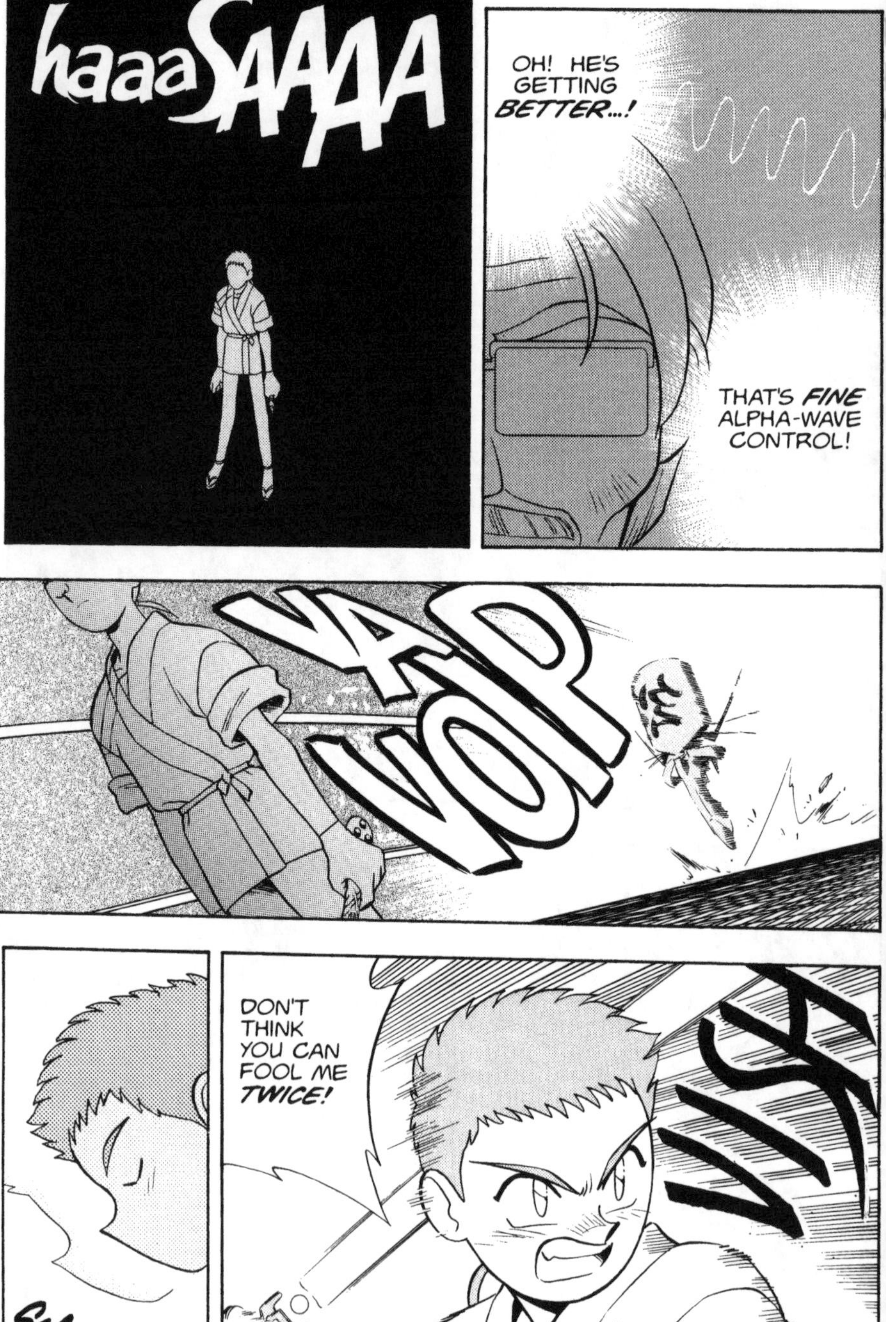
haaaSAAAA
OH! HE'S GETTING *BETTER...!*
THAT'S *FINE* ALPHA-WAVE CONTROL!
YA VOIP
SAAAA
DON'T THINK YOU CAN FOOL ME *TWICE!*
VISH

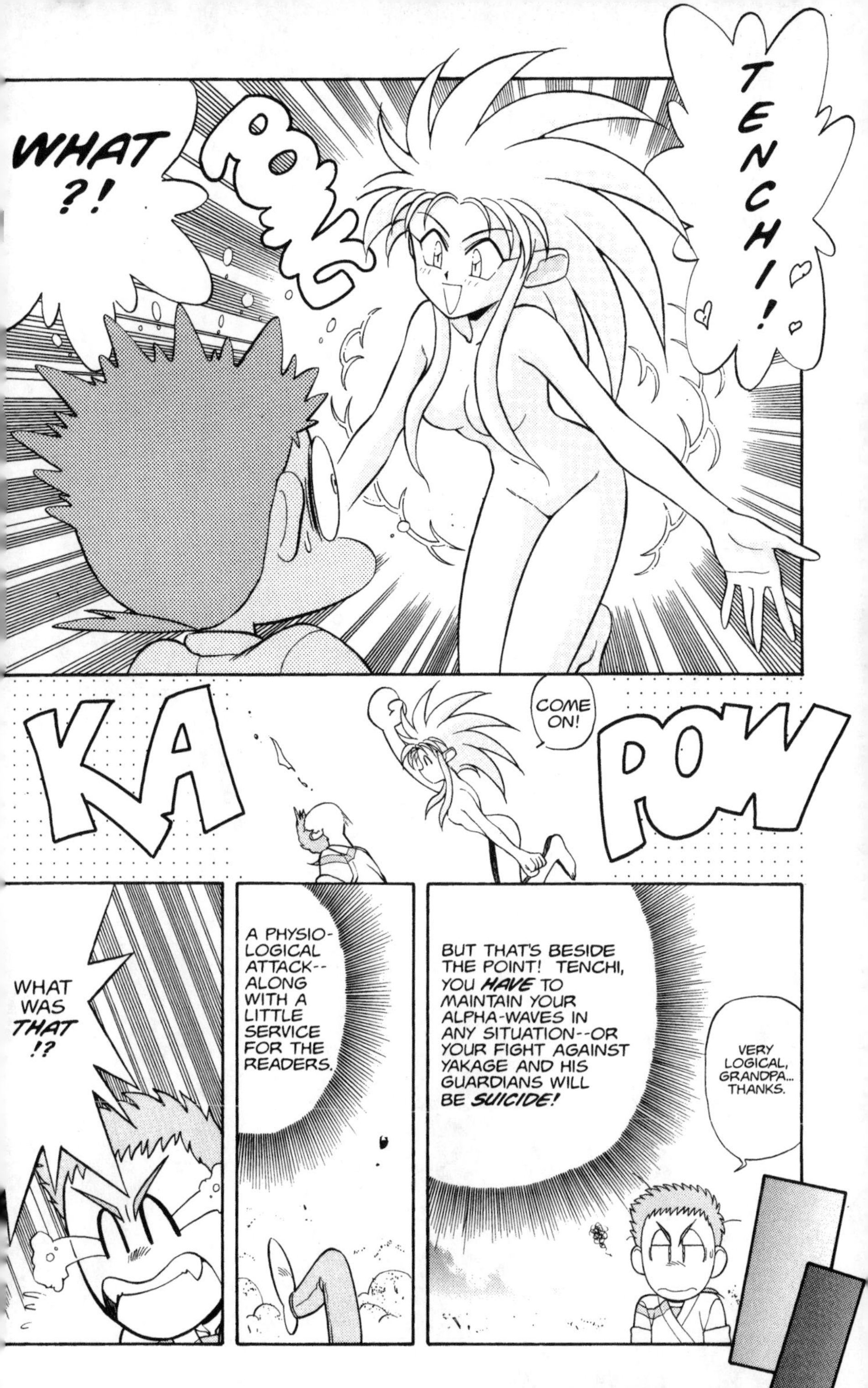
WHAT ?!
POW
TENCHI!
KA
COME ON!
POW
WHAT WAS THAT !?
A PHYSIO-LOGICAL ATTACK--ALONG WITH A LITTLE SERVICE FOR THE READERS.
BUT THAT'S BESIDE THE POINT! TENCHI, YOU *HAVE* TO MAINTAIN YOUR ALPHA-WAVES IN ANY SITUATION--OR YOUR FIGHT AGAINST YAKAGE AND HIS GUARDIANS WILL BE *SUICIDE!*
VERY LOGICAL, GRANDPA... THANKS.

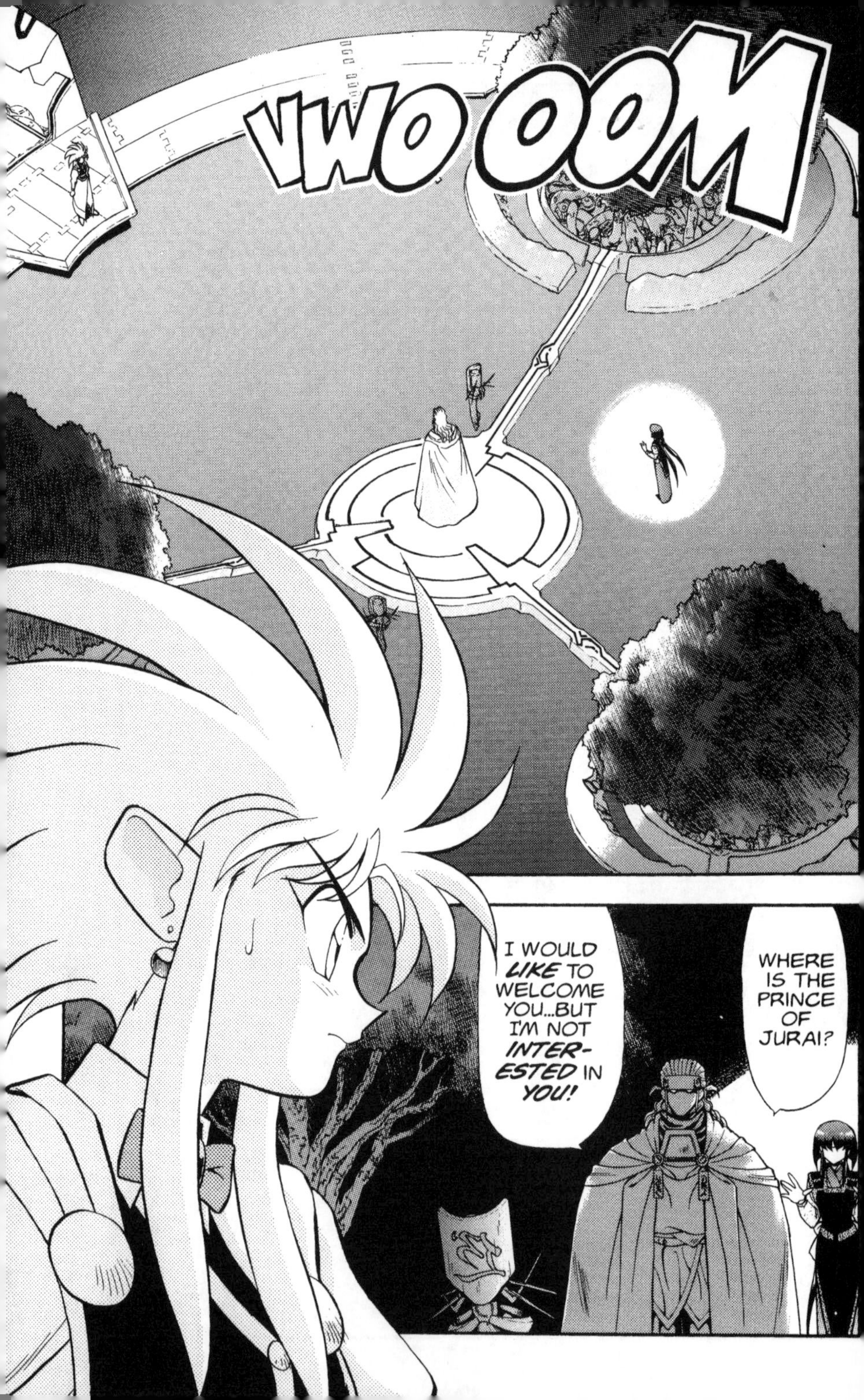
VWOOOM
I WOULD LIKE TO WELCOME YOU...BUT I'M NOT INTER-ESTED IN YOU!
WHERE IS THE PRINCE OF JURAI?

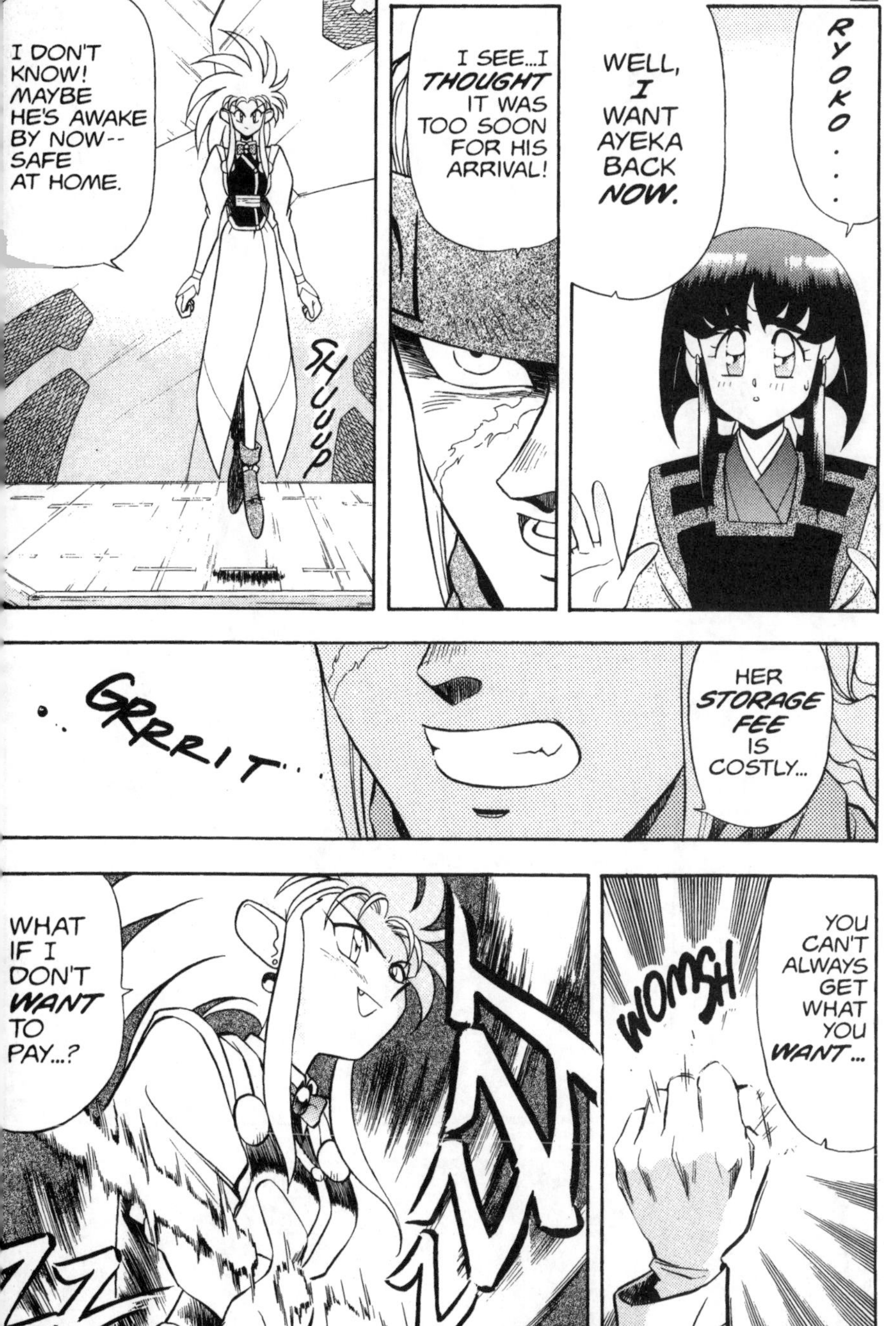
I DON'T KNOW! MAYBE HE'S AWAKE BY NOW-- SAFE AT HOME.
SHUUUP
I SEE...I THOUGHT IT WAS TOO SOON FOR HIS ARRIVAL!
WELL, I WANT AYEKA BACK NOW.
RYOKO...
GRRRIT...
HER STORAGE FEE IS COSTLY...
WHAT IF I DON'T WANT TO PAY...?
WOMSH
YOU CAN'T ALWAYS GET WHAT YOU WANT...

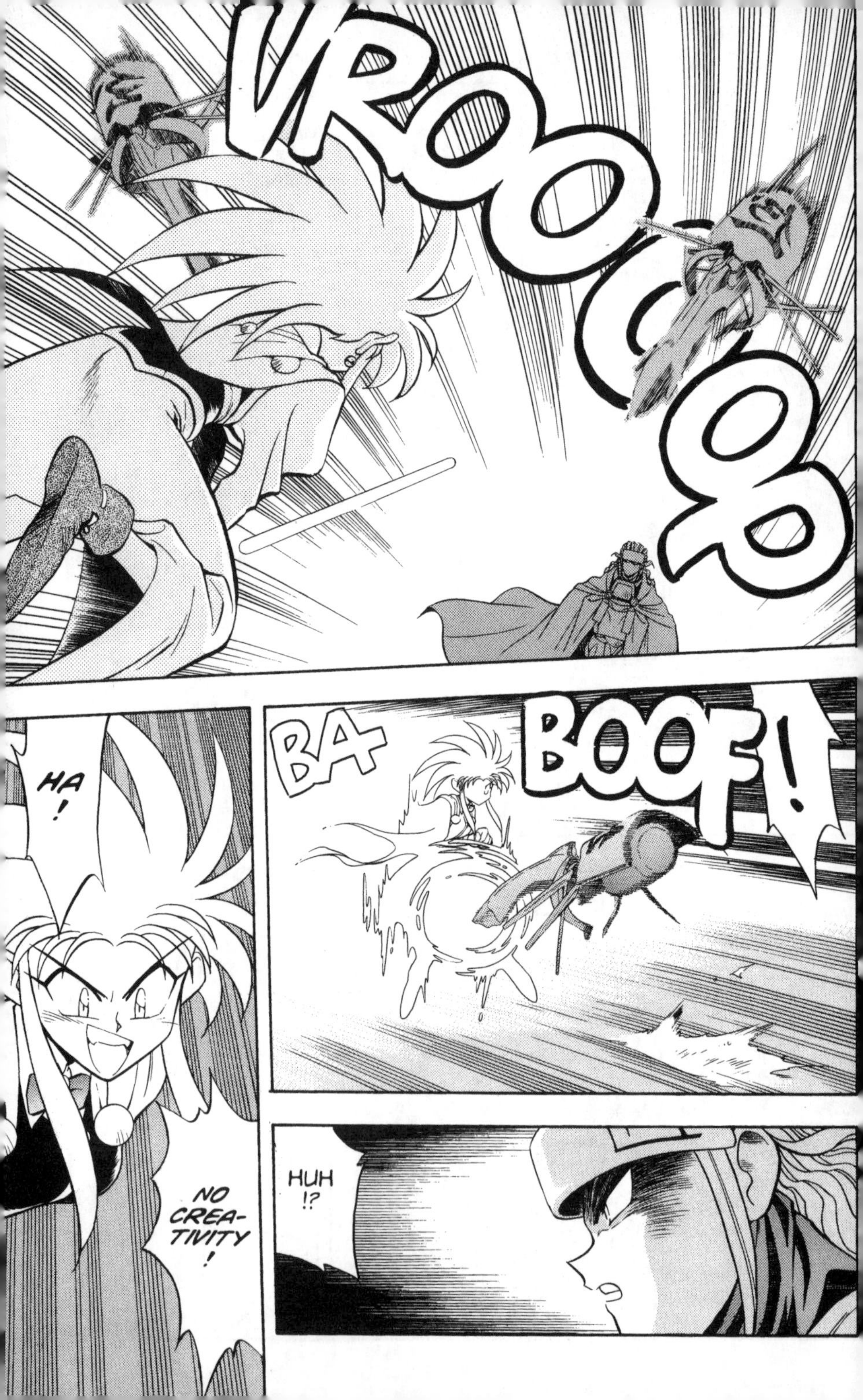
VROOOOOOP
HA!
NO CREA-TIVITY!
BA
BOOF!
HUH!?

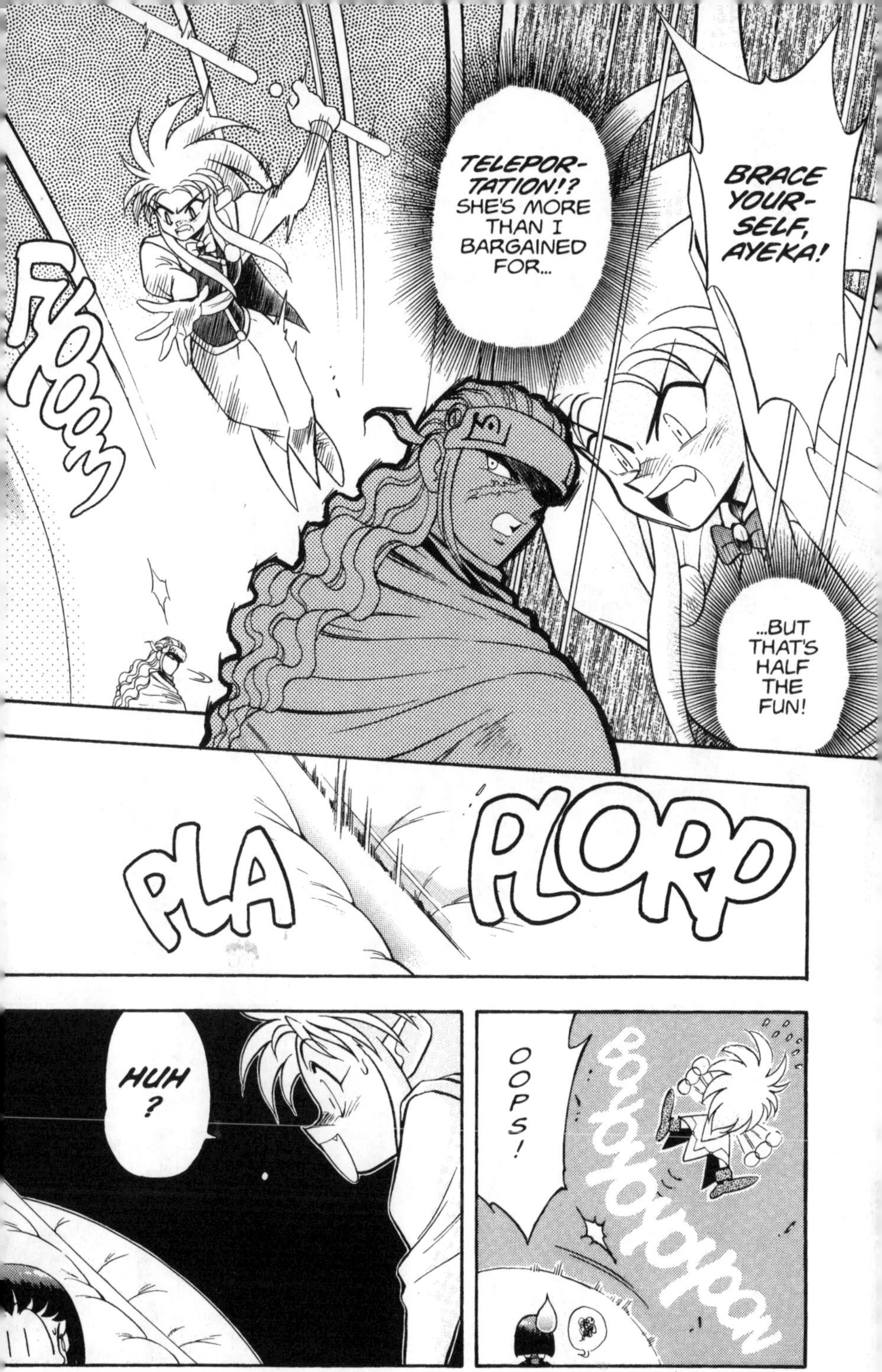
FZOOOM
TELEPORTATION!? SHE'S MORE THAN I BARGAINED FOR...
BRACE YOURSELF, AYEKA!
...BUT THAT'S HALF THE FUN!
PLA PLORP
HUH?
OOPS!

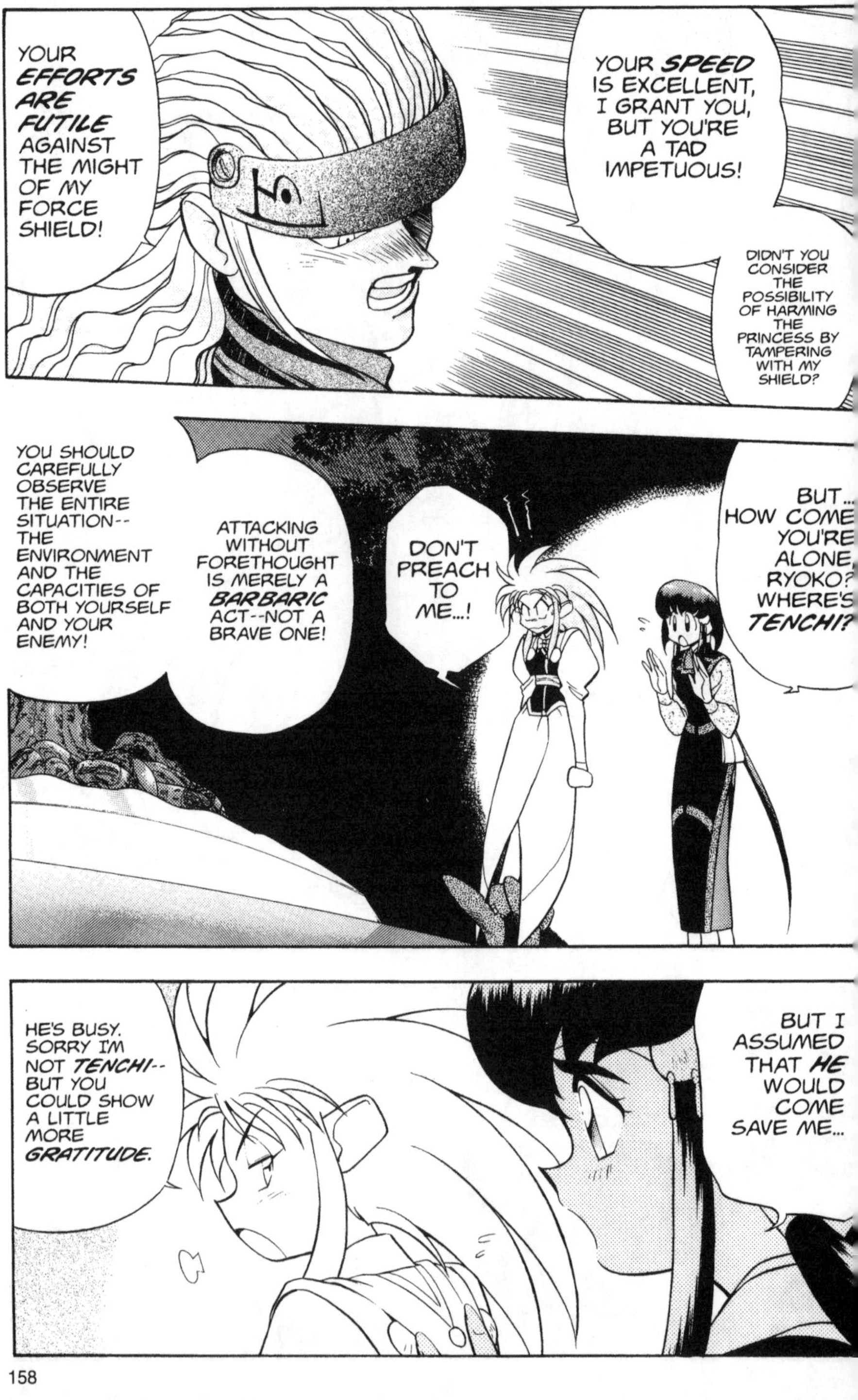
YOUR EFFORTS ARE FUTILE AGAINST THE MIGHT OF MY FORCE SHIELD!
YOUR SPEED IS EXCELLENT, I GRANT YOU, BUT YOU'RE A TAD IMPETUOUS!
DIDN'T YOU CONSIDER THE POSSIBILITY OF HARMING THE PRINCESS BY TAMPERING WITH MY SHIELD?
YOU SHOULD CAREFULLY OBSERVE THE ENTIRE SITUATION-- THE ENVIRONMENT AND THE CAPACITIES OF BOTH YOURSELF AND YOUR ENEMY!
ATTACKING WITHOUT FORETHOUGHT IS MERELY A BARBARIC ACT--NOT A BRAVE ONE!
DON'T PREACH TO ME...!
BUT... HOW COME YOU'RE ALONE, RYOKO? WHERE'S TENCHI?
HE'S BUSY. SORRY I'M NOT TENCHI-- BUT YOU COULD SHOW A LITTLE MORE GRATITUDE.
BUT I ASSUMED THAT HE WOULD COME SAVE ME...

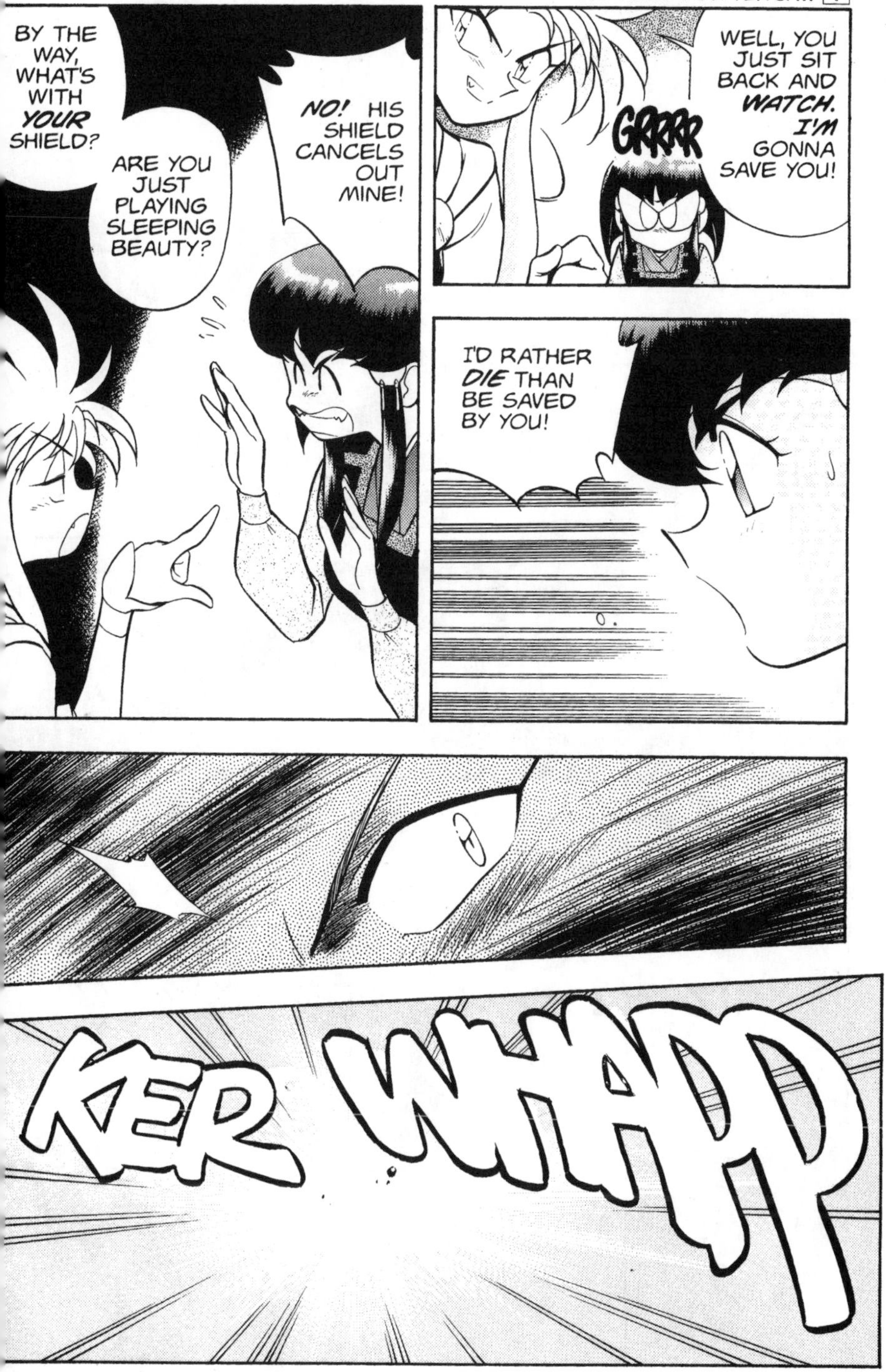
BY THE WAY, WHAT'S WITH *YOUR* SHIELD?
ARE YOU JUST PLAYING SLEEPING BEAUTY?
NO! HIS SHIELD CANCELS OUT MINE!
WELL, YOU JUST SIT BACK AND *WATCH. I'M* GONNA SAVE YOU!
GRRRR
I'D RATHER *DIE* THAN BE SAVED BY YOU!
KER WHAPP

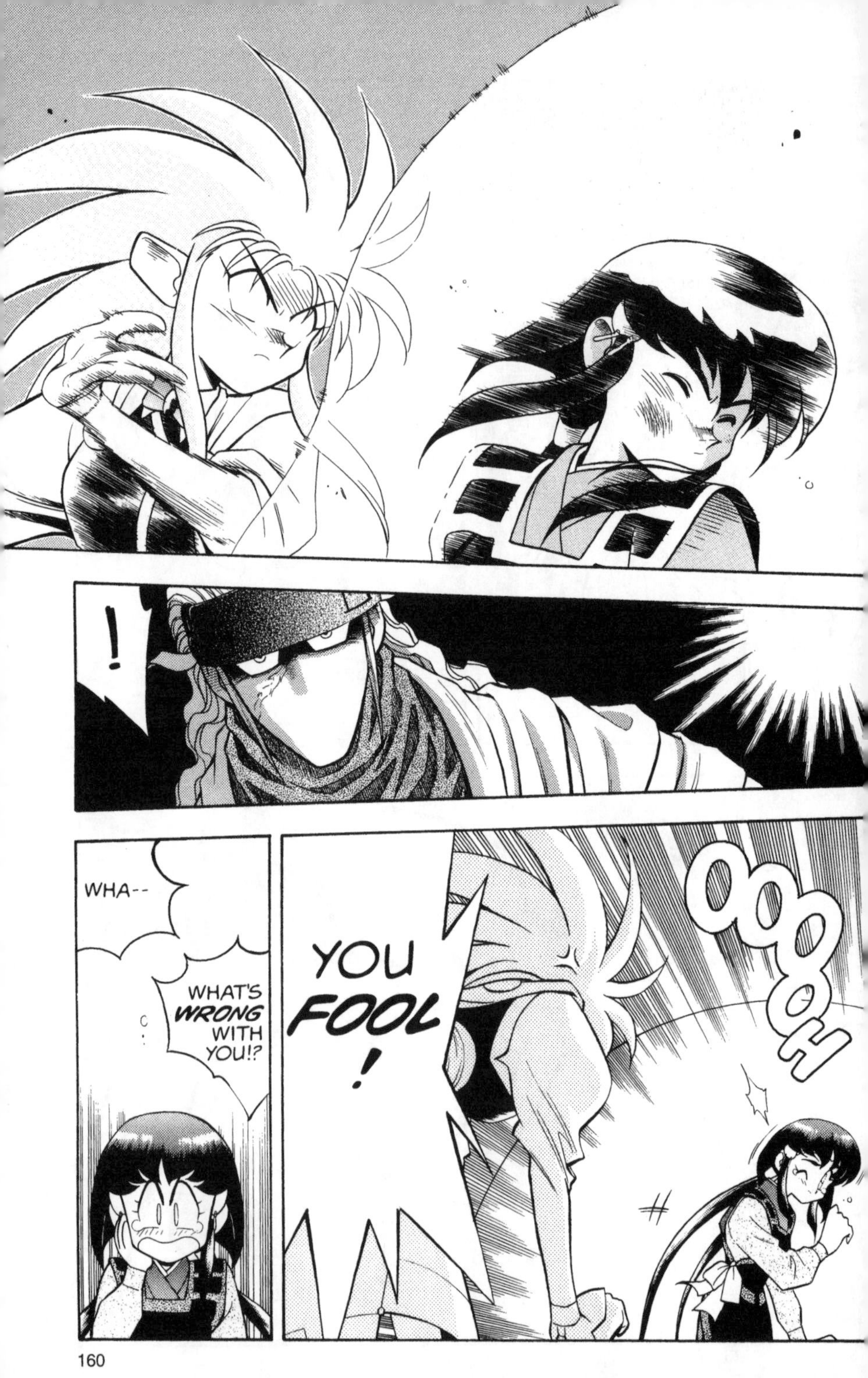
!
WHA--
WHAT'S **WRONG** WITH YOU!?
YOU **FOOL**!
OOOOH

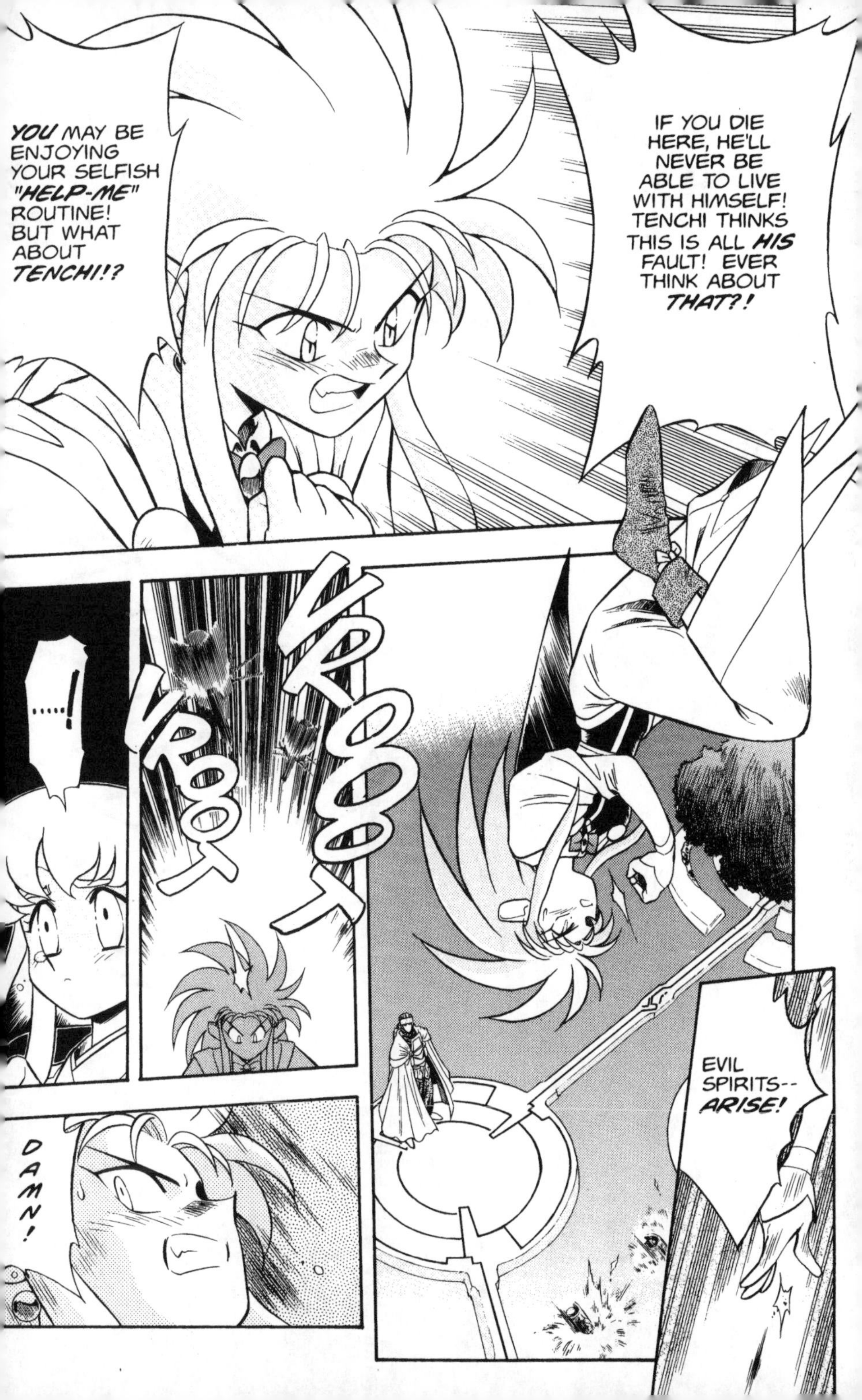

YOU MAY BE ENJOYING YOUR SELFISH "HELP-ME" ROUTINE! BUT WHAT ABOUT TENCHI!?
IF YOU DIE HERE, HE'LL NEVER BE ABLE TO LIVE WITH HIMSELF! TENCHI THINKS THIS IS ALL HIS FAULT! EVER THINK ABOUT THAT?!
......!
VROOOT
VROOOT
EVIL SPIRITS--ARISE!
DAMN!

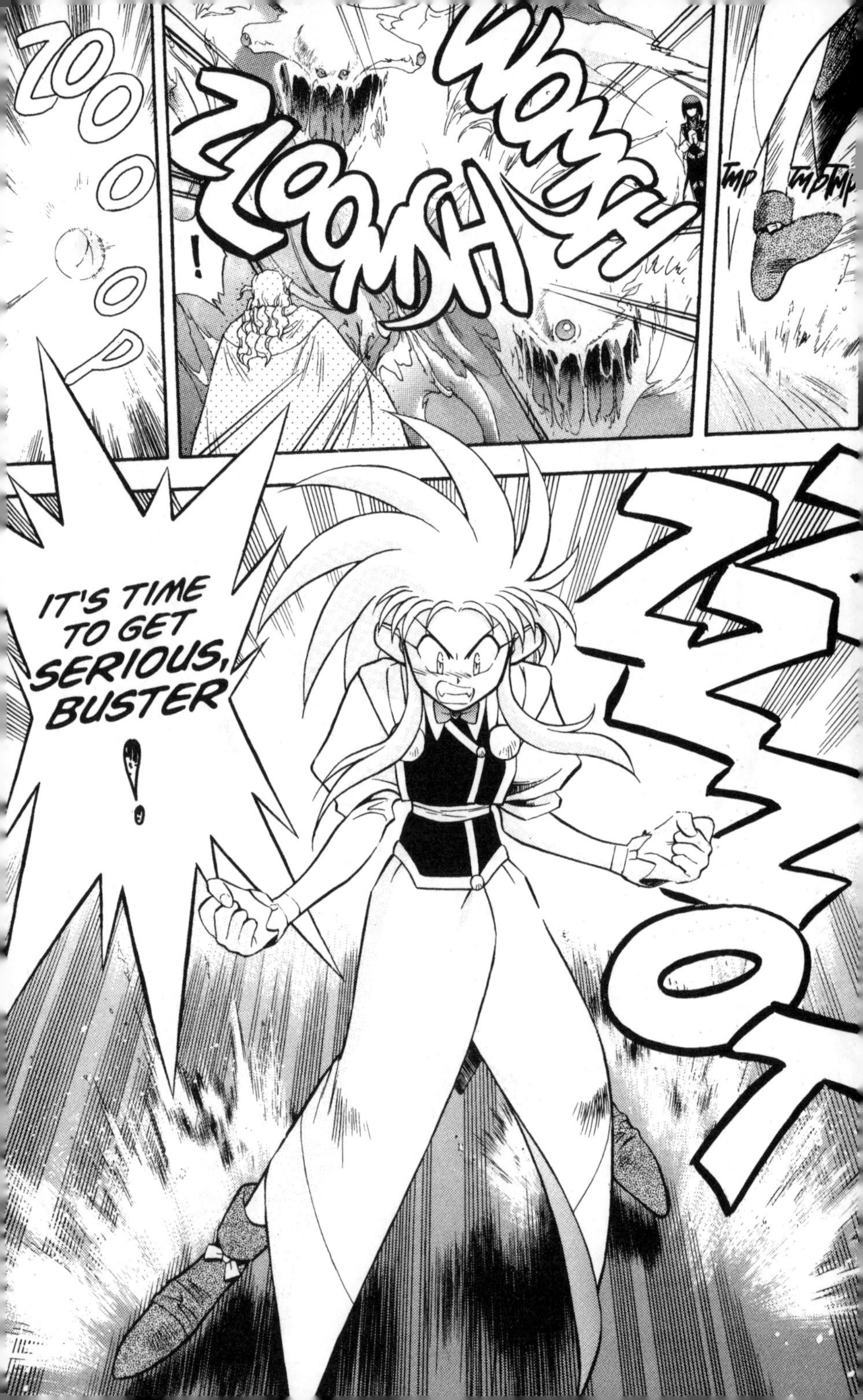
ZOOOOOP
ZLOOSH
!
TMP TMP TMP
IT'S TIME TO GET SERIOUS, BUSTER!

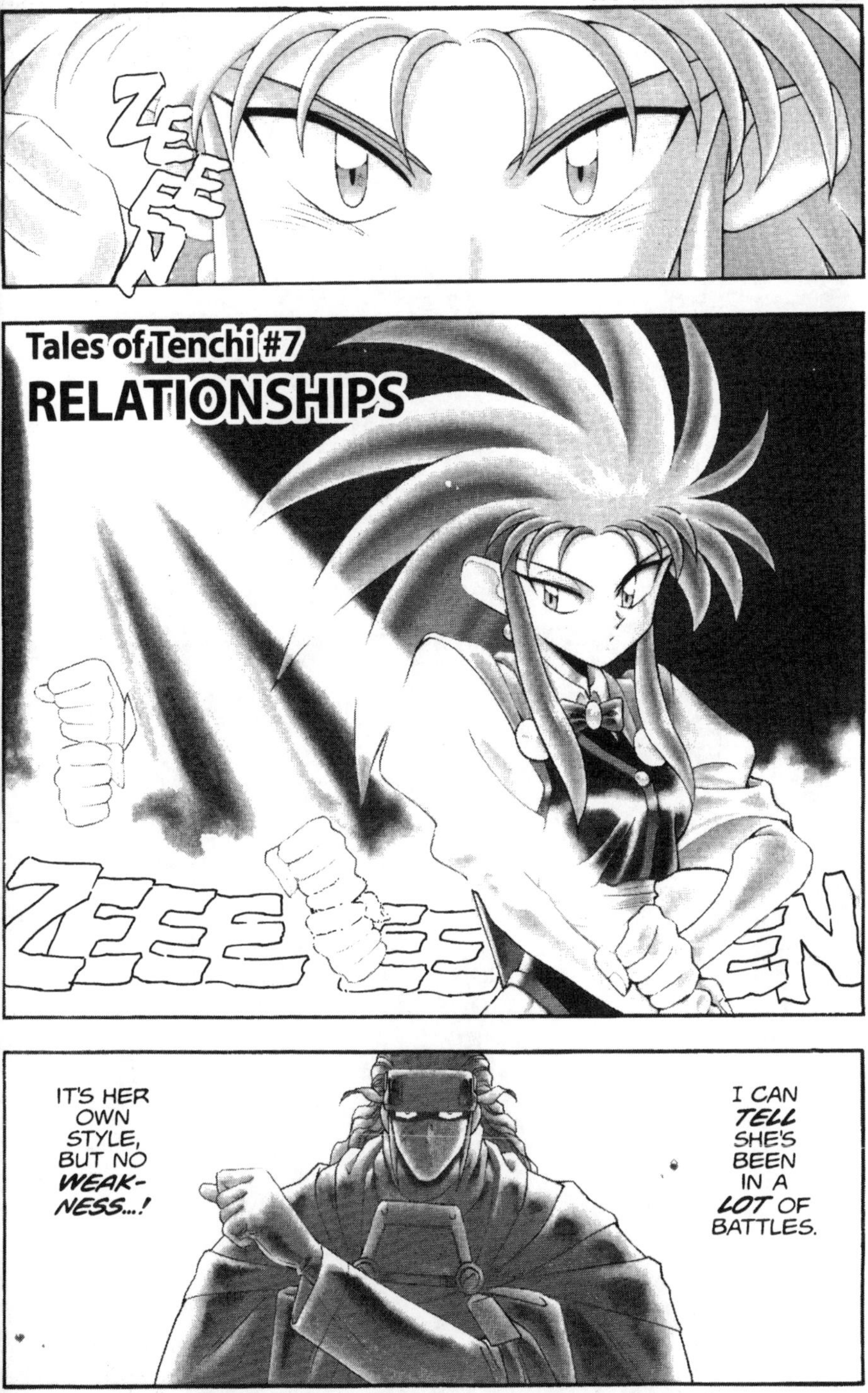
ZEEEN
Tales of Tenchi #7
RELATIONSHIPS
ZEEEEEEEEN
IT'S HER OWN STYLE, BUT NO WEAK-NESS...!
I CAN TELL SHE'S BEEN IN A LOT OF BATTLES.

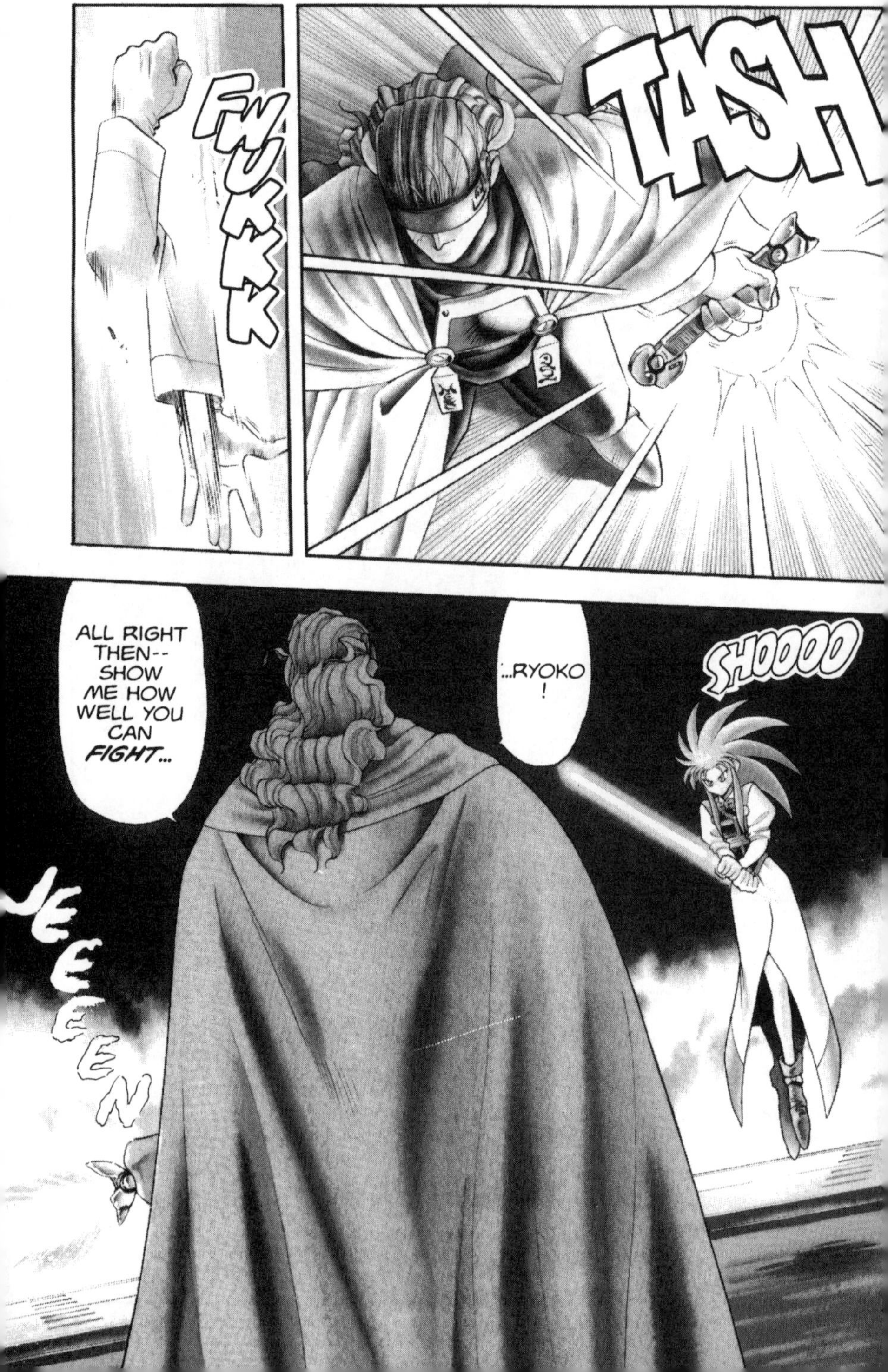
FWUKKKK
TASH
ALL RIGHT THEN--SHOW ME HOW WELL YOU CAN FIGHT...
...RYOKO!
SHOOOO
JEEEEN

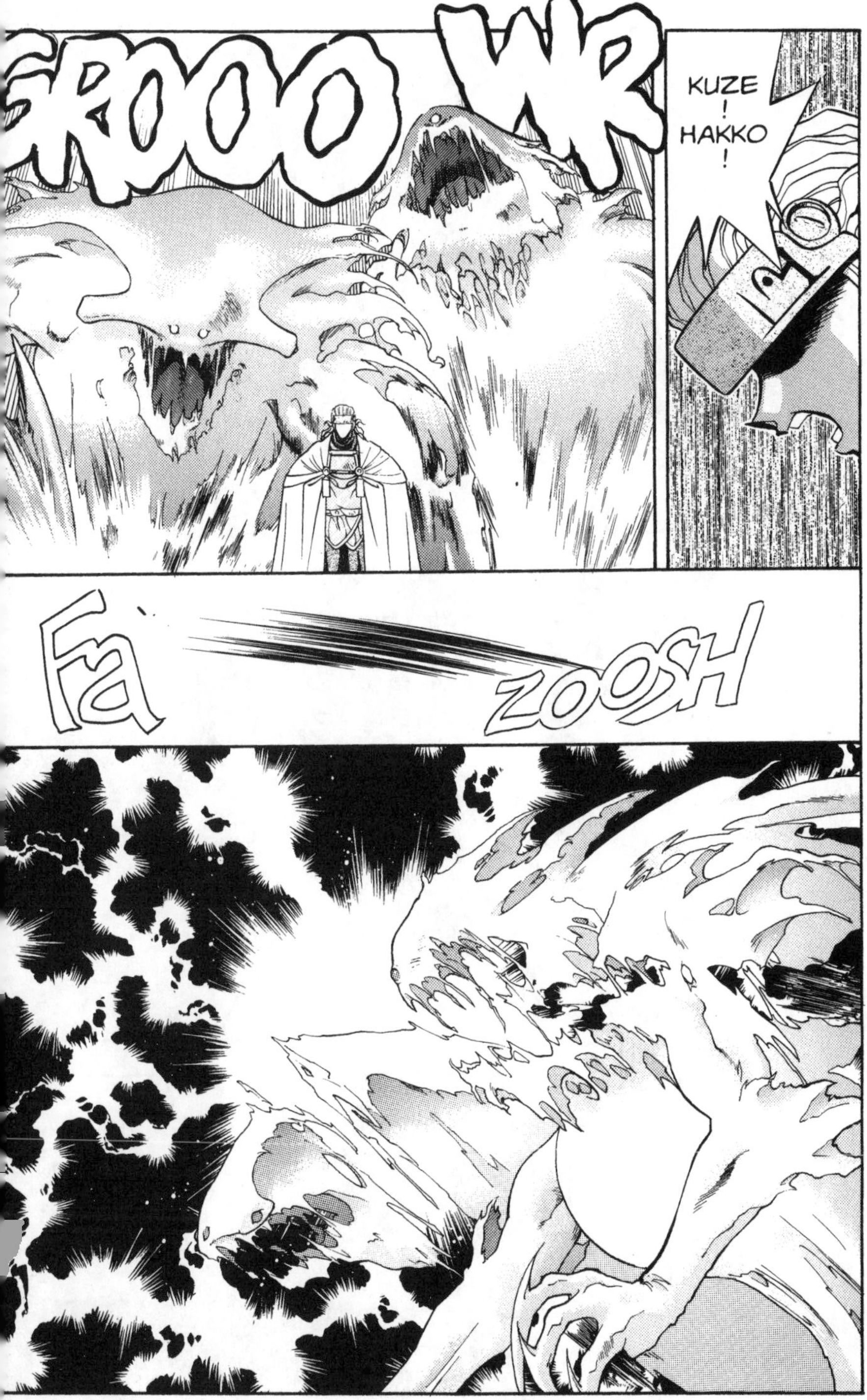
GROOOWR
KUZE! HAKKO!
Fa
ZOOSH

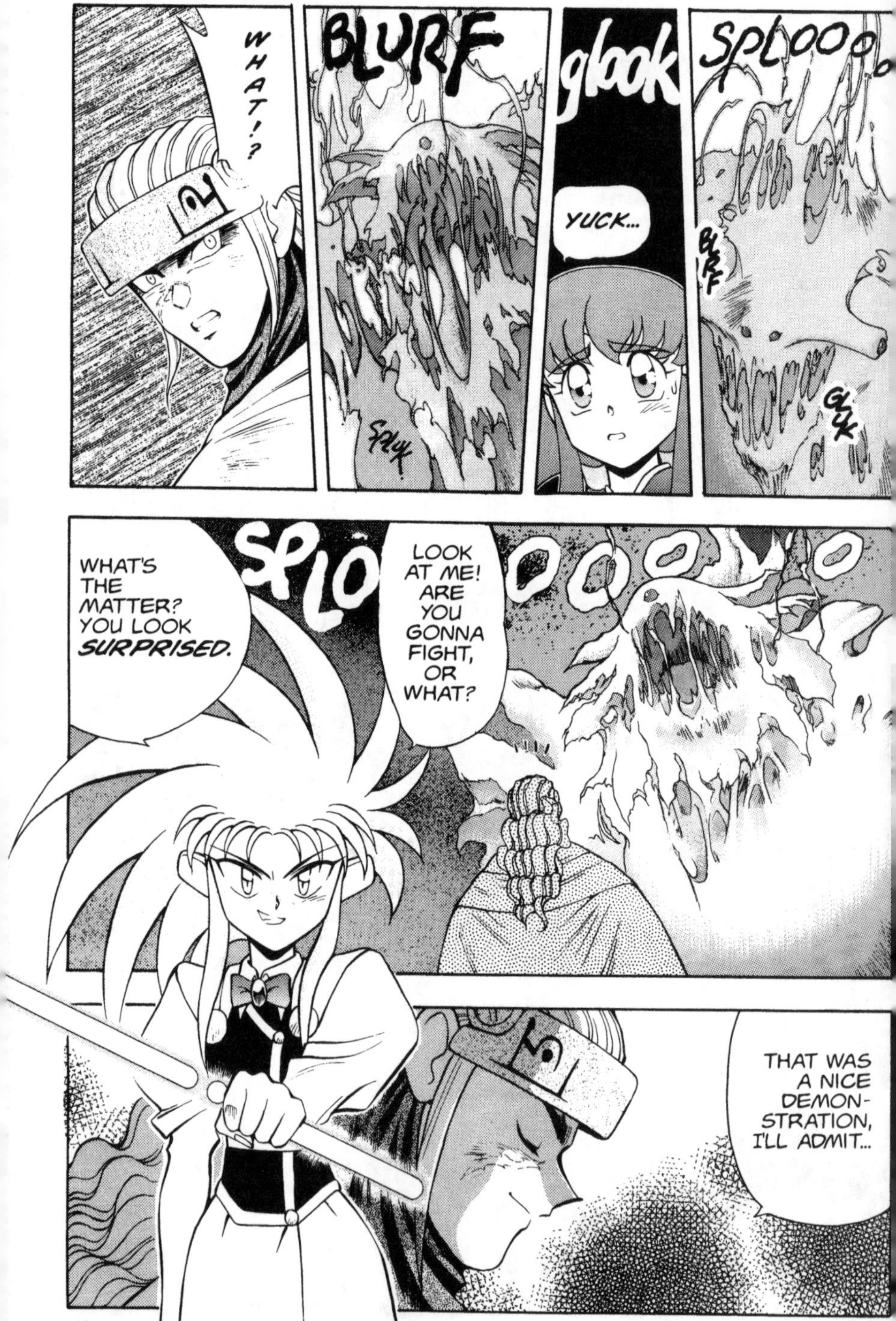
WHAT!?
BLURF
SPLUK
glook
YUCK...
SPLOOOoo
BLURF
GLUK
SPLOOOOOOO
WHAT'S THE MATTER? YOU LOOK **SURPRISED.**
LOOK AT ME! ARE YOU GONNA FIGHT, OR WHAT?
THAT WAS A NICE DEMON-STRATION, I'LL ADMIT...

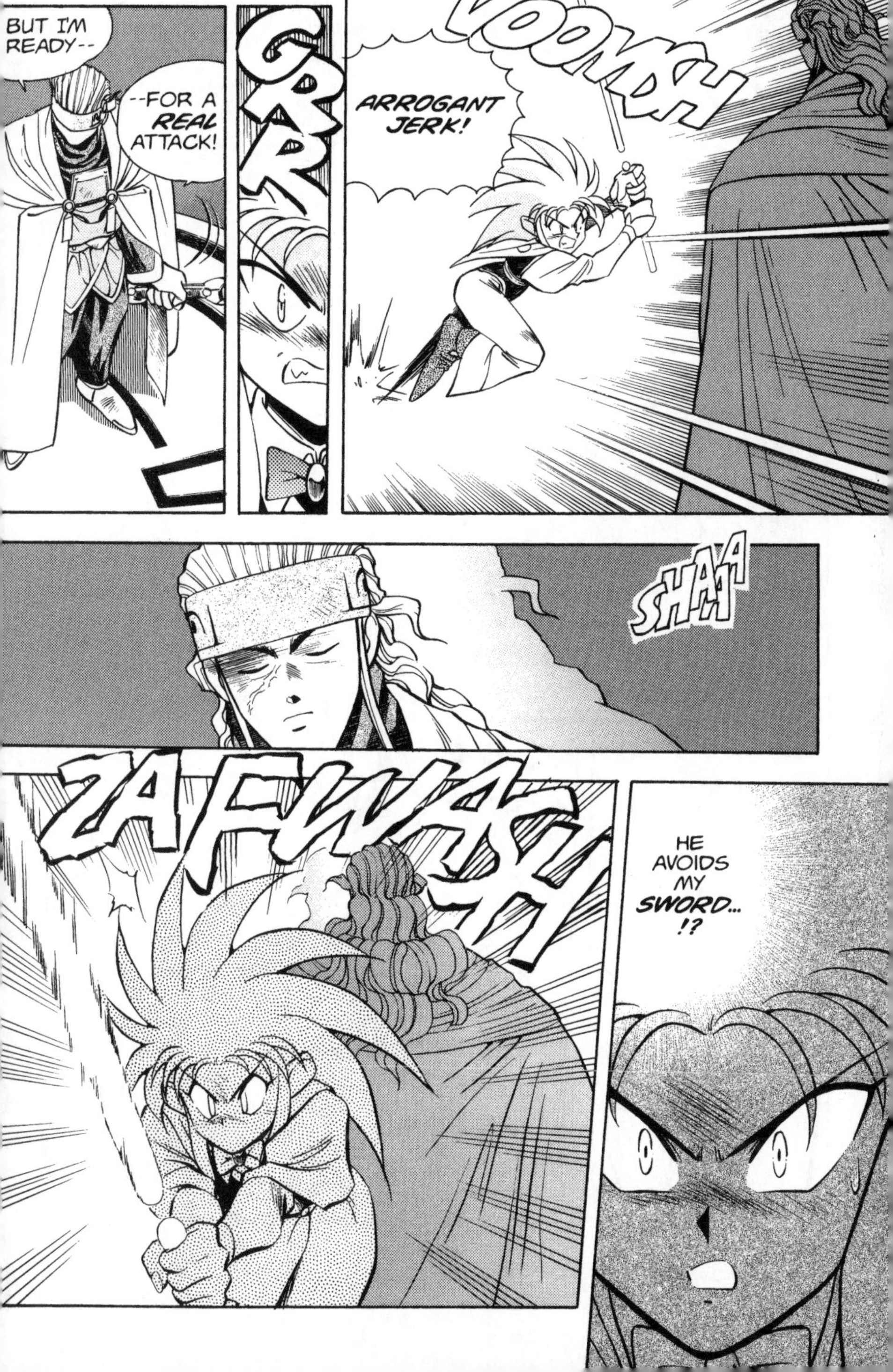
BUT I'M READY--
--FOR A REAL ATTACK!
GRRR
VOOMSH
ARROGANT JERK!
SHAAA
ZAFWASH
HE AVOIDS MY SWORD... !?

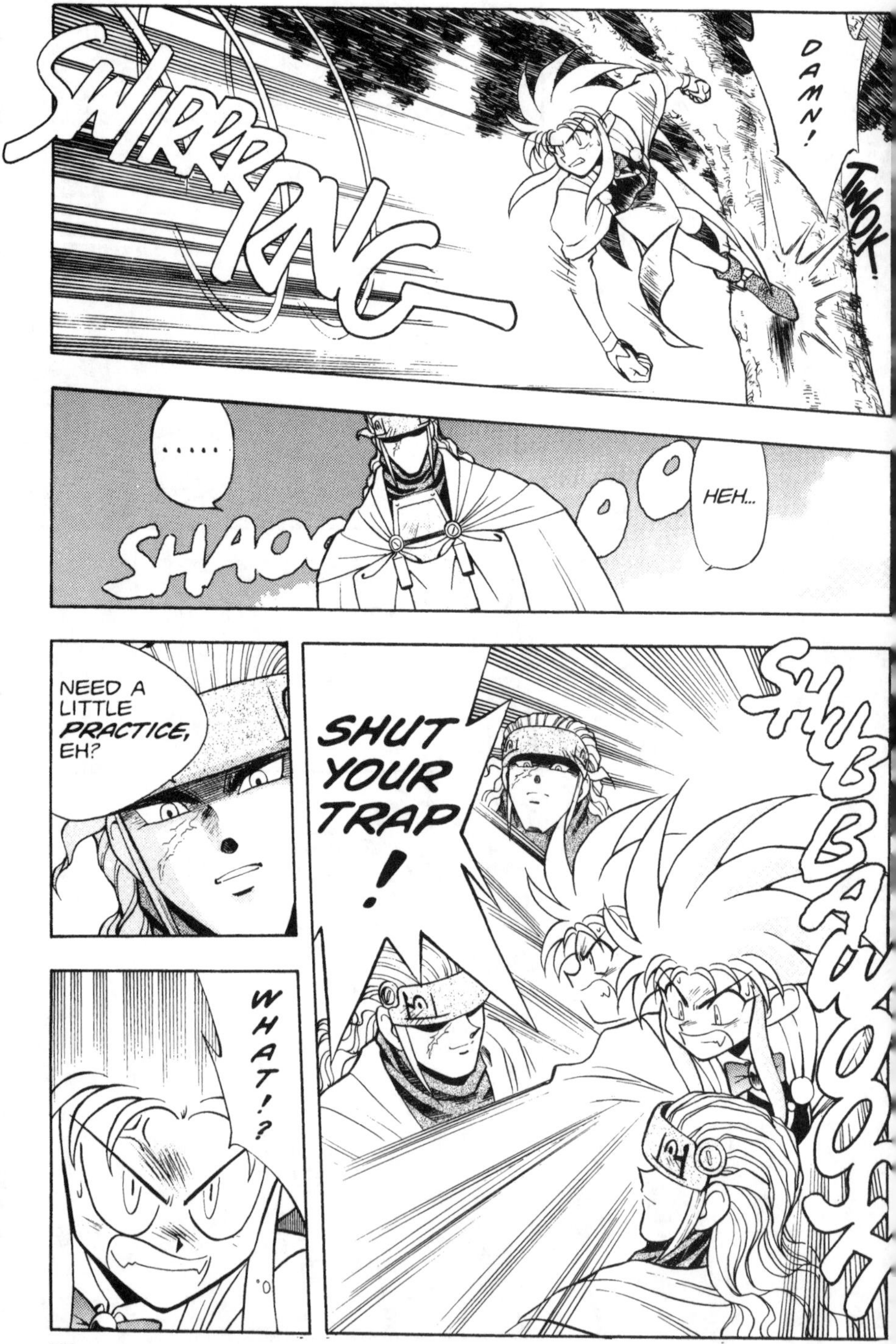
SWIRRRRING
DAMN!
TWOK!
......
SHAOOOO
HEH...
NEED A LITTLE *PRACTICE*, EH?
SHUT YOUR TRAP!
SHUBBABOOOM
WHAT!?

ALL THIS *UNNECESSARY MOTION!*

AS SOON AS YOUR FIRST ATTACK IS DODGED, YOU MUST CHANGE GEARS *IMMEDIATELY.*

DON'T TELL ME WHAT TO DO!

KATANG

CHANG

POW

HEH...

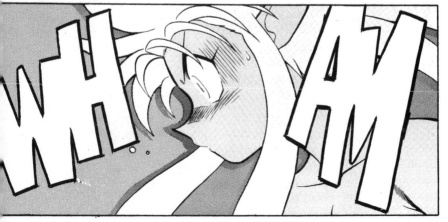

WHAM

169

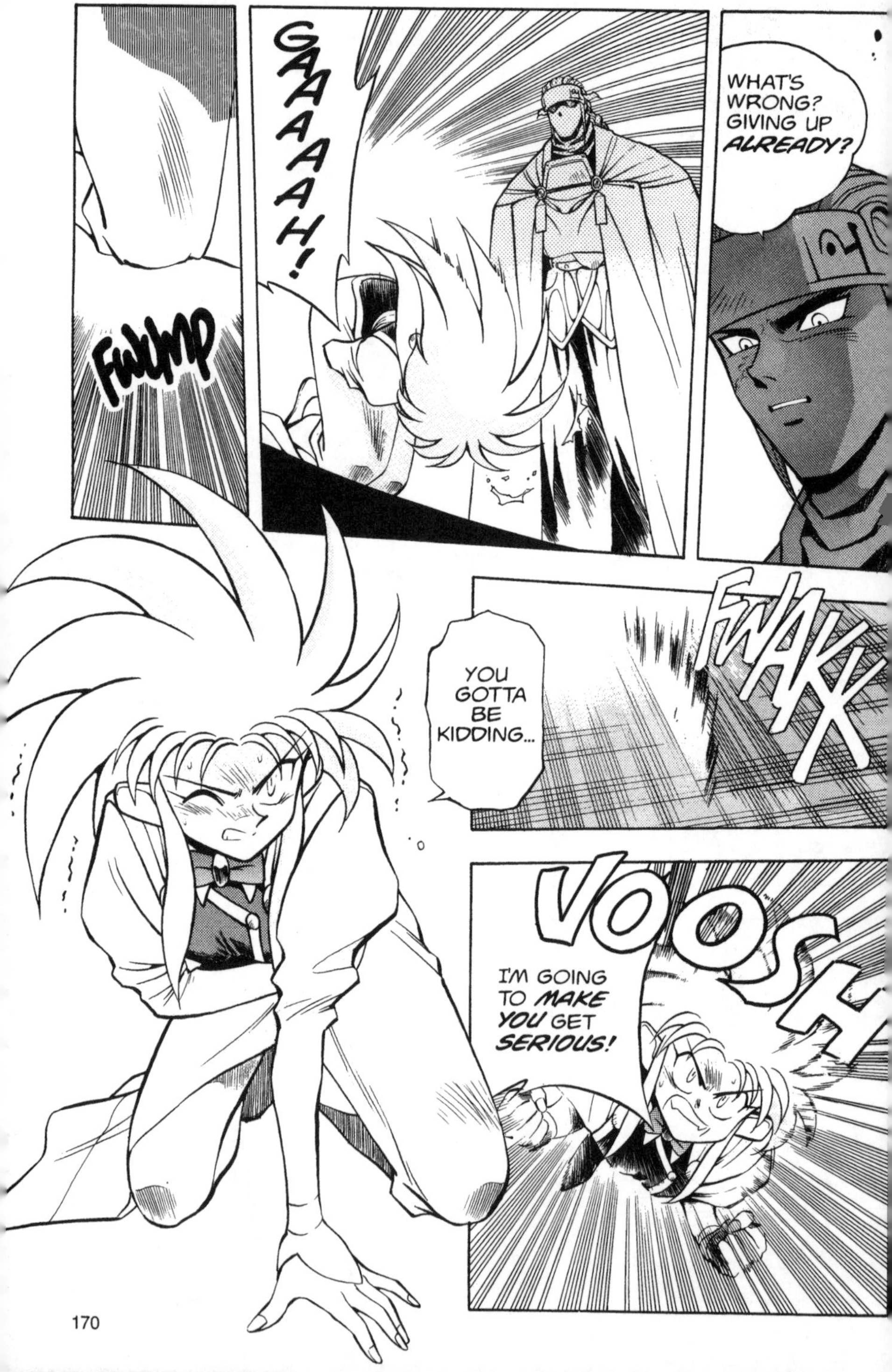
FWUMP
GAAAAAAH!
WHAT'S WRONG? GIVING UP ALREADY?
YOU GOTTA BE KIDDING...
FWAKK
VOOSH
I'M GOING TO MAKE YOU GET SERIOUS!

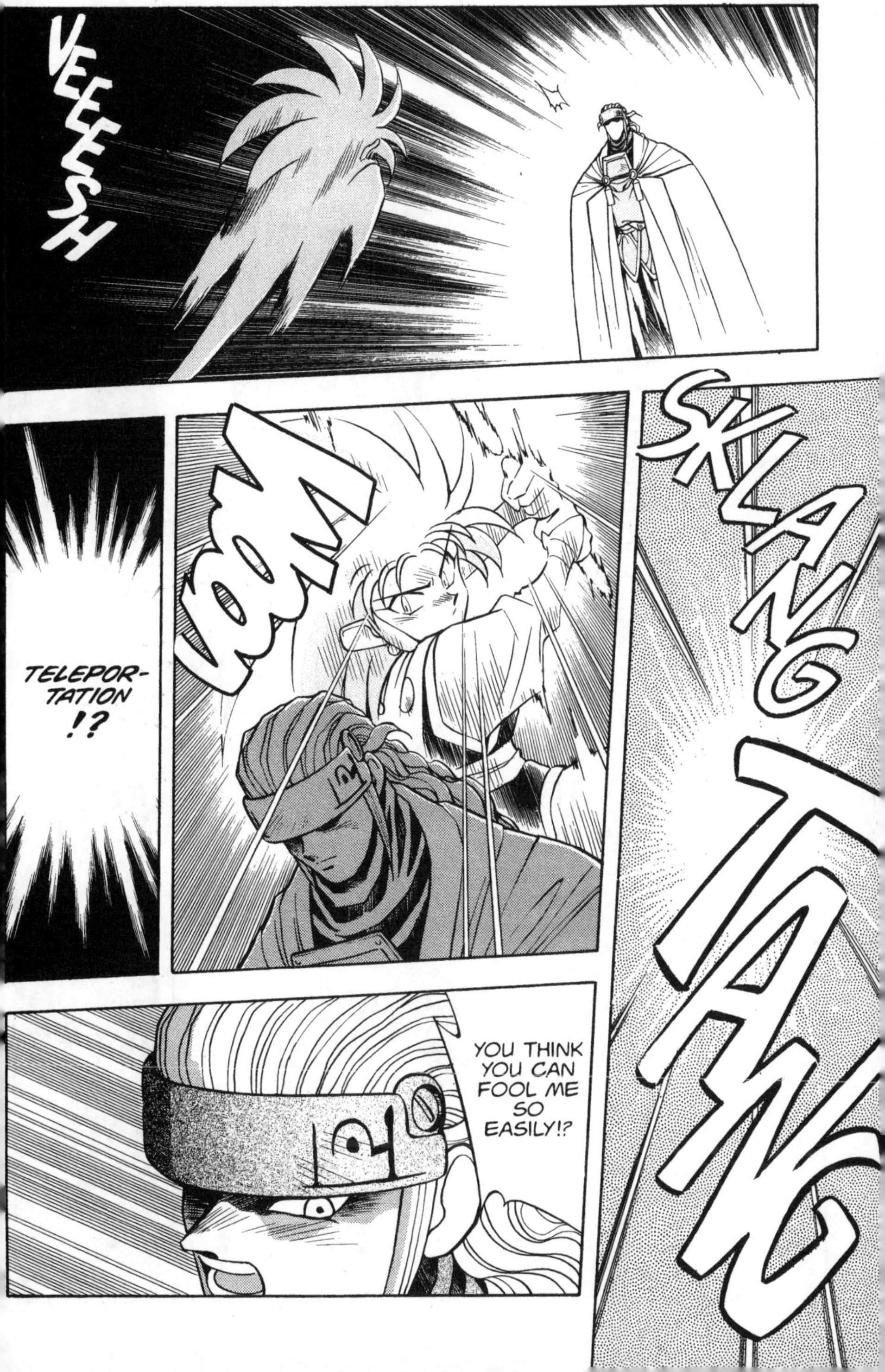
VEEEESH
TELEPOR-TATION!?
VOOM
YOU THINK YOU CAN FOOL ME SO EASILY!?
SKLANG
TSANG

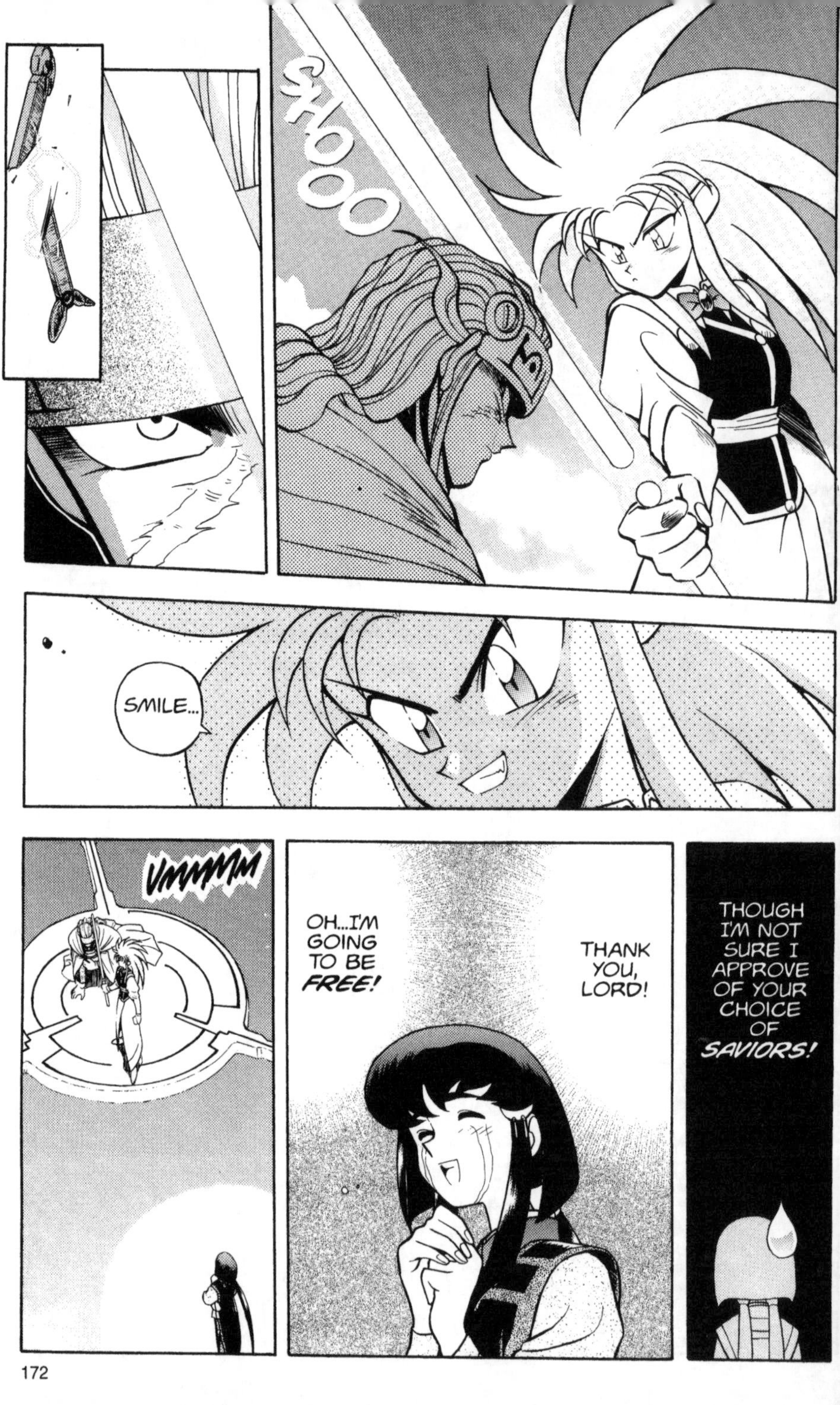
SHOOO
SMILE...
VMMMM
OH...I'M GOING TO BE FREE!
THANK YOU, LORD!
THOUGH I'M NOT SURE I APPROVE OF YOUR CHOICE OF SAVIORS!

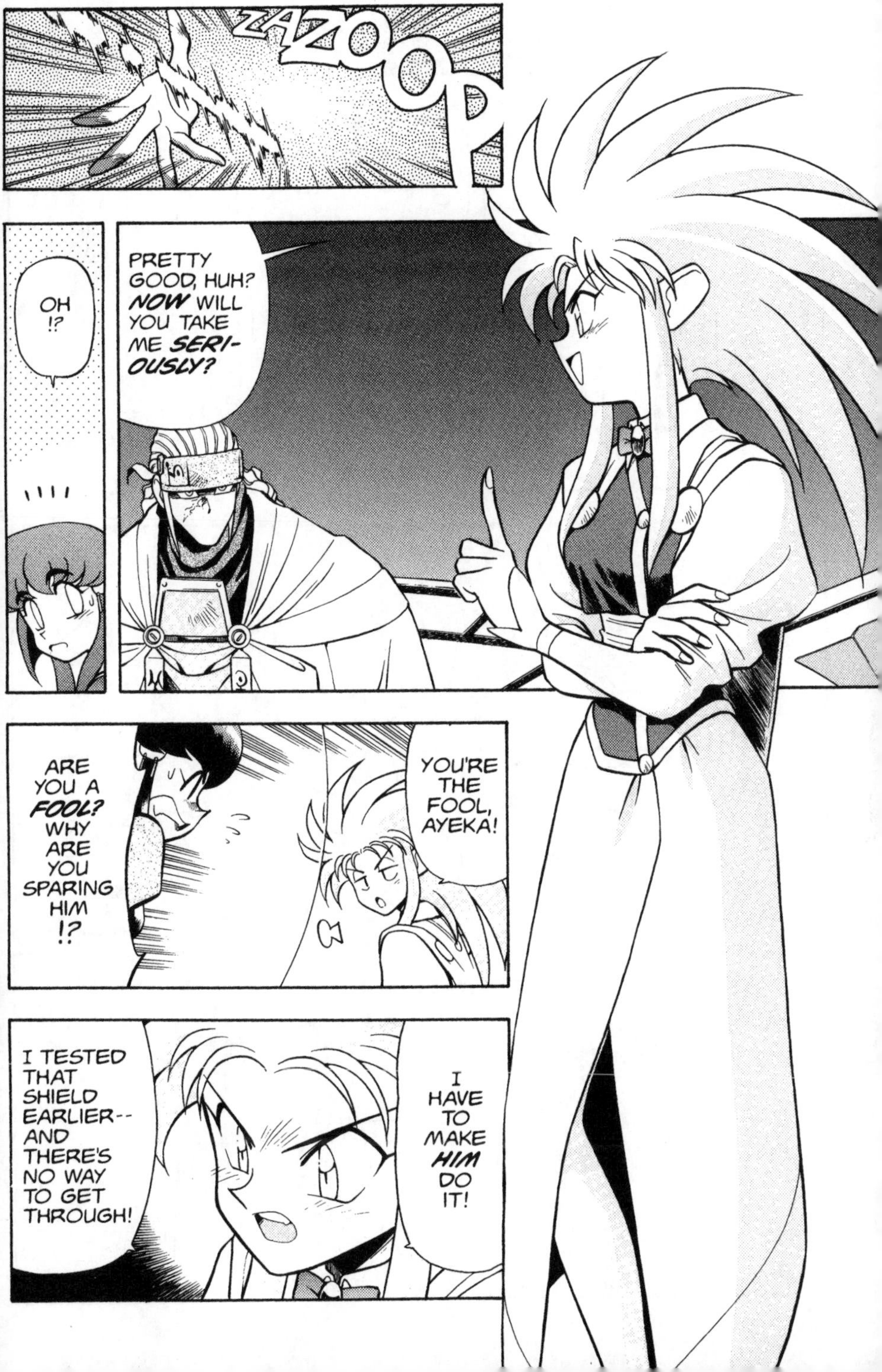
ZAZOOOP!
OH !?
PRETTY GOOD, HUH? NOW WILL YOU TAKE ME SERI-OUSLY?
ARE YOU A FOOL? WHY ARE YOU SPARING HIM !?
YOU'RE THE FOOL, AYEKA!
I TESTED THAT SHIELD EARLIER-- AND THERE'S NO WAY TO GET THROUGH!
I HAVE TO MAKE HIM DO IT!

WELL, WELL...! GOOD FOR YOU...!

NOT SO EMPTY-HEADED AFTER ALL.

I *APOLOGIZE* FOR MY *RUDENESS.*

OKAY! ♥

ALL YOU MUST DO IN ORDER TO BREAK THE SHIELD--

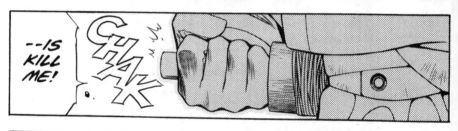

--IS KILL ME!

CHAK

AND THIS TIME, I'LL TAKE YOU SERIOUSLY INDEED.

BAS *HEEEN*

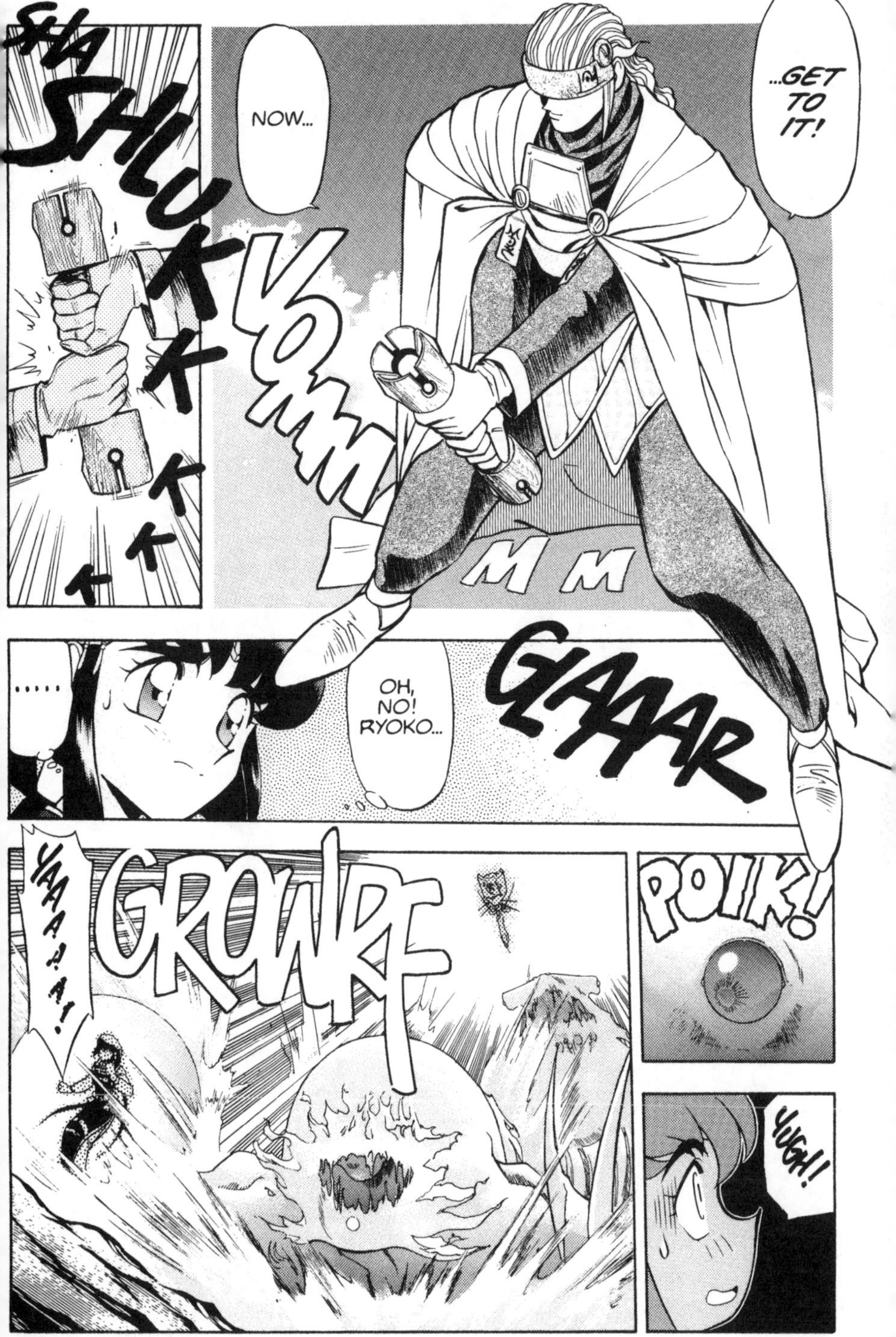
SHA
SHLUK K K K K
NOW...
VOMM M M
...GET TO IT!
.....
OH, NO! RYOKO...
GLAAAR
YAAAAAAA!
GROWRF
POIK!
YUGH!

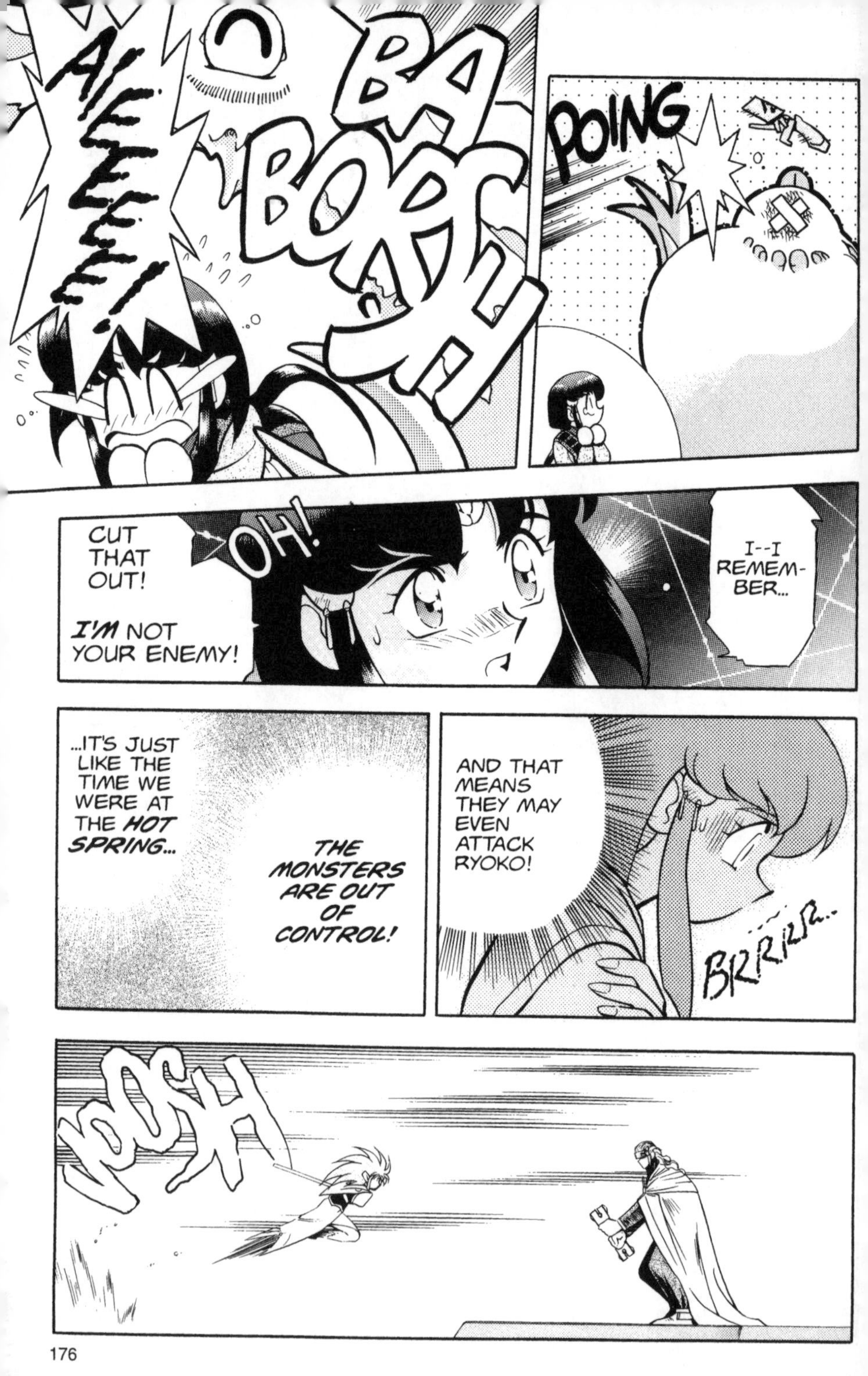
AIEEEEEE!!
BA BOOSH
POING
CUT THAT OUT!
I'M NOT YOUR ENEMY!
OH!
I--I REMEMBER...
...IT'S JUST LIKE THE TIME WE WERE AT THE HOT SPRING...
THE MONSTERS ARE OUT OF CONTROL!
AND THAT MEANS THEY MAY EVEN ATTACK RYOKO!
BRRRR...
WOOSH

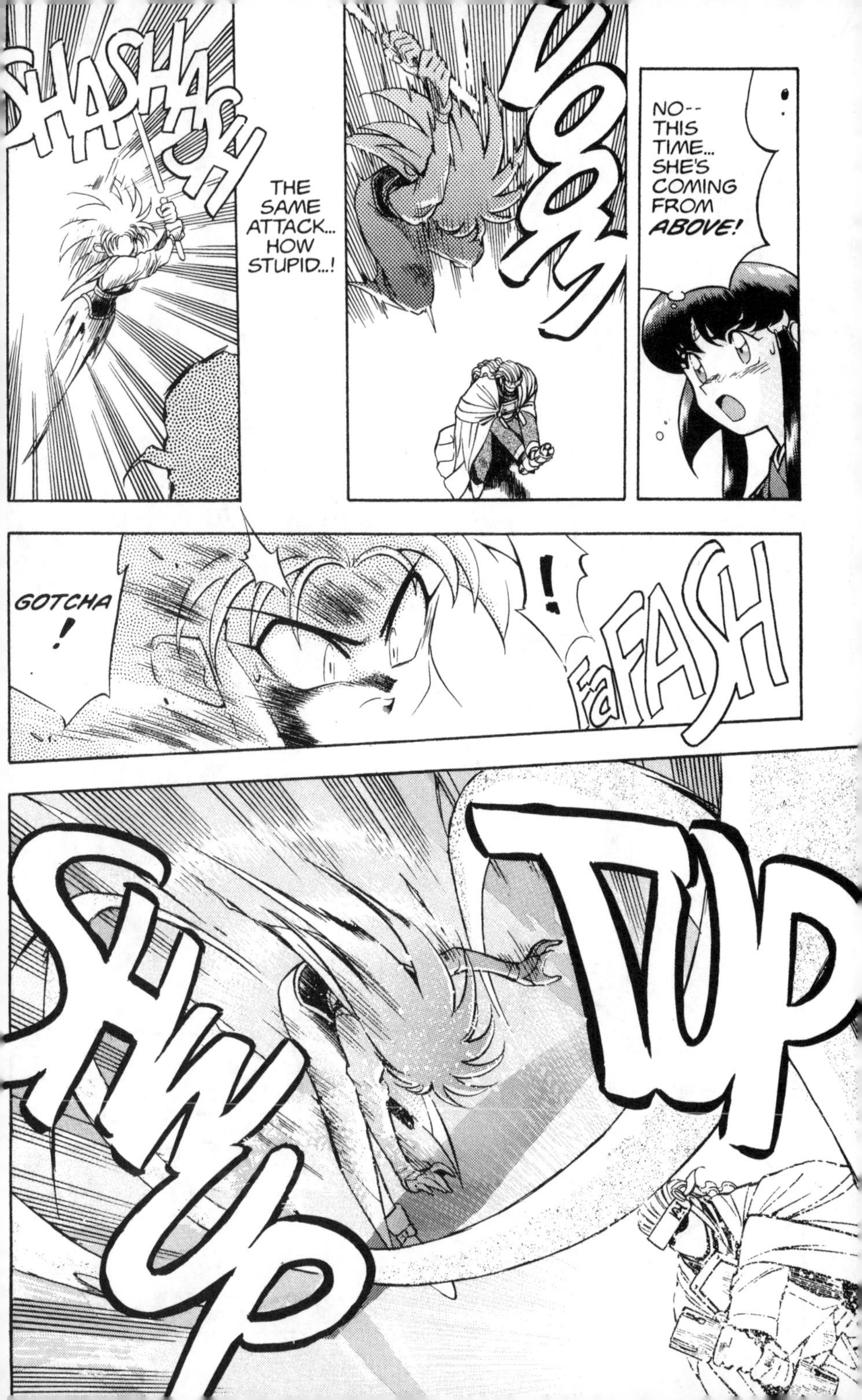
SHASHASH
THE SAME ATTACK... HOW STUPID...!
VOOM
NO-- THIS TIME... SHE'S COMING FROM *ABOVE!*
GOTCHA !
!
FaFASH
SHWUP
TUP

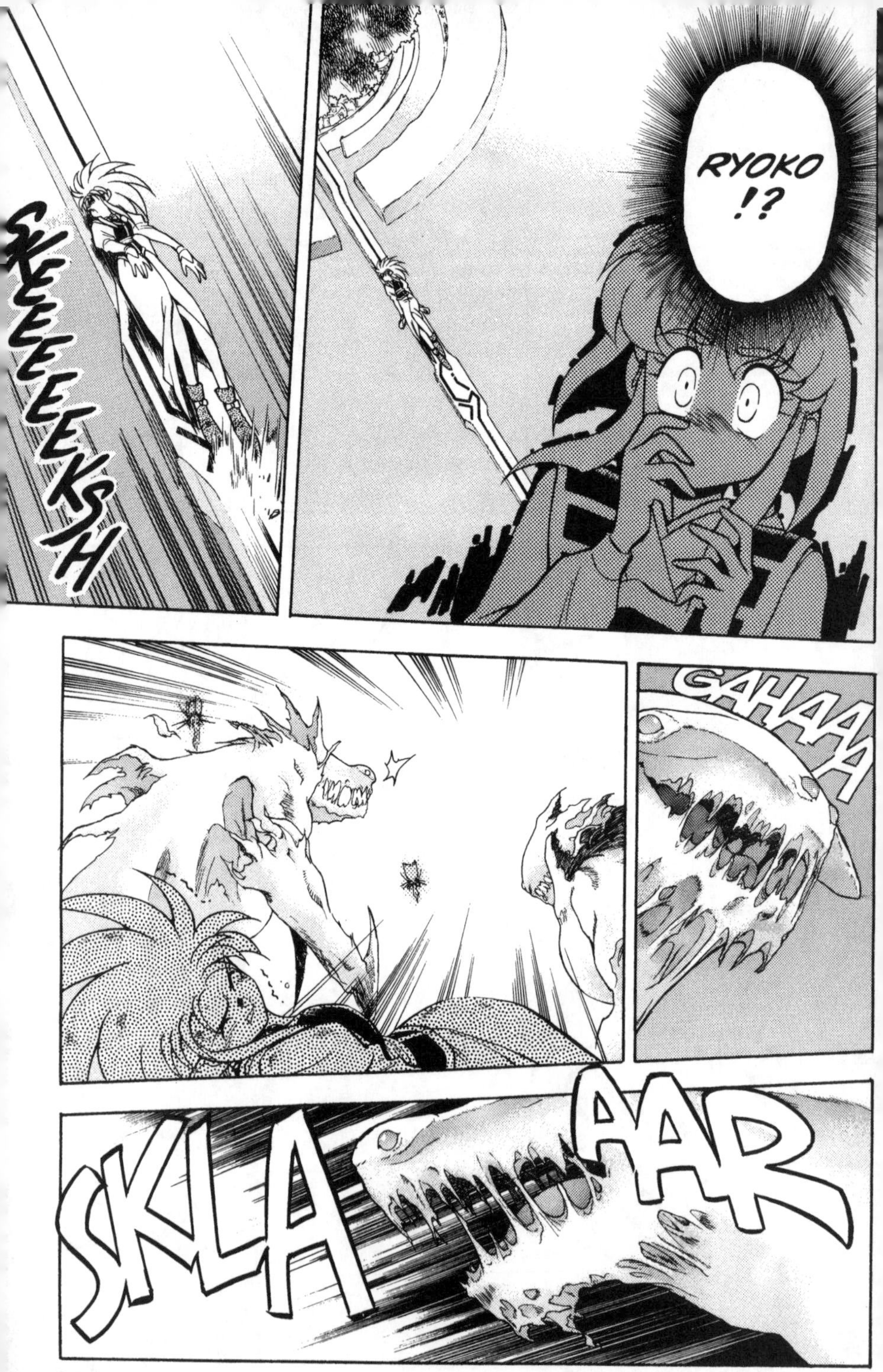
SKEEEEEEKSHH
RYOKO !?
GAHAAAA
SKLAAAR

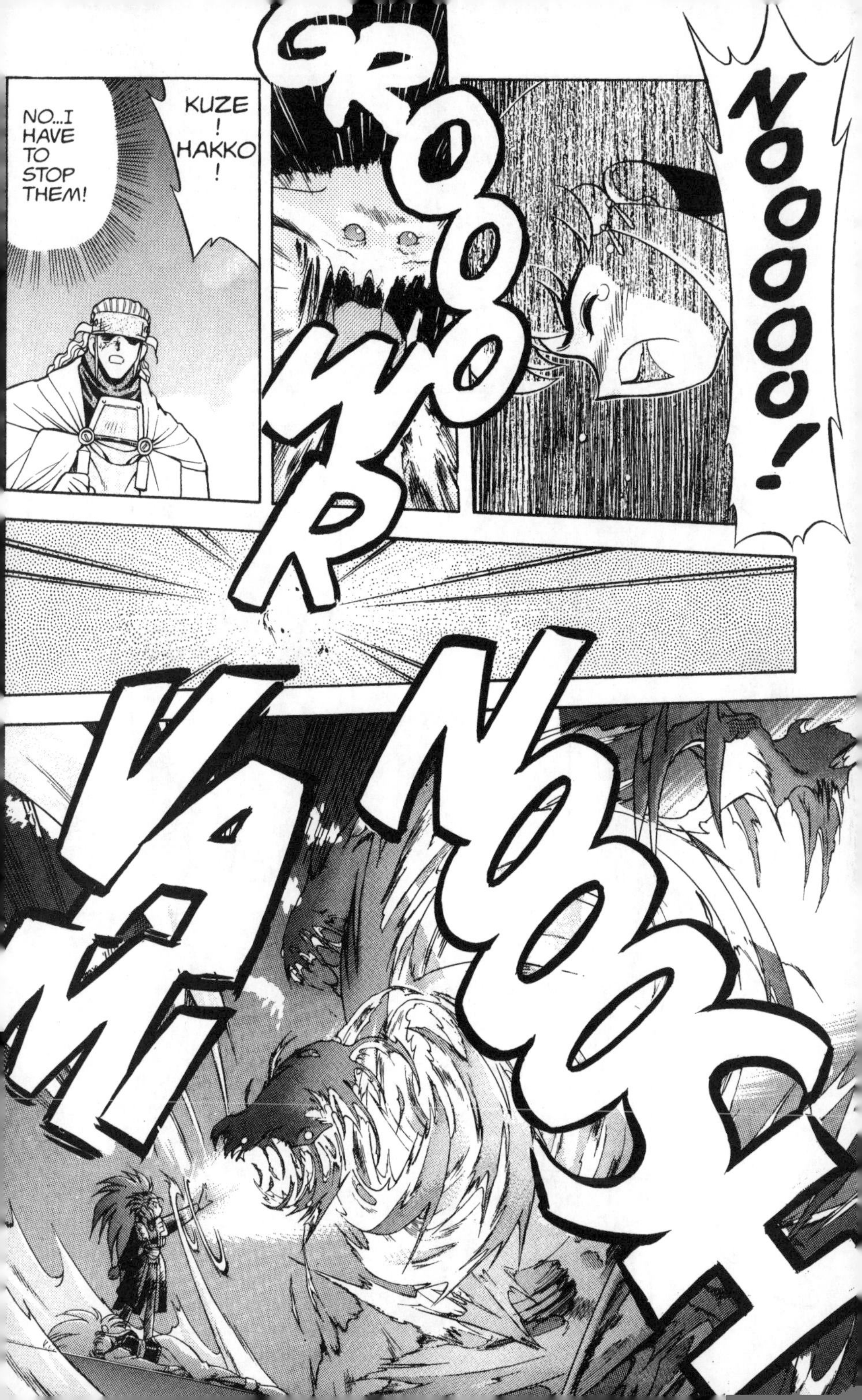
NO...I HAVE TO STOP THEM!
KUZE! HAKKO!
GROOOWR
NOOOOOO!
VAM
NMOOOCH

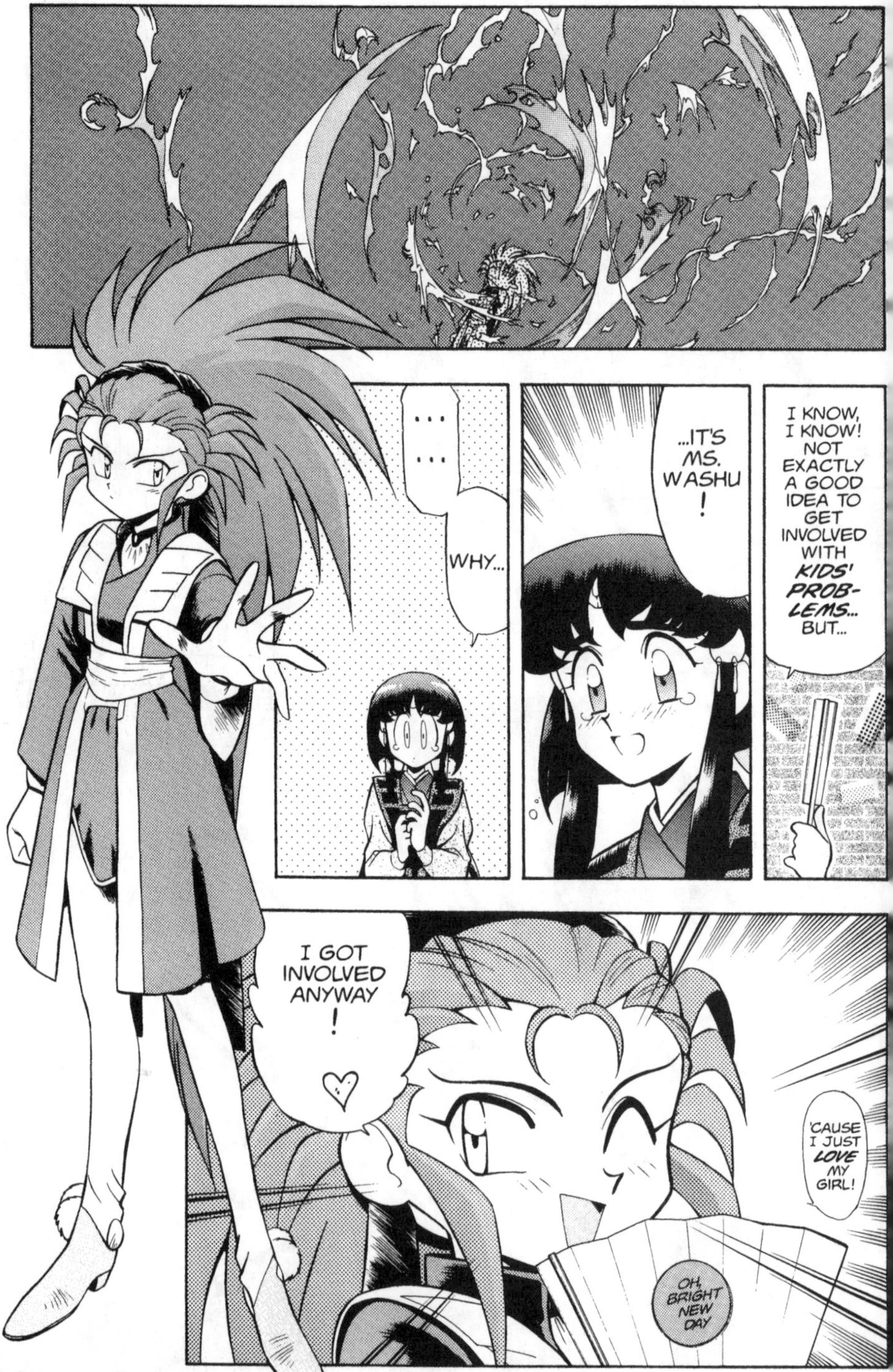
...
...
WHY...
...IT'S MS. WASHU!
I KNOW, I KNOW! NOT EXACTLY A GOOD IDEA TO GET INVOLVED WITH KIDS' PROBLEMS... BUT...
I GOT INVOLVED ANYWAY! ♥
'CAUSE I JUST LOVE MY GIRL!
OH, BRIGHT NEW DAY

FWUP

MS. WASHU, I'M SORRY... RYOKO IS...

RYOKO IS...

OH! IT'S ALL *MY* FAULT...!

I, FOR ONE, *KNEW* YOU WERE WITH HER, PROFESSOR. SO--HOW ARE YOU?

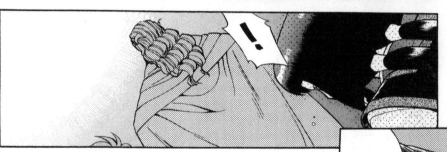

!

I SAW *MINAGI* AND REALIZED...

SHUP

...THAT IT *HAD* TO BE YOU. I WAS RIGHT, AS ALWAYS.

SO, WHAT ARE YOU GOING TO DO *NOW?*

WELL, YAKAGE...?

SPEAK UP...

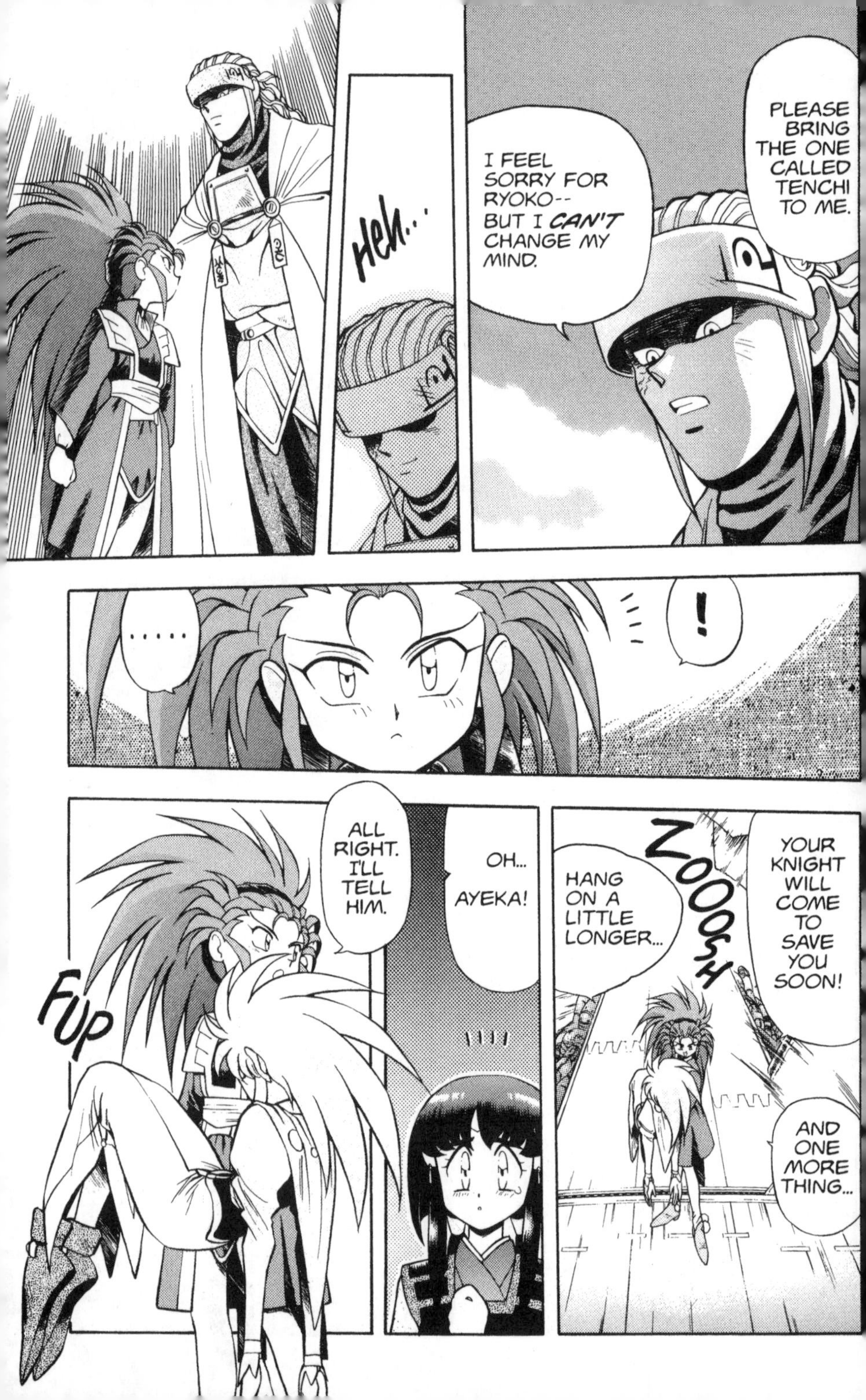
Heh...
I FEEL SORRY FOR RYOKO-- BUT I CAN'T CHANGE MY MIND.
PLEASE BRING THE ONE CALLED TENCHI TO ME.
......
!
ALL RIGHT. I'LL TELL HIM.
FUP
OH... AYEKA!
HANG ON A LITTLE LONGER...
ZOOOOSH
YOUR KNIGHT WILL COME TO SAVE YOU SOON!
AND ONE MORE THING...

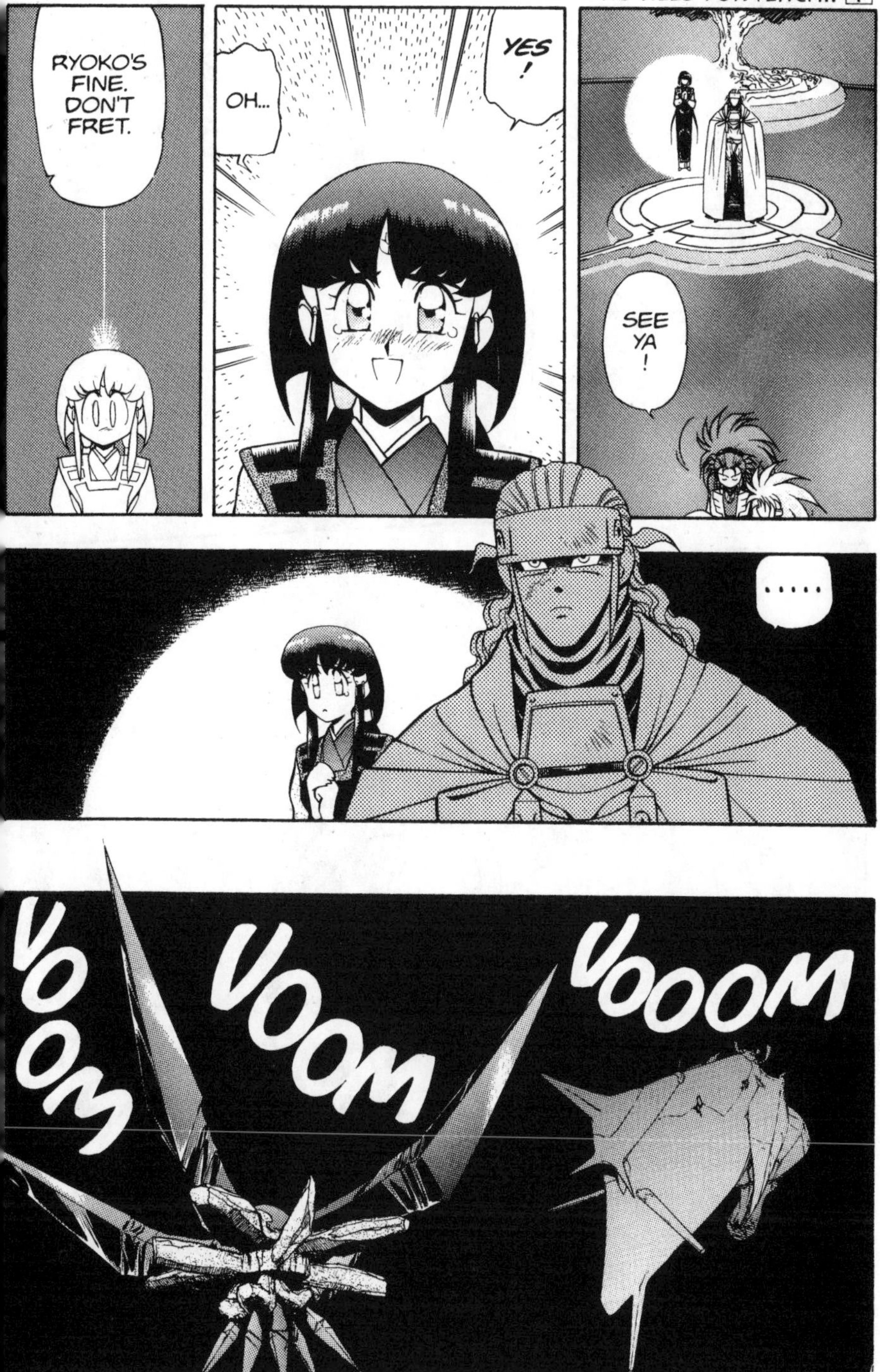
RYOKO'S FINE. DON'T FRET.
OH...
YES!
SEE YA!
.....
VOOM
VOOM
VOOOM

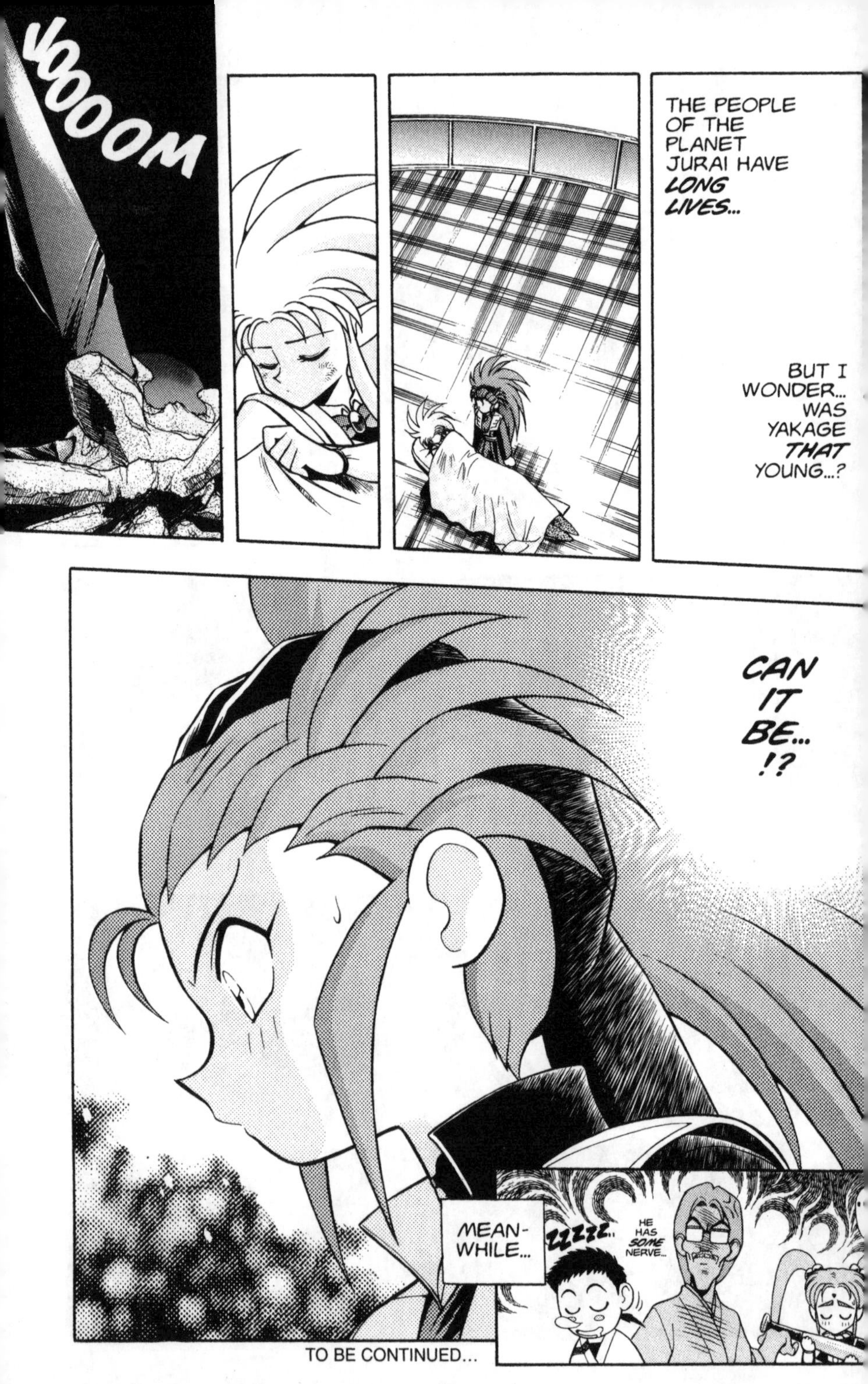
VOOOOM
THE PEOPLE OF THE PLANET JURAI HAVE LONG LIVES...
BUT I WONDER... WAS YAKAGE THAT YOUNG...?
CAN IT BE...!?
MEAN-WHILE...
ZZZZZ..
HE HAS SOME NERVE...

TO BE CONTINUED...